CONSERVING NATURAL RESOURCES

Principles and Practice in a Democracy

CONSERVING NATURAL RESOURCES

Principles and Practice in a Democracy

SHIRLEY W. ALLEN

Professor Emeritus, Department of Forestry
School of Natural Resources
University of Michigan

McGRAW-HILL BOOK COMPANY, INC.

New York Toronto London

1955

CONSERVING NATURAL RESOURCES

Library of Congress Catalog Card Number 54-9689

THE MAPLE PRESS COMPANY, YORK, PA.

Preface

For a number of years I have looked for a textbook on the conservation of natural resources with the following specifications: (1) it should be on the college level; (2) it should preferably be written by one author; (3) it should point out frequently the social and economic aspects of conservation practice; (4) it should cover the nonrenewable or irreplaceable natural resources as well as those which are replaceable.

Two excellent texts which approach these specifications have served in my classes at the University of Michigan since 1929: *Conservation of Our Natural Resources* by Van Hise and Havemeyer, published in 1930 by The Macmillan Company, New York (a reworking of Van Hise's earlier work of 1910 in symposium form by a similar title), and *Conservation in the United States* by Gustafson and associates, also a symposium-style text by four Cornell University authors, published first in 1939 by Comstock Publishing Associates, Inc., Ithaca, N.Y., and revised several times since. Other texts used for cognate reading have included the original, *Our Natural Resources and Their Conservation* by A. E. Parkins and J. R. Whitaker (editors) and eighteen other authors, published first in 1936 by John Wiley & Sons, Inc., New York, and revised a number of times before it came out under the editorship of Guy Harold Smith as *Conservation of Natural Resources* in 1950; and two other texts that emphasize the social aspects of the subject, *Foundations of National Prosperity* by Richard T. Ely and his associates, Hess, Lieth, and Carver, which ran through only one edition, published by The Macmillan Company, New York, in 1923, and *American Resources* by Whitaker and Ackerman, published in 1951 by Harcourt, Brace & Company, Inc., New York. Some dozen other texts have also been used for cognate reading, and all have had their own individual value.

Somewhere in each one of these texts, however, there has seemed to me to be a gap between chapters or a difference in the philosophy of various authors of one text and a loss of the unity necessary in presenting so broad a subject. To recover such unity is the reason for writing this book. An earnest attempt has been made to keep always in mind three essentials of a sound conservation program: use with minimum waste, increasing productivity where possible and desirable, and seeing to it that natural resources are equitably distributed now and hereafter.

I have been disturbed by the growing tendency among conservation writers to use the term *resources* in a passion for brevity rather than accuracy when they mean *natural resources* and by the almost universal emphasis on the replaceable natural resources. Certainly we should be helpless without tools and energy which come largely from the irreplaceable stores. If, therefore, my language in writing of minerals is not the language of the geologist and the engineer, at least I have emphasized the importance of mineral resources. I hope also to have made the point that our technological demand for minerals will require some rearranging of the landscape if we are still to have a decent world to live in.

It would have been impossible to prepare this book without the help of hundreds of agencies which deal with natural resources, and indeed much of the text must contain material which I have accumulated in the past twenty-five years and for which I could never give proper credit. I do want to express my gratitude to the following whom I can definitely identify: to my colleagues in the School of Natural Resources at the University of Michigan and particularly to Prof. Karl F. Lagler and Prof. Warren W. Chase for reading the section on wild-animal life and for valuable suggestions from the former on the fisheries portion; to Prof. Stanley A. Cain, for the use of certain diagrams worked up by him; to Prof. Dow V. Baxter for the use of several excellent photographs obtained on his Alaskan expeditions; and to Prof. Kenneth K. Landes of the University's Department of Geology for critical reading of the section on minerals. My thanks are due to a number of Federal and state bureaus for information and illustrations, including the Soil Conservation Service, the Soil Survey, and the Forest Service in the Department of Agriculture; the Bureau of Mines, the Fish and Wildlife Service, the National Park Service, the Bureau of Reclamation in the Department of the Interior, the Office of the Chief of Engineers, Department of the Army, the Tennessee Valley Authority, and the Michigan State Department of Conservation. Magazines which have lent pictures include *American Forests, Industrial News, Public Works, Du Pont Magazine, Journal of Forestry, Michigan Conservation, Reclamation Era,* and *Capper's Farmer.* Pictures were also furnished by the Bituminous Coal Institute, Lake Carriers' Association, American Forest Products Industries, Inc., American Potash Institute, American Petroleum Institute, Georgia Power Company, National Audubon Society, Kern County (California) Board of Trade, *Ann Arbor News,* Ann Arbor Water Department, Devereux Butcher, James P. Gilligan, and Ernest F. Brater. Special thanks are due to my publishers, McGraw-Hill Book Company, Inc., not only for the use of certain published material but for unfailing patience and helpfulness in my entire task, and to Prentice-Hall, Inc., for the use of maps and tables from their publications. Drawings were executed by Michael Bailey and William L.

Cristanelli. The typing was done accurately and faithfully by Bernice Murray and Ethel Huntwork. Many others have given help and encouragement from both public and private fields. Finally, I want to remember my students, whose interest and challenge are really important reasons for setting down the material in this book.

Should the reader wonder at the title, let me say that conserving natural resources in a free country is anything but automatic. The one best hope for it in a democracy is the very fact that our sort of government is founded on the agreement of a great people to live fairly together.

Shirley W. Allen

Contents

CHAPTER 1

Introduction

Productive power is one of the secrets of a successful nation, and its vast potentialities have been demonstrated over and over in this democracy. Those who believe in the idea of private enterprise will say that the freedom granted to the individual and to his corporation in a democracy is the reason for the high state of productive power in this country. Those who believe, even to a moderate extent, in the partial public ownership and operation of the means of production will point to the abuses of individual and corporate freedom in the handling of natural resources and will assert that our economy is not in balance and that really our productive power has not been fully drawn upon. Somewhere between these extreme views, even with the slow and cautious machinery of democracy, lies the opportunity to use, build up, and distribute equitably, in terms of public benefit, what we call the natural resources of the country.

To maintain such a program means that people must understand their natural environment, must recognize self-interest to the extent of practicing good management where its benefits are demonstrable, must submit to police power where restraints in use and exploitation are necessary, must be ready to encourage and finance the search for knowledge and the development and employment of the skills to apply such knowledge in the management of great publicly owned natural resources, and must collectively insist that any private individual or corporation claiming a right to "own" and manage natural resources must consider them a trust held for the people and must manage them in the national interest. Finally, if the citizens of a democracy want a continuing flow of benefits from use and management of natural resources, the proportional importance of various uses of natural resources in terms of human welfare must be recognized. Skill rather than rule of thumb and wisdom rather than prejudiced self-interest must here be invoked. Many sciences, arts, and procedures are involved. There is in such a program no place for *laissez faire*, politics in its evil sense, nor failure to use scientific knowledge, forethought, and organization.

Our record in the management of the natural resources of a great democracy is none too good, but it is improving. Something of this record will be discussed later, but such treatment will be more intelligible following a look at natural resources as factors of production and in their natural groupings.

Natural Resources

Natural resources in a narrow sense are those uncaptured natural stores which are useful to mankind in any way. They are most commonly grouped as waters, soils, forests, grasslands, wild-animal life, and minerals. In so far as they constitute collectively one of the factors of production, the economist speaks of them as "land." Manipulated by human powers which in turn are aided by tools and other operating devices, three factors, "land, labor (including enterprise), and capital," swing into action, and what the economist calls "production" gets going. Forests become houses, railroad ties, fuel, paper, or pencils; grass and other forage become meat and leather; waters become available for drinking, cooking, cleansing, transporting, and actually make up an important part of the volume of many useful articles and materials; wild-animal life becomes food, fur coats, quarries, photographic targets, trophies, or museum specimens; minerals become household fuel, abrasives, fertilizers, paper clips, automobiles, and bulldozers.

But the six groups mentioned above may well be rearranged for convenience, and they might line up this way:

- Inexhaustible natural resources
  - The atmosphere
  - Water in its cycle
- Replaceable and maintainable natural resources
  - Waters in place
  - Soils
  - Land in its spatial sense
    - For human activities
    - For the scene and other amenities
  - Forests
  - Forage and other cover plants
  - Wild-animal life
  - Human powers[1]
    - Those of the body
    - Those of the spirit

[1] There is nothing unnatural about human powers, and the term "*human powers*" makes their consideration here more appropriate than the more common term "*human resources.*" Either term is different from and broader than "labor" or "enterprise."

Irreplaceable natural resources
- Minerals
  - Metals
  - Mineral fuels and lubricants
  - Miscellaneous nonfuel, nonmetallics
- Land in natural condition[2]
  - Natural study areas
  - Specimen wildernesses

Each of these groupings is worth brief discussion in this introduction.

Inexhaustible Natural Resources

The Atmosphere. There is plenty of air. It is indispensable to life. There are places where it carries distressing impurities. Its moisture content, temperature, and movements in the great mass known as *atmosphere* constitute what is called *climate,* and this makes it important in determining the character of the soil and land in its spatial sense and how it may be used. It is therefore a natural resource which affects profoundly other natural resources. In a local and limited sense it can perhaps be managed, but the fact that it is in continual circulation puts it beyond all but the most superficial efforts in this direction.

Water in Its Cycle. Rainfall, runoff, circulating ground water, rivers, lakes, and oceans, and atmospheric moisture constitute an inexhaustible supply of water. It is indispensable to life, but whether or not this moving supply is made to serve mankind adequately is a question of control and management of regional and local supplies. Not infrequently temporary or permanent local or regional shortages are experienced through waste or through need for special amounts and qualities. Of course, also, the original availability of water as a natural resource depends on climate.

Replaceable Natural Resources

Waters in Place. Waters in the particular places where they are needed and can be used may be maintained or augmented in supply through seeing to it that rainfall reaches underground storage, that runoff is retarded by vegetation and is impounded and distributed, and that land use and occupancy do not dissipate or pollute water supplies. Water which we see, use, and consider indispensable, therefore, is replaceable.

Soils. Because most of the food and clothing and much of the shelter required by mankind must come from plants that grow in the soils or from animals that feed on such plants, soils are indispensable to life. They are replaced very slowly in nature but to some extent can be "rebuilt" and maintained in quality and fertility by human effort. "Main-

[2] Maintainable perhaps, but questionably replaceable.

tainable" rather than "replaceable" therefore more accurately characterizes soil as a natural resource.

Land in Its Spatial Sense. Space or land surface is required for human activities, if only enough to stand on. Where cornfield and farmstead stood in 1941, perhaps a vast war plant occupied the space in 1943. The city of today stands in the marsh or forest of yesterday. Here again, land as space is maintainable in the sense that it may be kept in shape to endure intensive human use and prevented from becoming "blighted" for such use.

FIG. 1. Need for space for human activity is constantly on the increase. Here the city crowds and passes fair grounds and farm land. Subdivision for residence will probably take the remaining open land. (*Ann Arbor Daily News.*)

Occasionally its most important use may be to furnish a restful or inspiring scene, but even here its availability for the purpose may depend upon care and protection. The airport and the testing grounds for atomic-energy developments are modern examples of space demand.

Human Powers. It is obvious that human powers such as strength, dexterity, and the physical skills which may be grouped as powers of the body are necessary to existence. In no less degree, certainly, men's power to reason and to live in peace and justice with their fellow men, which may be grouped as intellectual and moral powers or powers of the spirit, are essential to existence. There is nothing *unnatural* about these powers. They are capable of renewal and maintenance and may well be considered the greatest of *natural* resources when physically sustained.

Irreplaceable Natural Resources

Minerals. The metals, the mineral fuels and lubricants, and the numerous useful nonmetallic, nonfuel resources are truly irreplaceable. They are necessary surely to the present technological stage of human living, and they affect profoundly the convenience and comfort of such

FIG. 2. Land in natural condition. Cougar Lake with House Mountain in background, near Goat Rocks Wild Area, Washington. A road zigzagging up the face of this mountain or a raised lake level for industrial power would make it impossible to recapture this scene. It is irreplaceable. (*Photo by James P. Gilligan.*)

living. Only in the most limited sense are the metals maintainable in use. The mineral fuels and lubricants are of course destroyed in use, while the maintainable nonmetals such as the building stones, sands, and clays are comfortably plentiful.

Land in Natural Condition. In the cultural life of any nation, certain appreciable areas in natural and undisturbed condition may be said to be indispensable for purposes of study and for those inspirational values which can come only from combinations of scenery and solitude—the two latter are not the same. Once radically exploited or modified, the original or natural values in such lands cannot be wholly recaptured. Even a great part of a dedicated "wilderness area" can lose, through overuse, certain values which cannot be fully restored.

Conservation

Original Abundance of Natural Resources. With this background in mind, it is well to consider the attitudes of the settlers who started our democracy and how those attitudes have persisted and influenced the use of natural resources up to the present.

The nation still ranks high in the occurrence of all essential natural stores except for a few of the indispensable metals. Forests of vast extent, fertile soils, inland waters for any important purpose, wild-animal life in abundance, and minerals for the taking greeted the settler and made him feel perhaps that here at last was a land of inexhaustible resources. They might not be arranged just the way he wanted them, for forests stood where he needed arable land for food crops; the crude water-wheel mills for grinding could not always take advantage of falling water where he wished; the game animals for food and skins had to be hunted and trapped; and even the trees he needed were of inconvenient size. When it came to minerals, he had little of the wherewithal to convert them into use. But it was good land and rich, and the settler did what other pioneers throughout the world had done before him. He used lavishly of natural resources to make up for the scarcity of the other two factors of production. Labor in terms of his own puny strength was scarce. Capital in terms of tools, money as a device of exchange, buildings, and transportation equipment was scarce. Under these circumstances it is not strange that natural resources suffered.

Forests gave way over a period of 200 years to farms and pastures until the original area of forest has been reduced from 822 million acres to 624 million. Not all this produces usable timber, and local scarcities exist in many places. Use and exploitation here were characterized by terrific waste both through failure of reasonably complete utilization of products and through fire as an incident of human activity often followed by tragic losses from insects and disease.

Water, plentiful at first for all uses, has served one of its greatest purposes, that of transporting human and industrial wastes, to such an increasing extent that the pollution of streams and underground waters has made many of them intolerable for us for any other purpose save transportation and power production. Concentrations of population have overused underground accumulations of water to an alarming degree.

Land cleared so the soil could be used for crops is frequently found in service after 200 years of cropping, but increasing amounts of soil have been lost through water and wind erosion brought on by ignorance and carelessness in cultivation. Likewise the nutrient materials essential to plant growth have been removed in the form of crops and through failure to prevent loss of the actual soil by erosion and failure to return available plant residues, animal manures, and other soil builders.

Not everybody wants to see the country too plentifully supplied with wild-animal life. Even the sportsman is inclined to battle for the maintenance of his favorite quarry only and to advocate the destruction of certain predators which may also have economic importance. But game and fur animals occurred in marked abundance in this country and still exist to form the basis of hunting and fishing which support an equipment, supply and servicing business running annually into the billions. Furs too are taken in great numbers each year, and millions of Americans get thrills from seeing, hearing, and photographing wild creatures all the way from butterflies to mountain lions. Certain of the fisheries are of great commercial importance. But the history of wild-animal life in this country is one of destruction and in some instances of extinction.

Minerals are difficult and expensive to recover from the earth, and at first thought this should influence men to use them sparingly, take good care of them, and seek the more ready-at-hand replaceable and easily exploited substitutes. But men have a lot of audacity in their make-up, and if convenience, profit, and comfort to the human race can result from reckless and wasteful exploitation of minerals, that is the course their use is likely to take. So far, whatever we have in the way of mineral policy in this country has, with rare exception, placed the mineral resources in private ownership for exploitation with few safeguards against wasteful development. This has resulted in dangerous depletion of certain minerals such as lead, zinc, and petroleum. Not all this depletion is due, however, to wasteful exploitation at the sources. Merchandising and use aggravate it in such a manner that it would seem that the public has assumed a perpetual availability and low price.

Human powers pose a persistent problem. In a democracy, particularly, every citizen has the right to expect opportunity to maintain health, to work productively and for a sufficient reward to assure a reasonable living and financial security, to learn what he needs to know to make him fit into his environment and to become increasingly useful to society. And certainly he should expect every encouragement to his pursuit of freedom from fear and want and to freedom of religion and speech. In no form of government do these opportunities and encouragements exist to such an extent as in a democracy. Yet even our own country has need to increase them. Through them come the availability and to some extent the development of human powers to assume the role of natural resources.

Conservation as a Definite Movement. It is frequently said that the scientists of the country are responsible for the definite movement toward the conservation of natural resources. The thought and leadership of political economists and of certain statesmen, however, have been gen-

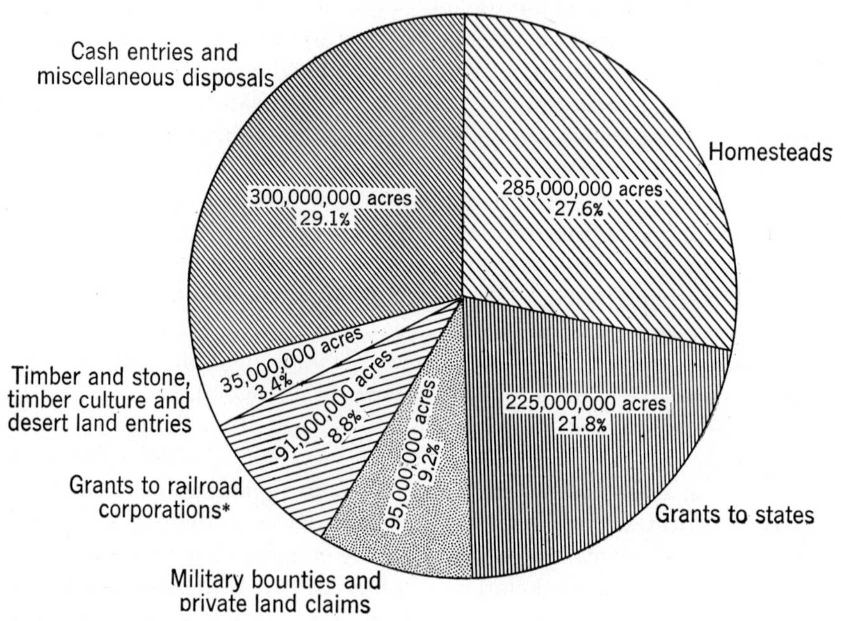

Fig. 3. More than one-half the total land area of the United States has been disposed of to private holders and to the states. (*Bureau of Land Management.*)

erous and just as nearly indispensable. Moreover, none of these groups could have been effective without an awakening among the people, and this still is not sufficiently widespread.

"Economy of natural resources" preceded the more popular term "conservation of natural resources" which came into general use in the administration of Theodore Roosevelt about 1907. The suggestion of the term *conservation* is said to have come from English visitors to the United States who had long used the title "conservator" in managing the land resources of India.

The movement assumed definite shape on a country-wide scale with the meeting of a conference of governors called by President Theodore Roosevelt in May, 1908. Here are some of the events that led up to it:

1. The various laws governing disposal of the public domain and their operation. These include among others the Homestead Law of 1862, the mining laws, and the Timber and Stone Act of 1878 (Fig. 3).

2. The spectacular lumbering operations which were beginning to alarm observers as the industry plowed through the Lake states from 1870 on.

3. Consideration of forest exploitation by the American Association for the Advancement of Science and presentation of memorials to the Congress in 1870 and again in 1890, resulting in the establishment of a Forestry Bureau in the U.S. Department of Agriculture in 1890 and in the legalizing and withdrawal of the first "forest reserves" in 1891.

4. Studies and publication of a report by Major J. W. Powell on *Lands of the Arid Region* in 1879 and the establishment of an irrigation division in the U.S. Geological Survey.

5. Recommendations by the National Academy of Science in 1897 strengthening forest-reserve policy and the resulting legislation.

6. Long agitation for, and passage of, the Reclamation Act in 1902.

7. Rapid growth of population from 1890 on, predictions that the United States would have more than 200 million people by 1950, and a growing fear that the country was not managing its resources wisely to take care of all these people.

8. Appointment of the Inland Waterways Commission by President Theodore Roosevelt in 1907 and its first report emphasizing the interrelated character of water, forest, transportation, and fuel problems.

The White House Conference of 1908 itself was no usual gathering, and it was the first one to which the governors of all the states had been invited for consideration of any question of national policy. Members of the Senate and the House of Representatives, the judges of the U.S. Supreme Court, representatives of the important scientific societies, members of the Inland Waterways Commission, and certain prominent citizens at large contributed to an unusual meeting of minds expressed in a "Declaration of Principles." This document left no doubt as to their conviction that some order should come into the use of natural resources.

It should be noted here that this declaration took no account of wild-animal life and apparently gave consideration to human powers only in terms of safety for mine workers. (One speaker at the conference brought up the subject of the natural scene and the importance of conserving it but was listened to, apparently, only with politeness.)

The leadership of two dynamic characters was everywhere seen at this conference, Gifford Pinchot, Chief of the United States Forest Service and Chairman of the Inland Waterways Commission, and President

Theodore Roosevelt, whose fighting idealism so frequently led to vigorous action.

Two important and immediate results of the White House Conference were (1) the appointment of a fifty-man National Conservation Commission composed about equally of scientists, businessmen, and statesmen, which reported back to the governors in December, 1908, with an inventory of the country's natural resources; (2) the appointment of state conservation agencies in forty-one of the states by governors who had become convinced that such agencies were necessary.

One other very important result was the use of the inventory, by the President, as a basis for the withdrawal from further settlement and entry (pending private acquisition), of vast areas of the public lands for study, looking to permanent dedication as public mineral, timber, and water-power "reserves." A total of some 200 million acres was thus withdrawn, but not until 1920 were the Mineral Leasing Law and the Federal Power Law enacted to provide for administration of a character similar to that already available for the "forest reserves." Following careful study, some 50 million acres of mineral reserves and more than 148 million acres of forest land and water-power sites were finally reserved permanently out of the above total withdrawals.

The inventory submitted by the National Conservation Commission would not have been possible without the help of skilled scientists and others in the various Federal bureaus, whose services were prompt and of a high order. Subsequent analysis and planning on a creditable scale by the Commission required an initial appropriation of $25,000, which was requested from the Congress. The attitude of the Congress, however, was not unlike that of a Middle Western state official who, a few years ago, referred angrily to the work of the State Conservation Department as "that conservation devilment." Not only was the requested appropriation refused, but Federal bureau employees were forbidden to participate further in the work of the National Conservation Commission. Thus passed out of existence a body which might have become a great natural-resource planning agency appropriate in that particular period of the life of a democracy.

The North American Conservation Conference. In February, 1909, upon call of President Theodore Roosevelt, a conference of North American nations met in Washington with representatives present from Canada, Newfoundland, Mexico, and the United States, to consider natural-resource questions on an international scale. Here, as in the White House Conference of Governors, conclusions were embodied in a "Declaration of Principles" which was broader and more specific than the one adopted by the earlier conference. Public health, "game preservation . . . and special protection for such birds as are useful to agriculture" were mentioned. Drainage of wet lands and the control of grazing on nonirrigable public lands were recommended. The suggestion of calling a world conference on conservation was approved. The powers of the world were, therefore, requested by President Theodore Roosevelt in February, 1909, to meet at The Hague to consider world natural-resource problems. He went out of office, however, in March, 1909, and lack of interest on the part of the Taft administration which followed resulted in failure to carry through. That world conference was never held. It is interesting to speculate on what such a meeting at that time might have meant to world cooperation and peace. After 40 years and two terrible world wars, a conference of somewhat different character, *was* held at Lake Success in 1949 and known as the United Nations Scientific Conference on the Conservation and Utilization of Resources. This conference was first suggested by President Harry S. Truman in 1946, to the United States representative on the Economic and Social Council of the United Nations. It was a direct outgrowth of the idea which Gifford Pinchot had kept alive until his death the same year. The opportunity for using such a conference for the enlightenment of international statesmen appears to have been overlooked, but better cooperation among scientific workers of many nations is likely to result from it.

The period from 1909 to 1933, as far as conservation activity is concerned, was characterized by somewhat slow but steady progress in the acquisition of forest lands at the headwaters of navigable streams and elsewhere in the eastern United States and the establishment of the principle of Federal, state, and private cooperative attack on forest fires, both authorized in the Weeks Law of 1911; by an increasing interest in the protection and development of wild-animal resources; by recognition of, but inadequate provision for the handling of, water-power resources; by the development, under Federal lease and regulation, of mineral resources on public lands; by a slow and steady awakening of certain industries and corporations to the duties and advantages of better natural-resource management; by healthy growth in state conservation agencies; by a recognition of the value and indispensability of the scenic and inspirational resources of the country and a considerable extension of national and state park areas; and by continuing failure to see clearly in human powers the greatest natural resource of all.

Conservation since 1933. With the inauguration of President Franklin D. Roosevelt in March, 1933, the plight of large numbers of people who had lost their possessions and jobs during the years after the financial crash and the physical disaster of wind erosion dramatized the appropriateness of a great public-works program to furnish employment and to accomplish useful work in managing natural resources. This Roosevelt had not attended the governors' conference at the White House in 1908, but two years later, as a young and newly elected assemblyman in New York, had been appointed by Governor Dix to the chairmanship of a reputedly "innocuous committee on forest, fish and game" which had straightway improved its reputation through the interest and energy of its chairman. He was also at this time close to Thomas Mott Osborne, who had been appointed Commissioner of Forests, Fish and Game in New York on the doubtful qualification of a great knowledge of penology and the more natural one of a great desire to learn what conservation of these natural resources was about. Whether or not this association and the struggle of these two men together to master their assignments are reflected in

FIG. 4. A Civilian Conservation Corps Camp. During the 1930s more than 2,000 of these camps were in operation, and almost 300,000 young men were enrolled at one period.

President Franklin D. Roosevelt's program of conservation, a combined interest in conserving human powers and other natural resources at the same time is unmistakable.

The President's first stroke was the establishment of the Civilian Conservation Corps under authority of an act passed by the Congress Mar. 31, 1933, granting broad powers to employ young men for the purpose of conserving natural resources. The "enrollees," many of whom had never had opportunity for remunerative employment, were organized into companies of 200 under army officers who operated the camps and cooperated with project superintendents, who with their staffs supervised the work on forest protection, construction, forest research and forest planting and care, soil-erosion control, pest control, recreational developments, flood control on Federal public lands and on state, county, and private lands where the Federal government was legally authorized to cooperate. Mobilization was surprisingly swift, more than 1,500 camps of 200 men each being established throughout the country within 3 months.

Records of accomplishments are impressive. So are the records of improved health, skill, and reduction of delinquency among the men enrolled. By 1935 the number of camps had increased to more than 2,600, and many enrollees were currently leaving for employment of their acquired training in industry.

The Civilian Conservation Corps was reauthorized for 3 years in 1937, with more emphasis on vocational training prescribed, and finally closed out as no longer necessary in 1940, having enlisted some 2½ million young men.

Other relief organizations authorized during President Franklin D. Roosevelt's administration include the Works Progress Administration (WPA), which enlisted unemployed people of all ages and classes and which accomplished a considerable amount of work in conserving natural resources along with other types of activity. It was considered "smart" during this period to ridicule the WPA, but it should be remembered that some of the best citizens in the country through no fault of their own found themselves on its rolls, that it was considerably less demoralizing than the dole, that it did accomplish useful work, and that the necessity for maintaining it is no compliment to our economic system. Then there was the Prairie States Forestry Project, involving the area otherwise known as the "shelterbelt," extending along the 100th meridian from the Canadian boundary in North Dakota through the panhandle of Texas. This project, started in 1934, developed into a program of farmstead tree planting to obtain protection from hot and cold drying winds which damaged the land, the crops, and the very lives of men and livestock. Here again there is a human-relief angle in the fact that the drought-persecuted people were employed in establishing the belts of trees, fencing them against grazing, and sometimes watering them until they became established. The total accomplishment of this project is impressive in terms of better crop and living conditions.

Establishment of the Soil Conservation Service in the Department of Agriculture through the Soil Conservation Law of 1935 was preceded by the action of President Roosevelt in setting up the "Soil Erosion Service" in 1933 as an emergency organization in the Department of the Interior. Thus 27 years after the brave pronouncements of the governors at the White House Conference of 1908, soil conservation came into its own as a Federal policy. Later the emergency bureau was transferred to the Department of Agriculture as the Soil Conservation Service and its work greatly expanded.

Other significant conservation events which occurred during the administration of President Franklin D. Roosevelt include: operation of the somewhat short-lived National Industrial Recovery Act of 1933, under which, in adopting a "Code of Fair Competition," the lumber industry committed itself to the practice of crude forestry in its logging operations and continued these practices after the act was declared unconstitutional in 1935; establishment of a National Planning Board in 1933 which was succeeded by the National Resources Board and finally became the National Resources Committee and published in 1934 a second attempt at an inventory of the country's natural resources; establishment of the Resettlement Administration, concerned with allocating marginal and submarginal lands to appropriate nonagricultural uses and to directing and helping people located on these lands to better economic opportunity; establishment of the Tennessee Valley Authority in 1933, which has undertaken the entire readjustment of the economy of a great river valley; strengthening the administration of the Federal Power Commission under the law of 1920 by authorizing in 1935 the appointment of five full-time commissioners instead of passing the job to busy ex-officio cabinet officers; calling the first North American Wildlife Conference at Washington in 1936 to unite the efforts of scientists, sportsmen, trappers, and lovers of wild animals, and which representatives from Canada, Mexico, and every state in the Union attended and achieved better understanding of the complex problems of conserving wild-animal life; enactment of the Flood Control Act of 1937 which, among other things, recognized the importance of cover in headwater control and brought other bureaus besides the Office of Engineers of the U.S. Army into the research and alleviation picture; passage of the Guffey Coal Act of 1937, which authorized the industry itself to bring some order into its operations through so-called production control but which failed of necessary reenactment in 1943; authorization of curtailments of civilian use of many materials during wartime, which dramatized the individual's duty to conserve finished products and thus the natural resources involved. The net effect of this was of course somewhat offset by tremendously wasteful war uses of natural resources of every kind.

Conservation since the End of World War II. With a hungry world desperately in need of everything from food to shelter, the natural resources of a rich country like the United States are looked to for continuing heavy use.

Soil conservation, river development, justified opening up of hitherto inaccessible public forests, and a mildly militant realization by the man in the street that shortages in comforts flowing from natural resources *can* occur even in a strong democracy—all these ideas are bound to obtain increasing attention. It is also encouraging to know that an agreement on the international management of Great Lakes commercial fisheries has been reached between the United States and Canada. Recent and more accurate appraisals of the forest resources of the country have been finished. Corporations and individuals controlling the timber-growing business of the country are making steady if somewhat slow progress in putting private timberlands under forest management. State conservation departments are assuming increasing responsibility for managing timber, wild animals, and mineral resources. Conservation materials are beginning to find their way into public-school teaching.

But natural resources as well as mankind took an inevitable beating during the Second World War. Losses will be offset slowly, and so far (1953) it has been difficult to advance or to defend established national conservation policies from amendments and reinterpretations which are likely to favor exploitation rather than conservation of natural resources. Typical of these are: a temporary breakdown of all-out Federal, state, and private cooperation in attacking interlocking conservation problems on a river-valley scale such as would be appropriate for the Missouri River Valley; a definite attempt by a certain small but powerful element of the livestock industry of the West to gain control of all western public lands now used for grazing and thereby to obtain permanent subsidy and to establish grazing as the *only* beneficial use of such lands; efforts to amend and thus weaken the Mineral Leasing Law of 1920 and stubborn resistance on the part of the mining industry to revision of the mining law of 1872 which is subject to shocking misuse and fraud; attempts to circumvent or amend the Reclamation Act of 1902, which has always limited purchase of irrigation water from federally built projects to family-size farms; lack of interest in any but weak and temporary legislation on control of pollution of streams and underground water supplies; pressure to abolish or invade parts of certain national parks and monuments for exploitation purposes; increasing resistance to any Federal regulation of private forest exploitation with an inadequate showing of state legislation and private initiative as a substitute; severe curtailment by the Congress of certain important conservation activities such as those of administering the grazing resources of the public lands outside the national forests and managing the wild-animal life occurring on national forests; the 1953 submerged oil-land legislation releasing to some of the states certain mineral resources belonging to all the people; the tendency to discard, with questionable justification, long-established public power policy.

While these setbacks may be charged in part to reaction against wartime restrictions and against policies of a party long in power, they serve notice on the citizens of this country that needed reforms in handling natural resources not only will fail to materialize but that ground already gained can easily be lost unless the public is alert. Understanding is one essential of such alertness, and it is well therefore to express here certain inescapable principles before taking up the natural resources separately.

Principles of Conserving Natural Resources. *Beneficial Use.* Natural resources are for the benefit of society, and any control of such resources places upon the "owner" an obligation to use them beneficially and with minimum waste.

Variability of Waste. What is waste either in production or consumption may vary under numerous conditions where the factors of production are out of balance or adequate physical distribution is impossible, but deliberate waste for purposes of profit only is seldom justified.

Substitution. In general, the substitution of replaceable for irreplaceable and plentiful for scarce natural resources, where the former will serve adequately, is sound practice.

Harmonious Property Relations. Pooling of ownership and operation of adjoining natural-resource properties to any extent practicable and with safeguards against predatory monopoly tend to assure opportunity for most effective conservation.

Providential Functions of Government. Governments by their very nature must do certain things for their people, which private enterprise cannot or will not do because such services are marginal as profit producers. The control and even the operation of many natural resources are activities of this character, and in many situations conservation can be achieved only under public control.

Productive Powers. The productive powers of natural resources, capital, and human strength and talent are subject to maintenance and increase through positive direction, and *conservation* of natural resources to serve this end is the exact opposite of the laissez-faire attitude toward them.

Individual Responsibility for Conservation. The prized freedom and dignity of the individual in a democracy must be balanced by a high sense of understanding and assumption of reponsibility by every citizen, if along with other blessings, natural resources are to be conserved in a democracy.

BIBLIOGRAPHY

Allen, Shirley W.: An Introduction to American Forestry, McGraw-Hill Book Company, Inc., New York, 1950.

American Forests, monthly magazine of The American Forestry Association, Washington, D.C.

Bennett, Hugh Hammond: Soil Conservation, McGraw-Hill Book Company, Inc., New York, 1939.

Butler, Ovid M.: American Conservation in Picture and Story, American Forestry Association, Washington, D.C., 1935.

Cameron, Jenks: The Development of Governmental Forest Control in the United States, Johns Hopkins Press, Baltimore, 1928.

Conservation of Renewable Natural Resources, Proceedings of Inter-American Conference, Denver, 1948, U.S. Department of State publication 3382.

Dewhurst, J. Frederic, and associates: America's Needs and Resources, The Twentieth Century Fund, Inc., New York, 1947.

Ely, Richard T., and associates: The Foundations of Our National Prosperity, The Macmillan Company, New York, 1923.

Gabrielson, Ira: Wildlife Conservation, The Macmillan Company, New York, 1942.

Gustafson, A. F., and associates: Conservation in the United States, Comstock Publishing Associates, Inc., Ithaca, N.Y., 1949.

Krug, J. A.: Report (as Secretary of the Interior) on National Resources and Foreign Aid, 1947.

Lovering, T. S.: Minerals in World Affairs, Prentice-Hall, Inc., New York, 1933.

Munns, E. N., and Joseph H. Stoeckeler: How Are the Great Plains Shelterbelts? *Jour. Forestry,* **44**:237–257, 1946.

Parkins, A. E., and J. R. Whitaker: Our Natural Resources and Their Conservation, John Wiley & Sons, Inc., New York, 1939.

Pinchot, Gifford: Breaking New Ground, Harcourt, Brace and Company, Inc., New York, 1947.

Shankland, Robert: Steve Mather of the National Parks, Alfred A. Knopf, Inc., New York, 1950.

Soil Conservation, monthly magazine of U.S. Soil Conservation Service.

Van Hise, Charles R., and Loomis Havemeyer: Conservation of Our Natural Resources, The Macmillan Company, New York, 1930.

Whitaker, J. Russell, and Edward A. Ackerman: American Resources, Harcourt, Brace and Company, Inc., New York, 1951.

CHAPTER 2

The Land, the Soil, and Conservation

The land and the soil are not the same thing. Both terms are used loosely and with more than one meaning. Land as popularly understood is the broader term always and carries the idea of surface or spatial, rather than cropping or extractive, use. Soil on the other hand is the surface layer of decomposed and disintegrated rock combined with organic matter supporting a biological population of its own and varying widely in its ability to produce crops under favorable climatic conditions. It is sometimes transported so that it is not from the underlying parent material in its present location.

Land in the above sense is more stable than soil, for soil can be washed or blown or carried away and may become sterilized or compacted. It can of course also be accepted as space only, rather than for cropping.

The uses of land, therefore, of which the use of soil for cropping is only one, would appear to require the strictest application of conservation principles and devices if human welfare is to result. One figure in Table 1, page 19, is particularly significant with respect to spatial use of land, namely, the 5.4 per cent of the entire land area of the United States devoted to cities, parks, roads, railroads, airports, nonfarm home sites, and the like, an impressive total of 105 million acres. Within farms the figure of 27 million acres in farmsteads, roads, lanes, etc., also is impressive. In a broad sense practically all other lands, even including the 84 million acres shown in deserts, swamps, and dunes, are to a greater or lesser extent producers of wild or cultivated "crops." The former may be only wild-animal life or unusual plants, or again the use may be spatial in certain instances, an example of which would be water storage aside from reservoirs. Of the entire land area of 1,904,000,000 acres, it is well to note that 59.6 per cent is within farms, though not all is plowable, and 40.4 per cent lies outside this classification but is used to a considerable extent for grazing purposes.

Soils

Even the most generalized classification of the soils of the United States presents a complex picture and somewhat startling terminology. Color, origin, location, and chemical content figure in group names used in soil classification, and perhaps the simplest generalized map is the one made up of Figs. 5 and 6, adapted from Marbut's original one. Such a grouping as here shown is useful in understanding efforts to conserve soil as a

Table 1. Distribution of Land Area of the United State by Primary Use

Primary use	Million acres	Per cent
Agricultural:		
Cropland	478	25.1
Open pasture and nonforest range	631	33.1
Farm yards, farm roads, fence rows, etc	27	1.4
Total, agricultural	1,136	59.6
Commercial forest land*	457	24.0
Total used for products of the soil	1,593	83.6
Noncommercial forest land, not otherwise classified†	122	6.5
Land committed to special uses:		
Urban and industrial land	25	1.3
Rural nonfarm home sites	10	0.5
National and state parks	16	0.8
National and state wildlife refuges	9	0.5
Transportation right of ways and airports	14	0.7
Reservoir and other water-project lands‡	12	0.6
Military reservations	19	1.0
Total, land committed to special uses	105	5.4
Desert, rock surface, swamps, sand dunes, etc	84	4.5
Total surface area	1,904	100.0

SOURCE: By special permission from mimeographed conference paper, "Competing Demands for Use of Land" by Resources for the Future, Inc.

* This estimate may be revised considerably as the nationwide survey of forest land is brought to completion.

† Most of this noncommercial forest area is used for grazing. An additional 41 million acres of noncommercial forest land is used for parks, wildlife refuges, and other primary uses.

‡ Of the 12 million acres shown here, 3 to 4 million acres is in reservoirs and surrounding reservations; the rest is in floodways and in land temporarily held for development in authorized reclamation projects. It is estimated that an additional 6 to 7 million acres of land is inundated by reservoirs, but this is excluded from the 1,904 million acres total land-surface area. The total area inundated by reservoirs and in the surrounding reservations is probably between 9 and 10 million acres.

resource, for the uses to which land is put are influenced by the character of the soil and the natural vegetative cover as well as by location, temperature, and rainfall. On the other hand, temperature, rainfall, and vegetative cover have been powerful influences in the development from the

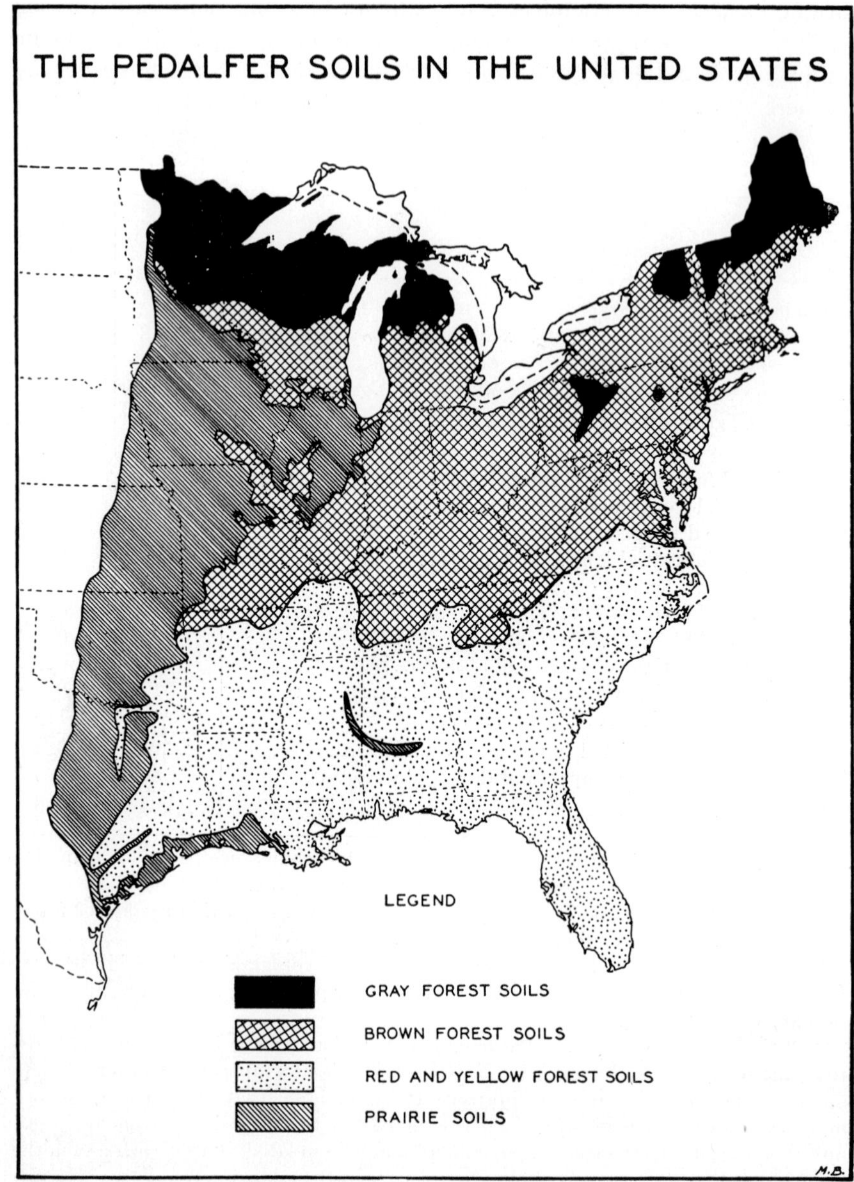

Fig. 5. Generalized map of the soils of Eastern United States. (*Adapted from an early map by the U.S. Soil Survey.*)

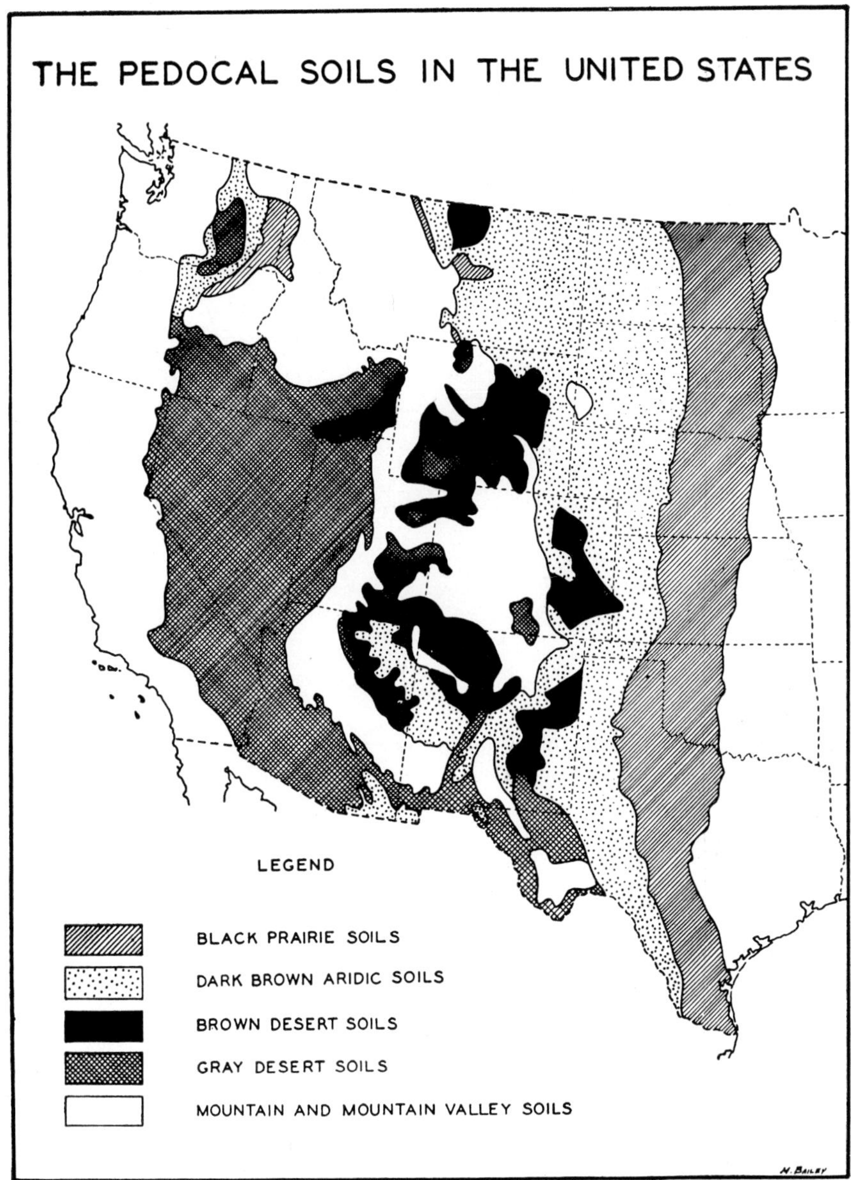

FIG. 6. Generalized map of the soils of Western United States. (*Adapted from an early map by the U.S. Soil Survey.*)

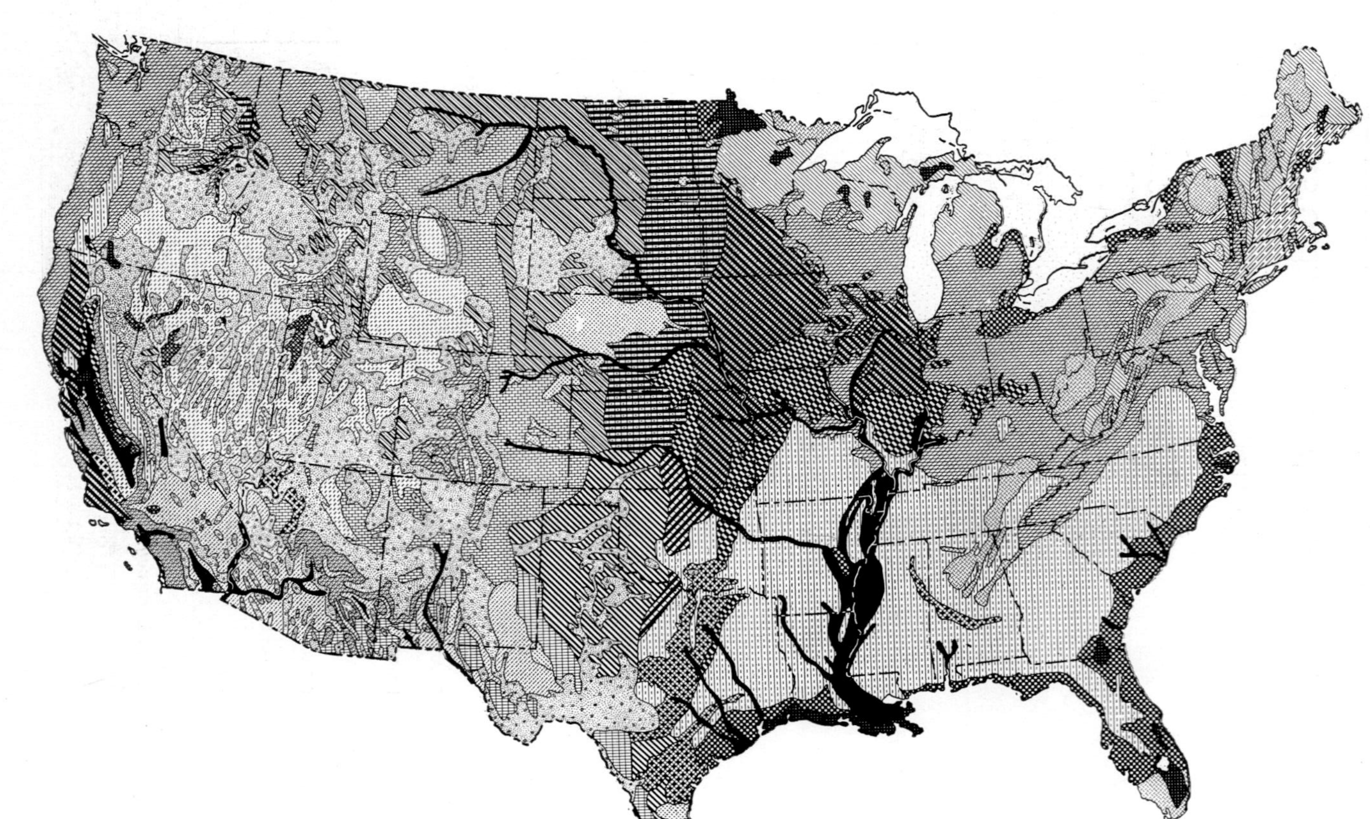

Fig. 6A. Recent map of the general pattern of great soil groups of the United States, indicating their wide variety in character. (*Map by U.S. Soil Survey.*)

ZONAL

Great groups of soils with well-developed soil characteristics, reflecting the dominating influence of climate and vegetation. (As shown on the map, many small areas of intrazonal and azonal soils are included.)

PODZOL SOILS
Light-colored leached soils of cool, humid forested regions.

BROWN PODZOLIC SOILS
Brown leached soils of cool-temperate, humid forested regions.

GRAY-BROWN PODZOLIC SOILS
Grayish-brown leached soils of temperate, humid forested regions.

RED AND YELLOW PODZOLIC SOILS
Red or yellow leached soils of warm-temperate, humid forested regions.

PRAIRIE SOILS
Very dark brown soils of cool and temperate, relatively humid grasslands.

REDDISH PRAIRIE SOILS
Dark reddish-brown soils of warm-temperate, relatively humid grasslands.

CHERNOZEM SOILS
Dark-brown to nearly black soils of cool and temperate, subhumid grasslands.

CHESTNUT SOILS
Dark-brown soils of cool and temperate, subhumid to semiarid grasslands.

REDDISH CHESTNUT SOILS
Dark reddish-brown soils of warm-temperate, semiarid regions under mixed shrub and grass vegetation.

BROWN SOILS
Brown soils of cool and temperate, semiarid grasslands.

REDDISH BROWN SOILS
Reddish-brown soils of warm-temperate to hot, semiarid to arid regions, under mixed shrub and grass vegetation.

NONCALCIC BROWN SOILS
Brown or light reddish-brown soils of warm-temperate, wet-dry, semiarid regions, under mixed forest, shrub, and grass vegetation.

SIEROZEM OR GRAY DESERT SOILS
Gray soils of cool to temperate, arid regions, under shrub and grass vegetation.

RED DESERT SOILS
Light reddish-brown soils of warm-temperate to hot, arid regions, under shrub vegetation.

AZONAL

Soils without well-developed soil characteristics. (Many areas of these soils are included with other groups on the map.)

LITHOSOLS AND SHALLOW SOILS
(ARID-SUBHUMID)
(HUMID)
Shallow soils consisting largely of an imperfectly weathered mass of rock fragments, largely but not exclusively on steep slopes.

SANDS (DRY)
Very sandy soils.

ALLUVIAL SOILS
Soils developing from recently deposited alluvium that have had little or no modification by processes of soil formation.

INTRAZONAL

Great groups of soils with more or less well-developed soil characteristics reflecting the dominating influence of some local factor of relief, parent material, or age over the normal effect of climate and vegetation. (Many areas of these soils are included with zonal groups on the map.)

PLANOSOLS
Soils with strongly leached surface horizons over claypans on nearly flat land in cool to warm, humid to subhumid regions, under grass or forest vegetation.

RENDZINA SOILS
Dark grayish-brown to black soils developed from soft limy materials in cool to warm, humid to subhumid regions, mostly under grass vegetation.

SOLONCHAK (1) AND SOLONETZ (2) SOILS
(1) Light-colored soils with high concentration of soluble salts, in subhumid to arid regions, under salt-loving plants.
(2) Dark-colored soils with hard prismatic subsoils, usually strongly alkaline, in subhumid or semiarid regions under grass or shrub vegetation.

WIESENBÖDEN (1), GROUND WATER PODZOL (2), AND HALF-BOG SOILS (3)
(1) Dark-brown to black soils developed with poor drainage under grasses in humid and subhumid regions.
(2) Gray sandy soils with brown cemented sandy subsoils developed under forests from nearly level imperfectly drained sand in humid regions.
(3) Poorly drained, shallow, dark peaty or mucky soils underlain by gray mineral soil, in humid regions, under swamp-forests.

BOG SOILS
Poorly drained dark peat or muck soils underlain by peat, mostly in humid regions, under swamp or marsh types of vegetation.

The areas of each great soil group shown on the map include areas of other groups too small to be shown separately. Especially are there small areas of the azonal and intrazonal groups included in the areas of zonal groups

FIG. 6B. Legend for map of great soil groups.

parent material of the soil of what is known as the soil itself. Marbut[1] points out as direct characteristics of the soil (1) that it is the surface layer of the unconsolidated rock material and (2) that it differs from the material beneath it and the material from which it was originally derived in color, texture, and structure, chemical composition, physical constitution, biological composition, number and arrangement of parts, and general morphology. (Otherwise, and in a geological sense, the differences are not so significant.)

The breaking down of parent material, or what is thought of as rock, occurs through weathering. This process includes *disintegration,* a physical process which is helped along by such forces as changes in temperature, changes in volume, friction through movement in stream beds and glaciers, and action of waves and winds, and *decomposition,* a chemical process effected by exposure to oxygen, water, and to a very small extent to weak acids in rainwater. Actually both processes go on at the same time.

Expansion and contraction through heating and cooling occur at differing rates, with various mineral constituents of rocks producing strains which break down the rocks themselves. Water penetrates cracks and depressions and in freezing and expanding as ice exerts a cumulative breaking force. Glaciers not only transport soil material from one location to another but actually pick up rocks and use them in their movements as gouging, planing, and abrasive "tools" to disintegrate rocks over which they pass. Roots of plants also penetrate cracks in rock, manage to find moisture and soil nutrients enough to keep the plant growing, and sometimes actually split huge rocks apart. These forces and their action are physical, and they produce disintegration of rock into soil materials.

Iron and other minerals which occur in rock readily take on oxygen when exposed to air and moisture in the process of oxidation. In doing so they increase considerably in volume so that there is a physical change as well as a chemical one, both disintegration and decomposition taking place. Carbonation is a somewhat similar process which may also increase the solubility of minerals. Perhaps the most important decomposition process, however, is hydration, in which water enters into chemical combination with minerals, changing old and producing new compounds, some of which are highly soluble. Dissolving is still another decomposition process.

Disintegration and decomposition of rocks have not now produced soils but *soil materials,* and if development were halted here there would be no soil. There would be only a layer of unconsolidated minerals.

[1] Marbut, C. F., Soils, Their Genesis, Classification and Development, lectures before the Graduate School of the U.S. Department of Agriculture, February to May, 1928. (Unpublished.)

Accumulation of these materials, populating them with microorganisms, and incorporation of organic matter into them from the plant and animal wastes must follow.

Soil materials may be accumulated residually or may be transported by wind, water, gravity, or glaciers from the place where first broken down to the place where further soil formation proceeds. From then on comes the action of vegetation, which in turn attracts animal life and

FIG. 7. Southwest Butte near Mesa Verde, Colo. Erosion here is geologic and not brought about or accelerated by the activities of mankind. (*Photo by Soil Conservation Service.*)

other biological forms, all the way from single-celled protozoa to angleworms and even burrowing mammals, and finally the soil material becomes a mature, living soil. It should be noted here that numerous factors have been at work and that even men in their selection of crops, their cultivating methods, and their return of plant and animal wastes may have been active in trying to manage an immature soil to an extent that amounts to actual soil building.

But the significant fact in this story of the development of soil from parent material is the slowness with which it proceeds in nature and the *relative* helplessness of men to hurry it along. Various estimates of the rate of soil building geologically run from $\frac{1}{600}$ inch a year to 1 foot in 10,000 years. The latter figure amounts to more than 140 long human lifetimes. The human race, therefore, needs to be alert that soil does not wash or blow away, does not lose its fertility, and that it gets all the help in actual development that human effort can supply.

Problems of Conserving the Soil

Two great physical problems challenge the thinking and the energy of those who use the land and the wider circle of people who live from the products of the land: (1) keeping the soil in place through controlling removal by erosion from water and wind; (2) maintaining the nutrient materials in the soil which make cropping successful, through cultivation, fertilizing, and cropping itself.

These two problems overlap to some extent because soil removal by erosion amounts also to the removal of nutrient materials. A third great problem, which is most important though not a physical one, is bringing about understanding and action on the part of those who control the soil resources of the country.

The two physical problems involve learning through observation, research, and inquiry, and actually practicing what is learned on the land itself. The third problem is one of influencing the minds of men and working out procedures, cooperative and other, by which determination to conserve may be translated into action.

Men will understand and act only when they know what brings about loss of soil and its nutrient materials, something of the extent to which such loss is occurring, and what such loss means in terms of their own and other human welfare. Such considerations should therefore be taken up next.

Erosion

Factors Which Influence Erosion. Normal or geologic erosion is a natural and age-old process of development on the earth's surface and is generally thought to proceed over the ages no faster than soil formation. It is not to be confused with accelerated erosion induced by the activities of men. It is with the latter that conservation practices are concerned, but many of the factors influencing erosion apply to both types. Climatic factors such as temperature variations, rainfall, and wind are powerful. Freezing and thawing loosen the surface of the soil and subject it to easy removal by washing. Rainfall, except of the gentler kind, has a beating and loosening effect on the surface which is almost explosive, and when it cannot be absorbed rapidly (Fig. 8) runs off in excess, carrying loosened soil particles with it. Amount, frequency, and character of rainfall are all, therefore, important factors. Character of the soil itself as to permeability, texture, and content of organic material may limit or multiply the erosive effect of rainfall both by failure to absorb water quickly or by the ease with which soil particles may be suspended in water. Vegetative cover such as trees, grass, shrubs, and weeds affects erosion by breaking the beating power of hard rains so that water drips rather than beats on the soil, by cushioning with leaf litter or sod the beat of raindrops, and by increasing the absorptive capacity of the soil through networks of roots and the building up of organic content. Slope, because water runs downhill, is obviously important as a factor affecting erosion. The steeper the slope, the faster will be the flow of the stream of whatever size and the greater its carrying and grinding power. Since accelerated erosion is being considered, the action of men in connection with the above factors is

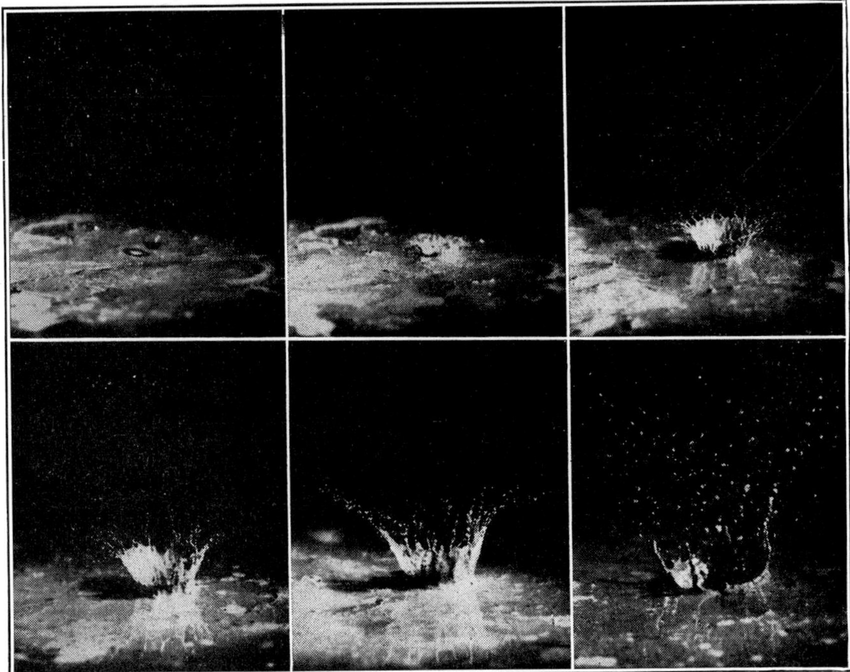

FIG. 8. The beating and soil-moving power of a raindrop (*Photo by Soil Conservation Service.*)

assumed and, as their manipulators, men become the most powerful factor affecting erosion. This is particularly true with respect to wind erosion, which is most severe where men have removed vegetative cover and paid too little attention to safe cultivation practices.

Kinds of Erosion. Wind erosion is more spectacular as regards the soil which is on the move than water erosion, but water erosion leaves frequently a more striking set of scars on the landscape; it may be designated as sheet erosion, rill erosion, gully erosion, and riparian or riverbank erosion.

Sheet erosion is the removal of soil in small but uniform amounts as it

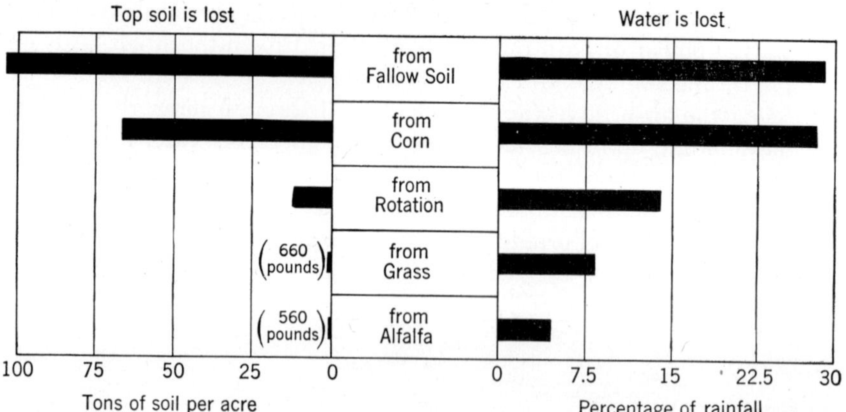

FIG. 9. Diagram of soil and water loss from 4 years' observation under differing conditions of cover at Bethany, Mo., on Shelby loam of 8 per cent slope with a 40-inch average annual rainfall. (*Photo by Soil Conservation Service.*)

FIG. 10. Rill erosion near Howell, Mich. Corn planted in rows up and down 10 per cent slope. (*Photo by Soil Conservation Service.*)

becomes suspended in excess rainfall and is carried away over slight slopes from the entire area. The very fact that it goes on unnoticed puts the landowner off guard, and it therefore becomes important in amount with repeated storms. About the only evidence one can see is small accumulations of washed soil in some low flat spots in the fields.

Rill erosion is more severe than sheet erosion and creates many individual small streams over the surface which start or follow some mark or depression and cut rapidly (Fig. 10). Total soil removal is heavy even during a single storm.

Gully Erosion. Uncontrolled rills become gullies which are wider V-shaped channels broadening and deepening as they descend. Gullies may also start almost suddenly where heavy rainfall and runoff strike a depression or weak spot on the soil surface. Enormous amounts of soil are removed, and great canyonlike gashes appear which make plowing impossible (Fig. 11).

FIG. 11. A gully in southeastern Michigan. (*Photo by Soil Conservation Service.*)

Riparian or riverbank erosion consists of weakening and undercutting by river currents of banks and caving of these banks into the stream. It is really a variation of gully erosion where the gully becomes or consists of a regularly flowing steam, but the cutting is more lateral than vertical (Fig. 13).

Wind erosion will be considered as only one type, since it varies more with intensity than with the pattern it leaves on the surface. The wind may produce the general dust storm which fills the air to a great height and carries the finest soil particles for many miles, or it may pick up and carry for short distances soil particles which are too large or heavy to be called "dust," or it may succeed only in rolling or causing to hop certain particles too heavy to move otherwise. In the latter instance soil not only is removed from the place where it belongs but is caught against some fence, building, or other obstruction and accumulates until it covers valuable improvements or forms a dune which moves slowly but powerfully, burying at least temporarily anything in its path, be it farm, forest, or village. While any one of these movements may be a part of geological erosion, any one may also be accelerated by removal of the vegetative cover such as the native sod in wind-swept territory. This occurred in the so-called "dust-bowl" section in northern Texas, western Oklahoma, and southwestern Kansas, and in other parts of the Great Plains, following the breaking of the native sod for wheat growing during

FIG. 12. Rill erosion on northern Rocky Mountain range land. (*Photo by U.S. Forest Service.*)

the First World War (Fig. 16). Soil particles from this region were identified in Eastern states and even on ships out in the Atlantic Ocean. Great suffering followed the economic breakdown of wheat farming in this region, and many families were forced to move out.

The Effects of Erosion and the Threats of Damage. Remembering that men have it within their power to control soil erosion to a great extent, the need for prompt action becomes apparent from figures on soil loss and its accompanying human suffering.

The map in Fig. 14 shows the distribution of erosion in the United States and reveals (1) a comparatively small area unaffected or subject only to slight wind erosion; (2) certain areas grouped as mountains, mesas, canyons, and badlands which yield little even in the way of pasture

Fig. 13. Riparian or stream-bank erosion near Richford, N.Y. Unprotected stream-bank cutting into the farmer's best field. In the background, a bank protected by vegetation is not affected. (*Photo by Soil Conservation Service.*)

and on which erosion, though severe, is not a critical economic problem; (3) areas of moderate erosion; and (4) areas of severe erosion.

A more detailed summary is given in Table 2 from estimates based largely on reconnaissance surveys and assembled in 1938.

Table 2. Distribution of Erosion Damage in the United States

	Acres
Total land area (exclusive of large urban territory)	1,903,000,000
Erosion conditions not defined (such as deserts, scablands, and large Western mountain area)	144,000,000
Total land area (exclusive of mountains, mesas, and badlands) divided into:	
Ruined or severely damaged	282,000,000
Moderately damaged	775,000,000
Cropland (harvested, crop failure and lying fallow):	
Ruined for cultivation	50,000,000
Severely damaged	50,000,000
One-half to all topsoil gone	100,000,000
Erosion process beginning	100,000,000

Hardly any major agricultural region is unaffected, and in some degree production of every staple commodity has felt the blow. Heavily farmed areas in rolling country where crops are planted in rows and where cotton, corn, and tobacco dominate the market suffer most severely from water

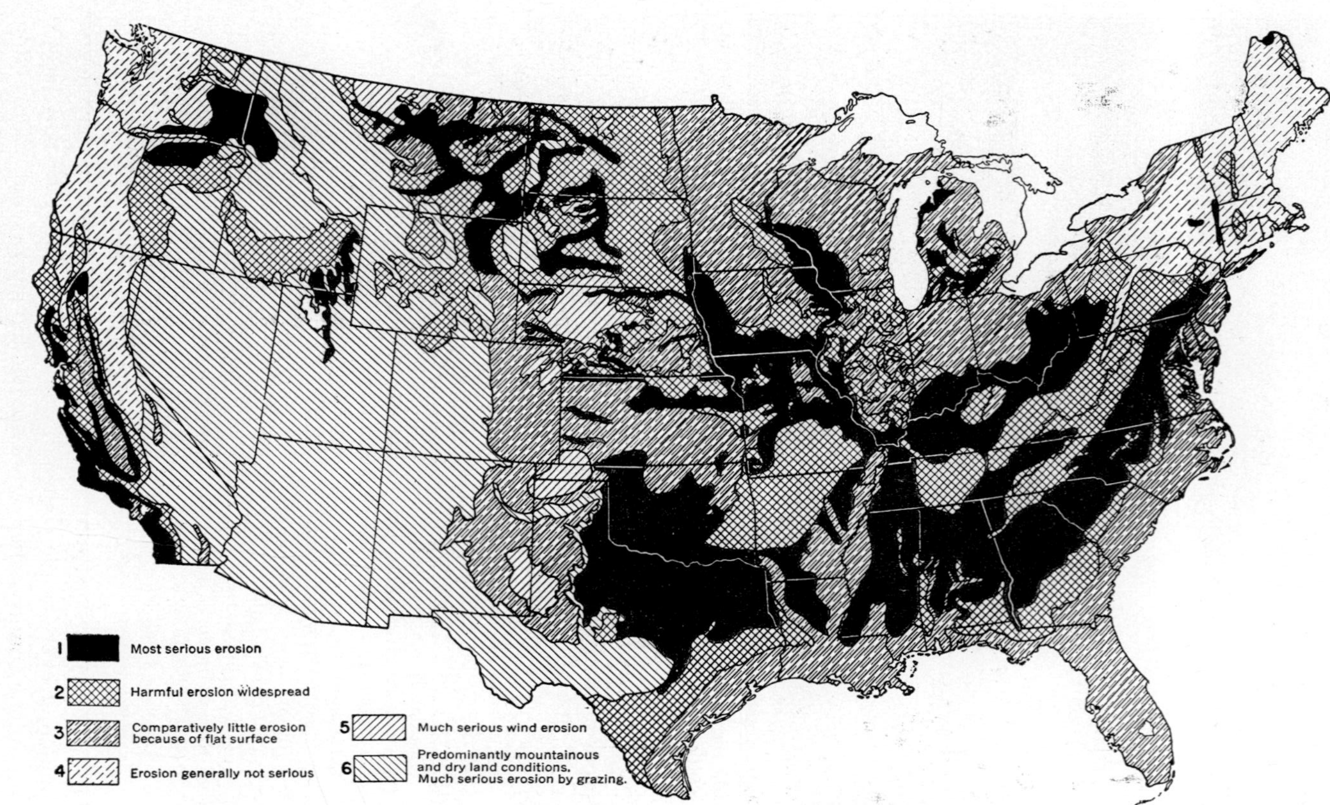

Fig. 14. Map showing distribution of erosion in 1933. (*Soil Conservation Service.*)

erosion. Wind erosion is most severe in the Great Plains and in high level country farther west.

Estimates based on a large number of measurements on experimental plots at soil-erosion experiment stations throughout the country put the amount of soil removed annually by wind and water from the crop and pasture lands of the United States at 3 billion tons. This includes the top layer, which is the most productive part of the soil, and amounts to the removal of 7 inches of soil from an area of no less than 9 million acres. "Where does it go?" one may ask, and the answer is that it may blow half

FIG. 15. Erosion ruins reservoirs at times by filling them with silt. Mono Dam, Los Padres National Forest, California. Watershed is frequently burned. (*Photo by U.S. Forest Service.*)

way across the continent and be so scattered as to rest at no point where it represents a usable accumulation; or it may blow out to sea as it was observed to do in the 1935 dust storms; or it may become a part of the 730 million tons per year that represent the silt discharge of the Mississippi River at its mouth; or it may be deposited in a reservoir built to store water for power or irrigation (Fig. 15) where it not only is lost to cultivation but reduces the water-storage capacity behind the dam; or it may cover cropland or improvements now in use to ruinous depth; and finally it may clog the channels of streams previously capable of carrying flood waters, interfere with navigation, or otherwise defeat the control and harnessing of runoff waters.

Controlling Erosion

To keep the runoff from washing away the soil and the wind from blowing it away is obviously a matter of managing the soil. This means putting it to use so that it serves mankind, but always taking advantage of cultivation methods, maintenance of cover, and devices for mechanically curbing surface runoff and wind.

Tillage. The preparation of the soil for putting in a crop includes plowing and other mechanical methods of turning over and breaking up the surface layer. Whether such treatment is shallow or deep may affect

Fig. 16. Wind erosion in Colorado. The dust storm is approaching from abused land. (*Courtesy American Forests.*)

the rate at which rainfall will be taken up by the soil and the resulting surplus that may bring about surface damage as it runs off. Whether the direction of plowing or "fitting," as the final process is sometimes called, follows an up-and-down-the-hill direction or follows the contour convenience will effect the power of the tilled soil to absorb water and the speed and power which it attains. Whether the residues of former crops such as cornstalks, straw, and other unharvested materials are incorporated into the soil in tillage practices or are burned or removed for convenience will affect the power of the tilled soil to absorb water and to resist removal by wind. Whether the surface is finely divided or left in clods will certainly affect the removal by wind, and whether the surface is leveled or left in furrows will affect the settling or accumulating of soil particles as they blow over the surface (Fig. 18). Tillage, therefore, offers an opportunity to defend the soil from both water and wind erosion and at the same time to provide for the peculiar soil-preparation requirements of any important crop.

Cover. Whether the vegetative cover maintained or alternated with clean tillage to keep down weeds is forest, brush, sod, sparse herbaceous growth, orchard, hay, grain, or some crop such as corn, cotton, tobacco, or potatoes, each planted in rows—the use and pattern of cover is an

FIG. 17. Contour plowing in Texas. A tillage method designed to prevent erosion. (*Photo by Soil Conservation Service.*)

important key to holding the soil in place (Fig. 19). The value of cover lies not only in actually covering and reinforcing the soil layer, but in assuring that the portion of the rainfall which penetrates the soil shall reach it as relatively clear water. Otherwise it becomes laden with surface particles of soil which clog the tiny "pores" and slow down or stop the *infiltration,* a term used to denote the passage of water into the soil. Study of the rates of infiltration and of the results of rainfall on soils under varying treatments has yielded some of the most useful data now available for practical application. Duley and Miller[2] at the Missouri Agricultural Experiment Station found that over a period of 6 years, on plots of similar

[2] Duley, F. L., and M. T. Miller, Erosion and Surface Runoff under Different Soil Conditions, *Mo. Agr. Expt. Sta. Res. Bul.* 63, p. 44, 1923.

soil and slope, the one kept in sod lost less than ⅛ of the rainfall, eroded at what appeared to be 11/1,000 inch in 6 years, and at this rate would lose 7 inches of soil in about 3,500 years. The plot kept devoid of cover and spaded 4 inches deep, on the other hand, lost close to ⅓ of the rainfall, almost 1⅔ inches of soil in 6 years, and at this rate would lose 7 inches of soil in 24 years. Five other plots ranked in soil and water conservation from best to worst approximately as follows: rotation of corn, wheat, and clover; wheat annually; corn annually; not cultivated;

FIG. 18. Wind erosion and deep furrows to collect the blowing soil in Oklahoma. Cloddy condition of soil in furrows resists removal of wind. (*Photo by Soil Conservation Service.*)

spaded 8 inches deep. (In the last instance rainfall loss was greater than in the plot not cultivated.)

Lowdermilk found in laboratory tests that certain soils would lose 75 per cent of their absorptive power in a period of 8 hours when turbid water was used in place of clear water.[3]

In a crude set of demonstration plots in Livingston County, Michigan, the average annual loss of soil in a period of 8 years, from 1938 to 1946, was 36.24 tons per acre from plots of various crops planted in rows up and down slope, and 5.82 tons from those planted on contour, more than six times as great a loss just from unwise direction of cultivation and planting. Soil loss per acre on the up-and-down-hill plots for the period of

[3] Quoted by E. N. Munns, Forests and Floods, *South. Lumberman*, **138**:60, 1930.

Apr. 1, 1945, to Apr. 1, 1947, for various crops amounted to corn, 6.05 tons; oats, 2.15 tons; hay, 0.1 ton. On contoured plots the losses were corn, 1.35 tons; oats, 0.05 ton; hay, 0.05 ton.[4]

Many claims for soil- and water-holding efficiency are made for the so-called "trash agriculture," where all plant residues are left on the soil. No turning of the soil as in ordinary plowing is done, but the trash is cut into the soil and the entire soil layer loosened before planting.

The rotation of crops in farming offers an opportunity to provide the particular crop with its tillage needs in alternate or occasional years

FIG. 19. Aerial view of strip cropping on contour. Winneshiek County, Iowa. (*Photo by Soil Conservation Service.*)

whether it is planted in rows with the intervening soil exposed or sown as grain crops so that something resembling a temporary sod is produced. Thus there might in succeeding years be rotations of corn, oats, clover, alfalfa—or alfalfa, corn, oats—or cotton, cowpeas, corn, wheat.

Because direction of tillage effects some mechanical control of the power of water and wind to erode, its discussion is taken up later.

Strip Cropping. The traditional practice of dividing up farms into rectangular fields to match and parallel property lines is slowly giving way to division on a band or strip pattern. Here one crop alternates with another in a sort of ribbon pattern, with the strips sometimes following

[4] *Annual Report,* 1946. Fenton Soil Conservation District, Fenton, Mich., p. 6.

the contour and with the *close-grown* or sodlike crops alternating with those planted in rows and sometimes spoken of as *intertilled.* Strips may be placed on contour, or may traverse the existing fenced field parallel to a boundary line (Fig. 20) or be placed so as to protect some particular spot or strip where erosion is starting, or be placed at right angles to the direction of the prevailing wind. They would then be designated, respectively, as (1) contour strips, (2) field strips, (3) buffer strips, and (4) wind strips.

Maintenance of permanent vegetative cover other than grass pasture or what has so far been spoken of as sod involves, for example, the use

Fig. 20. Wind strip in field strip pattern near Muskegon, Mich. (*Photo by Soil Conservation Service.*)

of the soil for forest crops; stock raising on Western ranges where sagebrush and intermittent grass and herbaceous growth may take the place of continuous sod; and use of the surface soil spatially in road cut banks and fill banks, parkways, and parks and lawns. So important is the prevention of erosion in these uses that vast sums are invested in such road-maintenance features as sodding, in retiring watershed lands entirely from use other than water catchment and storage, and even in forest planting of large areas.

Mechanical Methods and Devices. Vegetative cover has its limitations in soil-conservation practice but may frequently be used to advantage in connection with mechanically constructed devices for "making the water walk" off the land, retarding its flow until it can be absorbed, diverting it from vulnerable spots on the surface of fields, and protecting stream banks, roadsides, and shore residence and commercial sites from current and wave action. The simplest of these devices is really a tillage practice and consists of plowing "around the hills" on the contour, instead of up and down the slopes. Regardless of the crop to be planted, this direction of plowing and fitting avoids the kind of incipient channel which starts the surplus rainfall downhill on a destructive journey. Moreover if strip cropping follows contour plowing, high water-retarding efficiency

FIG. 21. Terracing in Tennessee. The upper white line indicates the slope of land, while the lower line gives an idea of the cross section of the ditch below the terrace, which will act as a diversion channel. (*Photo by Caterpillar Tractor Co., courtesy Tennessee Valley Authority.*)

is obtained from any strips planted to close-grown crops such as alfalfa or wheat, and even the intertilled crop strips such as tobacco and potatoes have a better chance to retard and absorb runoff. Contour plowing in dry country has also excellent possibilities for conserving rainfall which would otherwise run off and cause some erosion. Deep wide furrows catch and hold excess rainfall, and by use of an implement known as a damming lister or basin-forming lister, a furrow can be made which throws the soil to both sides and leaves a dam at intervals in the furrow. The effect is to dot the contour-following plowed area with hundreds of tiny ponds or basins, which assure good distribution of the saved rainfall.

Terracing. In regions of heavy rainfall and soils particularly subject to erosion, terraces (Fig. 21) may be used at the foot of any one or more crop strips. These devices are wide shallow channels approximately on contour but designed with enough fall *along* the contour to lead any surplus runoff around the slope to an outlet into a grassed or paved waterway usually located along the edge of the field. The latter channel may end up in an open drainage ditch or a stream, but it disposes of the surplus runoff safely and, of course, must frequently be definitely constructed and always maintained in sod or pavement. Terraces as just discussed are of the sort illustrated in Figs. 21 and 22. There are also bench terraces constructed in various parts of the world on steep slopes, maintained with heavy sodding or with masonary retaining walls, and permitting agriculture on otherwise prohibitive sites.

Fig. 22. Terrace with diversion ditch in action almost too soon. Strips are to be planted both above and below the ditch and the ditch and terrace seeded, fertilized, and limed. Livingston County, Mich. (*Photo by Soil Conservation Service.*)

Diversion Ditches. A terrace usually amounts to a diversion channel because it "walks" the water off the land instead of holding it for further absorption (Fig. 22), but a diversion ditch may be a more abrupt channel curving around the head of a set of rills or an incipient gully. In this form surplus runoff is diverted quickly onto safe sod or level areas where it can be absorbed (Fig. 23).

Fig. 23. Sodded waterway in corn strips, Muskingum County, Ohio. Excess rain water drains from the lower edge of strips into grassed waterway and leaves the field undamaged. (*Photo by Soil Conservation Service.*)

Fig. 24. Contour furrows on a seeded field, Okanogan County, Washington. Severe runoff has occurred without evidence of erosion. (*Photo by Soil Conservation Service.*)

FIG. 25. Gully erosion checked by the growth of kudzu vine. Second year's growth. Near Marion, Ga. (*Photo by Soil Conservation Service.*)

FIG. 25A. Checking wave erosion by means of rock-filled timber cribs which act as groins. They are placed at right angles to the shore line; the ones shown are already partly covered with sand and are building up good beach. (*Photo by E. F. Brater, courtesy Engineering Research Institute, University of Michigan.*)

Contour Furrows. Differing from continuous contour plowing, terraces, or short diversion ditches, contour furrows are usually single deep furrows at wide intervals and as nearly as possible on exact contour (Fig. 24). They are designed not to divert surplus runoff but to catch and retain it until absorbed. They amount, therefore, to elongated ponds, intermittently wet and dry, depending on rainfall. They are of special value on drier sodded pastures for moisture retention.

Gully-reclamation Devices. Reinforcing the banks or surfaces of the gully side walls with brush or straw, and using such material particularly

FIG. 26. A 66-year-old red cedar windbreak or shelterbelt, Seward County, Nebraska. Field and farm home protected. (*Photo by Soil Conservation Service.*)

at the vulnerable heads of gullies, is perhaps the simplest "gully-choking" method. Brush, log, and masonry dams across the path of the gully vary in cost but are all expensive of labor and material. If well constructed they bring about accumulations of silt, thus stabilizing the surface for revegetation and of course reducing the cutting power of runoff waters.

Any and all of these methods and devices again tie in well with the use of vegetative cover, which is difficult to establish otherwise (Fig. 25). Rebuilding of a real soil in a gully is a slow process, but forest crops of some value will sometimes take hold and eventually produce revenue in addition to their service in reinforcing and protecting the gully surface.

Riparian or stream-bank erosion requires heroic measures for control, and costs are high. Mankind frequently is competing with the stream for its natural "playground." The very old jetty device must be used where the current is swift and piling barriers or jetties can be established. Still another method is somewhat like the surface treatment of gully walls. Here the stream bank is sloped to a degree where it can be more easily stabilized, and a network or blanket of brush, fence wire, or rock, or a combination of the three, is anchored in place, and willow trees or cuttings are planted in and above the blanket. Stone riprap or sloping wall must occasionally be used near the low water line if the current is swift and the jetty type of structure impracticable.

FIG. 27. Sunflowers because they are taller than the bean crop are used in this Hendry County, Florida, field as a wind strip on blowing muck soil. (*Photo by Hermann Postlethwaite, courtesy Soil Conservation Service.*)

Wave erosion on lake and ocean shores indicates even more expensive control works if valuable residence and commercial establishments and public works are to be sure of their space. Frequently builders have stubbornly refused to realize that oceans and lakes are not through with their natural game of geological erosion and that man cannot hope to compete with nature in occupying the shores. Breakwaters, masonry walls, groins, and tree planting have been resorted to. While beyond the customary field of soil conservation, the problem is locally of vast importance and requires increasing study, planning, and action.

Windbreaks and Shelterbelts. A windbreak may mean anything from a fence to a forest, and the term is frequently used to designate one or more rows of trees planted in a direction which is at right angles to that of the prevailing winds and designed to prevent soil blowing and severe evaporation of soil moisture and to moderate the temperature locally. The term *shelterbelt* is more narrowly used to designate a belt consisting of several rows of trees and shrubs but located as just described for a windbreak. The prevention of wind erosion on a local scale is practiced all the way from using bands or strips of grain or hay to reduce the blowing of muck soil particles with their cutting effect on tender truck crop plants (Fig. 27) to the use of 165-foot-wide shelterbelts consisting of as many as twenty or more rows of shrubs and trees. Sometimes in the Great Plains region such plantings must be fenced from livestock and watered systematically until they become established. It is generally agreed that the effects of wind in soil removal, accelerated evaporation, and temperature

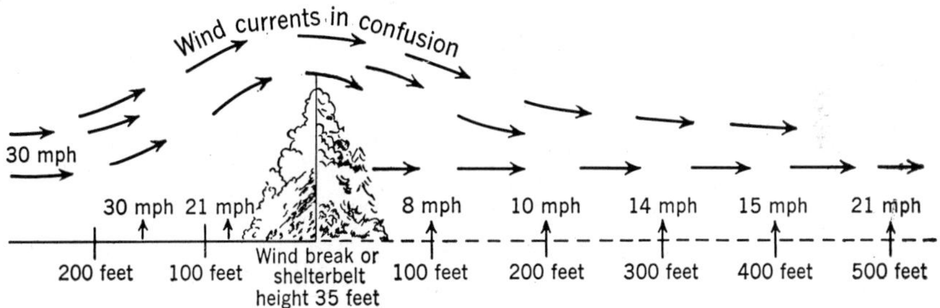

FIG. 28. Diagram showing the effect of a shelterbelt. (*Kansas State Board of Agriculture.*)

change are felt to a leeward distance equivalent to twenty times the height of the shelterbelt. Thus, a square field ¼ mile or 1,320 feet on each side and having an area of 40 acres might benefit over a large portion of its area from a 60-foot-tall shelterbelt. The planting would have three rows of cottonwood trees in the middle of it and be placed at the windward edge of the field. (See Fig. 28 in which the cottonwoods have not yet reached that height.) It should be borne in mind that the effect of these shelterbelts is local and that it would take a vast program of checkerboard outlining of the dust-bowl region with them before dust storms could be influenced appreciably. The work of the Prairie States Forestry Project in attacking wind erosion will be discussed later, as will other means by which action on soil conservation problems can be brought about.

Maintaining the Nutrient Materials in the Soil

If soil waste were completely halted and water made available to all soils, they could still be reduced to very low productivity through cropping unless the elements essential to the plant growth could be maintained in adequate measure. This is the second great soil conservation problem. Plants require considerable quantities of nitrogen, potassium, phosphorus, carbon, calcium, oxygen, hydrogen, and sulfur, although not necessarily in the order named. Lesser amounts of iron and magnesium are required, and very small amounts of cobalt, zinc, copper, manganese, and boron have been shown to be necessary to certain plants. The first three of these, nitrogen, potassium, and phosphorus, have come to be called *fertilizer elements* in the commercial fertilizer industry, and when a bag of fertilizer contains, for example, the label "3-12-12" or "0-10-4," the figures indicate the proportions, in the order given, of available nitrogen, phosphorus, and potassium compounds in the total fertilizing material. The last five elements mentioned above, cobalt, zinc, copper, manganese, and boron, are known as the *trace elements,* even though their absence may reduce profoundly the rate of maturing, resistance to disease, or some other factor influencing successful production of a given crop.

The ordinary person not particularly interested in farming or gardening probably reads and hears more about calcium than any other element important in plant growth, but usually the term *lime* or *liming the soil* is what he hears, since lime is a material composed mostly of calcium. This element together with nitrogen, potassium, and phosphorus comprise the more common ones needed and most frequently used in agriculture.

Nitrogen, oxygen, hydrogen, and carbon come nearest to being inexhaustible in nature. They occur or circulate in air and water and enter into most of the minerals found in the soil. Making these elements available to plants, however, is another matter, tied in, as will be understood later, to the grower's knowledge and practices on the land.

Nitrogen varies in amount from one-twentieth to one-fifth of 1 per cent by weight in the better forest soils to as much as one-fourth to three-tenths of 1 per cent in the black prairie soils, and even greater amounts in certain of the peats and muck soils. In actual weight per acre to a depth of 6 to 7 inches known as the plow layer, this would mean an average of something like 4,000 pounds (out of the total 2 million pounds of soil per acre to a depth of 6 to 7 inches)—hardly a load for a small dump truck.

Potassium is widely and generously distributed in the soils of this country, though lacking in certain of the lighter ones. The average for the general run of soils is 2 per cent by weight in the top 6 or 7 inches in the plow layer. This amounts to 40,000 pounds of potash (K_2O) to the acre, whereas the amount of nitrogen does not exceed 10 per cent of such a figure, and the phosphoric acid content is even lower.

Phosphorus is in greater demand than potash by certain crops grown generally, such as grains, and unfortunately is not too well distributed in the important farming soils. The average amount per acre in the plow layer for soils in general is 3,000 pounds. This somewhat scant supply plus heavy removal in crops which leave the farm, and traditional neglect in maintaining the supply through fertilization and crop rotation, make the phosphorus problem relatively serious.

Loss of Essential Nutrient Materials. Uneven occurrence of essential nutrient materials is not the only trouble met in this phase of soil conservation. Progressive loss through cropping, leaching in drainage water, removal by erosion (Fig. 29) when the soil itself is lost, and modification by fire are evidence of the deficit caused by removal as against systematic replenishment. Examples of heavy removal of phosphorus are most con-

FIG. 29. Loss of river bank is also loss of nutrient materials. Winooski River, Vermont. (*Photo by Soil Conservation Service.*)

vincing and include that which leaves the farm in the grain, the livestock, the poultry, and the dairy products which are sold. Frequently the only return is that contained in the animal manures and plant wastes which the owner plows under. These in turn are drawn upon by the next crop. While complete exhaustion of a soil is rare, the abandoned farmhouse with idle acres about it is eloquent of thoughtless cropping practice as well as of erosion or of bad judgment in the original selection of the land.

Nutrient elements contained in certain soluble minerals may also be lost by leaching and escape in surplus waters from drained land.

A further loss occurs in ground fires which follow or accompany forest fires and grass fires or in muck fires such as those which occur in the

Everglades and in drained marshlands in the Middle West. Sometimes in the latter instance the entire soil is reduced to ash or is so modified as to be unproductive.

How Nutrient Materials May Be Maintained in Soils

Crop residues such as cornstalks, straw, vegetable tops, and stubble; special crops such as soybeans, grasses, clover, and buckwheat which are plowed under while green (called green manures); animal manures made up of solid excreta, urine, or straw or other bedding material; guano; leafmold; compost; agricultural lime and marl; rock phosphate; potash

FIG. 30. Fall disking of wheat stubble in Oregon. An example of adding organic matter to the soil in the form of crop residue. (*Photo by Soil Conservation Service.*)

salts; ammonium sulfate; compounds of peat and mineral salts; ground dry sludge from sewage systems; and a great many other materials comprise the fertilizers and modifiers of the soil which may be added or returned in cropping practice. In general too little of these materials is used to replace the nutrients lost to the soils when the crops are sold and removed.

Examples of sources and procedures in applying these materials, starting with the simpler ones, follow:

Adding Organic Materials. Crop residues (Fig. 30), green manures, animal manures, guano, and peat compounds are used both to modify the physical condition of the soil to gain greater aeration, water absorption, and easier working qualities and to supply certain nutrient elements, particularly nitrogen, potash, and phosphorus. The living organisms in the soil also perform their function of making nutrient materials more readily available in soils which contain generous supplies of organic materials.

What goes on in a living soil is difficult to understand or even to believe until one thinks of the organic material as "fuel for bacterial fires in the soil, which operates as a factory producing plant nutrients." The organic material in this "burning" process produces among other things carbon dioxide and ash. The former makes possible a supply of acidified soil water which acts as a solvent for many otherwise unavailable mineral nutrients. In the whole process, nitrogen and other nutrients in the organic material itself become available. The use of the term "burning" is appropriate when one realizes that he may be standing on an acre of ground warmed up to its job on a hot July day and burning carbon at the rate equivalent to 1.6 pounds of good-grade soft coal per hour, and perhaps generating as much as 1 horsepower of energy. Organic matter then is the source of indispensable power to change nutrient elements into forms available to growing plants.

Crop Residues. Enormous quantities of the crop residues mentioned are produced and, while formerly burned in many instances in order to make plowing and fitting more convenient, are now returned to the soil in increasing volume. New types of machinery as well as better knowledge of the value of the materials have influenced this trend. Cornstalks can be quickly broken up and leveled, the straw and chaff from such crops as grain and soybeans can be returned at once to the surface by the combine harvester which threshes as it cuts, and devices for practicing "trash agriculture" include those which stir but do not turn over the soil and which "cut into" the soil the residues left on the surface (Fig. 30). In harvesting oats, rye, barley, and wheat with the older "binder," the straw is removed, blown into a stack at a later threshing site, and infrequently returned to the field, except as it gets there as bedding in manure. The same is true when "fodder corn" or silage corn is removed and fed to stock at distant barns or feed lots.

Green Manures. Clover, cowpeas, soybeans, and other legumes used as green crops to plow under not only add organic material to the soil but have the power to fix nitrogen from the air. This will be discussed later. Winter wheat, rye, buckwheat, and certain of the vetches are also used and are particularly valuable when they can be seeded with regular season crops to grow slowly through the colder seasons. In this way they "salvage" certain nutrients which might otherwise be lost by leaching during the wetter parts of the year, but are thus returned when the manure crop is plowed under. Commercial products using peat may or may not be "sweetened" with some mineral fertilizer; they are sold for use on specialized crops and have their principal values as soil modifiers. Middle Western cities with a problem of removing heavy street-tree and lawn-tree leaf fall find an outlet for this material to nearby lands devoted to specialized crops. Similarly, organic wastes are "composted" for use by commercial gardeners and nurserymen. Composting is a process of accumulating leaves, straw, and other plant residues with soil, keeping the heap or pit moist and aerated, and allowing the material to heat and decompose before adding it to the soil. Addition of animal manures and commercial fertilizer materials in small amounts hastens the process.

Animal Manure. Animal manure accumulated on the farms contains nitrogen, phosphorus, potash, calcium, sulfur, and traces of other nutrient materials needed by plants. It also serves as organic materials needed by plants and in improving the working quality and water absorption of the soil. Whether or not it increases crop production depends upon the way it is stored and allowed to decompose before it is applied to the land. Manure should be considered at this point as organic material which introduces certain microorganisms into the soil and modifies the soil in addition to supplying it with nitrogen and other elements.

Leaching from storage piles exposed to heavy rainfall, improper fermentation, and drying out before being incorporated with the soil are common sources of loss of nutrient materials in manure. With 1 billion tons of manure available yearly on American farms, capable of producing 3 million dollars' worth of increase in crops and equivalent to $440 for each of the country's 6,800,000 farm operators, it is probable that not until recently has more than one-third of the potential value been realized.

Rotation of Crops. Advantages of alternating crops as against growing a single crop continuously or having no plan whatever include plant-disease and insect control and erosion control, as well as the maintenance of fertility, but rotation is discussed here as a means of maintaining organic matter and plant nutrients in the soil. It must be "a good" or "the right" rotation to accomplish this, and good rotations do not always agree with the farm operator's idea of what is due to him in return for his effort. This conflict gives rise to the expressions "soil-building crops" and "soil-depleting crops," the planting of which was the basis for much of the subsidy payments to farmers under the old Agricultural Adjustment Administration's program (now the Production and Marketing Administration). Including a legume and a sod crop along with such crops as corn, oats, wheat, sugar beets, tobacco, or cotton can accomplish two things: (1) the fixation of nitrogen by the legume crop and (2) maintaining the organic-matter content of the soil to some extent. Clover, peanuts, soybeans, cowpeas, alfalfa, and other legumes have the power to bring about a fixation of nitrogen from the air somewhat in the following manner: With certain bacteria present or introduced, and with favorable soil and moisture conditions, legumes form bodies on their roots in which the bacteria live and develop, taking their nourishment from the plant and nitrogen from the air which they supply to the plant, some of which is bound to remain in the roots and stubble or vines even if the entire crop is not plowed under.

The turning under of grass sods naturally adds organic matter, and it is in a form which is quite properly incorporated into the soil. If the entire crop is plowed under instead of being harvested for hay or seed, so much the better.

FIG. 31. Turning under Balboa rye in Tennessee. This is an example of using a green manure for soil improvement. Near Murfreesboro, Tenn. (*Photo by Soil Conservation Service.*)

What happens to the crops in rotations, whether manures and other fertilizers are applied in the course of the rotation, what kind of tillage is practiced, and how irrigation water is used, all may affect a chosen rotation for better or for worse. Care must of course be exercised that in gaining nitrogen the complete removal of a crop without even returning wastes from animals to which it may have been fed does not amount to loss of critical amounts of phosphorus or potassium.

Results from a rotation are more difficult to identify than those from fertilizing and other practices used at the same time, but crop rotation, skillfully practiced, can amount to very effective soil conservation.

Supplying Lime as a Nutrient and Soil Amendment. Sight should not be lost of the fact that lime supplies the calcium necessary as an actual nutrient material in plant growth, as well as acting to "sweeten" an acid soil. The latter effect is the better known of the two and is important in amending a sour soil condition which is unfavorable to the growth of beans, peas, alfalfa, clover, and certain other important crops. In growing legumes the high calcium requirement is also very important. Perhaps the reason for thinking of lime primarily as a soil amendment is that lime as a nutrient material is present in sufficient quantities for that purpose in many soils, and yet lime leaves the farm under general farming conditions in the North Central states to the extent of 100 to 500 pounds per acre per year over the amount returned in manure and crop residues. Just how it "amends" the soil concerns, for example, the prevention of an actual toxic or poisoning effect of acids on plant tissues and the rendering available of needed phosphorus to growing plants. Calcium as a nutrient and also iron, manganese, copper, zinc, and magnesium are known to be less available in highly acid soils.

The chief sources of lime are ground limestone and marl, a natural product underlying certain marshes. Both of these materials vary in purity and calcium content and are applied to the land without refinement. Prepared lime includes burnt lime or caustic lime and slaked lime or hydrated lime. The latter is prepared by adding water to burnt lime which in turn is a product of burning raw limestone. Limestone deposits are widely distributed, and agricultural lime in its natural forms is available at reasonable prices. Many such deposits are developed by groups of farmers on a cooperative plan. Lime has also been supplied on a subsidy basis under the Production and Marketing Administration program. The town or city resident learns to respect lime when his garden requires it or where his lawn is concerned.

Maintaining Nitrogen in the Soil. In addition to the nitrogen returned to the soil in manures, plant residues, and green manure crops when they are plowed under, all of which are most important, numerous commercial products are applied directly to the soil where the locally available materials are insufficient. These may include ammonium compounds, of which ammonium sulfate is well known as a by-product of the coke industry, cottonseed meal, dried blood, fish scrap, linseed meal, garbage and slaughterhouse tankage, urea, sewage sludge, and sodium nitrate, much of which is imported from Chile in the form of the relatively pure "Chile saltpeter." Synthetic sodium nitrate is also manufactured in this country (see Fig. 52, page 95). Guano is imported from South America and while rich in nitrogen is also valued for its content of phosphorus. Deposits from caves frequented by bats in the southwestern United States are also being marketed.

Some of these materials are unstable under certain circumstances met with in agriculture and particularly in truck and greenhouse enterprises.

The techniques of applying them are varied and require care and planning.

Maintaining Phosphorus in the Soil. Inherent deficiencies of phosphorus in certain soils, removal in soil erosion, and removal by crops, all emphasize the importance of maintaining an adequate supply in the soil. Phosphate rock which occurs in considerable quantities in the Southeast and in the Northern Rocky Mountain territory of the United States is the principal source of phosphates as they are called by the fertilizer manufacturers. Where the phosphorus content is low in the rock, processes

FIG. 32. Home-made rig for applying phosphate fertilizer to the soil on a Western irrigation project. (*Reclamation Era.*)

of concentrating the product into "superphosphate" bring about savings in shipping and application costs. The phosphorus content, expressed as phosphoric acid, of these products may run as high as 48 per cent by weight. Animal bones furnished an early source of phosphorus for use on the land, and bone meal for fertilizer is now an important by-product of the meat-packing industry. Farm manures and recovered sewage materials are important sources. Much convincing experimental work has been done on the use of phosphorus in growing and improving the quality of important crops, and it is comforting to know that such an important element occurs in such abundance in the United States, even though the supply is not inexhaustible. Skill in the use of phosphorus fertilizers is necessary in order to be sure that they are readily available to plants and do not form insoluble compounds with other minerals present in or added to the soil.

Maintaining the Potash Supply. Potassium, or "potash" as it is commonly called in the fertilizer industry, while widely distributed, is deficient in certain leached sandy soils and in most muck soils and must be added to them in some form of cropping practice. Manure is a ready source of this element, particularly where used for fertilizing alfalfa and other heavily rooted plants with vigorous "feeding" habits. Commercial potash fertilizers were formerly imported into the United States in large

Fig. 33. Experimental fertilizer plant operated in the Tennessee Valley. (*Photo by Tennessee Valley Authority.*)

quantities from the Stassfurt fields in Germany and the Alsatian fields nearby, which are vast in extent. Deposits in New Mexico and Texas now yield considerable quantities, and by-product sources include the cement, sugar, and blast-furnace industries. A large number of the mixed commercial fertilizers contain potash, and while not so nearly the limiting plant nutrient in many soils as phosphorus is said to be, it is still important and presents a real maintenance problem.

Maintaining the Trace Elements. While knowledge of the necessity of copper, cobalt, zinc, boron, lead, iodine, fluorine, and nickel in the soil is comparatively recent, the addition of these elements has paid good dividends in crop increases and to some extent prevented failures from disease or other nutritional causes. These elements are usually purchased as mixed fertilizers or are blended before application to the soil. The mixtures are somewhat expensive and must be used in connection with soil analyses and thorough knowledge of the needs of the particular crop.

Increasing Productive Power through Maintaining Nutrient Materials in the Soil. It is well to remember here that conservation involves not only use without unnecessary waste but improving the productivity of any given resource where possible and desirable. Certainly the use of all the soil-amending and nutrient-returning materials mentioned in the foregoing pages offers examples of this very part of the conservation process as far as the soil is concerned. If dumping and distributing mineral salts on a field, year after year, and removing them in large part the same season in the form of a crop sounds like a tiresome and futile business, these considerations should be emphasized: (1) the results per unit of human effort are increased; (2) human life is made more abundant in terms of food, clothing, and health; (3) the soil resource is passed on to the next generation in sustained productive condition.

Influencing People to Conserve the Soil

Having discussed the physical problems of keeping the soil from washing away and of maintaining the nutrient materials in the soil, the question arises, "How shall the absentee landowners, the farmers, the bankers, the statesmen, and the people—all of whom have a stake in soil conservation—bring it about?"

Self-interest even when highly enlightened does not bring about automatically the action which such enlightenment calls for. In a democracy, therefore, where it is not the custom to punish men for inadequate stewardship of natural resources, people seek out ways to employ mild restraints and rewards as incentives to good stewardship of land. Examples of these are found in the practices of certain banks which base credit in the form of crop loans on agreements to use certain erosion-control measures; in the premium prices sometimes offered in the purchase of high-grade farm products; in the supplying of advice and demonstration by state and Federal agencies to landowners and farm operators; in offering actual subsidies of cash or fertilizer for the growing of soil-building crops; in encouragement through loans and technical assistance of cooperative farm operator groups who may help themselves to practice soil conservation through the common use of specialized machinery, group buying, and the pooling of operations on adjoining properties; in publicly guided resettlement programs to help failing farm operators to better chances of success; in the passing of mild laws which make easier the operation of the devices just mentioned and which authorize research and educational measures.

Such incentives may be grouped into three broad programs: (1)

research and education, (2) promotion, and (3) technical and financial assistance. They are more characteristic of the attack on soil conservation problems than on those of conserving other natural resources, but because soil conservation programs must reach so many individual owners and operators, the success or failure of these measures is a good indication of how conservation gets along in a democracy.

Research and Education in Conserving Soils. The tremendous mass of research data on the two great problems of keeping the soil in place and maintaining its content of nutrient materials has resulted mainly from the work of three kinds of publicly supported experiment stations, the state agricultural experiment stations, the forest and range experiment stations of the U.S. Forest Service, and the soil-erosion experiment stations of the U.S. Soil Conservation Service. The two latter are in the Department of Agriculture, and the former enjoys liberal Federal support. Scientists and other scholars of considerable number and located with agencies too numerous to mention have also made their contributions. Such research must go on constantly even though there is bound to be a lag between what is known to be good practice and what is actually practiced. The available methods and devices discussed so far are the results of such research.

Education strictly considered would perhaps be confined to preparing certain men as scientists, leaders, and actual farm operators and would be centered at schools of agriculture, forestry, range management, and to a less extent to those of engineering and public administration. Technically educated people are indispensable in a soil conservation program. More broadly considered, education involves interpretation of what is known, to farm operators particularly, but also to bankers and investment companies, to lawmakers, and to the ordinary citizen who in a democracy may never know, or may forget, that his life depends upon the soil and the way it is managed. Demonstrating economic benefits is important. This kind of education must be more systematic and less evangelical in character than the thing we know as *promotion*, which will be discussed further on. It goes forward through the itinerant teacher's efforts as an "extension" worker from state colleges of agriculture; through factual and carefully prepared scientific publications both technical and popular; through field demonstrations to groups of farm operators; through youth groups such as 4-H clubs, Future Farmers of America, particularly in "club" projects where actual projects are carried out; through lectures, particularly to nonfarm people; through better understanding of fundamental accounting principles; and through press and radio in their more serious and factual articles, news, and forums. (Remember that this is not yet promotion and that an attempt is being made to describe *education* in the sense of interpreting known facts and accepted principles.)

Rarely, a bank, implement company, fertilizer concern, railroad, or colonization company will employ on its staff men technically equipped to educate both employer and customer and give them a free hand. They can accomplish wonders under these conditions.

Promotion. Creating in people the desire to conserve the soil is certainly not to be accomplished through research and education alone. Citizens of a democracy, unfortunately, are inclined to value liberty and happiness more than life based on good management of natural resources. Evangelism in the sense of clever advertising (Fig. 34) and other selling techniques not only is necessary, but citizens of a democracy like it. Appeals are made to self-interest, patriotism, desire for recognition, pride in offspring, religious convictions, and any other human desire or

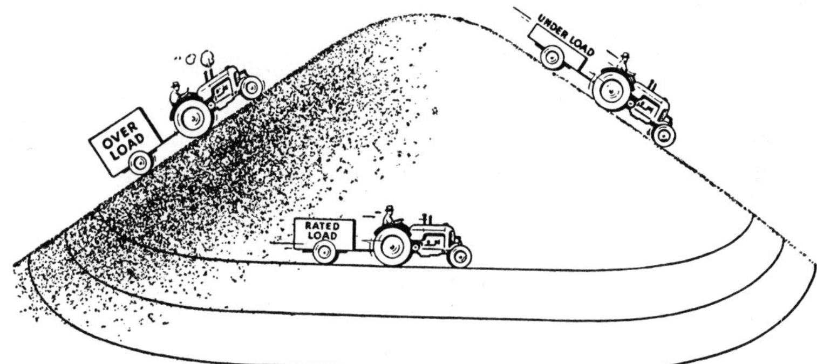

FIG. 34. Contour farming saves power. Cartoon from the bulletin, "Level Farming on Sloping Fields," a promotion device used by J. I. Case Co. (*Kansas State Board of Agriculture.*)

emotion that can be identified. Everything from a photograph of an ill-nourished child in front of a bleak home on eroded land to an illustrated lecture to picked businessmen in a great city may be called into play. If such *promotion* can precede, accompany, or follow what we have called education, so much the better. Announcing of rewards such as easier bank credit, subsidy in cash or kind, available technical advice and help, opportunity to join in a cooperative movement, in so far as they amount only to publicizing such incentives, also come properly under the head of promotion.

Having recruited technical talent and leadership and prepared the mind of the farm operator, there remains the action phase in which technical assistance and convenient financing and procedure are indicated.

Technical and Financial Assistance. How a farm operator or landowner is to conserve soil and make a living at the same time, with assurance of increased long-range values, are frequently questions the public must help to answer. The public through its government at various levels makes this answer with the service of its technicians; with incentive payments for the use of good practices; with credit, seed, fertilizer, trees, shrubs, and other material needs. All these things, when furnished to a landowner, amount to subsidy, a thing which various *industrial* concerns in this democracy have enjoyed in one way or another for many years. In discussing the many laws and procedures involved in such a program, subsidies will be mentioned in connection with the retirement of submarginal land, agricultural adjustment, and soil conservation districts.

Retirement of Submarginal Lands and Resettlement. In conserving the human powers of families who have selected and settled on land which had no power to support them, the Federal government in the 1930s, through its Resettlement Administration, purchased and retired considerable acreage, allocating it to other uses and helping the family by resettling it on better and sometimes more land, or otherwise furnishing opportunity for self-help. All land purchases were made with the consent of the owner and under the authority of the Jones-Bankhead Farm Tenant Act. Later the Farm Security Administration was assigned the task of continuing this improvement of economic opportunity through operation of its Rural Homestead projects and assisting certain families to improve land-use practices or to rent better land on which to live and work. Rehabilitation loans used in this way have an encouraging record of repayment and through various other incentives both human powers and soil have been conserved.

Agricultural Adjustment. Designed to bring farm income into proper relation with industrial income, the Agricultural Adjustment Act of 1936 authorized the payment of subsidies to farmers, presumably as a measure of controlling production of crops where lack of demand tended to depress prices. Actually the payments were made at first in the name of an "Agricultural Conservation Program" for decreasing acreage of soil-depleting crops such as cotton, corn, wheat, and tobacco. Lesser total amounts were paid for positive soil-building practices and erosion control. Later these practices, such as terracing, using fertilizers and soil amendments, and seeding sod-forming grasses and legumes, were emphasized although reductions in acreages of soil-depleting crops were also paid for. Such a program was authorized in an amended Agricultural Adjustment Act of 1938, and the total accomplishment, through use of subsidy, is impressive. Similar programs are now continued under the Production and Marketing Administration.

Soil Conservation Districts. Under the Soil Conservation Act of 1935, the Soil Conservation Service in the Federal Department of Agriculture was assigned tasks of research, survey of soil erosion and possibilities of water conservation, demonstration, dissemination of information, cooperation with other public agencies on national, state, and local levels, and finally cooperation with local soil conservation groups formed under state enabling acts. It is in this last assignment that soil conservation in farming districts throughout the country has gone forward most rapidly. Any state legislature may enact a law authorizing the setting up of soil conservation districts where landowners may vote themselves into cooperative soil conservation programs in a manner similar to that used in establishing drainage districts or school districts. Such groups can then accomplish things which as individuals they would not be equipped to do. Most of the states now have such laws, and more than 2,000 soil conservation districts are in operation at this time (1953).

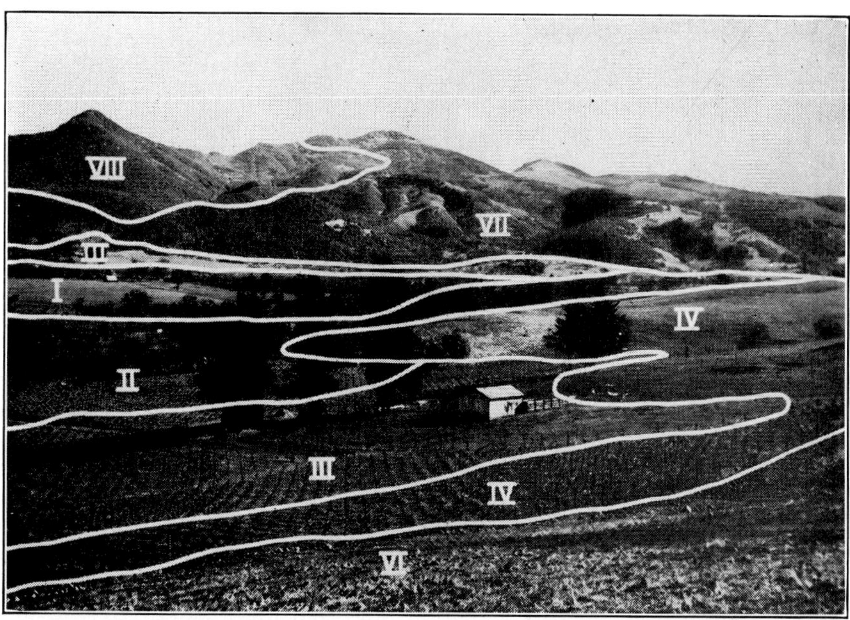

FIG. 35. Division of California ranch into land-capability classes. (*Photo by Soil Conservation Service.*)

When a district is organized it may request technical assistance and loan of heavy machinery, purchase trees and shrubs collectively and distribute them to its members for planting, and carry forward a program of soil conservation practices in accordance with farm plans which are worked out by the farm-operator members and the technical staff assigned by the Soil Conservation Service. These plans include furnishing the individual operator with a map showing soil types, degrees of soil depletion, present and recommended boundaries of fields, and "land-use capability" classifications of all land involved. There are five or more classes of land-use capability depending upon locality (Fig. 35), and they are so important as a basis for recommending soil conservation practices that one of the lists is given:

Class I. Lands which can be cultivated safely with good local practice and assurance of fair yields of adaptable crops, but requiring no special soil conservation practices.

Class II. Lands which if cultivated with expectation of fair yields require simple soil conservation practices such, for example, as contour cultivation and simple rotations.

Class III. Lands which can be safely cultivated only with use of intensive practices such as terracing, strip cropping in very narrow bands, heavy fertilization, or tile drainage.

Class IV. Lands which can be cultivated only in a limited way and kept as nearly as possible only in pasture and hay.

Class V. Lands which cannot be safely cultivated at any time and must be kept in permanent cover such as pasture or forest.

Three more classes are recognized in various localities where unusual conditions obtain (Fig. 35).

Individual farmers may sign 5-year agreements with the soil conservation districts, in which they assume reponsibility for definite practices each year and in which the respective parts of cooperator and district are set forth. Most of the state laws have no enforcement "teeth" in them, but compliance with these agreements has been remarkably uniform in applying land-use practices (Fig. 36). There is a vigorous and well-organized National Association of Soil Conservation Districts.

How Soil Conservation Can Be Assured on Non-farm Lands. While the most fertile lands of the country are in private ownership and in relatively small parcels, they do not comprise the whole soil conservation problem nor require the only exercise of the tools of research and education, promotion, or technical aid and financing. Public pasture lands or range lands in the Western states, Indian lands (public in the sense that each Indian tribe is literally a "nation" and that the Federal government as guardian has certain land-management obligations), cutover forest lands in large or scattered blocks, strip-mined coal and other mineral lands which may be private today and public tomorrow through tax reversion, exchange, or sale to public agencies—these are the lands that nobody loves but that need care if they are not to wash or blow away or become totally unproductive. Here the physical problems have to do with such things as grass, logging waste, and brush fires, with overgrazing, moisture conservation, and cloudburst floods, and with the use of more extensive soil conservation practices where the owner or custodian does not live on the land. The relatively low value of these lands, in spite of their indispensability to the livestock and recreation industries, and their watershed values operate against an intelligent interest in them on the part of the public. The Congress, for example, has taken the position that any administration of the public range under the Taylor Grazing Act of 1934

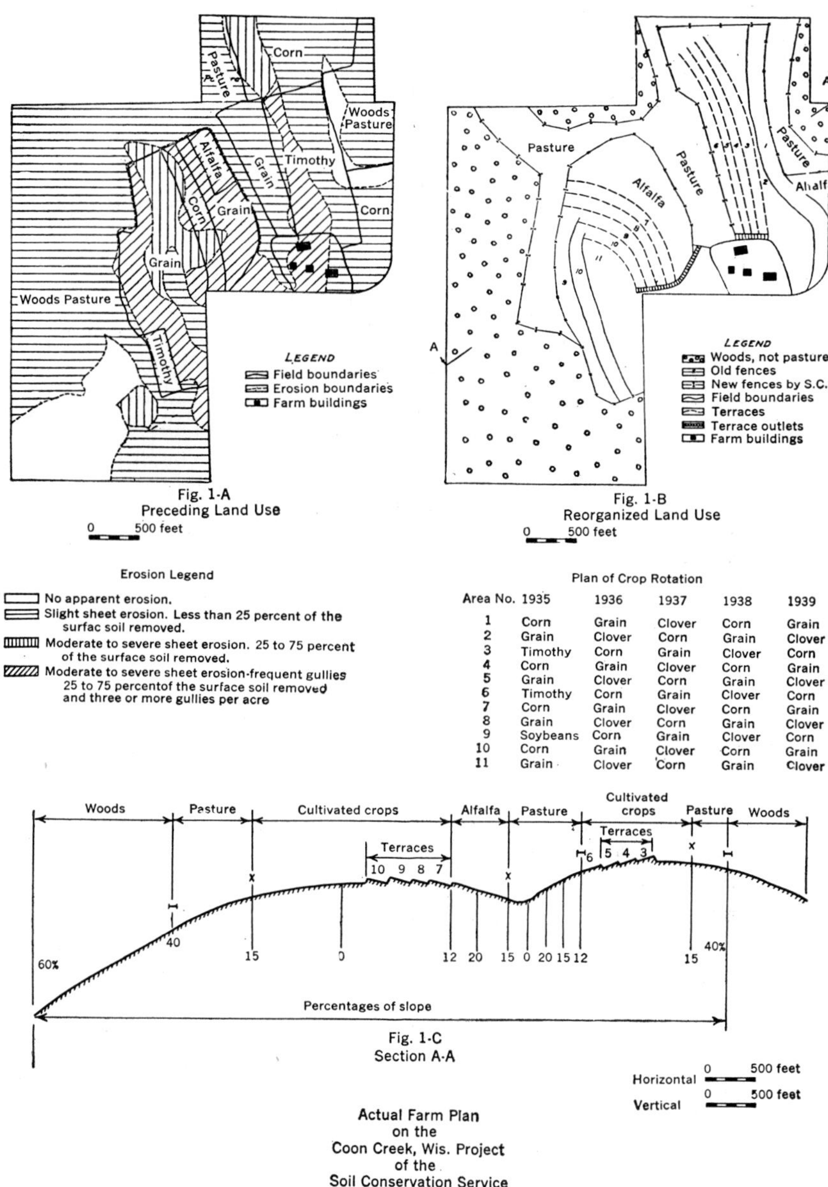

Area No.	1935	1936	1937	1938	1939
1	Corn	Grain	Clover	Corn	Grain
2	Grain	Clover	Corn	Grain	Clover
3	Timothy	Corn	Grain	Clover	Corn
4	Corn	Grain	Clover	Corn	Grain
5	Grain	Clover	Corn	Grain	Clover
6	Timothy	Corn	Grain	Clover	Corn
7	Corn	Grain	Clover	Corn	Grain
8	Grain	Clover	Corn	Grain	Clover
9	Soybeans	Corn	Grain	Clover	Corn
10	Corn	Grain	Clover	Corn	Grain
11	Grain	Clover	Corn	Grain	Clover

FIG. 36. Farm plan prepared by a Wisconsin Soil Conservation District technical adviser and the farm owner. Narrative portion will contain directions concerning rotations, etc. (*Soil Conservation Service.*)

must pay its way on the basis of grazing revenue alone. Presumably, as representing the people, the Congress speaks for the people. In so speaking the Congress used some of the "education" it received from a former cabinet officer who testified that it would be only moderately costly to administer these lands and implied that revenue was not important. The results of the failure of *education* in this instance are evident in failure by the Federal government to assume adequately its role of proprietor and to provide adequately through skillful and thorough control of livestock grazing and management of the range for conserving the soil. Tremendous possibilities for rehabilitating and improving the public ranges exist in the language of the Taylor Grazing Act, and increasing good is being accomplished in spite of meager appropriations. More technical assistance dictated by better educated congressmen, range users, and the people as a whole is the crying need. Grazing lands, consisting of the brush areas, open meadows, and other scattered areas within the national forests and managed under a different system and much more intensively by another Federal department, are generally in better condition. Their soils are being conserved.

The story in the preceding paragraph is one of somewhat unsatisfactory conservation effort in a democracy. One of the reasons it *can* happen is that education in its broad sense can fail even under a type of government which believes profoundly *in* education.

Indian lands in New Mexico, Wyoming, and other Western states totaling close to 35 million acres, suffering from overgrazing and located on watersheds contributing to great irrigation projects, require widespread public efforts at erosion control. Here the attack, while similar to the district and demonstration procedure used in humid regions, must emphasize low costs and far-flung efforts to reestablish vegetative cover and to reduce grazing injury. This means interference with an established, if unsound, local economy and the way of life. The answer is not to be found in resettlement or in meager appropriations. The Soil Conservation Service cooperates here with the Indian Service, the states, the private owners, and the water users.

Tree planting and pasture development on strip-mined coal lands, stream-bank control in some of the cutover areas, reforestation of cutover lands, sodding and shrub planting on highway cuts and fills, reinforcing of ocean and lake shores and influencing thoughtless citizens to realize that the oceans and the Great Lakes are still in the process of geological erosion and that some shores are not to be invaded by cottages and hotels, and the acquisition and management of reservoir lands by cities and by such agencies as the Tennessee Valley Authority—all these are examples of miscellaneous efforts at soil-erosion control. Such undertakings are variously financed and administered, and technical skill and advice are being increasingly employed.

Research, education, promotion, and furnishing of technical and financial aid on these nonfarm projects are more difficult than in the close-knit groups of farm cooperators. Nonresident owners and custodians of land are not apt pupils, nor do promotion tactics affect them so successfully. These lower-value lands will enter the soil conservation picture more and more with the development of the great river-valley projects to be discussed later.

BIBLIOGRAPHY

Bennett, Hugh Hammond: Soil Conservation, McGraw-Hill Book Company, Inc., New York, 1939.

Duley, F. L., and M. F. Miller: Erosion and Surface Run-off under Different Soil Conditions, *Mo. Agr. Expt. Sta. Res. Bul.* 23, 1923.

Gustafson, A. F., and associates: Conservation in the United States, Comstock Publishing Associates, Inc., Ithaca, N.Y., 1949.

Holes in the Ground, *Cornell Rural School Leaflet,* Vol. 35, November, 1941.

Kellogg, Charles E.: The Soils That Support Us, The Macmillan Company, New York, 1941.

Lyon, T. Lyttleton, and Harry O. Buckman: The Nature and Property of Soils, 3d ed., The Macmillan Company, New York, 1937.

Marbut, C. F.: Soils, Their Genesis, Classification and Development, Lectures before the Graduate Schools of the U.S. Department of Agriculture, February to May, 1928 (unpublished).

Our Public Lands, quarterly magazine of Bureau of Land Management, U.S. Department of the Interior, April and July, 1951.

Parkins, A. E., and J. R. Whitaker: Our Natural Resources and Their Conservation, John Wiley & Sons, Inc., New York, 1939.

Piemeisel, Robert L., Francis R. Lawson, and Eubanks Carsner: Weeds, Insects, Plant Diseases, and Dust Storms, *Sci. Monthly,* **73**:124–128, August, 1951.

Soil Conservation, monthly magazine of U.S. Soil Conservation Service.

Soils and Men, Yearbook of U.S. Dept. Agr., 1937.

Van Hise, Charles R., and Loomis Havemeyer: Conservation of Our Natural Resources, The Macmillan Company, New York, 1930.

CHAPTER 3

Water

The water which we take today as a matter of course for a thousand uses may last year have been part of a cloud, a tumbling mountain stream, a falling rain, or may have been at rest in a quiet lake or deep in the earth as a liquid or as frost. It moves in a "hydrologic cycle," described admirably 2,000 years ago in the Scriptures: "All the rivers run into the sea; yet the sea is not full; unto the place from whence the rivers come, thither they return again." Less poetically explained, starting at the surface of a lake or stream, the essential features of the cycle are the following: evaporation which is supplemented by the moisture transpired from plants, storage in the atmosphere as vapor, condensation, precipitation in the form of rain, hail, or snow which is absorbed by the surface soil of the earth, impounded as ground water, or collected into streams, rivers, lakes, and oceans, where it is again subject to evaporation.

Evaporation is spoken of as *flyoff;* the movement downhill whether over a flat surface, in tiny rills, or as great rivers, as *runoff;* the movement into the ground as soil moisture or finding its way to the underground reservoirs, as *cutoff*. But there can be no "off" without an "on." Perhaps, with apology to some of the geologists, we should speak of precipitation as "fall on."

In the hydrological cycle which is represented in the diagram (Fig. 37), any control or manipulation of the inexhaustible supply of water which men can exert must occur principally at the stages of runoff and cutoff, and men have much to learn at both stages. The supply and availability at any given point are variable and may easily become uncertain. They can cause suffering by their absence or by their overabundance. Along with atmosphere, sunshine, and soil, they are essential to human life. The conservation of water, therefore, is of compelling importance, even down to keeping the household faucets in repair.

Men speak of "harnessing" rivers, of "controlling" and "alleviating" floods, of "delivering" water for irrigation, of "improving" lakes and streams to maintain good fishing, of "softening" and "metering" water for domestic and industrial use, of "impounding" water for power, recreation, and stock raising, and of "charting" waters of proper depth and freedom of obstruction for navigation. All these activities are the efforts of men to conserve water as a natural resource, and it is not strange that various uses conflict at times and that conservation in one direction may become waste in another.

How Water Is Measured. In order to understand and appreciate the problems of water supply, some notion of the quantities needed and of the terms in which they are expressed must be held in mind. Water is measured by volume and by rate of flow. The simplest unit to remember,

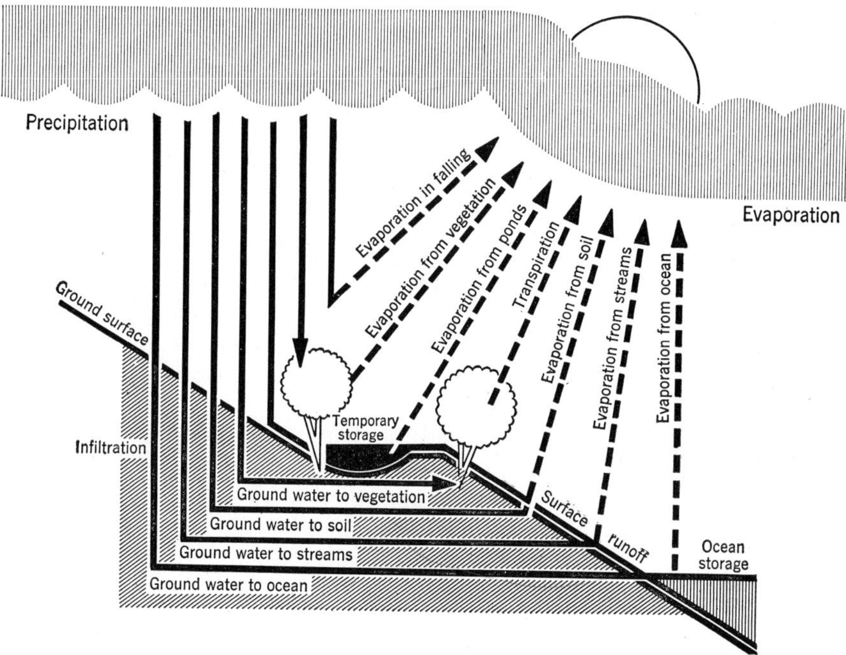

FIG. 37. The hydrologic cycle. (*Soil Conservation Service.*)

and the basic one, is the cubic foot. Reduced to gallons, 7½ of them would make a cubic foot, or if you can only think in "fifths" it would figure out 37½. Now remembering that a football field is about the size of an acre, the unit known as an acre-foot of water means the equivalent of water 1 foot deep covering an entire acre, or 43,560 cubic feet. If the term acre-inch is met, one-twelfth of this volume is indicated.

Now passing to the units indicating rate of flow, the cubic foot per second is the basic unit. Here, water moving at the velocity of 1 foot every second will fill a flume 1 foot wide and 1 foot deep. Gallons per minute (abbreviated g.p.m.) may be visualized as a flow unit by remembering that 450 gallons per minute is equivalent to 1 cubic foot per second. Such a flow would produce about 1 acre-inch per hour or 2 acre-feet per 24 hour day.[1]

The "miner's inch" is also a flow unit but is not uniform in the various Western states where it is used. The number of miner's inches to the cubic foot per second varies, for example, from 38.4 in Colorado to 40 in Oregon and 50 in southern California.[1]

Annual Rainfall on the United States. Assuming 30 inches as the mean annual rainfall over the United States, 5 billion acre-feet of water comes down on the country every year. That amounts to almost 35 acre-feet for every inhabitant, or to the entire annual flow of the Mississippi River ten times over. What happens to it? Well, it is estimated that one-half of it evaporates, giving no opportunity for capture; one-sixth gets away in the runoff, some of it having been temporarily captured and used along its journey to the sea; one-sixth is used and transpired into the atmosphere by plants; another sixth joins the "reservoirs" of uderground water from which it may be captured to some extent for use.[2]

Uses of the Runoff and the Cutoff. There is some virtue in an attempt to classify the uses of water at those stages of the cycle where men can exercise some control and management of the resource.

No one has successfully challenged the statement Frederick H. Newell[3] made in 1930 on the uses of the runoff ranked in order of importance to the comfort, health, and prosperity of mankind, as follows:

1. Water supply for domestic and municipal purposes
2. Transportation of waste, or sanitation
3. Food production: irrigation, drainage
4. Water power: hydroelectric development
5. Recreation: fishing, boating, swimming, skating
6. Navigation: lakes, rivers, canals

Because Newell, however, was confining his classification to the runoff and because of startling changes since 1930, in the demand for and uses of water supply from whatever stages of the cycle, the following classification and ranking of uses for water which is subject to a measure of capture is suggested:

1. Water supply for domestic and municipal purposes
2. Transportation of waste, whether pathogenic or industrial
3. Manufacture and processing of natural-resource materials

[1] Lewis, M. R., Practical Irrigation, *U.S. Dept. Agr. Farmers' Bul.* 1922, p. 16, 1943.

[2] McGee, W. J. Water as a Resource, *An. Amer. Acad.*, **33**:521–534, 1898.

[3] Newell, Frederick H., Water, p. 134 in Conservation of Our Natural Resources by Loomis Havemeyer and associates, The Macmillan Company, New York, 1930.

4. Food production, including the growing but not the processing of plant and animal crops
5. Water power, both hydroelectric and steam
6. Recreation: fishing, hunting waterfowl, boating, swimming, winter sports, enjoying scenery
7. Navigation, for whatever purpose save recreation and on any water

In any such grouping as the above, the uses overlap, supplement, and sometimes interfere with each other. For examples, municipal use includes along with supplying drinking water the transportation of certain wastes; food production may be the dominating purpose of impounding water in arid regions, and yet a reservoir may offer recreation all the way from furnishing a restful scene to attracting waterfowl for the hunter; and a navigable, power-producing, waste-transporting stream may surrender, because of these services, any recreation values otherwise inherent.

It should also be remembered that, unless water can be in a measure captured, controlled, and outguessed in its variability of supply, any one use may be sharply and sometimes suddenly curtailed. Just how well men succeed in managing this natural resource will be discussed later, and a special section on alleviating floods is included later in this chapter.

Water for Domestic and Municipal Purposes

Relatively few people in the United States have suffered long from thirst or from lack of water for personal cleanliness, for cooking, or for other comforts and conveniences. Nor have many lived in communities where water supply was critically short for fire control, watering of lawns and gardens, operation of laundries, and other small, essential service businesses. These are "domestic and municipal purposes" and require on the average more than 100 gallons of water per day per person. Such uses are recognized as of first importance, and the supplying of communities with adequate amounts of water is not infrequently the limiting factor in their growth and development. Problems of supply run all the way from finding new sources to augment inadequate systems to treating water for safe human consumption and for "hardness," regulating amounts used, and developing separate mains through which untreated supplies may be obtained for fire control. These are problems of conserving water as a natural resource.

Communities obtain their water supplies from streams and lakes and from wells and springs which tap underground accumulations. Settlements along any range of mountains are likely to enjoy supplies diverted from mountain streams or pumped from gravel cones at the mouths of canyons. Large cities along the Great Lakes take their supplies from these cold and never-failing bodies of water. In the South and Middle West the village or city water tower or standpipe is frequently the most prominent skyline feature and may indicate that the water supply is pumped from wells. Here also some renovated water from polluted streams may be used. In the arid West and Southwest domestic and municipal supplies often come from the same sources as water for the irrigation of agricultural crops. These include both reservoirs with their canal systems and their pumping stations drawing on underground water. Increasing industrial use of water from village and city systems has raised

FIG. 38. A Middle Western city's water supply comes from a dammed river and wells. Two pumping plants are seen in the foreground. Other wells are used also. Water-power plant is in the upper center. (*Ann Arbor City Water Department.*)

the old figure of 100 gallons per person per day considerably in those systems which are considered adequate.

Requirements for Household Water. Satisfactory household water besides being adequate in amount must be clear, free from harmful bacteria, odorless, free from disagreeable taste including "flatness," and "soft," *i.e.,* free from excess calcium and magnesium salts.

Clearness adds to the attractive appearance of water and, while not a dependable indication of purity, does dispel the idea that turbid water conveys, namely, unfitness for use. Freedom from harmful bacteria is fundamental, and while the cynic may say, as a Western water consumer did, that he'd just as soon drink an aquarium as a graveyard, treatment with chlorine gas or other chemicals which kill bacteria, coagulation which entangles and removes them, and boiling which destroys them are methods of assuring "purity" in the sense of making any pathogenic organisms harmless. Disagreeable odors in drinking water may come from sulfur compounds, algae, gases from the accumulation of organic matter in a reservoir, or the presence of traces of industrial wastes which have found their way into underground water supplies. Sometimes chlorine and

FIG. 39. Water-softening plant of the city of Ann Arbor, Mich., settling and coagulating basins in the middle foreground, bank of reservoir at extreme right. Water from various sources runs 180 to 400 parts per million of calcium and magnesium salts. This content is reduced to 80 parts per million. (*Ann Arbor City Water Department.*)

other reagents used to make water safe also make it disagreeable in taste. Other tastes are closely allied to the odors and their causes mentioned above. Water should not be "tasteless" to the degree of "flatness." So-called hard water contains more than 60 parts per million by volume of calcium or magnesium salts which are deposited on pipes and utensils and which interfere with the cleansing function of soaps. The amount of these salts can be reduced by precipitating them at central or household plants, both of which methods are common in inland Lake states communities. One such city, supplying water to 50,000 people and a few small industries, removes 10 tons of salts, including some treating materials, each day from its water and is paying for its plant by a small monthly charge accompanying the citizens' water bills.

In addition to assuring a supply which measures up to the above specifications, a problem of carelessness and waste must be met in conserving the water of any community and avoiding the cost of delivering, if indeed it can be done, more water than necessary. With all the good intentions and propaganda imaginable, it is still found to be good practice with water users to measure the amounts used and charge on the basis of meter readings.

In the plan for paying off the cost of the water-softener plant mentioned above and in the device of metering the use of water, two methods of assuring equitable distribution of a natural resource are evident. Fairness in distribution, in other words, is assured, and this is a part of good conservation.

Still another problem in conserving water for community use involves both amount and quality and has to do with too great depletion of underground supplies. Here through lowering of water levels or unregulated drilling for oil or brines, the water supply becomes at the same time inadequate and unfit for human consumption. Two examples will make this clearer:

Drilling for oil, gas, brines, and water itself and mining coal and other minerals in many parts of the United States frequently tap the wrong deposit or encounter brine, for example, when oil is sought. Sometimes this occurs at great depths. Then when an oil well, a gas well, or a test drilling for any purpose is left "unplugged" or inadequately closed with concrete, salt or mineral waters migrate upward into beds containing fresh water. The heavier the use from such beds, the faster the brackish condition of the fresh water will develop, but in any event the supply for community use is ruined. The only remedy for such a situation is a law, rigidly enforced, regulating the drilling and leaving safe of such wells. Michigan has such a law.

The second example involves an area of several hundred square miles in a Pacific coast state where the use of water by a score or more of communities exceeds the return to the underground sources by approximately one-half each year. This has brought about a critical lowering of the water level until it is now estimated to be 25 feet lower than sea level. The underground basin is close to the Pacific Ocean, and the invasion of salt water from the ocean is estimated at the rate of more than a mile a year. Here overuse threatens the entire supply and may make it necessary to "import" water for the area from a great distance and at all but prohibitive cost.

Failure to foresee a situation of this kind seems now to be indefensible, but it is part and parcel of the sort of public indifference which is likely to occur anywhere in a democracy through ignorance and through a tendency to neglect the responsibilities of citizenship. On the other hand, no other type of government shows the stubborn refusal to give up, once a problem is understood.

Farm Water Supplies. Before leaving the subject of domestic water supply, it should be remembered that not everyone lives in a town or city and that domestic water systems on thousands of farms which are not served by a publicly operated irrigation project represent problems of supply and quality second only to those of densely populated communities. Again wells and springs are drawn upon and problems of surface pollution must be guarded against. Because it is difficult, however, to separate human use of water on farms from use in producing plant and animal crops, farm water problems will be further discussed under Water for Food Production.

Water for Waste Transportation

Flowing water is not only the inevitable vehicle for getting rid of waste matter but also the means for the ultimate and proper oxidation and dilution when the solid waste is removed or the liquid form properly treated before being started on its "journey to the sea."[4] Sewered communities and most of the manufacturing and processing industries, particularly those dealing with food, animal products, chemicals, and minerals, *must* have water outlets for their wastes. Certain tub-thumping advocates of fishing as a sport need to realize this and to start thinking about ways and means.

The admirable growth of public interest in the prevention and abatement of stream pollution and the regulation of all waste disposal emphasizes the stark truth that *there can be no satisfactory disposal of human and industrial wastes without the use of water.* Unless this fact is accepted, the importance of preventing pollution has not been squarely faced. Waters may be used for waste transportation and at the same time pollution can be stopped, and the determination and ability of a democracy is just the combination to do the job, at whatever cost, and cost is bound to be great.

Treatment of Sewage. Interesting and beautiful in architecture and landscaping as it usually is, few people ever exhibit the intellectual curiosity to visit a modern sewage-disposal plant. The steps involved in sewage disposal, an important municipal task, should be understood by everyone. First the sewage must be collected and delivered to a point for treatment. These involve waste transportation in which water is necessary all along the route. Next comes the quick removal by settling of the inor-

[4] Adams, Milton P., Water in Its Relation to Pollution, p. 69 in Michigan's Water Problems, Michigan Department of Conservation, Lansing, Mich., 1944.

ganic solids such as sand, gravel, glass, and bits of metal and the screening out of these materials. This is followed by one of the several primary treatment processes which remove by settling and skimming the organic matter whether floating or settled. Now, if the remaining liquid or sewage effluent is still too high in "organic loading" or too great in amount to be safely merged with receiving waters, secondary treatment follows. This is accomplished by one of several so-called purification or oxidation processes. Before this, a treatment intermediate between primary and secondary may have been used as sufficient. Expense increases usually with the amount of organic matter removed, and sanitary disposal of

Fig. 40. Close-up of filters and settling tanks of industrial sewage-treatment plant. Tanks may be seen between the two round filters and building. Calmar plant of Link-Belt Co. (*Public Works.*)

accumulated grit, screenings, skimmings, and sewage solids must be provided for. The sewage solids constitute what is called *sludge* and have some fertilizing value when reduced to a form easily applied to the land.

The effluent discharged to receiving waters at best contains a considerable loading of harmful bacteria, unless it has been completely disinfected at the point of treatment. Waters of the receiving stream or lake are not considered safe for water supply or for swimming unless chlorinated. This much, however, should be said: the oxidation which occurs through merging the effluent with natural water does reduce the bacteria count, following in general the percentage of the removal of organic matter. The actual process of oxidation is discussed later under industrial wastes.

Treatment of Industrial Wastes. In addition to sewage discussed above, organic wastes from slaughterhouses, canneries, creameries, paper mills, and tanneries constitute the principal industrial wastes which require oxidation. These wastes, whether diluted before reaching the receiving waters for transportation or not, contain large proportions of putrescible liquid which is oxygen-demanding in the presence of natural water. If the receiving stream is not overloaded, it can assimilate these liquids without injury, but the key to this result is the small amount of dissolved oxygen in natural water. This totals 9 to 13 parts per million, depending upon the time of year and the temperature. The warmer the water, the less the amount of dissolved oxygen available. This is why the odor of polluted waters is more offensive in summer and early autumn. From these facts it may be reasoned that, unless the stream can take these wastes during the warmest months of the year, the so-called "oxygen-balance control" will not be satisfactory. In other words, the stream has broken down as a safe transporter of waste.

Oil refineries and certain chemical industries discharge phenolic wastes which are to some extent oxygen-demanding but which certainly do not yield to oxidation so far as the taste and odor which they impart to water is concerned. Similar trouble accompanies the discharge of creosol wastes from wood-distillation plants and the "black liquor" from pulp and paper mills using the sulfate process. One of the ironies of conservation effort is that chlorination of waters so polluted accentuates the taint, one part of chorinated phenol in 500 million parts of water sometimes proving objectionable in a domestic water supply.

Salt brines, though frequent pollutants, are neither oxygen-demanding nor of bacterial significance, and yet when they are discharged into waters needed for other purposes they produce a condition frequently almost seven times saltier than sea water, which contains 30,000 parts per million of chlorides. Salt brines from oil fields and chemical plants are made up of chlorides of sodium, calcium, and magnesium dissolved, of course, in water. They produce an artificial hardness besides making the water unfit for drinking and injuring fresh-water fish in concentrations after dilution of 4,000 parts per million or greater. Here the problem is neither one of bacteria nor of poisoning but can be solved only by tremendous dilution, usually prohibitive in cost, or by storing and finding some by-product use for the chlorides.

The cyanide, acid, and alkali industries also discharge pollutants which must be dealt with, and dilution here again is a discouraging prospect, the most minute amounts of cyanide salts having been known to cause the death of both fish and livestock in Michigan.

Inert industrial wastes, including sands from stamp mills treating gold and copper ores, coal- and gravel-washing wastes, stone-crusher plant waste, and actual eroded soil, limit sharply the use of the receiving and transporting waters for *any* other purpose. All but the least valuable fishes are likely to be suffocated. Streams themselves are turbid and unattractive for sport. Then in addition to this peculiar kind of "pollution," channels are clogged in all but the swiftest of streams and much of this waste ends up eventually in reservoirs constructed for irrigation, power, flood control, and the improvement of navigation. Expensive settling and return of these wastes to worked-out mines, gravel pits, and quarries sounds fantastic but may not be beyond the range of human need. "Polluting the landscape" has been turned to by certain enterprises of this character and may constitute the lesser of two evils, slag-, culm-, and chemical-waste piles not being unknown at present, particularly in mining regions. Control of water on the land has been discussed under soil conservation and holds out some hope for keeping streams clearer.

A final peculiar kind of water pollution comes from petroleum transportation and automobile servicing rather than from the refinery and oil-field wastes mentioned earlier. This is actually waste oil, it has to go somewhere, and not infrequently it may be seen on the surface of streams and harbors. Not only does it pollute the water, but it has been known to catch fire and to threaten shore structures. Greater salvage of such refuse offers one chance to limit it as a nuisance.

By-products from Water-borne Waste. The cost of transporting both municipal and industrial wastes will no doubt increase with time, and any application of scientific knowledge and ingenuity to this problem is bound to help. Development of by-products from waste is perhaps the most fruitful of these efforts.

One city of the Great Lakes has developed a nitrogen fertilizer from its sewer sludge and a sales program which returns a good revenue to the city treasury.

Sugar-beet companies struggling with four or five concentrations of pollutants which must be disposed of find a market for dried pulp and certain by-products of lesser volume. One such company reported in 1943 a gross return on a single by-product equivalent to 10 per cent of the payment for beets, and another which had returned the cost of its safe disposal.

Reclaimed pulp from the so-called "white water" of paper-pulp mills as well as the reclaiming of water used as a vehicle in the plant itself have shown favorable results.

Hair and fleshings from tanneries have some value and, when reclaimed, relieve transporting waters of a considerable load of putrescible materials.

Administering Safe Waste Transportation. At present the responsibility for safe transportation of waste by water is a state responsibility.

The Federal government has no authority, even over interstate waters, in this particular. Highly organized boards, commissions, or committees cooperating with other appropriate state and national agencies are in operation in Connecticut, Illinois, Indiana, Louisiana, Michigan, Oregon, Pennsylvania, Washington, and Wisconsin. Generally the cooperation of the offending municipalities, institutions, and industries is sought, and the laws, weak in many instances, are enforced with varying vigor. Stubborn resistance to a moderate Federal law has developed on the part of state authorities and industries in the name of "states rights" without adequate

Fig. 41. Paper-mill apparatus for salvaging waste material that would otherwise be discharged into a stream. Chemicals are added to the "white water" from the paper machines, and a froth is thus formed in which the waste particles are caught and skimmed in a manner similar to the flotation process used in the recovery of metals, see Fig. 164. (*Photo by Michigan Water Resources Commission.*)

assumption of *states responsibility*. After more than a decade of waste-transportation problems occasioned by war industries and growing industrial populations, the Taft-Barkley law of 1948 was enacted by the Congress. This law which was to run for 3 years was extended in 1951 and provides for grants-in-aid from the Federal government to local governments and for furnishing advice on the abatement of water pollution. Aside from encouraging cooperative effort, this law provides no help for the lack of uniform regulations on the part of the states.

A more carefully drawn law, firmly and adequately enforced, with subsidy if necessary where problems were particularly acute and expensive to meet, would seem to be the least that a democracy could do to meet the problem of waste transportation by water with safety to health and to other water values. The average state has had 100 to 300 postwar construction projects in this field to which their planning bodies might well have assigned higher priorities.

Safe Waste Transportation Is the Problem. Because so much is said and written from the viewpoint of the sportsman and nature lover, the real issue is frequently lost sight of in plans concerning the use of water for safe transportation of waste. Whatever can be done to reduce even the amount of treated waste which is delivered to streams, lakes, and harbors is desirable. Every possible effort to find by-product uses for waste must be made. Vast sums must be invested in the treatment of waste before it is released; the ideal to be achieved is that all waste will be so treated as not to pollute the water which finally transports it. Problems of greater water supplies for treating and initial transportation of wastes arise. Spatial use of land for screened solids is neither easy nor escapable. New industries and increasing populations add to the difficulties. Heavy responsibility rests on the informed citizen. Water will always be used to transport waste, and this use is appropriately ranked second only to domestic and municipal use.

Water for Manufacture and Processing

It is not easy to identify or segregate uses of water for the manufacture and processing of ores, foods, textiles, chemicals, pulps, and beverages and for refrigeration, for such uses overlap domestic and municipal and waste-transportation groupings. On the other hand, a few examples will indicate that this consumption of water is large.

Perhaps the steel industry is the greatest user of water in manufacture, for 65,000 gallons is required to make 1 ton of iron ingots into steel and 18,000 gallons is used in the first place to make the ingots.

To produce 1 ton of aluminum 120,000 gallons of water is required, and a World War II bomber contained 30,000 pounds, or 15 tons, of aluminum. That means 1,800,000 gallons in the building of one bomber for the aluminum alone. An additional 27 million gallons was used in other operations before the ship was complete.

Passing over to aviation fuel, 25 gallons of water is needed to produce 1 gallon of aviation gasoline and 2,500,000 gallons to produce enough fuel for 1 hour's flight of 1,000 fighter planes. Bearing in mind that an acre-foot is the equivalent of more than 300,000 gallons, these quantities of water begin to take on real significance.

In the pulp and paper industry, water is used not only in reducing wood to pulp and pulp to paper but as a vehicle for moving material in various stages, from the actual wood right through to paper. A large mill may use as much as 50,000 gallons in the total processing of a ton of finished paper.

Laundries are naturally heavy industrial users of water, any immediate salvage of which is impracticable. Creameries, breweries, distilleries,

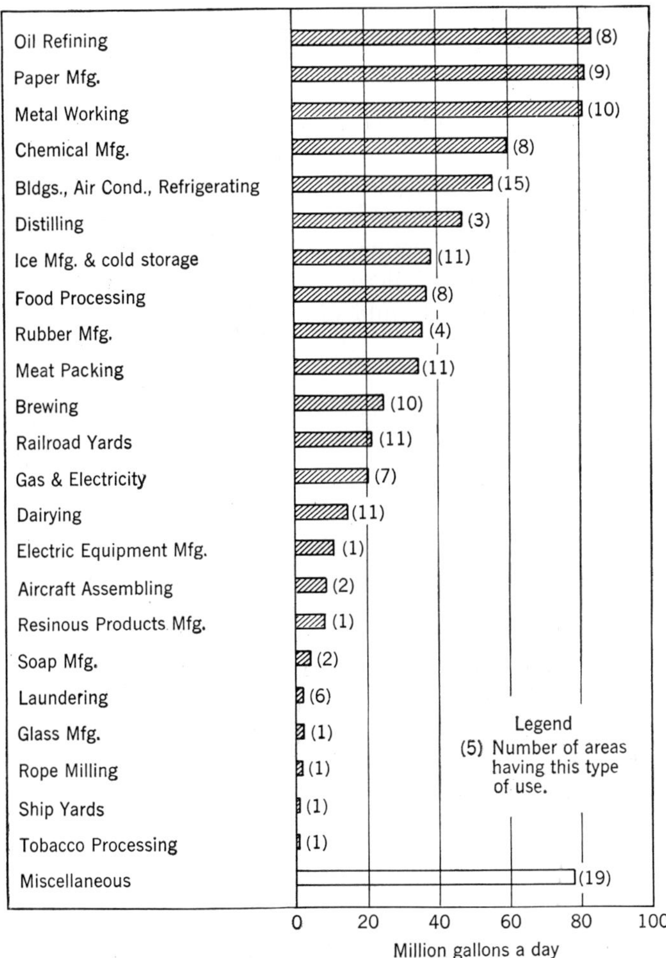

FIG. 42. Use of ground water by industries in twenty selected metropolitan areas. (Not including water from municipal systems.) (*Data from U.S. Geological Survey Cir. 114, 1951.*)

sugar factories, packing houses, and canneries are among the food-processing plants utilizing large quantities and facing heavy problems of pollution abatement.

Condensation water use for individual steam plants in thousands of manufacturing enterprises overlaps the "power" group of uses and perhaps "domestic and municipal" uses, but is really a firsthand industrial use. The same is true for the increasing use of water for the artificial production of ice and for the air-conditioning of buildings, although many wells have been drilled by individual building proprietors as a less expensive means of obtaining a supply for this purpose. Department stores, theaters, and office buildings, while hardly considered industrial, present an unusual demand for water and in their efforts to conserve it sometimes return cooling water to the underground reservoir. In some cities this is mandatory. Unless this return is accomplished so that it reaches a different formation than that producing the water originally, the entire underground supply is raised in temperature so that it is unfit for drinking without further cooling. Research on the application of less wasteful adaptations of refrigeration methods to the cooling of buildings is needed.

Conservation problems in all the uses of water for manufacture and processing are numerous and difficult. Supply, quality, safe disposal of used water and treatment for hardness and high sulfur and iron content follow pretty closely the necessity of providing safe domestic and municipal supplies, and certainly, as a vehicle for processing and a transporter of waste, the difficulties met are greater.

Water for Food Production

Milk is 87 per cent water, vegetables run from 80 to 97 per cent, eggs contain 65 per cent, meat contains 60 per cent, and fish somewhat more. A fat steer needs about 80 pounds of water a day, and that amounts to about 10 gallons. It takes one-half that amount, or 5 gallons, to water 40 chickens for a day.[5] Of the familiar farm crops, a pound dry weight requires 300 to 500 pounds of water for its production. Somewhere along the line, this much water has been taken up, transpired, or stored by the plants. Counting the water necessary to produce the crops consumed and the amount taken directly by the animal, 1 pound of beef has required 15 to 30 *tons* of water in its production. Food cannot be produced without water and lots of it.

In discussing the use of water for food production, the term *production* will be used in the strict sense of growing rather than processing food crops, whether plant or animal. (If the term *crop* seems strange when used in connection with livestock, the reader should know that the expression "calf crop" is common on the Western range.) Food production, then, involves the use of water for producing food fishes, livestock, and waterfowl and for irrigation in arid portions of the country. To a less extent also and with different methods, water is increasingly used for irrigation in the humid regions.

[5] Water for the Modern Farmstead, Rural Electrification Administration, Government Printing Office, 1946, p. 1.

Animal Crops. *Fishes.* Almost any stream or permanent body of water which is reasonably free from sewage and industrial wastes contains, or may be planted with, food fishes. Oyster culture is frequently spoken of as "farming," and the definite growing of warm-water fishes for food in farm ponds has become a popular practice in the last decade. Yields up to 250 pounds per acre of water are possible with intensive management, and the farm food supply can thus be varied and increased (Fig. 43). These uses of water will be further discussed under wild-animal-life resources.

FIG. 43. Farm pond near Troy, Idaho, constructed in 1944, planted to fish in 1946, and having a capacity of 4.47 acre-feet. (*Photo by Soil Conservation Service.*)

Livestock. On any farm supporting animals for supplying beef, pork, mutton, or fowl, the work and meat animals will consume much more than one-half of all the water used. A glance back at the figures in the opening paragraph of this chapter will give the reason. The production of eggs and dairy products and the considerable quantities of water used, aside from watering the animals on a dairy farm where milk is not processed, add to the amounts of water necessary in this branch of food production.

On the Western range the availability of water is frequently the limiting factor in the use of natural forage by the vast numbers of cattle and sheep grazed there by the livestock industry. The stories of the range wars between sheep and cattle outfits had often to do with the control of meager supplies of water, and much of the expenditures of public and private funds today in improving the range goes for developing and protecting water supplies.

Waterfowl. Although waterfowl are taken almost entirely for sport, their size and number represent considerable food value, and they can be grown and a crop assured only if waters are provided for resting, breeding, and feeding while in the latitudes of the United States. Commercial raising of waterfowl requiring generous and unfailing water supply is handled as a poultry business and really is a type of farming. Other aspects of this food crop will be discussed under Wild-animal Life later in the text.

Water for Irrigating Food Crops. While the foregoing uses of water for the production of food are taken for granted by the well-informed but not widely traveled citizen, he will be impressed and perhaps startled to see for the first time a green orchard or alfalfa field in an arid part of the West. And regardless of anything he has read about them, the great dams, reservoirs, "hillside rivers," and other intricate systems of canals, flumes, and small ditches which are commonplace in a region of irrigation agriculture will drive home the idea that no food is grown without water.

Of all the definitions of irrigation, the most succinct is the one settled on by Etcheverry,[6] "The artificial application of water to lands whenever the rainfall is insufficient to meet the full requirements of crops." This puts even the "watering" or "sprinkling" practices, as they are commonly spoken of in the humid regions, into the group of practices correctly known as irrigation. (Whether with hose or gadget, one "irrigates" a lawn in the West, rather than "waters" or "sprinkles" it.)

Irrigation has been practiced for centuries. It has been known on the North American continent, if traces of irrigation systems are correctly interpreted, since the Mayan culture in Central America, and later it is known as a matter of definite historical record in connection with the early Spanish mission enterprises and in trading and mining settlements. The first extensive use of water in a strictly agricultural economy occurred when the Mormons settled in the Salt Lake Valley in Utah in 1847, just more than 100 years ago. All users of water for this purpose have had to learn how to apply it, how to make its distribution equitable, how to overcome concentrations of alkali and siltation of reservoirs and ditches, and dozens of other things which make irrigation agriculture complex and exacting.

From practically nothing the irrigated acreage in this country increased

[6] By permission from Irrigation: Practice and Engineering by B. A. Etcheverry and S. T. Harding, 2d ed., Vol. I, p. 1. Copyright 1933 by McGraw-Hill Book Company, Inc., New York.

from 1847 to more than 3½ million acres in 1889, to 7½ million in 1902, and to 21 million in 1946. The period of greatest increase in acreage, amounting to more than 12 million, stretches from 1899 to 1919, at which time the United States census reports arrive at the figure 19,191,716 acres. This interval matches closely the period from 1901 to 1921, when population seemed to many national leaders to be heading for a growth that would outrun potential food supplies.

Early efforts at irrigation were made individually or by neighborhood partnerships and informal cooperative agreements. Law and custom

FIG. 44. An irrigated cotton field in the Rio Grande Project where water from Elephant Butte and Caballo reservoirs serves 155,000 acres. (*Photo by Bureau of Reclamation.*)

developed in arid and semiarid regions dictated the "location" of water rights in terms of "miner's inches" or other units. The water was guided by ditch from some point along a stream above the land to be irrigated and distributed as needed by gravity. Little pumping was known. In more recent years vast systems of dams, reservoirs, and canals have been constructed both publicly and privately, and pumping of irrigation water has become highly developed. Examples of some of the public projects will be discussed further on in this chapter.

The thoughtful reader, having heard much of the difficulty of farming in general to achieve "parity" with industry in the prices of products, will begin to inquire how the expense of bringing water artificially to land can be anything but prohibitive. The answer lies in the accumulated and unleached mineral salts which make newly irrigated land much more productive, the greater periods of sunshine and growing weather prevalent in arid and semiarid regions making possible more than one crop a year, the specialized character of the appropriate crops and their high market values, and the control which it is possible to exercise in the application of water. This last feature has more recently brought about increasing, though still hardly extensive, use of water in humid regions, where it is usually applied by sprinkling systems. Thus some control over crop failure in dry years can be exerted.

While the proportion of irrigated croplands to all croplands, about 4 to 5 per cent, follows somewhat closely the same figure for tonnage, the value of both land and crops is much higher and the importance to local Western economy, usually dominated by livestock, mineral, and lumber enterprises, is tremendous. On the U.S. Reclamation Bureau projects alone, which amount to less than one-fifth the entire area, the alfalfa and forage crops were sufficient during the period covered by the Second World War to have produced 150 pounds of meat per man for an army of 4 million men for 4 years.[7] Grass-crop values alone per acre on 4,195,832 acres in cultivation in 1945 were $103.72.[8]

How Irrigation Water Is Provided. Individual, cooperative, and publicly financed irrigation projects have been mentioned briefly, but it is well here to set down all the procedures employed and to discuss their relative significance, so far, as a democracy's way of handling one natural resource for one specific purpose.

Individual and cooperative projects were the result of a struggle to live a bit more abundantly in pioneer days. Miners who held placer claims on river bars and gravel deposits at the mouths of canyons raised vegetables and alfalfa in small areas in summer and used the water from the same source for hydraulic mining in winter. Stockmen needing water for cattle and sheep at ranch headquarters developed all the water they could and irrigated meadows and pastures. Fruit growing came early into the picture and demanded more ambitious irrigation works. Observation of neighbors' crops and joining up with successful growers finally became unwieldy and probably led to the next method.

Collective action to obtain and distribute water took on the same course as the need for schools, drains, fire control, sanitation, and more recently, soil conservation, namely, the establishment of a district following the majority vote of the landowners within a given territory. The district be-

[7] Natural Resource Problems, *Annual Report of the Secretary of the Interior*, 1946, pp. 23–24.

[8] *Ibid.*, p. 60.

comes a sort of governmental unit to accomplish a specific purpose—in this instance to gain control of water and bring it to the land. On the theory that each property owner benefits from the district's activities, costs are assessed in much the same manner as taxes. (A full discussion of soil conservation districts may be returned to on pages 58 to 60.)

FIG. 45. Raw land changed to a home and farm by irrigation. Yakima Project, Washington. (*Reclamation Era.*)

In perfect good faith, twelve of the Western states were put into the arid-land-reclamation business in the 1890s with the passage of the Carey Act in 1894. Federal lands in any of the public-land states could be selected up to a million acres per state, acquired without cost by the state, and developed for colonization and sale under the supervision of state officers who necessarily took this duty on as a side line. Private enterprise could come into the picture with somewhat dangerous financing arrangements and with no guarantee that the development would be sound or that water would be sufficient for permanent agriculture. The total area selected, developed under this arrangement, and passed into private ownerhip is relatively small—less than a million acres. Forgivable ignorance probably defeated the objective.

No phase of conservation effort in a democracy is more likely to intrigue the public or to enlist its support than the sort of thing which steps up productive power and extends opportunity for a greater number of citizens to make a living. It is not strange, therefore, that after long agitation to get around financial and other obstacles the Reclamation Act was passed in 1902. This law put the Federal government squarely into the irrigation-water development business and charged it with ironing out large-scale questions of water rights, property relations, construction, water distribution, and settlement of irrigated land. Money was to come from a revolving fund, to be replenished from the sale of developed lands, from settlement fees, and from earmarked revenue from the sale of public lands of whatever nature.

Coming on the heels of the exhaustion of the better homestead lands in the Middle West, the authorized program was prosecuted with vigor both for the development and serving of Federal lands to be homesteaded and for delivering water to existing and badly served farms and communities.

The story of the operation of this act and its various amendments is long and complicated, but it has proved that a democracy can work out devices for developing its latent productive powers and spread equitably the economic opportunities which its citizens demand. One may risk the opinion that its original purpose, which was *not* the production of power, might have avoided much trouble in its achievement if the Department of the Interior in the past two decades had not used it so enthusiastically as a power-production agency. This action resulted both from local needs for power and from increasing difficulty met by water users in paying off the cost of irrigation projects. (Power revenues of course cut down the costs of the latter.) But the act in letter and in spirit is now a far cry from the ideas held in 1902.

Little has been published on the development for commercial sale of irrigated land, and yet some very successful projects, taking particular care to select rich and easily watered lands, were carried out. The 1919 United States census reported more than 1,900,000 acres of this type under irrigation, with an investment of more than 85 million dollars.

The United States as guardian, and to some extent manager, of properties held in trust for the Indian tribes has developed water for irrigation on a number of reservations, slightly more than a quarter of a million acres total having been reported in 1919. This had grown to 850,000 in 1946, and development of 750,000 more is in prospect.

A few thousand acres of state and institutional lands and properties in miscellaneous ownerships have their own water locations and irrigation systems. These will never bulk large in the total area of irrigated lands.

How the Reclamation Bureau Projects Are Administered. Lands in newly developed irrigation projects under the management of the Bureau of Reclamation of the Department of the Interior are subject to entry under the homestead laws, but costs for the developed irrigation water, since assurance of the supply goes with title to the land, must be paid for in annual installments spread over 50 to 60 years. Sale of power developed

Fig. 46. Food production through the use of water, Boise Project, Idaho. Main Black Canyon Canal in the foreground. (*Photo by Bureau of Reclamation.*)

at the dams lightens this load on the settler, but he must still be a good farmer and businessman to pay out. The local project office of the Bureau operates the water distribution and power features of the areas, promotes sound irrigation and farming practices, and otherwise seeks the productive use of the water and land resources. The Bureau operates in twenty states, and its many projects vary in area to be served from a few thousand acres to more than a million. Since its establishment in 1932 and until June 30, 1946, it has out-Bunyaned Paul of the lumber woods by constructing reservoirs with a total capacity of almost 69 million acre-feet, 15,325 miles of canals, 33 power plants with a combined full-year output in 1946 of more than 13.1 billion kilowatthours (equivalent to the household consumption of 9.5 million of the water users of the entire country),

335 pumping plants with a pumpage of almost 1.5 million acre-feet per year, and moved more than 625 million cubic yards of material in all classes of excavation.

Europeans who count the potato tremendously important in their food supply would be amazed, and even the ordinary American citizen interested, to know that the reclamation farmers of the Pacific Northwest produced in 1945 a total of 49 million bushels of potatoes (enough to provide a year's supply for 23 million people).

Fig. 47. The use of water for food production must be understood. Here light, frequent irrigation providing fairly constant moisture to soil grows quality potatoes in Idaho. (*Photo by Bureau of Reclamation.*)

New Irrigation Projects. While there are considerable fragments of unsettled land which can be served by existing reclamation projects, vast new ones are planned and some of them already started to provide additional homes for veterans and others whose way of life will be tied into the land in the seventeen Western states. It appears possible to make available more than 45,000 family-size irrigated farms in the near future on about 4 million acres of productive lands. New projects envision, to a much greater extent than those established early in the century, multiple-purpose use of water frequently involving not only irrigation but power production, improved navigation, flood alleviation, recreational development, and municipal water supply, all rivaling the *food-production* purpose which is the basis of this immediate discussion, and indeed of the original Reclamation Act of 1902. All these new projects have extremely interesting features, from the tunnel under the continental divide—and incidentally under a national park—of the Colorado–Big Thompson Project, to the great earth-filled dam at Fort Peck or the Lucerne pumping plant, which takes water from the Big Horn River in Wyoming to irrigate 14,400 acres in the Owl Creek Valley. Meanwhile, as an example, one of the oldest projects in the United States, the Carlsbad in the Pecos River Valley in New Mexico, embracing a little more than 25,000 acres, 459 farms, and a population of 1,954 people, is being studied economically to see what can be done to rehabilitate it and to put the brakes on slipping crop returns following water shortage.

Three of the larger projects or systems will now be considered.

Following somewhat the example of the great icecap of former ages, in plugging a canyon of the Columbia River and diverting it so that it cut a great trough or coulee, through which it went its own way for a while, the people of a democracy have built the biggest structure in the form of a dam. By referring to Fig. 48 it will be seen that the river through the coulee and other breakovers deposited a vast delta before the ice plug gave way and allowed it to resume its path in the great bend. Eventually the coulee and the deposit were left high and dry, and the former with a dike at each end will now serve as a "balancing" reservoir into which waters from the backed-up river will be pumped for use in irrigating the delta lands. Power generated at the dam will be used for this purpose. Water will be available for more than a million acres. The first excavation on the main canal was well under way by July 1, 1946, and the six giant pumps on the river were in action for the eventual delivery of water to 66,000 acres during the 1952 irrigation season. Meanwhile the year's opening of 176 full- and part-time farming units of Federal land to settlement on the project found 110 applications for each one.

This whole Grand Coulee development, which is a part of the Great Columbia Basin plan, will be mentioned again later under Power Production.

At the head of the list of Western states in irrigation agriculture, California has still to achieve the unified management of her two great river valleys, the Sacramento and the San Joaquin. Excellent progress has been made, however, and the Central Valley Project's great Federal Shasta Dam already delivers water to 250,000 acres and the San Joaquin Valley Federal developments to 420,000 acres. There remains only to be worked out the proper state and Federal cooperation. The Bureau of Reclamation from all its projects will eventually furnish water to more than a million and a half acres requiring supplemental water, including the above acreages, and to 550,000 acres of new land in the Central Valley. This project will be vast in cost and significance and, like the Grand Coulee and other

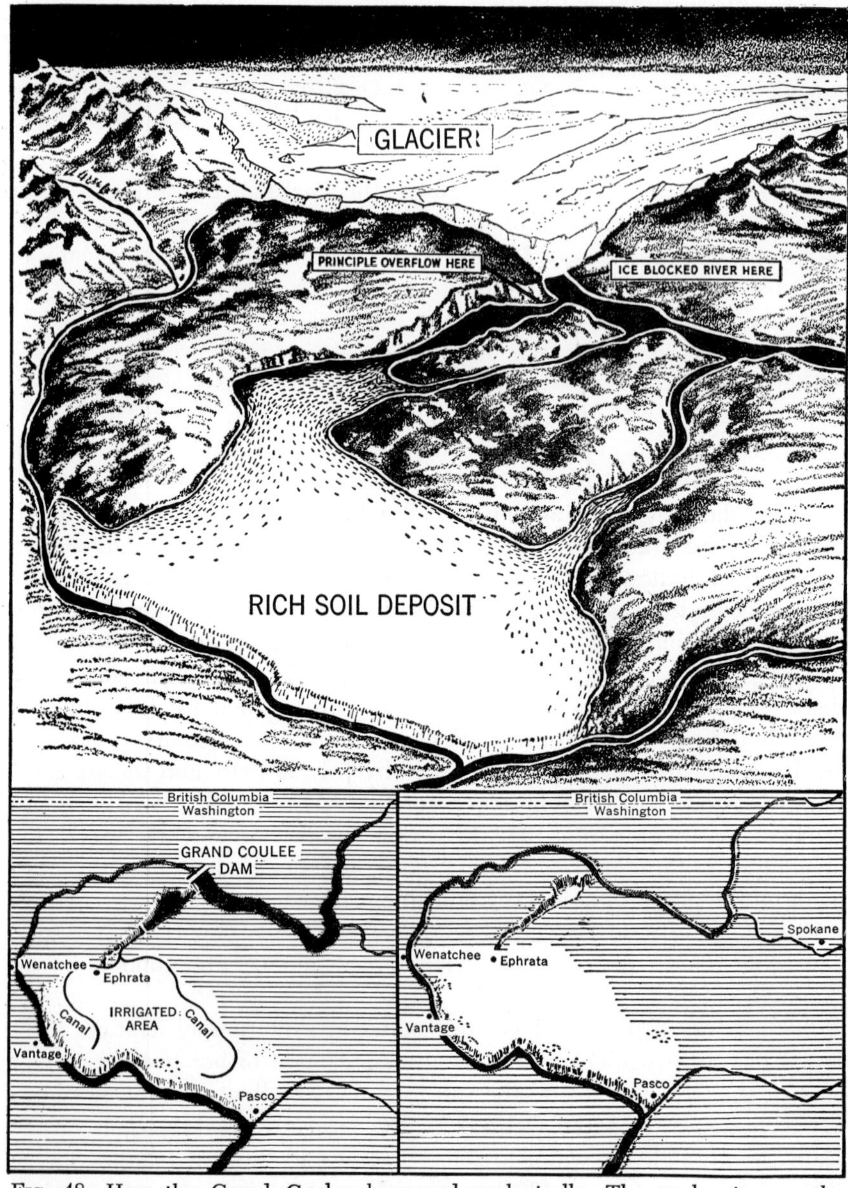

FIG. 48. How the Grand Coulee happened geologically. The coulee is now the equalizing reservoir into which Columbia River water is pumped by power generated at the dam and from which water flows to irrigate the ancient "delta." (*Industrial News, published by Gates Rubber Co.*)

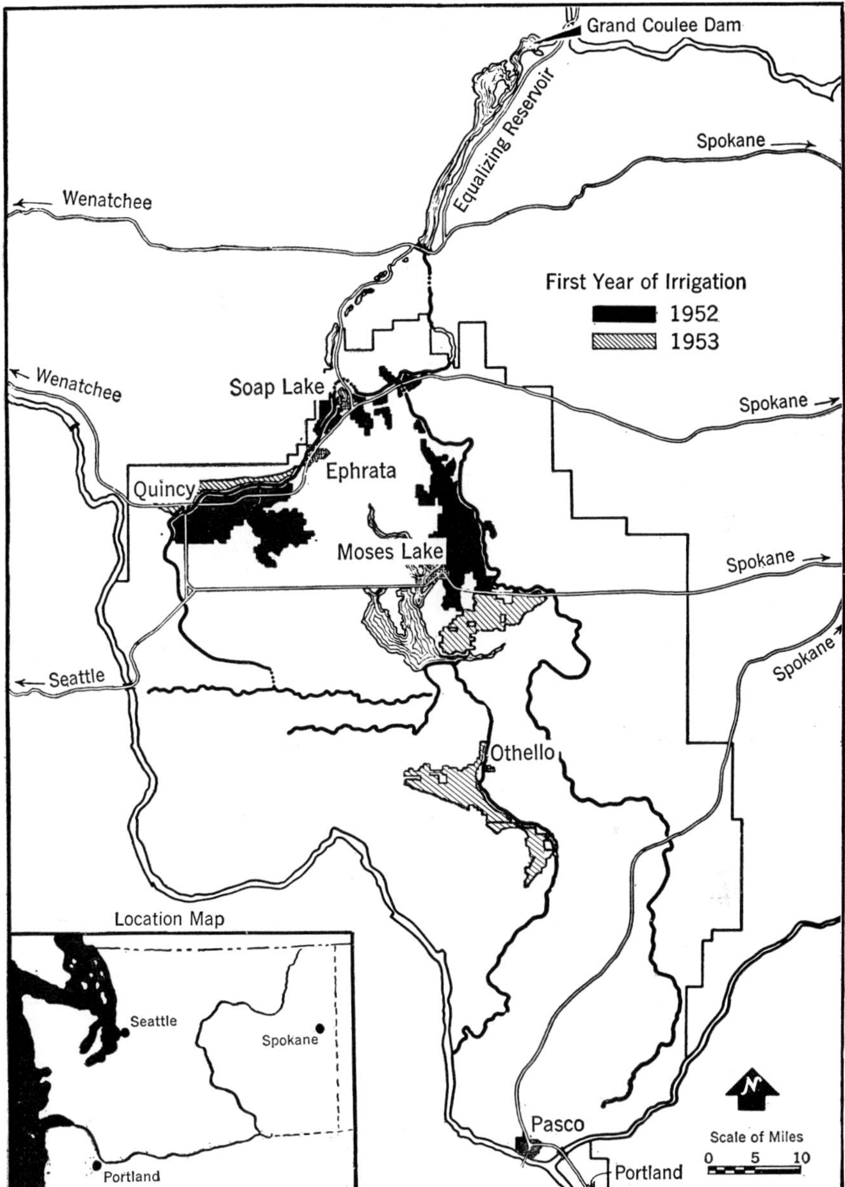

FIG. 49. Columbia Basin Project, Washington, showing irrigation for 1952 and 1953 from Grand Coulee Project. Compare with map on p. 88. (*Bureau of Reclamation.*)

Columbia Basin enterprises, is for multiple purposes, including all those mentioned in connection with the one to the north and perhaps being even more significant in supplying water for municipalities.

The heat and high local blood pressure generated in the last few years by discussions of a Missouri Valley Authority have for the present leveled off into piecemeal attack on the problem of improving the economy of about one-sixth of the area of the United States and about one-twentieth of its population, for that is what the Missouri River, touching ten states, represents. The so-called "unified" Pick-Sloan plan battled out by General Lewis Pick of the Corps of Engineers, U.S. Army, and W. G. Sloan of the Bureau of Reclamation is now in operation. The plan will involve the expenditure of 400 million dollars by 1966, the construction of more than 100 dams, eight of them high and large, an attempt to hold the river to its channel from Sioux City, Iowa, to St. Louis by bigger and better levees, production of power, improvement of navigation, and finally get around to food production almost as an incidental. The distressing feature of this somewhat hastily drawn plan, authorized by the Omnibus Flood Control Bill of 1944, is its assignment of the job to two bureaus of the Federal government, authorized to give no attention whatever to practices on the land but to start work at various points on the river. The only hope that the river will not continue to carry its 600 odd parts per million of soil materials, destroy many of the world's greatest waterfowl refuge grounds, and really fail to achieve a permanent agriculture for the valley is the existence of a Missouri Valley Inter-Agency Committee upon which Federal and state soil conservation, forestry, and wild-animal-life interests are represented along with the two *construction* agencies. So far (1953) the voice of this committee is heard, but its power is not evident. Its possibilities as a democratic way of doing things are great.

Critics of the Army–Reclamation Bureau setup, many of whom favor the proposed Missouri Valley Authority, believe that economy, unified action on the land where the rainfall troubles start, and valley-wide co-operation can best be achieved by an authority somewhat like the TVA but greatly modified. They get pretty bitter in terms of the evils of bureau jealousies, the ignoring of the national interest, the cry of states rights without state responsibility, and the pressure of power interests against the idea of an authority. Whether they are right or not, a democracy is the only kind of government in which they can say so with vigor and persistence, and the idea of an MVA is not yet dead.

Drainage and Food Production. While ridding land of too much water in order to increase its capacity to produce food is hardly using water for food production, it should be mentioned here. On the positive side something needs to be said to offset the frequent statements that land drainage is all bad because it destroys wild-animal habitats, fails to pay out in crop production, aggravates flood damage, and dries out the marshes so they can be destroyed easily by fire.

First of all drainage is necessary on other than marsh lands (1) because an excess of water frequently results from prolonged storms in humid regions, and there should be a way to remove it properly; (2) because irrigation practice often results in a concentration of mineral salts carried in received water, if too much is allowed to accumulate on crop lands. Most of the important crop plants will tolerate little alkali, and for their use the soil may be easily "sickened."

Drainage as a help to extensive growing of specified crops such as truck, mint, and bulbs usually involves major works, including great truck drains as well as the tiling and ditching of the fields and the clearing and straightening of natural waterways. Here the drainage district, similar to the irrigation district discussed on pages 82 and 83, is used and where well planned on tested soils and in appropriate terrain may bring into production new lands of great fertility. In addition to lands important because rich though arid, vast areas of potentially productive wet lands now in use for the more extensive production of wild animals, including fur bearers, and of timber and for stabilizing water levels may be looked to for new farms in the event of great need.

Mint, sugar beets, potatoes, onions, and celery now occupy thousands of acres in Indiana and Michigan where the early explorers and trappers had concluded that the country was one vast, dismal, worthless swamp. In fact the commander of the garrison at Saginaw in 1822 is reported to have written the War Department that nothing but Indians, muskrats, and bullfrogs could live there. (What a wildlife sanctuary!) Starting about 60 years later, however, 8 million acres had been drained by 1940 with an investment of 40 million dollars.[9] Many other areas available for drainage lie in the southeastern part of the United States.

It was estimated in 1927 that enough land was then drained to meet the demand for cultivation for 35 years.[10] That would bring it up to the year 1962, and the Soil Conservation Service of the Department of Agriculture since about 1946 has had a definite policy of promoting the drainage of new lands within farms. The Bureau of Reclamation of the Department of the Interior also looks toward extending its activities to this field as the need increases for providing homes for displaced cotton farmers in the South.

In 1920 close to 65,500,000 acres had been drained with an investment

[9] Ballard, C. V., Water in Its Relation to Agriculture, pp. 28–29 in Michigan's Water Problems, Michigan Department of Conservation, Lansing, Mich., 1944.

[10] Teele, R. P., Economics of Land Reclamation, A. W. Shaw Co., Chicago, 1927, p. 201. Also, Land Reclamation Policies in the United States, *U.S. Dept. Agr., Bul.* 1257, p. 28, 1924.

of $372,274,000. By 1940 some 87 million acres was contained in drainage projects representing an investment of $691,725,000. Figures for the same year show more than 70 million acres occupied and 49,614,000 planted.[11]

How much of the remaining 75 million odd acres of wet lands, many of which need clearing as well as draining, will eventually be brought under cultivation is not easily prophesied. Better planning to assure that land drained will be productive, that it will justify development costs, and that it will not disorganize programs of conserving other valuable natural

FIG. 50. Trapping muskrat and mink in an undrained marsh near Fenton, Mich. 166 muskrats and 3 mink were taken off this area in 1945. (*Photo by Soil Conservation Service.*)

resources point the only road to sound over-all wet land conservation. Some of the conflicts of use met in draining land will be touched upon under Flood Control and under Wild-animal Resources (Fig. 50).

Water for Power

The United States is well supplied with sources of power, from the muscles of its people and its mineral fuels to the vast volume of water flowing downhill and finding itself increasingly harnessed. This natural wealth is reflected in the power consumption of the nation, which has been estimated even before the Second World War to exceed that of Great Britain by 50 per cent, to be twice that of Germany, 10 times that

[11] Statistical Abstract of the United States, 1951, U.S. Bureau of the Census, p. 553.

of Japan, and 150 times that of China. It is a far cry from the crude grist mills and sawmills built along the streams by the colonists even to the small municipal steam plant owned and operated by any one of numerous communities, and farther to the vast installments of the public utilities or a TVA. And yet water has always been in the picture and will continue to be important in filling the demand for power. Condensation-water problems, even in the most efficient steam plant, are not easy. One company serving southeastern Michigan uses in just one of its four plants 300 million gallons of water every 24 hours—almost 900 acre-feet—and the water must be reasonably soft and free of algae.[12] Another in Georgia uses similar amounts (Fig. 51).

Power from flowing water has had an interesting development. The first mills had to be located near the streams, and any work to be performed by them delivered and collected at the site. The development of the steam engine made it possible to locate the power plant more conveniently. Then came the use of electric current for power and its transmission by wire for considerable distances to locations where it was required. Following this, unusual developments in high-pressure boilers for steam plants put steam back into competition with water power for producing electrical current. At present, the production of hydroelectric power is one of several multiple purposes of river-valley development coupled with new industrial and farm demands, and it has given added significance to the use of water for producing power. In fact, some of the great Federal river-valley projects almost exhibit the picture of the power "tail" wagging the multiple-purpose "dog."

How Hydroelectric Power Is Measured. Before discussing the status of hydroelectric power quantitatively, the units in which it is expressed should be understood. One horsepower, it has been agreed since the days of Isaac Watts, represents the power required to raise a weight of 33,000 pounds 1 foot in 1 second's time. A watt in measuring electrical power is equivalent to $\frac{1}{746}$ horsepower, and a kilowatt is 100 times that much, or approximately $1\frac{1}{3}$ horsepower. The kilowatthour then, which one eyes with varying degrees of weariness on his light bill, is equivalent to the service of one and one-third horses working for him for 1 hour. If the horses had to live on what this service costs, they would not do so well. But how can one visualize more clearly what one horsepower means in terms of falling water? Well, at 60 or 70 miles an hour, a 100-horsepower engine in an automobile will be doing just 100 times 1 horsepower's work. Now to get that ride from water power, a column of water falling a distance of $67\frac{1}{2}$ feet at the rate of 9 cubic feet per second would have to be

[12] Boomers, Lynes D., Water in Its Relation to Industry and Commerce, p. 49 in Michigan's Water Problems, Michigan Department of Conservation, Lansing, Mich., 1944.

employed. So that is water power and horsepower in terms of an automobile ride.[13]

Still another term used in computing the possible power output of a stream is *firm power,* sometimes also called *minimum* or *primary power.* This term is used in connection with horsepower and means the amount of water power constantly available at the rate of flow during the lowest two weeks of the year. When the flow of a stream is augmented by turning water from another source into it, the verb form "to firm the flow" or "firming up the stream" is sometimes used.

FIG. 51. Yates steam power plant of Georgia Power Company. This plant uses for each 24-hour period, 373,680,000 gallons of water for cooling (this is borrowed and returned to the nearby river), 420,000 gallons for replacement due to loss in the boiler-feedwater cycle, and 9,000 gallons of sanitary water. (*Georgia Power Co., and McGraw-Hill Publishing Company, by whom picture is copyrighted.*)

Recent Consumption of Power and Energy in the United States. The total amount of energy used for all purposes in this country each year increased sixfold in the 40 years from 1889 to 1929, then slumped until about 1937, when it went back to the 1929 figure. In this period water power produced less than 4 per cent of the *total energy,*[14] and this and similar figures are sometimes quoted to indicate that water power is unimportant. On the other hand, the percentage for power alone was much

[13] Gorrow, M. G., Water in Its Relation to Power, pp. 36–37 in Michigan's Water Problems, Michigan Department of Conservation, Lansing, Mich., 1944.

[14] Our Energy Resources, 1939, Natural Resources Committee, Washington, p. 3.

higher, and in 1920 the nation had a hydroelectric power production of 15.95 billion kilowatthours which increased in 1940 to 47.74 billion and in 1945 had reached 79.97 billion. The figures for proportion of total power production represented by water power are interesting. In 1920 this figure was 36.8 per cent, it slipped to 32.9 per cent in 1940, and by 1945 had climbed back to 36 per cent.[15] A convenient rounding off of the figure today can be remembered as slightly more than one-third of the total power production.

The figure for installed capacity is probably lower than this, since in 1945 only 16 million kilowatts of installed water-power capacity in a total

FIG. 52. Nitrate plant of the TVA with Muscle Shoals Dam and power plant in the background. (*Photo by Tennessee Valley Authority.*)

of 63 million is reported.[16] The Federal Power Commission, concerning which more will be said later, accounts for the healthy demand for electric power from all sources in four ways:

1. Growing demand of the country for the products of the relatively modern electrometallurgical and electrochemical industries
2. Increasing application of electricity to modernized processes in the older industries

[15] Natural Resources Problems, *Annual Report of the Secretary of the Interior,* 1946, p. 15.

[16] Federal Power Commission, *Twenty-sixth Annual Report,* 1946, p. 1.

3. Steadily increasing use of electricity in the home
4. Rapid development of rural electricity[17]

Extent of Water-power Resources. According to a National Power Survey, figures for which are given in Table 3, the undeveloped water power in the United States amounted to 88,070,000 kilowatts as of January, 1949. This figure for estimated undeveloped water power, however, cannot be added to the developed water-wheel capacity of installed water power to get a round figure for the total developed and undeveloped water-power resources, and Table 3 is principally valuable for showing the geographical distribution of these resources and the increase in their development from 1939 to 1949.

So to get a comparison between total water-power resources and those now developed, in terms of horsepower, both of which are on the basis of installed water-wheel and turbine capacity, the rounded-off estimate of 17½ million kilowatts as the 1949 total in Table 3 is used. This figure compared with 88 million for total possible installed water-wheel and turbine capacity[18] indicates that about 20 per cent of the total had been developed by 1949.

Further study of Table 3 will reveal something of a natural dislocation of water-power resources with respect to population and to concentrations of industry as they are usually visualized. By far the greatest proportion of undeveloped power, some 60 per cent, is in the two Western regions, while only slightly more than 24 per cent is available to the three Atlantic seaboard regions. Installed water-wheel and turbine capacity is also somewhat greater in the Western regions. The East and West North Central regions with heavy concentrations of population and industry are low both in water-power resources and installed capacity.

These relationships are significant in two particulars: (1) water power if unavailable cannot be used as a substitute for coal in the oversimplified long-time argument for using replaceable for irreplaceable natural resources; (2) potential water power offers, in regions where it is plentiful and adapted to development, a hope for new locations for industry and population with the widening of economic opportunity—one of the objectives of democracy.

Power from Multiple-purpose River-valley Development. None of the great river valleys of the United States is without a history of floods, many of the rivers are used for water transportation, most of them are used for power, all the western ones for irrigation, all for recreation to a greater or lesser extent, and river fishing for commercial reasons as well as for recreation is still of some importance. Rivers have a way of ignoring state

[17] *Ibid.*
[18] *Statistical Abstract of the United States*, 1951, U.S. Bureau of the Census, p. 479.

boundaries set by men, and they get their water from the runoff of rainfall from vast watersheds. The production of power is one beneficial use of water, but one which may or may not be thoughtfully and skillfully reconciled with control of a great river for other purposes. This situation

Table 3. Developed and Undeveloped Water Power in the United States

Region	Rated kilowatt capacity of actual installations of all water wheels and turbines		Estimated undeveloped water power (not directly comparable to other two columns)
	December, 1939	December, 1949	January, 1949
United States	12,075,000	17,662,000	88,070,000
New England: Maine, N.H., Vt., Mass., Conn., R.I.	1,115,000	1,170,000	3,249,000
Middle Atlantic: N.Y., N.J., Pa.	1,633,000	1,687,000	6,503,000
East North Central: Ohio, Ind., Ill., Mich., Wis.	790,000	836,000	2,385,000
West North Central: Minn., Iowa, Mo., N. Dak., S. Dak., Nebr., Kans.	537,000	633,000	5,807,000
South Atlantic: Del., Md., D.C., Va., W. Va., N.C., S.C., Ga., Fla.	2,224,000	2,687,000	8,184,000
East South Central: Ky., Tenn., Ala., Miss.	1,270,000	2,570,000	4,789,000
West South Central: Ark., La., Okla., Tex.	140,000	423,000	3,585,000
Mountain: Mont., Idaho, Wyo., Colo., N. Mex., Ariz., Utah, Nev.	1,581,000	2,202,000	23,426,000
Pacific: Wash., Oreg., Calif.	2,783,000	4,422,000	30,142,000

SOURCE: *Statistical Abstract of the United States,* 1951, U.S. Bureau of the Census, p. 479.

sets the stage for multiple-purpose river-valley development under unified leadership with the total welfare of people as the major objective.

Irrigation farmers and the Bureau of Reclamation look to the power developed on the Colorado, the Columbia, the Missouri, and in the Central Valley of California to reduce the costs of irrigation farming, both through a supply of power to lighten their work and increase their efficiency and through earning revenue from power sales, which will mean that a lesser amount must be paid for irrigation benefits. The people who live in the valley of the Tennessee enjoyed the benefits of an increase from 8.3 billion kilowatthours in 1930 to 15.8 billion in 1940 and from 1936 to 1944 a 630 per cent gain in electric service to farms. There were also healthy increases in salaries and wages and in manufacturing.[19] And because the Tennessee is the only river-valley project enjoying unit leadership in its development, the nationwide interest in its production of power makes this river appropriate for discussion here.

The Tennessee Valley Authority and Its Work. TVA are the letters which denote the type of administrative organization set up by the act of 1933 for the purpose of increasing the security, well-being, and productive power of the people through developing the basic resources of the Tennessee Valley and its river. In an authority, a commission (in this instance three trained and capable men) is granted broad gevernmental powers to accomplish a tough job, usually requiring a large organization, generous funds, and imperative cooperation with related agencies. But TVA is also the nickname for this vast undertaking on a regional scale as well as for the outfit in charge.

The heaviest rainfall in the eastern United States comes down in the Tennessee Valley. If it lands on a thick patch of forest or a well-established hayfield, its beating power does little harm and much of it sinks into the leaf mold, sod, and soil. But with heavy settlement, forest clearing, and mountainside farming, the destructive power of rainfall has been at work for nearly a hundred years, and by 1930 the valley was not supporting its millions of people adequately.

So the task assigned to the TVA in 1933 was first to stop this destruction of productive powers and second to make the water on the land and in the river more useful and productive than ever before. Soil, water, land and river, people and their resources contribute what the TVA calls a unity, and each of the various parts of its water-control tasks—navigation improvement, flood alleviation, power production, development and experimental manufacture of new mineral fertilizers, encouragement of modern forestry practice, and the management of private lands—is inseparably related to all the others.

The 15 billion kilowatthours of electric power which the Authority produced and distributed in 1947 demonstrates the interlocking character of all conservation undertakings. In 13 years of actual operation, TVA has built sixteen dams and integrated their operation with ten which had been constructed previously. And the integration brings about this desirable "chain reaction": it produces electricity with which it develops and demonstrates new mineral fertilizers. These are available to enable farmers

[19] An M.V.A. or Stagnation, National Farmers Union (undated pamphlet of about 1945). Denver, Colo., pp. 4–5.

on the land to shift to less destructive crops and forms of cultivation. The products of livestock farming and diversified soil-management and forest-management systems require electricity in their processing, both for power and refrigeration. People find employment in the new plants. Meanwhile fisheries, both sport and commercial, are improved in the nine long lakelike reservoirs at whose dams the electricity is produced. The sale of power to distributing companies and cooperatives puts more people to work, and revenue goes not only to the retiring of publicly advanced costs for construction but to augment local taxes in lieu of those lost from land occupied by conservation works.

FIG. 53. A catch of catfish by commercial fishermen. An incidental but important contribution from the artificial lakes of TVA. (*Photo by Tennessee Valley Authority.*)

Thus hydroelectric power from the Tennessee River, important as it is in the role which rates the greater part of TVA's publicity, affects the management of every other natural resource in the valley, including its people. And the Authority can see to it that power is equitably distributed and that its development complements rather than conflicts with other beneficial uses of the river.

The TVA will be referred to further in later sections of this chapter for it has made significant contributions in the fields of mineral developments, recreation, navigation, and fishery management.

The Missouri River Basin. The reader is here referred back to the discussion of the Missouri Valley Authority on page 90. Here with

44 years of construction work the Bureau of Reclamation finds itself now lined up under the 1944 Flood Control Act with the Corps of Engineers of the U.S. Army, whose legal water business is largely defined in terms of flood control and the improvement of navigation. The Corps of Engineers now, however, operates the power plant at the great Fort Peck Dam in Montana (Fig. 54) which in 1946 generated 100,900,000 kilowatt-hours of power. This was marketed by the Bureau of Reclamation. The Office of Indian Affairs, the various state agencies, the Fish and Wildlife

FIG. 54. Fort Peck Dam, built by the Corps of Engineers, U.S. Army, principally for flood control. The power it generates is marketed by the Bureau of Reclamation. (*Photo by Corps of Engineers.*)

Service, the Soil Conservation Service, mineral interests and livestock interests, all have a tremendous stake in the outcome of any plan for the Missouri River Basin. The device used to assure the "unity" which to a great extent is achieved elsewhere by the TVA is an interagency committee previously mentioned. This may or may not be able to assure adequate consideration for power production at the 100 dams and to relate it to the total conservation objective.

The Central Valley Project. Production of hydroelectric power looms large in the Central Valley of California even before agreement has been reached as to just how the development project as a whole shall be managed. The great Shasta Dam with its power plant operating 13.5 per cent overload during the entire year from July 1, 1945, to June 30, 1946, generated 1,486,578,600 kilowatthours, the major portion of which was sold to a large utility company under a war-duration contract. Here again a plan, this time worked out by the Bureau of Reclamation, has been submitted for review to the Governor of California and to other agencies. In final form, emphasizing the necessity for coordinated and integrated development "of the water resources" of the Central Valley, it will be presented to the President of the United States and presumably by him to the Congress. An interesting feature of this plan, which illustrates the complexity of river-valley problems and which must be integrated with desirable power production, is the need for a flow of stored water to prevent ocean-water encroachment on 450,000 acres of rich delta land at the mouths of the Sacramento and the San Joaquin.[20] Other river-valley projects which develop vast volumes of power are the Columbia Basin with its Grand Coulee and Bonneville power installations and the Colorado with its Hoover (Boulder Canyon) Dam. By whatever plans these river resources are controlled and brought into service, hydroelectric power, not only in its production but in its equitable distribution, offers the tough kind of problem that a democracy must face. Total river-basin thinking and planning are indispensable.

A radical change in policy with change of administration in 1953 tossed this problem into the laps of local agencies and public utilities, particularly with reference to the sale and distribution of power produced by publicly financed works. More significantly, however, the new policy frowns on construction at Federal expense, to say nothing of Federal operation of new projects which private capital may be able to undertake more or less on its own terms. Two examples may be cited to illustrate the trend under the new policy: (1) decision of the Secretary of the Interior in 1953 to turn over to a private corporation the sale and distribution of power generated by the Clark Hill federally constructed project on the Savannah River in Georgia. This is an interim decision which counts on the Congress to amend the Flood Control Act of 1944—an act providing that priority in the disposal of power produced by such projects be granted to public and cooperative agencies such as municipalities and rural electrification cooperatives. (2) A decision to abandon plans for Federal construction of the great Hungry Horse project on the South Fork of the Flathead River in Montana in favor of a number of smaller ventures financed by private capital.

How Water Power Enterprises Are Regulated. Because any control of large power resources can lead to natural monopoly, it is appropriate that development and distribution should be subject to a measure of public regulation just as trade, transportation, and the practice of the

[20] Natural Resource Problems, *Annual Report of the Secretary of the Interior*, 1946, p. 89.

professions are regulated. On the side of equitable distribution, which is an essential of conservation of natural resources, most of the states have long had a measure of rate regulation on the distribution of power under their "public-service commissions," "railroad commissions," and similar bodies. Federal regulation for conservation purposes was authorized in 1920 with the passage of the Federal Power Act, 12 years after the White House Conference of 1908 had included such a recommendation in its "Declaration of Principles." Meanwhile, however, withdrawal of water-power sites on Federal land had gone forward with other land withdrawals for study and possible reservation, and public interest had grown steadily in the nation's water-power resources.

The Federal Power Act signed by President Woodrow Wilson on June 10, 1920, assumed rightly that ownership of land at a power site and the duty of looking after the interests of the people of the United States as the owners justified licensing and regulation of water-power enterprises. The navigability of any stream might also be affected by power development and so put the commerce clause of the Constitution squarely behind the commission's powers. The Congress, however, assumed that any work which an ex-officio Federal Power Commission, created by this act, might have to do could be taken care of neatly by borrowing help from other Federal departments. Only a chief engineer and a small office force were provided to handle a mass of applications and inquiries. Lack of funds and personnel persisted for more than a decade, until finally in 1935 the law was amended to provide for five full-time skilled commissioners and for greatly expanding the technical force. The work of the commission was also defined more carefully to cover (1) passing upon applications for developing power on waters of the public lands and navigable waters elsewhere, (2) supervising interstate wholesale power rates, (3) devising and promoting the use of uniform accounting systems by licensed companies, (4) passing upon mergers and issuance of securities, (5) studying power resources and rates, and (6) cooperating with state regulatory commissions.

Since 1935 the duties of the Federal Power Commission have increased and now extend to certain power problems other than those wholly connected with water power. In 1938 Congress conferred upon the commission the jurisdiction over interstate natural-gas rates in addition to other duties in regulating the natural-gas industry. The Federal Inter-Agency River Basin Committee established in 1943, and from which the various local river-basin committees have developed, includes a representative of the Federal Power Commission to assist in obtaining more complete cooperation of all interests in river-basin development. The commission has also made numerous studies of power resources, typical of which is the one requested by the Senate Committee on Foreign Affairs on the marketability of the potential power output of the St. Lawrence River (12 billion kilowatthours annually). This study concluded that this output could be put to full use a short time after the completion of the proposed project. It showed also that the cost of producing and delivering the energy to load centers would be cheaper than the production costs alone (principally fuel and labor) of a like amount of energy at any existing steam-electric plant in the area if fixed charges on the steam plant were excluded.

Still another and very interesting study by the commission under its mandate in the Federal Power Act to "conduct investigations regarding the generation of electric energy, however produced" has to do with wind-power units. In this study it is estimated that power from efficiently designed wind-power generators scattered widely over the territory served could furnish 20 per cent of the energy of a large network.

In a study of rates, the commission found a situation Jan. 1, 1946, where in widely varying sizes of communities throughout the United States the lowest monthly bills for residential electric service ranged (for 100 kilowatthours of service) from $1.70 in the State of Washington to $7.10 in Oklahoma among those served by publicly owned systems. For residences served by privately owned utilities the lowest was $2.50 in Ohio and Kentucky, the highest $9.61 in Massachusetts.[21] In the general field of rate regulation by the commission, now well established as to constitutionality, reductions running in 1946 to nearly 40 million dollars in interstate wholesale rates were effected. This begins to bring equitable distribution of the benefits of conserving a natural resource right down to the ultimate consumer.

Water Power in Future Power Requirements. Projected by the staff of the Federal Power Commission[22] the total electric-power requirements of the country from all sources, with about 60 per cent of it going to industries large and small, is 376 billion killowatthours for 1952. This is more than double the production of 188 billion in 1940 and almost 27 per cent more than the 275 billion total power production of 1946. With these figures, and with the aluminum industry, for example, requiring about 10 kilowatthours to produce 1 pound of metal, water power by holding up its end has had to comprise a considerable part of a projected increase of some 20 million kilowatts of installation from 1948 through 1952. Table 3 on page 97 may be referred to for figures on potential water-power resources from which future needs must be met.

Power is a productive use of water, and wherever water can be stepped

[21] *Statistical Abstract of the United States*, 1947, U.S. Bureau of the Census, p. 488.

[22] Krug, J. A., Report (as Secretary of the Interior) on National Resources and Foreign Aid, p. 6, 1947.

up in this phase of its productivity, *with due consideration for other natural resources and values involved,* it is being conserved. Frequently also the same water that turns a wheel or a turbine may irrigate a crop, water a deer, float a barge, wash away a treated industrial waste, put out a city fire, and go on its way without tearing up soil or destroying buildings and even human life. In the course of these adventures it has saved irreplaceable mineral fuel at the power and transportation stages. This is conservation.

Water for Recreation

It is difficult to imagine satisfactory outdoor recreation, with its importance to the health and power, both spiritual and mental, of people, without water in the picture. A parched, waterless outdoor scene may exhibit gorgeous sunsets and a dry pine forest furnish fragrance and beauty, but men must have water to drink, to use in the simple necessities of outdoor camp and picnic activities, to look at, to swim in, and for recreational bathing and boating. The sound of running water is also pleasant in an outdoor setting, and in winter water in the forms of ice and snow offers opportunity for skating, skiing, tobogganing, and decorating oneself with clothing that would rival Solomon's in all his glory. Sport fishing and the hunting of waterfowl as the favored recreations of millions put increasing pressure on streams, lakes, ponds, and reservoirs which must serve other purposes as well.

It is not too much to say that water is indispensable to adequate outdoor recreation nor that almost all the bodies of water of whatever size in this country are used for recreation.

Water as a Part of the Natural Scene. A great many people get their only outdoor recreation through their eyes. A landscape with a stream or waterfall or lake near or far away proclaims its value in terms of dollars and even in terms of international agreement over use of the water. It is an actual fact that much of the price of lake lots or riverside residence property is represented in the unearned control of a water scene. Ridiculously small proportions of beaches, lake shore, and river shore throughout the country are in public ownership for exclusive recreational and scenic use. Isle Royale in Lake Superior, one of our most recently dedicated national parks, is a lovely land mass which would be just another stretch of northern country but for the great cold clear lake around it and its own inland waters. Cumberland Falls in Kentucky, now a state park, is valuable principally for the water scene. It was purchased and presented by a family of wealth to the state and just escaped being developed for power purposes. The decision of a Kentucky judge that the use of water to look at constitutes "no use at all" is no longer valid.

Niagara Falls with its 165-foot drop represents one of the world's greatest opportunities for the development of power, having a remarkably uniform flow of about 220,000 cubic feet per second capable of generating 5 million horsepower, which is something like 8 per cent of the total installed water-wheel capacity of the United States at present. Moreover, the falls themselves were once fenced off from view on the American side, and a fee was charged by private interests for a chance to view the scene.

FIG. 55. Water to drink is important and sometimes a limiting factor in the use of land for recreation. Here water is piped to a play area in the Nantahala National Forest in North Carolina. (*U.S. Forest Service.*)

Public sentiment through the years has asserted itself, with the result that public interests now control the view from both sides. A treaty has been entered into between the United States and Great Britain in behalf of Canada recognizing the equitable share of both countries in the flow of the stream but calling a permanent halt to further power and industrial encroachment on the scene. Actually the treaty reserves three-quarters of the water of the falls for scenery alone.

Further evidence of the public appreciation of water for its aesthetic values is evident over the years through spirited opposition to industrial invasion of Western national parks for the use of park waters for power and irrigation projects.

Water for Camping, Picnicking, and Sport. The little water the users of a pleasant spot may need for drinking and simple outdoor cooking has often been the limiting factor in the development of day-use or camping areas in public forests, parks, and other lands. Nor is such a problem confined always to arid regions, for too many streams and springs in humid localities are likely to be unsafe for drinking simply because of heavy concentrations of industry, agriculture, and population. Ironically enough, too, one of the great difficulties met in administering outdoor areas for picnic and camp use is maintaining the safety of the water supply against human carelessness in use.

FIG. 56. Toccoa Falls, Georgia, an example of water as a part of the natural scene. (*Photo by Soil Conservation Service.*)

Water sports include canoeing, sailing, swimming, rowing, motorboat racing, and organized games such as water polo, the latter being more commonly played in indoor pools. For these sports, clean, accessible, safe, and attractive waters are essential. Surveys of recreation preferences show a vast discrepancy in most localities between preferences for water sports on the one hand and opportunity to participate in them on the other. And frequently these sports themselves interfere with each other so that special waters are needed. Certainly the owner of a noisy motorboat has his rights, but they should not extend to all waters where they interfere with swimmers, canoeists, and seekers of wilderness solitude. Nor should airplanes for sport be allowed to invade wilderness waters. A considerable part of the reason for these conflicts and frustrations is unavailability of water facilities. State and Federal authorities are aware of this situation and have attempted to meet it in the following ways: (1) lease or purchase of additional waterfront sites for public use, (2) construction of dams for impounding artificial lakes exclusively devoted to recreational use, (3) organizing the recreational facilities on the growing number of multiple-purpose reservoirs, (4) promoting the cleanup and treatment of waters heretofore unsafe for recreational use, (5) developing with camping facilities and making accessible public waters all the way from ocean beaches to canoe landings and portage trails in state forests. On the municipal and county front, water for outdoor swimming pools becomes important, frequently making heavy demands on underground supplies.

Fishing and hunting, also important exclusively as sports, should be mentioned here as well at later on under Wild-animal Life because fishing and hunting of waterfowl are impossible without clean, accessible waters in vast stretches of stream and marsh and in well-managed lakes, ponds, and artifically impounded bodies. It is also important to know that the strongest leadership in behalf of preventing water pollution comes from organizations of sportsmen of the more constructive type. The Izaak Walton League of America deserves special commendation on this score. State leasing for public use of stream banks from the riparian owners and purchase and development of access sites for fishermen out of license receipts have become necessary in some states. It is not strange that one hears more and more the terms "rod pressure" and "gun pressure" in the discussions of conserving water for fishermen and hunters to use.

The conservation problems met in using water for recreation are those of (1) assuring availability and accessibility, (2) assuring freedom from pollution, (3) establishing recreation in its broadest sense as a major beneficial use of water, and seeing to it that such use is granted its share of priority.

Water for Transportation

One of the oldest uses of water is the one in which men have made it their highways for travel and burden carrying by boat, the floating of logs and pulpwood, and the carrying away of waste. Waste transportation has already been discussed, log and pulpwood driving will be covered in the chapter on forests, and there is left here the use of oceans, lakes, coastal inlets, and rivers and canals for shipping.

This subject involves a kind of conservation which, so far as inland waters are concerned, frequently appears as a sort of premium and non-conflicting result when waters are controlled and developed for other major uses. And yet the average American citizen through the years has been conditioned to think of rivers and harbor appropriations as pork-barrel legislation. Why? The answers to this question perhaps lie in the facts that much of this water is actually little used for this purpose as against other uses; that freight movements by water are slow and that

FIG. 57. Water transportation on the Mississippi near Memphis, Tenn. Barges in foreground are laden with oil, those in center with pipe. (*Photo by Corps of Engineers, U.S. Army.*)

they move from wharf to wharf and port to port rather than from warehouse, farm, or mine to plant, store, or home; that the vast scale of improvement and maintenance required has not attracted private investment; that in colder climates inland waterways are not open year long; and possibly that in a "free competitive economy" much more than just "the economics of the thing" have been used to oppose waterway development.

It should be pointed out here that historically transportation was the only use of water specifically mentioned in the Constitution of the United States and that the "commerce clause" is the basis for much important conservation legislation, notably in the fields of water power and forest resources.

To their credit, on the other hand, it may be said that ocean waters are indispensable to commerce and to much of the communication and most of the travel between continents; that inlets and larger rivers are convenient extenders of ocean transportation; that other transportation facilities, particularly in times of war and of great prosperity, are relieved of much tonnage and free to concentrate on more urgent hauling; that many of the great natural waterways in this country are so located as best to handle cargoes of great bulk and weight with assured return hauls, where speed of delivery is not important; and finally that improvement of rivers for navigation gears in well with a measure of control of floods with their long record of damage to life and property. One other long-time advantage touching the needs of future generations appears in the lesser use of irreplaceable metals and fuels by water than by other means of transportation.

Quantitative Significance of Water Transportation. In 1945, the total tonnage moved by railroads in this country amounted to 2,961,789,000 short tons[23] (2,000 pounds) as against 618,906,000 short tons[24] for all foreign and domestic water-borne commerce, 446,813,000 tons, or more than 72 per cent, of which was river, canal, connecting channel, and harbor transportation. The more comparable figures therefore, rounded off, are 447 for water and 2,962 for rail, or roughly as 1 to 6½. An easier way to keep this comparison in mind is to think of water haul as two-thirteenths as great as rail haul. The figure would be even more unfavorable to water transportation if truck haul and pipeline transportation were added to rail-haul figures, but the business of the country cannot lightly brush off an inland shipping capacity two-thirteenths as great as that of its rapid-transportation railroads.

In order to present a country-wide picture of water-borne commerce, excluding certain duplications and harbor commerce from the figures quoted above, attention is called to Table 4. It will be noted here that state and private canals account for a very small portion of the total tonnage while Federal canals and connecting channels carry the greatest part of the load.

Ocean Transportation. The several million men who constituted the military and naval forces of the United States in World War II learned some things about oceans which should be a part of the education of every well-informed citizen. Perhaps the most important lesson is that ocean routes form life lines throughout the world and that nations as well as armies look to these routes for supply and for profitable outlet of their products. Another one is that "freedom of the seas" is conservation of first importance in assuring any kind of world-wide equitable

[23] *Statistical Abstract of the United States*, 1947, U.S. Bureau of the Census, p. 517.
[24] *Ibid.*

distribution of natural resources. The depth and safety of harbors, constituting one of the limitations on the use of ocean waters for transportation, very properly become objectives in improvement and maintenance work, and meeting these objectives is a kind of conservation.

In 1944, United States ships carried 59 million long tons (2,200 pounds) of cargo, which was more than three-quarters of all our ocean shipping that year. This compares with 8 billion long tons in 1930, representing less than a quarter of that year's cargoes.[25] With more than 5,000 vessels in the country's merchant marine today, the conservation of ocean-harbor facilities assumes new importance.

Table 4. Commerce on Principal Rivers, Canals, and Connecting Channels of the United States, 1940 to 1945

In thousands of short tons. Excludes general ferry traffic, car ferry traffic, and cargos in transit.

	1940	1945
Grand total	414,787	432,937
Atlantic coast rivers	37,533	22,799
Gulf coast rivers	12,903	11,242
Pacific coast rivers	32,928	30,156
Mississippi river and tributaries	112,634	123,902
Federal canals and connecting channels	210,630	239,880
State and private canals	7,817	4,646

Source: *Statistical Abstract of the United States*, 1947, p. 543.

The Great Lakes and the St. Lawrence River. The five Great Lakes—Michigan, Superior, Huron, Erie, and Ontario—with their improved connecting channels form the world's greatest inland waterway. Those who want to see the St. Lawrence River Waterway authorized and completed envision Buffalo, Cleveland, Detroit, Milwaukee, and Chicago as great ocean ports. At present a healthy mild-weather commerce carries grain, limestone, and ore eastward, and coal westward, with interport, Canadian, and to a lesser extent small European shipments of pulpwood. Shorter hauls of sand, gravel, automobiles, and miscellaneous cargo are common. Such traffic is possible only because of the dredging, improvement, and maintenance of connecting channels, important among which are the Saint Mary's River between Lakes Superior and Huron, the St. Clair and Detroit Rivers between Huron and Erie, and the Welland Canal between Erie and Ontario above Niagara Falls. These improvements, on the other hand, and certain waterway hookups such as the Illinois Ship

[25] Dewhurst, J. Frederic, and associates, America's Needs and Resources, The Twentieth Century Fund, Inc., New York, 1947, p. 8.

Canal, which drains Lake Michigan water into the Illinois River and thence to the Mississippi, have introduced some lake-level problems which require constant attention.

Lake levels of Erie, Huron, and Michigan are believed by some authorities to have been lowered during a 30-year period some 5 to 6 inches by diversions at Chicago and elsewhere. This seems insignificant, but it is important enough to carrier companies using large ships to have brought about litigation to reduce the amount of water diverted from 10,000 cubic feet per second to 1,500. And as if this were not enough

FIG. 58. Lake boats passing in St. Clair River between Lakes St. Clair and Huron. Speed is regulated to prevent wave damage to shore property. (*"The Bulletin," Lake Carriers Association.*)

trouble, cyclical variations in lake levels, identified by studies of 125 years' records, must be dealt with in forecasting and maintaining navigability of this waterway.[26]

The importance of the Great Lakes to the steel industry will be understood in terms of transportation when it is considered that coal, iron ore, and limestone are the natural-resource materials needed and that in no one place in the country do they occur identically in the quantity and quality required except in northern Alabama. Great Lakes transportation, however, can load or meet them from short rail hauls so that the coke from

[26] Martin, Helen M., and others, They Need Not Vanish, Michigan Dept. of Conservation, Lansing, Mich., 1942, p. 201.

the coal fields of Illinois and Pennsylvania meets the lake-borne limestone and iron ore at Chicago, Detroit, and Cleveland. The mills at these centers thus rival those at Pittsburgh and Youngstown which have short hauls for coal but long hauls from lake shore for other materials.

The St. Lawrence River Waterway. Improvement of the St. Lawrence River from the eastern end of Lake Ontario to the harbor at Montreal, where it will be necessary to deepen canals around rapids, enlarge the locks, and otherwise provide for large ocean-going ships, will require agreement by treaty between the United States and Canada. Certain other improvements in connecting channels will be necessary farther west. Legislation has been introduced in Congress in some form every session for the past two decades and has been roundly opposed by power interests, by citizens who saw in it ruination for the Port of New York, and by others who feel that Canada will profit more than the United States. The estimated cost would be 260 million dollars for navigation improvements, of which the United States would pay 165 million. Recently, from the Eightieth Congress on, the proposal has been made to charge tolls and thus make the project self-liquidating, and on May 13, 1954, President Eisenhower signed a measure which authorizes the United States to participate in construction extending as far as Lake Erie at a cost of 105 million dollars to this country. Bonds would be retired in about 50 years from shipping tolls. (This pay-as-you-use plan assumes increasing importance when it is considered that two other proposals, one for the Intercoastal Waterway and one for expanding the Mississippi River system, would cost a total of 745 million dollars. Smaller projects would bring total proposed western expenditures up to $1,160,000,000.[27]

Coastal Navigation. For safe domestic and light international trade along the Atlantic and Gulf coasts, increasing attention is given to improvement of natural waterways paralleling the coast itself but back of headlands, where water is relatively calm most of the time. Depths of 9 to 12 feet would be maintained in the natural waters and connecting canals from Massachusetts Bay intermittently clear to the mouth of the Mississippi. It was in connection with, but as an addition to, this program a few years ago that the Florida Ship Canal was proposed. This would have been a deep water channel from the St. John's River across the narrow part of the peninsula to the Gulf of Mexico. Cost and threat to the quality of Florida's underground water supply appear to have discredited this plan. Meanwhile work progresses on various segments of this great intracoastal waterway with steady use by craft of light draft.

River and Canal Navigation. A considerable number of the canals built in this country have connected rivers with each other or with larger

[27] Dewhurst, J. Frederic, and associates, America's Needs and Resources, The Twentieth Century Fund, Inc., New York, 1947, p. 231.

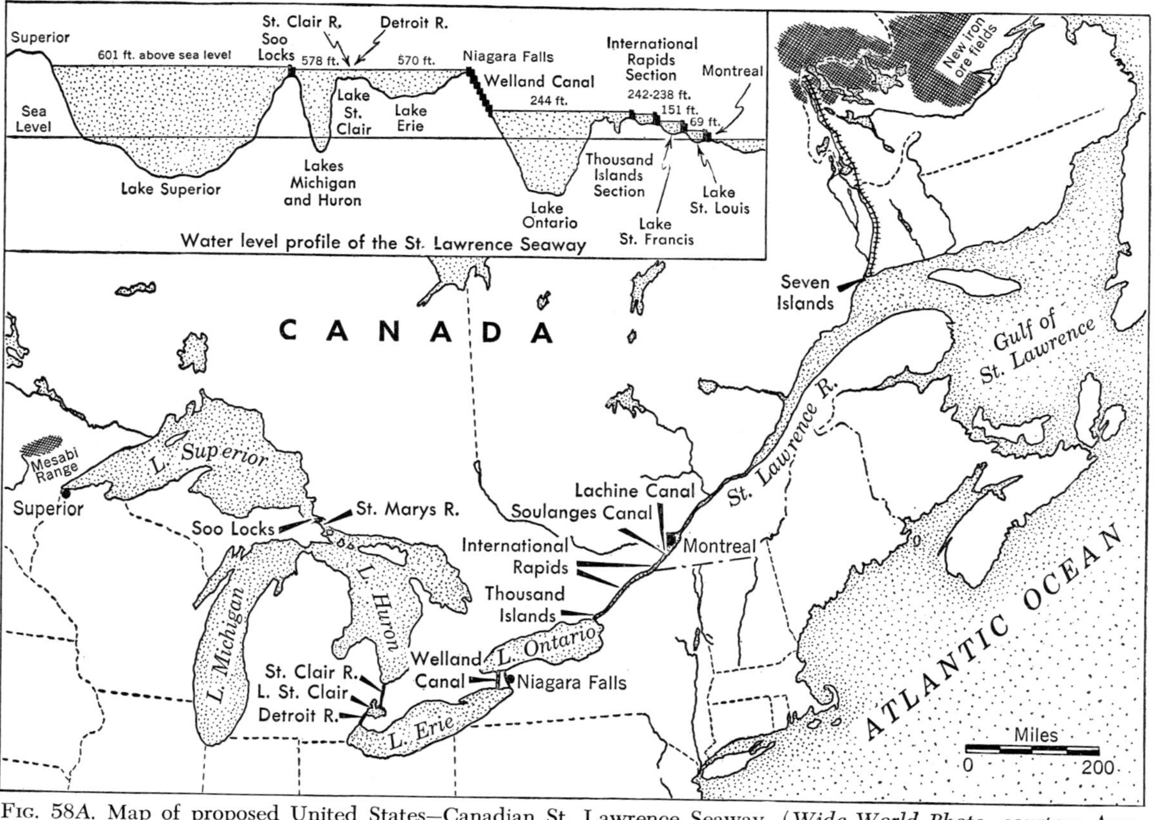

Fig. 58A. Map of proposed United States–Canadian St. Lawrence Seaway. (*Wide World Photo, courtesy Associated Press.*)

bodies of water or have followed existing river channels as a part of their improvement of navigation. Rivers and canals are therefore discussed together. The best known of the latter are the New York State Barge Canal, formerly called the Erie Canal; the "Soo" Canal at Sault Ste. Marie between Lakes Superior and Huron, which carries tonnage exceeding that of the Panama and Suez Canals combined; the Illinois Ship Canal, carrying away Chicago's wastes; and the Cape Cod Canal, connecting Massachusetts and Naragansett Bays, built privately and sold some years ago to the Federal government. Each one of these has its own peculiar distinction, and all persist against repeated charges of having proved uneconomic or of dealing out subsidy to shippers alone. Great expense for building and operating locks, slowness of traffic, uselessness during freezing weather, inability to compete with railroad, interference with water-level maintenance, and continual necessity of dredging because of siltation are stock arguments against canals in general as supplementing inland transportation in this day and age. Their use, however, is inevitable if rivers, lakes, and other inland bodies of water are to be employed for navigation.

Short, heavily used, and indispensable, the Soo Canal taps the rich Lake Superior country and is itself an improvement of a short river. Without this canal and the Welland Canal (wholly in Canada), the Great Lakes would be much less important as a waterway.

The New York State Barge Canal, once indispensable to the moving of crops and other cargo eastward during its days as the Erie Canal, greatly improved from 1910 to 1920 and now inadequately used, "canalizes" a portion of the Mohawk River and connects the Hudson River with Lake Erie.

The Illinois Ship Canal cuts through a low divide and reverses the direction of flow of a part of the Chicago River, leads to the Illinois River and thence to the Mississippi. It becomes a part of the Mississippi River system which with the St. Lawrence Seaway and the Intra-coastal Waterway are the three waterway projects of greatest promise.

In addition to the Mississippi River system which has been the scene of greatest study, experimentation, and development in river navigation, all the great river-valley projects include improvement of navigation as one of their objectives. On the Tennessee (independently from the Mississippi program), the Columbia, the Sacramento (Central Valley Project), and the Missouri (a part of the Mississippi program) navigation bids fair to increase in importance as a use of water.

The Inland Waterways Corporation. This corporation should not be confused with the Inland Waterways *Commission* mentioned early in the text and having an important role in the early days of the conservation movement. The Inland Waterways *Corporation* was created by the Congress in 1924 some years after a study of needed increase in transportation made when the Federal government took over operation of the railroads as a war measure. This study recommended the building and operating of two fleets of modern river barges, one for the lower Mississippi and the other for the Tombigbee and Warrior Rivers in Alabama, from the Gulf to the steel center near Birmingham. At first the War Department was to acquire and operate these barges experimentally as a demonstration to private enterprise of the economic feasibility of river transportation; it functioned with some losses until the corporation came into being in 1924. This was one of the early Federal corporations now so common as administrative devices in a democracy.

The act creating the corporation has this to say of its purpose: "To promote, encourage, and develop water transportation, service, and facilities in connection with the commerce of the United States, and to foster and preserve in full vigor, both rail and water transportation." As a means of implementing this policy, it has also recognized the need for interchange of water traffic with railroads through the medium of the establishment of "such joint tariffs with rail carriers as shall make generally available the privileges of joint rail and water transportation upon terms reasonably fair to both rail and water carriers.[28] In other words, whether a shipper or a buyer of a shipped commodity lives on a river bank or not, he is entitled to the benefits of lower cost water transportation. This smacks of equitable distribution in this kind of water conservation.

With such joint rates, modern terminal facilities, and improved barge and tow equipment, the corporation still has a chance to demonstrate transportation as a beneficial use of river water, but its record so far has been somewhat disappointing.

The corporation, with an initial appropriation of 5 million dollars, had an investment of 24 million dollars by 1930, steadily saved money for the shippers but lost for the public and still operates as an experiment, theoretically to be turned over to private enterprise when the demonstration is sufficiently convincing. During the war year 1944 the Director of the Office of Defense Transportation pointed out that the 5,000 barges operating on the improved channels of the Mississippi and its tributaries showed heavy traffic and that 95 per cent of the commodities carried were directly needed for war purposes. At present (1953) the corporation has proposed to Congress two alternatives for the future of the experiment. The first one emphasizes the insistence at recent hearings by certain shippers of bulk cargoes such as steel, sulfur, and grain and by numerous smaller shippers that the barge service is indispensable. It also points out that plans for modernization through barge design for integrated tow and other improvements would be possible with increased capital investment.

[28] *Annual Report*, Inland Waterways Corporation, St. Louis, Mo., 1944, p. 6.

Such capital if made available will definitely demonstrate the barge lines as a paying business and promote sale of the lines, with the Federal government retiring from the river-transportation business in favor of private enterprise. The second alternative offered is a recommendation that immediate sale without modernization be authorized.

The Congress, having created the Inland Waterways Corporation in 1924, must choose now what it will do with the experiment, which has demonstrated almost everything it was designed to do save some way of achieving joint rail-barge rates and other necessary types of cooperation from railroad carriers. Strangely enough, in deciding this the Congress will need to listen to the paradoxial argument from private enterprise which goes something like this: "We oppose government in business on principle. This corporation of yours is the only government corporation in competition 100 per cent with private enterprise. It has saved us money. Do not liquidate it." The Congress has not yet faced this need for decision, as of 1953.

Privately Operated Barge Lines. On the Mississippi and its tributaries, a number of privately owned barge lines are operated, and barge haul is important on the Tennessee River where modernized articulated barge units are used for high-speed transportation of automobiles. Here terminal facilities are new and efficient, but absence of joint barge-rail rates is a drawback.

Flood Control

Bearing in mind that floods are as old as the rivers themselves and that their "control" sounds like flying in the face of providence, it is still profoundly true that the human race, through its abuse of the land and its invasion of the natural valleys and bypasses through which flood waters must flow, has served as a multiplier of, and a target for, the fury of flood waters. And it is defeatist to conclude that nothing can be done to control the runoff when there are promising possibilities of accomplishment, first on the land from which the waters drain, and finally in the river bed and its immediate valley. So far this program has been in reverse with little attention being paid to the source of flood waters.

Heavy and unseasonable rainfall and early or sudden melting of accumulations of snow have accompanied many of the great floods in the United States in recent years. These phenomena are recurring and inevitable. But overuse of watersheds for the grazing of livestock, deforestation, injudicious partial clearing for agriculture and later abandonment, unplanned drainage projects, and unplanned and thoughtless farming—all these occur not in the stream but back on the land. Every one of them contributes to the rapid runoff of rainfall and the certainty of flood conditions.

How Important Is It to Control Runoff? Human life and useful, well-distributed accumulations of human efforts expressed in homes, businesses, and public works are regarded with more respect in a democracy than in any other form of government. Floods destroy every one of these things, over and over, while in many places the people have short water supplies within the same year.

Among the more spectacular floods it will be recalled that the Johnstown flood of May, 1889, which took many lives was increased in suddenness and destructiveness by the failure of the dam on the Conemaugh River in Pennsylvania. The largest flood record in the Tennessee Valley

Fig. 59. What a flood can do to a railroad. (*Photo by Tennessee Valley Authority.*)

occurred in 1867, destroying a community and making 5,000 persons homeless. Here for 70 years agriculture and lumbering had made only modest headway, but had such a flood happened today it is estimated that the city of Chattanooga would have witnessed 40 million dollars damage and its population of 130,000 would have suffered greatly. An Ohio flood in 1913 took 400 lives and destroyed and damaged 100 million dollars worth of property. In 1927 the Mississippi flood drove 700,000 people from their homes and destroyed millions in crops and property. The Pickens Canyon flood in southern California in 1938 took lives, homes, orchards, and public works, following a heavy rain over a burned-out watershed. In August, 1945, a rainfall of high intensity following grazing abuse of the contributing watersheds and a bad plant-cover fire the previous year brought Salt Lake City a flood which damaged homes and property to the extent of $347,000. These examples, chosen at random from a tremendous list, indicate the importance of investing money and effort to save life and property.

Engineering Works for Flood Control. "Main strength and awkwardness" or what the English call "muddling through" has worked so well in freedom-loving democracies that early flood-control statesmen and builders may be forgiven for a stubborn policy of "levees only," a belief that

Fig. 60. Nebraska farm flooded in May, 1950, by the Salt-Wahoo creeks. This flood took twenty-three lives. (*Reprinted from Capper's Farmer.*)

whatever is done must be in the form of earth walls to confine the river to its channel. Up to 1927 this policy was seldom challenged.

Required in the grants by the King of France as a condition of holding land, the planters of Louisiana were building levees on the Mississippi as early as 1717. Everyone who lived within 7 miles of the river had to help, and not until 1850 did the levee districts, similar to irrigation, drainage, and soil conservation districts discussed earlier in this text, come to be common and to take over the increasing task of building and maintaining levees.[29] After the war between the states through which levees were neglected and destroyed, the desperate extent of the flood problem led

[29] Ely, Richard T., and Geo. S. Wehrwein, Land Economics, The Macmillan Company, New York, 1940, p. 352.

to the establishment by the Federal government of the Mississippi River Commission in 1879. This body concluded, partly on a cost basis, that levees were the best way to meet the flood menace and suggested no other remedies. These devices served remarkably well until the 1927 flood broke through disastrously in so many places with such loss of life and damage to property as to shock the nation into more constructive thinking. In spite of convincing testimony, however, concerning the necessity of extending control measures back on to the land where the rainfall first becomes runoff, sometimes thousands of miles from the scene of flood damage, the Federal aid then granted and the Army Engineers' plans adopted *still* included only engineering works. Levees, to be sure, as an indispensable defense; storage reservoirs to hold surplus water for later use perhaps for power, irrigation, or maintaining depth required for navigation; retarding basins to be empty most of the year but available in times of flood to spread out the flow temporarily and cut down dangerous peaks; spillways and bypasses to be coordinated with the levee system—each one of these should be explained and its limitations emphasized.

Storage Reservoirs. Designed with flood control as the first objective, these lakes behind dams, unless of tremendous capacity, are useful for little else, are likely to depreciate rapidly by filling with silt, and usually present a sorry prospect for recreational use because of the changing and ugly shore line. Moreover, an enormous number are necessary to approach anything which can be called control, and as pointed out above, their economic and aesthetic values are likely to vary inversely with those exclusively tied in to flood control. This does not mean that some control is not realized from existing and proposed storage dams such as the Norris in the Tennessee Valley, which has enormous storage capacity over and above that needed for power production and other purposes; the Grand Coulee with its vast tributary watershed; the Shasta and other reservoirs which hold for the Central Valley's dry season use the waters which would otherwise produce flash floods; or the Santee-Cooper in South Carolina where the principal objectives served are power production and improvement of navigation. Only by thinking in terms of the cost of world wars could enough reservoirs be built and maintained to reduce the heights of flood levels at critical points in terms of feet instead of inches. At best they can serve only as one of many measures which must be employed.

Retarding Basins. The word *basins* is used in this connection because dams are established so that the basins behind them shall be empty as often and as long as possible. In the Miami Conservancy District in Ohio, this is recognized and the public kept advised. The loss of potential power production is paid for in prevention of flood damage. Useful on smaller rivers, these retarding basins would have to be on a vast scale throughout the Missouri and other tributary valleys if attempts were made to use them to control floods in the Lower Mississippi. Moreover, if they were functioning in this particular, they would be out of service for controlling local floods just below their locations. When the roof leaks into the attic, the ceiling into the second floor, and on into the living room and the basement, there are likely to be basins enough only for the attic. Again, however, retarding basins *are* one means among many which will be employed in flood control.

FIG. 61. Jefferson Parish, La., protection levee. Lake Pontchartrain on the right. Dragline in the foreground is constructing retaining dykes for hydraulic fill which will raise the level of the land to a considerable width. (*Photo by Corps of Engineers, U.S. Army.*)

Channel Improvements. Straightening, clearing of obstructions, and otherwise causing a stream channel to speed up the flow of water are obvious advantages to land on which water is being backed up, and if such improvement extends virtually to the mouth of the stream it means further rapid disposal of potentially destructive flood waters. Here the problems of siltation, city dumps, and accumulations of uprooted trees and of wreckage present a constantly recurring task in which the river current needs engineering help.

Levees and Spillways. Such structures are built at varying distances back from the actual river channel. They have served to hold many streams within harmless paths, except when crests become too high and pressure brings about breaks or crevasses causing the inundation of occupied lowlands. Like many of the gadgets about which men become enthusiastic, levees are useful within limits and must be supplemented in every way practicable. One of these ways which finds continuing favor is definitely to construct a break or spillway in the levee, sending a part of the flood on a detour or bypass which may be an old channel, a swamp, or constructed floodway. Handling a part of the flow in this manner is sometimes spoken of as the *outlet method.* There are a number of these "detours" on the lower Mississippi.

Vegetative Cover and Floods. It does not tax one's mental powers to appreciate that vegetative cover in any terms from moss to redwoods has some effect in retarding runoff of rainfall. Even sparse shrub and herbaceous growth on a steep slope exhibit a noticeable effect in reinforcing the soil and increasing *infiltration*—a term used for cutoff or taking up of rainfall by the soil. Fortunately quantitative figures are available on infiltration under vegetated and bare-soil conditions, and more and more data are becoming available for use in definite employment of revegetation for partial control of runoff. Some of these figures are given on pages 35 to 37 under the discussion of soil conservation. Unfortunately for flood control, however, the purposes for which men want to use or to neglect much of the land in the vast watersheds of the country which furnish flood waters give the vegetative cover a round beating or keep it removed. Fire following logging or on brush-covered slopes of the arid Southwest, the destruction of all vegetation by smelter fumes, overuse of mountain lands for grazing domestic livestock, poorly planned construction of anything from a road to a subdivision, ill-planned cultivation followed or not by abandonment—all these tend to diminish the protecting cover with its shielding, absorptive, and infiltrating effects. But the plant-cover people have finally made their voice heard, and the 1936 Omnibus Flood Control Act provides that the U.S. Forest and Soil Conservation Services and the Army Engineers are required to join forces in the study of flood control from the downstream works right back to the timber line on the highest mountain.

One example of the power of vegetative cover to retard flood waters in a limited area is worth recounting: the Pickens Canyon flood in southern California has been mentioned on page 117. It followed a fire which had consumed the chaparral cover on 5,000 acres. A few miles to the east lies San Dimas Canyon, one of the "experimental forests" of the Forest Service. Twelve inches of rain fell in 2½ days late in December, 1933, on both watersheds alike. New Year's Day saw the village of La Crescenta flooded, with 34 lives and 200 homes lost. The peak flow at crest was 100 cubic feet per second per square mile of watershed. The peak flow in San Dimas was 50 cubic feet, and no damage occurred.[30]

The Parrish Canyon flood in Utah exhibited a relatively small but convincing with-and-without flood-control lesson in 1930. Overgrazed and underprotected for years, this canyon spilled the waters of a sudden storm on the village of Centerville, wrecking seven homes, crashing in the walls of a schoolhouse, spreading 1 to 7 feet of debris over orchard lands valued at $600 to $800 an acre, and requiring the expenditure of $100,000 to open

FIG. 62. Parrish Canyon flood over village and farm lands of Centerville, Utah, in 1930. Better cover in the adjoining canyon took the same storm without damage. (*Photo by Forest Service.*)

and repair the damaged highways alone. Right beside it, Centerville Canyon, hit by the same storm but long protected and well covered, yielded no flood and accounted for no damage.[31]

Whose Business Is Flood Control? Historically the landowner first, then the states, and finally the Federal government have recognized obligations in attempting to control floods, but all have thought of the problem and worked at it from the wait-until-it-comes and multiple-purpose-with-flood-control-incidentally approaches. Now the Federal government has something in the way of policy as far as responsibility is concerned

[30] Silcox, F. A., Forests and Flood Control, pp. 10–11, in The Scientific Aspects of Flood Control, Supplement to Science 84, Science Press, New York, 1936.

[31] *Ibid.*, pp. 13–15.

and is definitely committed to the increasing use and encouragement of all useful works and practices on the land and multiple-purpose river development including flood control as an objective. The "pork-barrel" temptations in the requests for and appropriation of money for flood control are warned against in the recommendations of the Water Planning Committee of the National Resources Board.[32] Here the Federal appropriation of funds for flood control would be made under these conditions:

(*a*) Only where there is reasonable protection against maximum floods; (*b*) only when the total benefits justify the expense; (*c*) only where there are responsible and legally constituted authorities with which to deal; (*d*) to an extent not greater than 30 per cent of the cost of labor and materials where benefits are chiefly local; (*e*) to an extent greater than 30 per cent only in proportion to benefits applicable to recognized national interests; (*f*) to a full 100 per cent only where the benefits are almost wholly of national interest.

The application of these guides requires the wisdom of a Solomon, but it is well that they are somewhere set down.

In the final analysis, the user of the land as well as the rank-and-file taxpayer must hold up the hands of those to whom public office is assigned and of the skilled engineers and scientists to whom the actual task is given. The better the voter understands flood control, the better will be the control. Only in this manner, too, may the public be assured of an accounting from its servants.

BIBLIOGRAPHY

Annual Report, Inland Waterways Corporation, St. Louis, Mo., 1944.

Annual Reports of Secretary of the Interior, 1946–1952.

Dewhurst, J. Frederic, and associates: America's Needs and Resources, The Twentieth Century Fund, Inc., New York, 1947, p. 8.

Ely, Richard T., and George S. Wehrwein: Land Economics, The Macmillan Company, New York, 1940.

Etcheverry, B. A., and S. T. Harding: Irrigation Practice and Engineering, 2nd ed., McGraw-Hill Book Company, Inc., New York, 1933.

Krug, J. A.: Report (as Secretary of the Interior) on National Resources and Foreign Aid, 1947.

Lewis, M. R.: Practical Irrigation, *U.S. Dept. Agr. Farmers' Bul.* 1922, 1943.

McGee, W. J.: Water as a Resource, *An. Am. Acad.*, Vol. 33, 1898.

Martin, Helen M., and associates: They Need Not Vanish, Michigan Department of Conservation, Lansing, Mich., 1942.

Michigan Water Problems, Proceedings of Water Conference, Michigan Department of Conservation, Lansing, Mich., 1946.

Natural Resources Board Report, 1934, Government Printing Office.

Silcox, F. A.: Forests and Flood Control, in The Scientific Aspects of Flood Control, Science Press, New York, 1936.

Statistical Abstract of the United States, 1947, U.S. Bureau of the Census.

[32] National Resources Board Report, 1934, Government Printing Office, p. 273.

(Also published as H. Doc. 35, 80th Cong., 1st sess., with different pagination.)

Statistical Abstract of the United States, 1952, U.S. Bureau of the Census.

Van Hise, Charles R.: The Conservation of Our Natural Resources in the United States, The Macmillan Company, New York, 1923.

——— and Loomis Havemeyer: Conservation of Our Natural Resources, The Macmillan Company, New York, 1930.

Water for the Modern Farmstead, Rural Electrification Administration, Government Printing Office, 1946.

CHAPTER 4

Forests, Grazing, and Recreation

The Forests

A forest is a community of living trees and associated organisms covering a considerable area; utilizing sunshine, air, water, and earthy materials to attain maturity and to reproduce itself; and capable of furnishing mankind with indispensable products and services.[1] But what is a tree, and what are these other organisms? And are the benefits mentioned expected to keep coming from a forest automatically? Unless the answers to such questions are reasonably well understood, both by the people who make their living from the forest resources of the country and by the individuals to whom the forest is significant only in terms of shade, beauty, and a source of wood for whatever purpose, or of maple sugar, game animals, clear water, Christmas trees, and turpentine, there can be little understanding and less performance in conserving the forest as a natural resource.

Trees for purposes of this discussion may be thought of as woody plants that usually grow upright with single stems. Standing close to each other, their roots form a network deep into the soil, their trunks or boles have usually shed twigs and branches for most of their lengths, but their upper branches, twigs, leaves, and buds form a crown where the raw materials of growth from air, moisture, and soil meet for manufacture through the action of sunlight and for distribution to all parts of the plant. This process which we call growth appears to occur very slowly, but the total year's wood increment may vary from one cord per acre in the Southern pines with their long growing season to less than one-quarter cord in the spruce swamps of the Lake states. Meanwhile the forest wherever it may be located is improving the scene, protecting the soil from blowing and washing, furnishing a home for useful wild animals, developing a number of minor products useful in food, medicine, and the arts, increasing the water-holding capacity of the immediate surface cover

[1] Allen, Shirley W., An Introduction to American Forestry, McGraw-Hill Book Company, Inc., New York, 1950, p. 53.

and the soil, and like as not exerting some small influence on the local climate.

So far, the flow of "indispensable products" sounds as though it were all set to be automatic. But even before men have started to help themselves to the benefits available, storms, lightning fires, insect attack, decay, and possibly drought are at work, and when harvesting of products by men starts in earnest all these troubles are likely to increase. Some of the beneficial organisms in the soil may have a hard time adjusting to the commotion or may stop operations completely.

It may be said then of the forest, as of every other renewable natural resource, that its productivity in use depends considerably upon the way its benefits are reaped by men and that a continuing flow of these benefits dictates skillful, scientific management. This in the case of forests is called the science and art of forestry. Whether or not it is invoked and made to bring about conservation is also a matter of business management and of public policy. In these two particulars, understanding has been halted by the vast extent of the original resource, the fact that it was a crop that did not appear to require cultivation, and the fact that it was often in the way where agriculture seemed to be a land use of pressing need.

With these characteristics of the forest as a resource in mind, some attempt to measure its importance is appropriate.

How the Forest Resource Is Used

In 1944 the people of this country consumed and exported *the equivalent of* 65 billion feet board measure[2] of products from their forests. Not all of it was in the form of lumber. Indeed only 34.3 billion feet of it was sawed into boards, dimension stock, and heavy timbers. The remainder was in the form of pulpwood, fuel wood, miscellaneous products including those representing new uses, and in the form of losses. But reduced to board-foot measure—a foot square and an inch thick—the total consumption and export amounted to about 65 billion feet. To get some idea of the magnitude of this amount, one can go back to the playing area of a football field, which covers about 1 acre, and imagine such a field covered over with 1-inch boards. The gigantic total of 65 billion would cover more than 1⅓ million such fields. Or one may reduce the total to six-room cottages of average size, each of which would require about 10,000 feet board measure of lumber in its construction, and some 6½ million of them could be built. If these comparisons are not enough and the reader is ambitious statistically, he may start building himself one of those mythical to the moon or around-the-world-at-the-equator examples.

Per capita consumption of lumber for 1952 in this country amounted

[2] Adapted from Long Range Agricultural Policy and Programs, U.S. Dept. Agr., *Sup.* 4, 1947, following p. 12.

to 242 feet board measure, which would more than cover the floor of a room 11 by 22 feet in area with 1-inch thick boards; per capita consumption of paper and paper board reached 396.1 pounds in 1952, considerably more than twice the weight of an average-sized grown man; and for the same year each member of the population accounted for the use of 16 square feet of plywood. The latter would make a top for a 4-by-4-foot table.

From the viewpoint of variety, wood is used for not less than 4,500 purposes[3] in the United States. Its properties give it a versatility possessed by almost no other material. Among these, workability, combined strength and light weight, color and grain, insulating ability, response to sound vibrations, bending strength, and odor have been appreciated and used for centuries. Today new uses in the fields of plywood, plastics, and chemical derivatives give wood from the forest added importance.

Far smaller in volume than wood, actual tree products help to make up a long list of materials indispensable in modern technology and trade. Among these may be mentioned rosin and turpentine (known in the trade as "naval stores"), quinine, cascara, charcoal, acetic acid, rubber, maple sirup and sugar, Christmas greens, and nuts. These products are significant aside from their intrinsic usefulness because of the part they play, often unrecorded, in local economies.

Thus the use of the products of the forest alone would appear to make this natural resource indispensable.

But services rendered mankind by the forest, while more difficult to appraise, may overshadow values in the form of products and dictate exclusive use of the resource for protection, scenery, or management of wild-animal life. As in the field of river-valley development and water use, these producing and serving functions of the forest resource may or may not proceed simultaneously and on the same area in a multiple-purpose program.

The public values of forest cover in erosion control have been touched on under soil conservation and flood control on pages 27 and 121. It should be repeated here, however, that quality of water, steadiness of its flow from natural storage, and resistance of the soil to the erosive power of rainfall dictate the permanent maintenance of the forests in headwater areas of river systems and smaller streams and that restoring of forest cover frequently offers the only hope of arresting soil erosion in abused hilly country. Furthermore, a large proportion of the national forest area in the White and Appalachian Mountains has been acquired under the Weeks Law of 1911, which in turn is based on control of water in navigable streams under the commerce clause of the constitution.

[3] Hall, J. Alfred, and T. J. Mosley, Products of American Forests, Government Printing Office, 1946, p. 5.

Perhaps no use of the forest as a resource appeals to the average citizen more than recreation. Campers who enjoy the simplest hike or family picnic to a canoe trip or highly organized deer hunt, head for the woods and capitalize on its beauty, solitude, and mystery. Literally millions of persons use the national and state parks and forests for recreation, and more and more they are becoming indispensable for this purpose. Devoid

FIG. 63. The forest—an indispensable natural resource because of its many products and services. (*Photo by Tennessee Valley Authority.*)

of forests it is hardly too much to say that most of the attractiveness would be gone. Hunters and fishermen, whether they are after big game or small, use forests and waters, seeking big game particularly in the forests as such or in the openings and fastnesses surrounded by forest growth. To a remarkable degree the necessary safe breeding places adapted to the special needs of a particular animal, places of temporary refuge from predatory enemies while foraging and during both day and night, and food supply that is adequate and adapted to the use of the animal[4] are found in forests and their openings.

Forage from the forest and its openings, important as it is to the larger game animals, also supports great herds of domestic sheep and cattle during the milder months of the year. Some 6,320,354 animal months were used by cattle in 1947 on the national forest ranges alone, and sheep accounted for 10,731,459 animal months.

More than one-half of the total commercial forest area of the country and about three-fourths of that privately owned are in the hands of 4½ million owners. Only 2 per cent of these own more than 500 acres. Many of the tracts are parts of farms and are coming more and more to be handled as crop-producing areas. Fuel, repair material, and miscellaneous products are counted into farm income, and their harvesting furnishes profitable employment during slack periods. These facts, as well as the fact of wide distribution of farm-woods ownership, put the forest resource squarely into the agricultural economy of the country. Planted strips of "forest" in the form of shelterbelts, as discussed on page 45, hold the soil, conserve snowfall, and temper drying and freezing winds. Similar services are rendered by natural tracts of woods on many farms.

In addition to those who work only a part of their time on the smaller forest areas, more than a million men were employed in 1950 in the lumber and pulpwood industries, including the mills, and something like a million more in the fabricating industries and others using wood.

Perhaps the best short summary of the importance of forests was expressed by President Franklin D. Roosevelt in his message to the Congress on Mar. 14, 1938.[5]

> Forests are intimately tied into our whole social and economic life. They grow on more than one-third of the land area of the continental United States. Wages from forest industries support from five to six million people each year. Forests give us building materials and thousands of other things in everyday use. Forest lands furnish food and shelter for much of our remaining game, and healthful recreation for millions of our people. Forests help prevent erosion and floods. They conserve water and regulate its use for navigation, for power, for domestic use and for irrigation. Woodlands occupy more acreage than any other crop on American farms and help support two and one-half million farm families.

[4] Grinell, Joseph, Wild Animal Life as a Product and as a Necessity of National Forests, *Jour. Forestry*, **22**:840–841, 1924.

[5] Message from the President of the United States Transmitting a Recommendation for the Immediate Study of the Forest Problem, 1938, H. Doc. 539, 75th Cong., 3d sess., p. 1.

Extent of the Forest Resources

The United States is rich both in the distribution of volume and in the number of usable species of trees represented in its forests. Some 100 varieties are valuable enough to find their way into the lumber trade over a considerable territory. More than 200 are used locally, and many species once discarded have come into regular use as demand has grown. Eastern hemlock, for example, was formerly considered valuable only for the bark, which is used in the tanning industry. Now it holds a respected position in lumber markets. Balm-of-Gilead and aspen, two of the widely distributed and fast-growing poplars, were formerly good at best for pulpwood and excelsior. Now they command good prices as saw timber in certain localities. The better species, among which are the pines, Douglas-fir, redwood, oaks, birch, maple, hickory, and walnut, are large in size and produce wood of high quality. But whether they are the giant firs, pines, or redwoods on the Pacific coast, the pines or cypresses of the Deep South; the jack pines, birches, and aspens of the Lake states plains; the pinyons and junipers of the Southwest; or the oaks, hickories, elms, and maples of the Appalachians and the Northeast—products and services are taken from them as if they would always be there. They stand as forests unique among those of the entire globe.

Before taking up geographical distribution, it is well to go over some of the terms used in describing the forest resource: A *hardwood* tree, whether it produces a wood of peculiar hardness or not, is a broad-leaved tree. This is an established lumber-trade term which has persisted in forestry literature. Likewise, a *softwood* is a needle-leaved tree which may be evergreen like the pines or spruces or deciduous like the tamarack or bald cypress. Then, too, a *hardwood forest* is sometimes contrasted with a *coniferous* forest—the latter being made up of cone-bearing needle-leaved trees. The term *commercial forest* means, as one would suppose, a forest from which merchantable wood products can be taken in paying quantities. And *protection forests* are chiefly dedicated to watershed protection, *park forests* or *scenic forests* are those in which no cutting is done, and miscellaneous scattered areas bearing trees but which are relatively unproductive are known as *noncommercial forests*. The terms *national forest*, *state forest*, and *municipal forest* signify more than just ownership classification, for these are usually definitely organized and managed areas.

Forest Regions of the United States

It takes a good forester and a better student to keep abreast of the way in which the other foresters and the botanists divide the country into forest regions. The author believes that the older generalized division

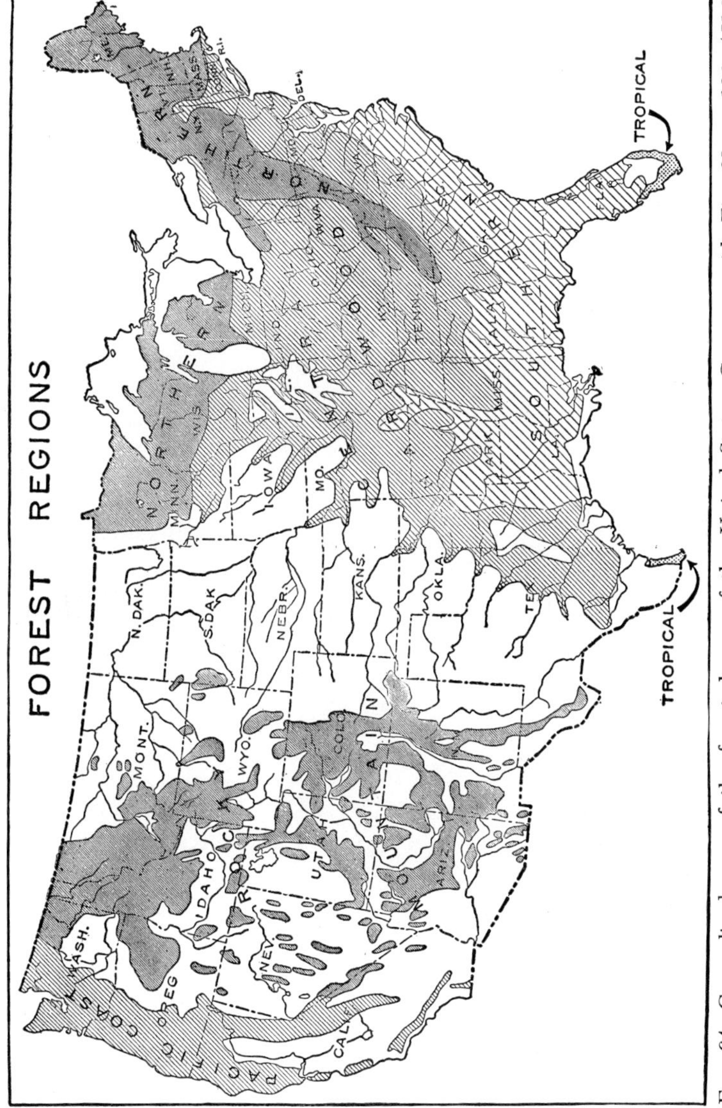

Fig. 64. Generalized map of the forested area of the United States. Compare with Fig. 69, p. 136. (*U.S. Forest Service.*)

shown on the map[6] on page 131 is convenient and logical and will follow it in briefly describing the forests of the United States. Another map designed to show specific features of distribution will be found on page 136.

The Northern Forest. It will be observed that the Northern forest gets pretty far south in the Appalachian highlands. Otherwise it is well in the northern border of the northeast quarter of the country and is characterized by soils generally better adapted to forests than to agriculture. Although dairy farming and the raising of short-growing-season crops are common and widespread, a large part of the region is in forests of white,

FIG. 65. The Northern forest—a Michigan mixture of hemlock, pine, and hardwoods. (*Michigan Department of Conservation.*)

red, and jack pine; white, red, and black spruce; paper and yellow birch; maple, beech, elm, ash, and aspen. Eastern hemlock is also found in mixture with hardwoods, and white or balsam fir, white cedar, and tamarack are found in the swamps. Miscellaneous hardwoods are found throughout the region. White pine growing in this region, prized and marked for the king's navy in colonial times, dominated lumber production for the first 250 years of the country's settlement, and the region still figures importantly in the production of pulpwood and to a lesser extent other round products and lumber.

[6] Mattoon, Wilbur R., Forest Trees and Forest Regions of the United States, *U.S. Dept. Agr. Misc. Pub.* 217, pp. 34–35, 1936.

The Central Hardwood Forest. Stretching almost from the Rio Grande River to Cape Cod including the southern half of Minnesota, Wisconsin, and the lower peninsula of Michigan, the Central hardwood forest still grows some of the world's largest and finest hardwoods, although its richer soils have been the occasion for much clearing for agriculture. Here, white oak, hickories, white ash, walnut, and tulip or yellow poplar (well named except that it is not a true poplar and it is a soft "hardwood") reach their maximum development and highest quality. More than a dozen hardwood species in this region are of commercial value and

Fig. 66. The Central hardwood forest—mixed stand of oak, hickory, and yellow poplar. Anne Arundel County, Maryland. (*Photo by Geo. C. Lowary, courtesy Soil Conservation Service.*)

extent. Flying over this area, one is impressed with the vast amount of cultivation throughout still heavily wooded areas. Hardwood lumber, railroad ties, cooperage stock, and piling are characteristic products of this forest.

The Southern Forest. Following the coastal plain from southeastern Maryland to eastern Texas, the Southern forest is characterized by four pines—longleaf, shortleaf, loblolly, and slash. Also in the swamp and river bottoms cypress, gums, and other lowland hardwoods including river birch, laurel, live oaks, and swamp chestnut oaks are found in great abundance. Pecan and other hickories are common in better drained locations with good soil. Pine lumber, naval stores, and more recently pine pulpwood are leading products in this region, and huge volumes of wood are produced in record time because of the long growing season and abundant rainfall.

The Tropical Forest. Interesting botanically but small in size, without commercial value, and characterized by scrubby hardwoods, mangrove (helpful against wave erosion), and palms, the Tropical forest

FIG. 67. The Southern forest—loblolly pine and hardwoods in Arkansas. (*U.S. Forest Service.*)

occupies the southern tip of Florida and a small area in southeastern Texas.

The Rocky Mountain Forest. More far-flung but less continuous than any other region, the Rocky Mountain forest extends in large and small spots from Canada to Mexico and from the Black Hills in South Dakota and southeastern Colorado to the boundary between Nevada and California extended northward. Ponderosa pine, western white pine, Douglasfir, and Engelmann spruce are the principal commercial species in this region. Western larch, magnificent in size and quality, must in its limited range in the north compete with western white and ponderosa pines and has not yet come into its own. Lodgepole pine in heavy stands is of great local importance, and Engelmann spruce, long important only locally, is now finding its way into paper manufacture, with promise of increasing demand. The growing season which is relatively short and large stretches of low rainfall area introduce real handicaps to timber growing in this region. Grazing, water conservation, soil protection, and recreation, all

Fig. 68. The Rocky Mountain Forest—ponderosa pine in New Mexico. (*U.S. Forest Service.*)

depending heavily on the forest, are highly developed in the Rocky Mountain forest.

Pacific Coast Forest. Smaller in area but producing greater volumes per acre and larger single specimens than other regions, the Pacific coast forest yields lumber from Douglasfir in the Northwest, redwood along the northern half of the California coast, and ponderosa and sugar pine in the Cascade and Sierra ranges at higher elevations and extending to the drier eastern slopes. Species of great value but of lesser volume include Sitka spruce and Port Orford cedar along the Oregon and Washington coast, western hemlock intermingled with Douglasfir and western red cedar and alder in the moist heavy-rainfall Northwest. The size and weight of these giant specimens in virgin stands has required powerful

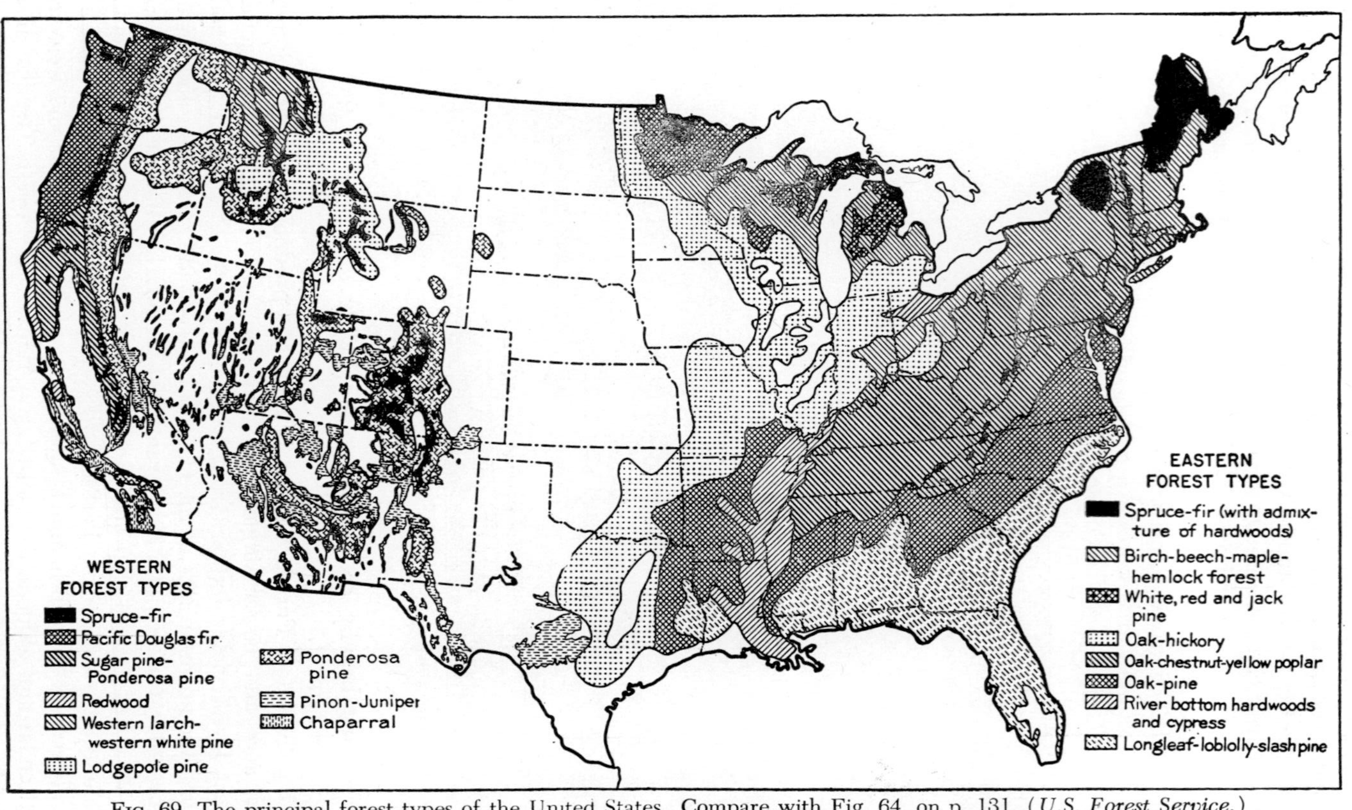

FIG. 69. The principal forest types of the United States. Compare with Fig. 64, on p. 131. (*U.S. Forest Service.*)

logging equipment, and only in the heavy rainfall and productive forest soil is there hope for adequate regeneration. Logged forests do, however, come back rapidly, forestry practice yields good results, demand for products is high, and the Pacific forest will continue as the Southern forest to be a major forest-growing region. Scenic and recreation values are high and increasingly recognized in management.

FIG. 70. The Pacific coast forest—Douglasfir and western hemlock in Oregon. (*U.S. Forest Service.*)

Territorial Forests. Most important among the forests of the outlying United States possessions are those of Alaska, the commercial portion of which are at low elevations and extend only a short way inland. Western hemlock, Sitka spruce, and Alaskan red cedar are the important species. Practically all the forest is in Federal ownership. The principal product is lumber for packing cases used by the salmon industry. Early prospects for a great paper industry are bright.

Charcoal burning is the only important forest industry in Puerto Rico, with its "wet forest" in the north and its "dry forest" across the range to the south. Small areas of saw timber of various tropical species are included in a small national forest, but most of the needed lumber for a crowded population must be imported. Such unfamiliar names as mountain palm, muskwood, and bullet wood designate species important in the wet forest.

The wet and dry forests of Hawaii have suffered from fire and overgrazing and while in Federal ownership in a national park or territorial forest add more to the scene than to the economy of the islands. *Koa*, one of the acacias, and *ohia lehua* are used commercially, the former being prized as a cabinet wood.

Problems and Needs in Forest Conservation

Some measure of the productive ability of the existing forest resource is needed to match actual growth and estimated demand for products and services. Heavy utilization of products combined with minor dedications to noncommercial uses hasten the time when most of the forest will be "second growth" rather than "virgin." Growth under these circumstances should be faster on the same area basis because fewer trees will have reached the old-age period during which they mark time rather than grow in wood volume.

This sounds as though everything were neatly arranged and that demand for products and services would be met automatically. But in the words of a recently popular song: "It ain't necessarily so." Again, therefore, one may ask, "What do we know of the productive capacity of the forests of the country?" "Can it be made to meet the probable demand?" "What are the technical and economic hurdles to be cleared?" "How well are we doing?" And "What more is necessary?"

Productive Capacity of Forest Resources. In appraising the ability of forests to continue their important services to humanity, a short historical summary is in order.

Early settlers in this country were too busy to philosophize much about future flow of products and services from a forest that seemed always to be in the way. They did turn its products into early cash commodities of trade such as lumber, staves for casks, and naval stores, and they used it for buildings and fuel. There is little evidence that up to 100 years ago any thought had occurred to the people concerning the forest as yielding any important benefits save wood products. The fur trade and game for food figured to some extent in the economy of the times, but surely water conservation was not a recognized service. The Rip Van Winkles who hunted and fished and the Thoreaus who explored for recreation were considered time wasters. Skis and toboggans, if any, were for the serious purposes of travel. The necessity of burning the resulting forest waste in clearing for agriculture may have influenced an attitude of fatalism toward forest fires. "Waste" had less to do in the thinking of the times with natural resources and more with the precious results of long hours of labor in terms of actual items of food, clothing, and shelter. Land given away to railroad, canal, and wagon-road companies and to the states (see Fig. 3, page 8) was expected to be settled and worked by an agricultural population to whom it would be sold in relatively small parcels. The settler, too, could acquire land, whether timbered or not, a

Fig. 71. Some logged-off lands in the Lake states have recovered from fire and are reproducing the original pine forest. (*Michigan Department of Conservation.*)

little later by living on it and "homesteading" it, taking certain areas for timber and stone, planting trees on a "claim," or taking land for other alleged purposes off the hands of the states which had acquired it by various grants from the Federal government. If he wanted to be a miner, he was given a rather free hand to claim, and later acquire, land whether timbered or not. All this led to forest destruction and to concentration of forest ownership on a grand scale in a rather free and easy interpretation of the laws and customs and the duties of citizenship in a democracy. The logger in his natural haste to meet a demand for lumber used the old device of making one factor of production carry the other two. Capital and labor were scarce, "land" or natural resources in the shape of forests were abundant and took the heaviest beating. The logger left inflammable "slash" from the unused portions of the trees and abandoned his camp structures. These frequently caught fire at once, or as the settler followed the logger. Burned-out soils refused to "blossom as the rose" with new forests, or if they did grow up, exhibited inferior types of forest. Meanwhile insects and disease were beginning to take toll.

Mild interest, early expressed by President John Quincy Adams and others, in reforestation by planting had died down. Trespass on Federal lands was severe in the Lake states. No legal way of purchasing standing timber apart from the land or of timbered lands for purposes of utilizing the forest had been worked out. The states had shown less interest in the forests even than the Federal government. There were no trained foresters in the country. The American Forestry Association, a group of public-spirited citizens interested in adequate forest resources, had not yet been organized, and even informed scientists had paid little attention to the march of forest exploitation. People were probably not saying as many conservation writers insist, "Our forests are inexhaustible." They were saying nothing. The nation was a busy, toiling people bent on "developing" the natural resources in terms of transportation, trade, settlement, and agriculture, with even the interest of the nation's early years in forests for building and maintaining a navy pretty thoroughly forgotten up to 1876. And while there was then an awakening, to be discussed later, the exploitation of forests for the next 30 years has probably not been duplicated anywhere in the world. A historical summary of this period will be given later in this chapter, but against the background so far, productive capacity may be discussed.

Productive Capacity of Original Forests. It is not difficult to figure out that white pines, large and straight enough for the king's navy in colonial days, had been growing for hundreds of years before the Atlantic seaboard was settled. Giant oaks, chestnuts, and elms 200 to 400 years old were no doubt standing in the Ohio Valley. The larger trees dominated the stand except where lightning fires had exposed the soil and younger forest was coming on. Productive power was there on a grand scale from the viewpoint of growing conditions, but the forest was stagnant because crowded. Had the spectre of timber famine disturbed their rest, the early settlers might have kept one acre out of every six in forest and drawn upon it as need arose. Indeed this is what William Penn required of those to whom he assigned land. As older trees were removed, young ones would take their places as natural reproduction. A sort of crude forestry would thus have been practiced and a part of the forest area actually cultivated by skillful harvesting. Two hundred to five hundred or more board feet might have been made to grow per acre per year, and local demand would have been met with much shorter haul and less expenditure of energy. But the productive capacity of forests disappeared rapidly in favor of agriculture and lumber production during this period, both through rapid reduction of commercial forest area and through abuse of the forest soils by fire. Justifiably in many respects, but surely at a considerable reduction of productive capacity, the area of forest has shrunk from its original 822 million acres to 625,828,000 acres, with only about 461 million acres of commercial importance or promise, in less than 350 years of settlement.[7]

FIG. 72. A vigorously reproducing forest of Port Orford cedar in southwestern Oregon. (*U.S. Forest Service.*)

Present Productive Power of Forests. Local scarcities of forest products still plague many localities in the United States, but on the whole the remaining forests retain the necessary productive power to serve the needs of the nation both for wood and for other services. Yet it will have to be fully used and so handled as to step up present rates of growth about 50 per cent. The figure given for the poorest of the lands in discussing original forests (page 140) was considerably higher than the 78-foot average annual production for the entire country's commercial saw-timber forests and even higher than the 156 feet board measure

[7] Basic Forest Statistics for the United States, 1946, U.S. Department of Agriculture (mimeographed), Table I (pages not numbered).

required if these forests are to produce enough to meet projected demand.[8] With moderate overcuts for a few years from remaining virgin forests in the West and from rapid-growth Southern forests, demand could probably be met by the time the majority of commercial forests, public and private, could be brought under good management and be protected well enough to make them permanent. The prospect for this on the large holdings is good. It is not so good on the small areas which comprise more than one-half the total, although it is improving and forestry has reached a high efficiency in many farming regions.

How Forest Productivity Is Maintained

Protection from Depleting Forces. Fire, insects, disease, storms, overgrazing, overcutting, and waste in utilization are the depleting forces which must be held in check if forests are to produce the returns which people demand. This particular problem may be stated as assuring for the use of mankind the forest products and services which would otherwise be wasted.

Fire as a Depleting Force. Fire is one of the greatest of discoveries. Certainly it serves men in enough ways to brand it as a blessing. Only when it is out of control does it turn into an enemy, and a forest is no place to let it get out of control. To its credit in forest management, fire can be used conservatively to expose mineral soil in some forest areas and so promote better germination of seed and natural reproduction of the forest. It is also available as a weapon against itself in "starving out" a destructive fire by backfiring so that the area ahead of the main fire will have nothing to burn and may so be controlled, or by disposing of debris which constitutes a fire hazard in a forest, or by consuming trees in which insects are "trapped."

In a general sense, moreover, fire as an industrial servant makes possible the manufacture of tools and equipment used in forest management and furnishes comfort to forest workers. And what would camping for recreation amount to in the forest without the campfire? Uncontrolled, on the other hand, fire destroys trees as potential wood products. It injures and weakens trees which may not be consumed or killed and so joins forces with insects and diseases which can attack more destructively. It consumes the duff or ground cover of leaves, twigs, and decayed wood and frequently burns into the soil itself, changing its physical character, reducing its water-absorptive capacity, and destroying beneficial soil organisms. It exposes the soil to the erosive effects of rainfall. It destroys the peculiar habitat necessary for many valuable wild animals and frequently the animals themselves. It ruins

[8] Long Range Agricultural Policy and Programs, *U.S. Dept. Agr., Sup.* 4, app., p. 12*ff*, 1947.

forest scenery. It destroys buildings and other structures and every year takes a toll of human life.

Forest fires which burn principally in the ground itself, consuming roots, peatlike soil, and other organic matter, are known as *ground fires.* Those which consume only the duff and low herbaceous and brushy growth are called *surface fires.* The forest fire usually pictured and the most terrifying and destructive burns in the branches, sweeps everything in its path, and is known as a *crown fire.* The word "crown" is also used as a verb in describing the behavior of a forest fire. The surface

FIG. 73. Lightning is the only unpreventable cause of forest fires. It is particularly prevalent in the western forests. This storm is in the Mt. Baker National Forest, Washington. (*U.S. Forest Service.*)

fire is the least destructive of the three and the commonest, but all three must be prevented or controlled if productive power is to be maintained.

For uniform statistical purposes, eight causes are recognized. Ranked from highest to lowest in number of fires for 1952, these are incendiary, 42,440; smokers, 25,666; debris burning, 25,816; miscellaneous, 13,711; lightning, 8,012; campers, 5,667; railroads, 3,611; lumbering, 3,074. Grouping the fires which occur under their causes is helpful in planning prevention work. Smokers may be warned, restrained by laws and regulations, and punished when apprehended for violation, informed of safety measures which they themselves can use, and even appealed to with some success during dangerous periods. The incendiary, who sets fire deliberately from a variety of motives rooted in ignorance, desire for thrill, grudge, or for personal gain and convenience, is a hard forest-fire causer to deal with. His record persists in spite of the work of psychologists, of law and its enforcement, and of efforts to enlighten his self-interest. Campers may be warned, furnished safe places for building campfires and directions and tools for safely extinguishing them, ap-

FIG. 74. Observers from both airplanes and towers are on the watch for forest fires during the hazardous season. This tower is in Michigan. (*Michigan Department of Conservation.*)

prehended and punished for violation of laws and regulations, and even excluded from forest areas by proclamation in dangerous periods. Debris burners may be required to obtain permits stipulating care and sometimes offering assistance when burning is to be done. Railroads are regularly required to use safety devices on locomotives operating in hazardous forest regions, required to reduce inflammable hazards on rights of way, and frequently are proceeded against for damages to forest cover and physical properties. Fires from miscellaneous causes such as an exploding plane in a crash, an automobile wreck, or various freak accidents are unpredictable and may be prevented only by steady progress in safety education. Lightning fires cannot be prevented but can sometimes be outguessed and controlled by prompt and vigorous attack. Unknown

FIG. 75. A Minnesota crown fire—a real danger to human life. (*U.S. Forest Service.*)

causes become yearly a smaller group as vigilance in fire protection and control improves.

Forest-fire Control. Somewhat oversimplified, the steps in forest-fire control, assuming a skeleton organization and service of supply, are detection, reporting, dispatching, travel, attack, control, and mop-up. Practically every forest fire is a potential conflagration. Observers from towers, to some extent from airplanes, homes, resorts, mines, logging camps, cattle headquarters, ranches, vehicles on public highways and any other available source are definitely employed or enlisted for detection service by cooperative agreement or informally. Instruments and maps of special accuracy are used on towers and other equipped and manned observation posts. Telephone and radio both are employed for reporting and dispatching. Elapsed time from detection to attack is counted in minutes and seconds. Transportation of men and equipment and supplies employs fast motorized equipment, boats, railroad, saddle and pack

FIG. 76. Forest-fire fiighting is hard and exhausting work comparable to actual combat in war. (*Photo by U.S. Forest Service.*)

animals, airplanes at times, and "shank's mare" or foot travel in wild and rough country. Attack resembles actual combat in war, uses water from back packs, tank trucks, natural bodies tapped by portable motor pumps, or shallow wells, driven by special equipment in appropriate territory in as little time as 15 minutes—all applied in the form of stream, spray, or "fog" to cool down or "knock down" the fire so that men can work on it. Dirt is also used to deprive the flame of oxygen and knock down the fire and is applied by a mechanical scattering device or by shovel and hand power. Depriving the fire of something to burn is the secret of control. This involves direct attack at the edges, clearing a line or break to mineral soil to which the advancing fire may approach and die, or burning out the space intervening between this line and the advancing fire. The latter method, called *backfiring*, is risky and inadvisable except in the hands of skilled men. Control is achieved in a technical sense when the spread of the fire is successfully checked. Extinguishing of islands of fire within the burned-over area and particularly near the extinguished edge both on the surface and underground constitutes mop-up. Long patrol is frequently necessary before abandoning the area.

Through all this "battle" and depending on weather, character, amount and arrangement of cover, slope, and local air currents, from one individual to several thousand men may be working on the fire itself. Skilled direction, ingenious equipment, and highly organized systems of communication, transportation, and supply are the result of long workouts. Lives, not only of travelers and residents in the area but of fire fighters, are occasionally lost. Damage is usually appraised in terms of value of merchantable timber, young growth projected into the future, physical properties, and repair costs to the public works. Scenic, game animal, and other recreation values are usually not included in damage figures.

In broad terms, then, fire control has one objective and that is maintaining the productive power of the forest. It accomplishes this by preventing waste in a physical sense, to be sure, but most significantly in protecting a growing forest from one force which curtails its growing power.

Forest Insect Damage and Control. Insects no doubt have their rights, but in arguing as to whether men or insects shall get the forests, it is important that men should win by preventing insects from curtailing the productive power of the forest. It is no easy task, for trees are subject to trouble in this direction from the time the weevil finds an edible tree seed right up to the day when a pine bark beetle cooperating with others of his kind has successfully girdled a great tree under its bark. In addition to these two forms of insect attack, the grub of the June bug, or May beetle, feeds on the roots of small trees, particularly the stock in forest-tree nurseries and that just planted for reforestation purposes; the larvae of numerous moths attack the leaves and buds of many forest trees; certain weevils and larvae of moths attack terminal shoots and buds and thus deform trees; scale insects get in their work on the sap of twigs and branches; borers injure trunk and branch mechanically; and finally the wood products, having safely escaped the forest insects, invite termites and powder-post beetles.

Prevention of insect attack is a matter of strict quarantine against forms which may be brought in from abroad and moved into uninfested domestic regions, maintaining the forest in healthy, growing condition, avoiding the logging and fire injury which expose live trees to insect attack; and threatened epidemic attacks can be halted to some extent by felling and barking the tree and exposing grubs and adult beetles to the sun or cold, or burning the bark or the trunk itself, sometimes with the tree still standing. A modification of the method is used in removing large jack pines of certain bushy form and supporting staminate flowers

FIG. 77. Oiling and burning a "bug tree" on Targhee National Forest, Idaho. This is a means of destroying trapped bark beetles in lodge pole pine. (*Photo by U.S. Forest Service.*)

upon which spruce budworm attack is concentrated. (The bark beetle is a girdler, the spruce budworm a leaf eater or defoliator.)

Planning on a broad scale, generous public financing, and employment of highly trained scientists as well as extensive survey and work crews make the control of insect attack a major undertaking as one means of maintaining the productive power of forests.

Control of Forest Tree Diseases. Attack on the forests by diseases is subject to the same principles to a large extent as those governing insect attack. Various rusts, cankers, and rots must be made subject to quarantine so far as practicable, and here again the attack may start at the seed and be met in some other form at all stages of growth and on all parts of the tree. In the control of disease, however, the most difficult ones so far encountered have come to America from other countries, and one, the chestnut blight, has so far proved too much for scientists. Its life history is well understood, but because it can be carried by birds and because of the rapidity of its spread after reaching this country from China, the American chestnut—a valuable species for wood, tannin, and nuts—appears to be doomed. Only by developing blight-resistant strains will the chestnut be reestablished.

Another baffling disease is the white pine blister rust, brought to this country from Germany on nursery stock and spread until it now

FIG. 78. Aerial spraying with DDT to destroy the Douglasfir tussock moth—a leaf eater—in an Idaho forest. The cost of such operations is now at a point where contracts for spraying may be let. (*Photo by American Forest Products Industries.*)

reaches the Pacific coast, attacking any of the "white" or five-needle pines. This disease selects what is known as an *alternate host*, maturing on the pines but starting all over again from them on currant and gooseberry bushes (*Ribes* sp.). It sounds simple, then, to catch it at a vulnerable point in its life history by destroying the bushes which serve as alternate hosts, but these form a host in another sense. There are vast numbers of them scattered throughout the range of these valuable pines. After an infected area is discovered, surveyed, and its control fully planned, the work of destroying the bushes both domestic and wild must be done with a "fine-tooth-comb" thoroughness. The citizen's garden is sometimes "invaded" in the interest of conserving forest resources, and he loses his currant bushes. A mountainside of scattered bushes or a deep rough canyon with junglelike growth of *Ribes* is attacked by digging tools, the gloved hands of the worker who pulls the thorny plants, or another worker carrying a heavy back-pack spray rig—and all these activities are part of the control task. Vast expenditure of funds and of energy has held down but not eliminated this disease.

Still another disease, which threatens the elms of the country, valuable in the veneer and other wood industries and outstanding as shade trees,

FIG. 79. Digging up *Ribes* (gooseberry) bush which is the alternate host for the disease known as white pine blister rust. It jumps from pine to *Ribes* to pine, not from pine to pine. Plumas National Forest, California. (*Photo by U.S. Forest Service.*)

is the so-called Dutch elm disease which reached this country in imported logs from Holland. Here an insect reinforces the attack of the disease by helping to spread it. Control dictates the location and destroying of infected trees.

Along with all this there must be more "barn-door-closing-after-*one-of the-horses*-has-been-stolen" in the form of quarantine enforcement, and the over-all program is just another necessary contribution to the maintenance of the productive power of the forest resource.

Dealing with Damage to Forests by the Elements. Men have not yet found a way to reduce hurricane damage to the forests (Fig. 80), lightning hazard, breakage from ice and snow, frost damage to reforestation stock or to alleviate, on an economic scale, the effects of drought. And yet every one of these natural phenomena may set back the productivity of a forest for years. Windfall in a managed forest can be lessened by care in the distribution of the removal of mature and "crop" trees (those designated for growth and eventual removal for a definite market) and to some extent by streamlining the windward edge of a forest by allowing it to grow or shaping it or using giant fences so that destructive winds will be deflected upward. The latter procedure is expensive and rarely used in this country. Salvage of fallen timber, cleanup of potential fire

FIG. 80. The kind of a salvage job left by a New England hurricane as it looked in 1938. (*American Forests.*)

hazard, encouraging natural reproduction of "wind-firm" species, or growing a crop of smaller trees on a shorter rotation are the alternatives to the prevention of storm damage. Avoiding low "frost pockets" with sluggish air drainage is indicated where frost damage has appeared in forest-planting projects. Drought can be combatted only on an immediate and local situation such as the establishment of shelterbelt forests in prairie country. Here actual watering until the trees are established is sometimes justified because of the great values inherent in addition to wood production.

Once more, whatever it is possible to accomplish is pointed toward maintaining the productivity of the forest.

So far various efforts to defend the forest from depleting forces have been discussed from the viewpoint of *maintaining* productive power and preventing waste of resources and products so that men instead of destructive forces should take them over. But certain manipulations of the forest are desirable, and these will often amount to a rude cultivation practice keyed largely to careful harvesting of products and to a less extent with artificial replacement or reforestation. Out of such practices an actual *increase* of productivity is possible, and such increase is one of the essentials of "conserving" the forest.

How Forest Productivity Is Increased

Having given due attention and effort to maintaining productive power, that power should be kept at work. Arrogant as it may appear, the co-operation and skill of men can bring about increased yields of forest products, and with much less intensive and backbreaking methods than farmers have used for centuries in obtaining progressive increases in soil productivity for food and fiber crops. The forester calls his art of growing timber *silviculture* and his application of this art to a forest business, *management.* Harvesting or cutting and removing trees for market figures strongly in these practices. A ship or vehicle, however it may be supplied with power, cannot be steered unless there is some place for it to move and unless it is moving. A forest in a physical sense does not move from place to place, but it moves in the sense of growth. Having been once established, it can grow if it has room. Periodic harvest of increment furnishes this room. How is all this planned and brought about?

First of all there must be a forest. Bare ground or grassy or brush areas sometimes yield slowly to the spread of natural forest from wind-blown seed or from seed carried by birds, rodents, or larger mammals, or even from seed or twigs floated on a stream or by temporary runoff. Where a forest must be established artificially, men usually grow in the forest nurseries large numbers of small trees about the size of the tomato plants purchased by the home gardener (Fig. 81). These are planted on the selected sites, using special tools or, more recently, motor-powered machinery (Fig. 82), and so placed in a more or less definite pattern of rows in order to assure proper spacing (6 by 6 feet or 6 by 8 feet is frequently decided upon). Technically this is known as *afforestation* if on a previously treeless site and *reforestation* if it is to reclothe a logged-off area or any other recently occupied by forest. After the plantation or new forest is thus started, it must of course be protected from the depleting forces mentioned earlier. When it reaches a growth where any of its products are marketable, the manipulation mentioned above is employed, first by thinning for small products—fence pickets, Christmas trees, cheap ornamental stock, greens for floral purposes—or thinning without using the material removed. Next and in rare instances where it will pay and where natural dying off and shedding of lower branches is not satisfactory, pruning may be employed. After this there may be a thinning on a larger scale as to size of trees with a yield of fuel, posts, pulpwood, chemical wood from which charcoal and distilled products are obtained, or of Christmas trees of larger size. In this thinning, "crop trees" are selected to be left and encouraged to grow for the main yield and to reseed the area. Things do not proceed so neatly as this, of course, except on relatively small planted forests located close to good markets or where the forestry or silviculture and management described are more intensive than usual. Once a new forest is established, with not only an

Fig. 81. State-forest nursery in South Carolina. (*Photo by South Carolina State Commission of Forestry.*)

increase in productivity of the original bare site but also of an artificial and tended forest, the immediate objective, as in the management of natural forest, is *sustained yield.* By this is meant the growing of as great a volume of wood and the assuring of as much other service during any given harvest period as it is proposed to cut and lose by damage, or to enjoy during the same period. Stated in a different way and with respect to wood harvest only, sustained yield means seeing to it that growth in volume balances removal in volume over any given period, be it year, decade, or 100-year rotation. (It is important that the emphasis be put on growing rather than on cutting.)

Starting with a natural forest "fully stocked," as a forester would say,

FIG. 82. Where the planting site will permit, planting machines are used generally in reforestation. Here the planter reaches for trees to insert in a slit made as a knifelike blade is pulled along by tractor. The two pinch wheels firm the soil about the tree roots.

FIG. 83. Norway pine plantation by private industry near Tomahawk, Wis. (*American Forest Products Industries, Inc., courtesy American Forests.*)

hoping that all productive ground was growing trees or serving its top purpose otherwise, or starting with any kind of promising natural stand of timber, silviculture and management have an immediate chance to show financial return. The need to await the first few years' growth (as in the planted forest) does not arise. The program of heading for sustained yield starts right off. Protection and periodic cuttings designed to maintain and increase productive power and yields may be much more difficult and costly in a natural forest because of terrain, distance from

FIG. 84. A timber sale on the Ouachita National Forest, Arkansas. Partial cutting left a residual stand of trees and released existing reproduction from shade so that growth has speeded up in 10 years since cutting. (*Photo by W. H. Muir, U.S. Forest Service, courtesy American Forests.*)

markets, legal restrictions, and extent of area which make control of trespass and other depleting forces hard to achieve. But the same general program is indicated. Any one of several systems of management may be used in harvesting and in so employing the soil, light, and moisture through spacing of trees left that natural reproduction rather than artificial reforestation will take place. A selection of specimens may be made and marked for removal, entire strips or blocks may be clear cut (all trees removed), small groups may be completely cut, species peculiarly adapted to the particular site may be favored in the cuttings and left to increase, certain portions may be dedicated for game cover, grazing, or scenic use and either left undisturbed or "man-handled" as far as timber production is concerned. And right here the reader should understand that in the process of "management" a forest may at times look like a bedraggled beauty, just as one might view an ugly, waterless retarding basin in a flood-control project, a field ready to be plowed and redolent with manure, or a farm pond full of fish but the color of dirty dishwater. Maybe after all this *is* beauty—the beauty of the laborer's muscle. For the labor of productive forces is increasing the flow of natural resources and, characteristic of our country's possibilities, making life more abundant in a democracy.

Conserving Forests on a National Scale

While the ownership pattern as regards the forests of the country involves a large number of individuals, the problem of conserving forest resources on a national scale differs in one marked respect: large ownerships require a different kind of attention than those, for example, located on farms. And so while an important part of the task is to influence individuals to practice good forestry, Federal, state, and local governments and large corporations must deal with forest resources as proprietors direct, in a manner almost unknown in managing agricultural soil resources.

The Federal Government as a Forest Land Proprietor. In the public lands the Federal government has long been the proprietor of large tracts of forest. In its use of lands of all kinds, and among them forest lands of great value, to subsidize the building of railroads and other international improvements and to encourage education, the Federal government made possible, unintentionally, the ownership by operating and nonoperating corporations of great concentrations of forest land. To a lesser extent but with similar effect, this Federal proprietor, through such laws as the Homestead Act, the Timber and Stone Act, and the mining laws, sketchily administered, followed democratic theory in attempting to distribute land ownership among large numbers of its citizens. Corporations did rather well in accumulating these individual "claims" into large timberland ownerships. Grants to the states frequently, though not always, were sold off as promptly as possible in order to obtain cash for education and other state expenses. Frequently the land bounced back into state ownership after being gutted of its timber and becoming no longer worth the taxes which the owner was called upon to pay. Thus the states accumulated large holdings and found themselves saddled with obligations of proprietorship once held by the Federal government.

But with all this shifting of ownership, the Federal government in 1876, as thought on forest conservation was being revived, found itself still the proprietor of vast tracts of public timberland in the West and with no legal way of operating the timber separate from the land or disposing of it on that basis. Selling the timber alone to be cut under conservative regulation had hardly been thought of. One "national park and forest reserve," the Yellowstone, had been withdrawn from entry under the various land laws and eventually put under superficial police protection by using the cavalry of the U.S. Army.

More will have to be said later about the Federal government's showing as a forest-land proprietor, but just here a short historical summary is in order.

Events Leading to the National Forest Movement. Mentioned in the introduction the memorial sent to the Congress by a committee of the

FIG. 85. A modern ranger station. Pine Valley, Dixie National Forest, Utah. (*Photo by U.S. Forest Service.*)

American Association for the Advancement of Science in 1874, under the chairmanship of Dr. Franklin B. Hough, not only emphasized timber values but the importance of public forest lands in maintaining favorable water conditions. The recommendations included the withholding from sale and the protection of public forest lands. They brought about the establishment of a Division of Forestry in the Department of Agriculture whose principal activities were the publication of forestry bulletins and later a service to forest-land owners in assisting them to practice forestry. Appropriations were scant, and this division had no jurisdiction over the forest reserves for many years.

In 1890 the American Association for the Advancement of Science persisted with another report to the President of the United States, again recommending the withdrawal of forest areas in the public domain from sale, settlement, and entry for timber and water-conservation purposes "until a permanent system of forest administration be had." Impressed by this memorial, Secretary of the Interior J. W. Noble, during the administration of President Benjamin Harrison, recommended action to the Congress. This resulted in the enactment of a law in 1891 authorizing the President to establish by proclamation reservations of public lands whether heavily timbered or not, but with no provision for their protection or administration. Some 13 million acres, therefore, promptly reserved by President Harrison in the Western states were for many years unattended.

By 1896 the Federal government had raised some money for one of its early "brain trusts," the National Academy of Science, to make a study and to recommend a national forest policy. Its report outlined a policy and plan for administering the existing reserves and others which it recommended to be established. The latter recommendation received the prompt attention of President Grover Cleveland, who in 1896 withdrew as new reservations 20 million acres. Apparently this action impressed certain interests in the West as anything but democratic, and out of the criticism and debate on the President's action came the important Organic Forestry Act of 1897 for administering the "forest reserves" (since 1907 called "national forests"). With authority in this act to regulate occupancy and use of forest reserve lands, to sell timber separate from land under proper cutting restrictions, and to protect the forest resources, the Federal government was beginning to roll up its sleeves as a proprietor.

Actual progress in organizing the reserves for administration was somewhat slow until 1905. At this time the responsibility was transferred from the Department of the Interior to the Department of Agriculture, and the Bureau of Forestry, which had been clothed with little authority and fewer duties since its creation as a Division in the Department of Agriculture in 1887, came into its own. By 1907 it was the "Forest Service," the forest reserves were "national forests," and the Federal government was taking its task as a proprietor seriously over a part of its domain. But this is only a part of the public-land story featuring principally the forest reserves.

Forest Lands Other Than National Forests. Considerable areas of forest land remained unreserved in the public domain, including millions of timbered acres of Indian reservations, for which the Federal government as guardian had certain responsibility, and vast railroad land grants bid fair to be back on the government's hands because of the refusal of the railroads to abide by the terms of the grants.

During this 30-year period also the forest lands in the hands of the states suffered continuing neglect in many instances, although Maine, Michigan, and Wisconsin had started some studies in the 1860s. In all, fourteen states had initiated some sort of forestry programs between 1885 and 1891, most of which had to do with protection and sale of state-owned timber.

Corporations showed an occasional spark of interest, a few in the Eastern and Southern states accepting help from the Bureau of Forestry in planning forest management on their lands. Little actual forestry, however, was under way on private lands, and there was a real exhibition of diligence in discussing why the private owner could not afford this new luxury on account of unfair taxation practices.

Federal Leadership from 1905 to 1933. As the Bureau of Forestry assumed its stride in the Department of Agriculture and became the Forest Service in 1905, the dynamic interest of President Theodore Roosevelt, influenced by his Chief Forester Gifford Pinchot, was reflected in new creations of national forests, more generous appropriations for their administration, and the beginnings of a forestry profession. The entire forestry movement received a real impetus from the White House Conference of Governors called by the President in May, 1908, and from the report of the National Conservation Commission (see page 10). Research in forestry and forest products was inaugurated, states became increasingly interested, and a series of important Federal laws were enacted. The latter will be here listed for convenience:

The Weeks Law of 1911. Urged for many years, the Weeks Law, enacted in 1911, established two important principles: (1) the purchase with Federal funds of lands to be managed as national forests at the headwaters of navigable streams, (2) cooperation in terms of finances and technical advice and assistance between the Federal government on the one hand and the states and private forest-land owners on the other in forest-fire control in the watersheds of navigable streams. Under this act considerable area was purchased and organized in the next decade in the White Mountains of New England and in the Appalachians. Definite cooperative agreements for fire control were entered into with most of the states, and Federal appropriations for the latter purpose had greatly increased by 1923. Fire and damage records were improving.

The Clarke-McNary Law of 1924. Following heated discussion throughout the country on the subject of Federal regulation of forestry practices (usually meaning timber cutting) on private lands, this compromise act was passed in 1924, dismissing the idea of enforced Federal regulation in favor of cooperation after the pattern of the Weeks Law. Emphasis was still on fire control, authority for which was broadened. Land for forest-demonstration purposes in growing timber, rather than for watershed protection only and particularly cutover lands, could be purchased and organized into national forests (but no financial program for these purchases was authorized). Federal cooperation with states in support of extension work in farm forestry and the distribution of forest-tree seed and reforestation stock was provided for. A study of the effect of taxation on forest perpetuation was authorized. Fire control was definitely strengthened as a result of this act, and farm forestry was stimulated. It

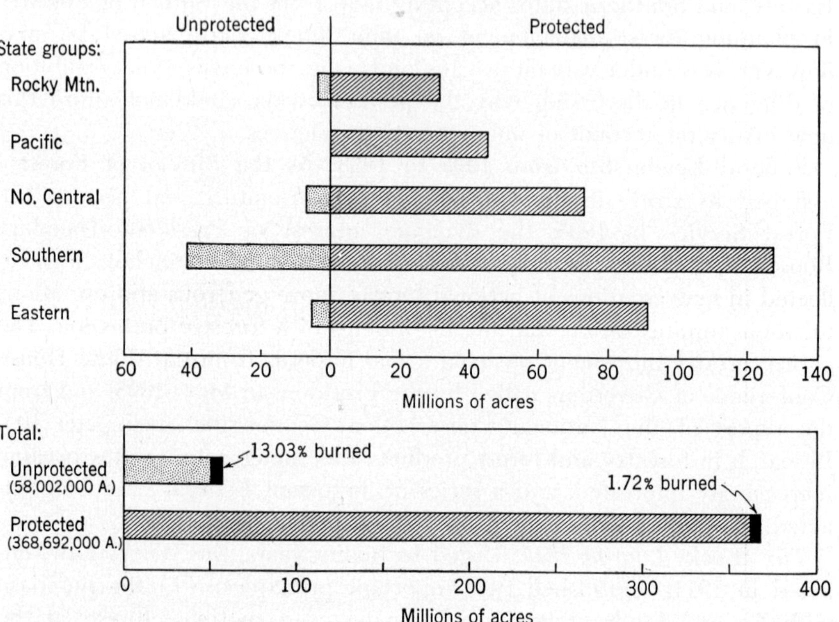

FIG. 86. Status of state and private forest land protection for the calendar year 1952. Cooperative effort under the Clarke-McNary Act is largely responsible for this record. (*U.S. Forest Service.*)

has also produced better working relations between the Federal government and private owners of forest land. It no doubt also cleared the way for a tremendous expansion of the forest-purchase program.

The McNary-McSweeney Law of 1928. Recognized as important since 1908 by the Forest Service, no policy, as such, on forest research had been adopted until the enactment of this law. In it a financial program authorizing forest research and having in mind particularly a scientific and thorough inventory of the country's forest resources was set up. Under it this survey has been pushed and a system of regional forest experiment stations set up.

Knutson-Vandenberg Act of 1930. A financial program authorizing funds for reforesting national forest lands was set up in this act. This followed long effort by the Forest Service to get adequate support for this work and carried another interesting provision: the earmarking of certain portions of the proceeds from national forest sales of timber for reforesting or otherwise improving these areas after cutting. This was particularly significant because the Civilian Conservation Corps with its wealth of labor, and which was later to figure importantly in this work, had not yet been mentioned.

Other Laws and Studies from 1905 to 1933. Not all the policy making and progress in public forestry concerned the Forest Service during this period. Agricultural lands within national forests could be homesteaded

FIG. 87. Experiment station for forest genetics where improved strains of forest trees are being developed. Placerville, Calif. This and other forest experiment stations are authorized by the McNary-McSweeney Act. (*Photo by U.S. Forest Service.*)

under an act of 1906. This led in 1912 to a complete classification and listing of such lands. Two Supreme Court decisions in 1911 sustained the contention of the Forest Service that it was authorized to charge for and to regulate the grazing of domestic livestock on national forests. In 1916 the Oregon and California Railroad grant lands to the extent of 2 million acres were repossessed by the Federal government for violation of the terms, and the sale of land and timber authorized under conditions inviting exploitation (this was corrected in 1939). The National Park Service was established in 1917 under an authorizing act passed in 1916. A study of the lumber industry by the Secretary of Commerce and Labor appearing in 1913 disclosed the startling concentrations of private timberland ownership and emphasized the speculative character and lack of forestry interest in the businesses of the holders. This led to the agitation for Federal regulation of timber cutting on private lands preceding the enactment of the Clarke-McNary Act of 1924. President Hoover's commission on the Conservation and Administration of the Public Domain, appointed in 1930, recommended in 1931 the turning over of vast Federal areas to the states and ignored anything but forest cover as an appropriate characteristic of land to be added to national forests. His Timber Conservation Board concerned itself with wasteful overproduction in the lumber industry and with competition of national forest timber with that privately owned and marketed. In March, 1933, the so-called "Copeland Report" was issued as a result of a congressional resolution, and it concluded among other things that, since most of the forestry problems in America center in or grow out of private ownership, public ownership of forests should be greatly increased. It recognized the need for private enterprise and ownership in the forestry picture but pointed out that such management was not enough.

Other events, laws, and reports affecting forest policy figure in the history of this period from 1905 to 1933, but this summary brings the general story up to March, 1933. Then with the inauguration of President Franklin D. Roosevelt, circumstances combined with the President's leadership brought about a fast and far-reaching increase in all natural-resource conservation. Forest resources received marked attention.

Further Progress in Maintaining and Increasing the Productivity of Forest Resources. The reader must here pause to remind himself that, throughout an account that seems to be endless historical summary, the discussion is still on ways in which maintenance and increase of forest productivity is brought about. He should also remember that, while accumulating and disseminating scientific knowledge and information on the techniques of forest management are vastly important, the way in which a democracy and its people make possible and get to work at the job of management determines whether or not it will be done. For this reason, the burst of physical accomplishment in all natural-resource conservation during the administration of President Franklin D. Roosevelt, mentioned in the introduction, merits further discussion strictly from the viewpoint of forestry.

Three considerations should be noted in the use of the Civilian Conservation Corps (and to a lesser extent in the use of other emergency labor organizations): (1) the long-planned, time-consuming, labor-consuming programs of reforestation, timber-stand improvement work, and building of fire control, recreation, and other administrative facilities on public lands both Federal and state; (2) the almost sudden granting of authority to use constructively, in both a social and physical sense, the labor of millions of unemployed young men who were in distress through no fault of their own; (3) the need for stimulating heavy industry and other business by furnishing a wartime-like market for their products.

Passing over the inevitable question of why millions of young men should be unemployed in a rich democracy, ever, their accomplishments in forestry may be listed briefly. Public forest nurseries were greatly expanded and many acres of Federal and state lands reforested. Promising young timber stands on 2,504,808 acres were thinned, released from overshading species, and otherwise set to growing faster. Forest-insect and forest-disease attacks were combatted on 13 million acres. Fire-control facilities, including observation posts, cleared firebreaks, low-grade roads for moving heavy equipment and men, water sources, airplane landing fields, warehouses, and headquarters for fire-control forces, in almost every instance were completed far in excess of anything that had appeared in all the preceding years. Recreation facilities in terms of camp grounds, water bodies, shelters, winter-sports areas, and improvements to hunting and fishing grounds received their first major attention in a physical sense. Grazing areas on the national forests were improved by the development of stock-watering facilities, fences to keep cattle from drifting off the assigned ranges, and control of damaging rodents. Terracing and revegetation of certain small but important watersheds were made possible. Certain forest research projects requiring large forces and vast physical effort were completed. And cutting across these activities the forests were defended from fire with a skilled force never before or since available.

Similar but very much smaller contributions were made by other labor organizations, including the WPA.

Frequently unappreciated too, this chance to get needed work done operated to increase the purchase of lands for national-forest purposes and to a lesser extent to increase the areas of the national-park system. Exchange of private, state, and Federal lands for the blocking up of the three types of forest holdings also went forward more rapidly than usual under a law of 1922 which authorized the trading of land or standing timber to state or private interests for lands owned by them in and along the border of national forests.

Still other unappreciated features of "emergency" work performed by the Civilian Conservation Corps and other public-work agencies are the capital-investment character of the properties developed and the increase in productivity of forest resources that were brought about. These will pay off to a much greater extent than assumed in actual returns measurable only in money. The vast gain in human welfare has already been evident.

In attempts at industrial recovery after the crash of 1929–1932, the various natural-resource industries learned a great deal about cooperation in trying to help themselves through the National Industrial Recovery Act with its "Codes of Fair Competition," of which the "Lumber Code" was one. It is hardly too much to say that the regional "rules" of forest practice which had a short tryout during the life of this act hastened a consciousness in the industry which has resulted in remarkable progress toward a sound industrial forestry program on the part of many large timberland owners.

Curtailing Waste in Forest Utilization. When a tree is cut for lumber, only about 43 per cent of it, on the average, is utilized. Getting heavy logs to a mill is ordinarily too expensive, whatever the transportation system

FIG. 88. Commercial logging operation in Washington Douglasfir. Looks bad because clear cut in large group, but it will reseed from the timber left. Apparent waste would offer good opportunity for "relogging" with market for salvaged material. (*Photo by K. S. Brown, courtesy American Forests.*)

used, to allow the kind of close utilization which would salvage tops, large limbs, or broken and cull logs. Certain unavoidable waste also occurs in milling. The sawdust, slabs, edgings, trimmings, and cull lumber accumulate much faster than they can be used for fuel by the mill's power plant or by the local community. Even in the harvesting of farm-forest crops considerable waste occurs, and the owners of a portable sawmill faced with an uncertain market for their products and with limited mechanical equipment at their disposal cannot be bothered too much with the unprofitable business of guarding against waste. Finally the fabricating industries experience losses in seasoning and storing stocks of lumber and other wood items and in manufacturing processes. The parts of the tree, therefore, that finally land in a residence or a finished manufactured article represent anything but full utilization. Figure 88A furnishes a graphic analysis of wood waste for the year 1944 in terms of tons rather than board feet and shows particularly well just what happens to logging waste, "primary" waste which is the kind occurring at sawmills and pulp mills, and "secondary" waste which is the kind occurring in the fabricating and other specialized manufacturing industries. The term *commodity drain* is used as distinct from loss through fire, insects, disease, and the elements. In this graph only the "not-used" portion constituting 34.5 per cent of the total commodity drain can be considered absolute waste. The 22.5 per cent "used for fuel" constitutes relative waste in the sense of being detoured into an inefficient "use" for which it was not purposely harvested.

All along the line from logger to builder or manufacturer this problem of inefficient utilization of the forest crop is a daily puzzle, and in recent years much has been accomplished toward finding economic use for greater amounts of the tree. In fact many larger companies look to the waste pile for a part of their business.

Integration of wood-using industries is one way to improve utilization practices. The same company or group of enterprises may set up at one place a sawmill, a pulp mill, a wood-distillation plant, a post and pole yard, a fuel yard, and a woodenware or furniture plant, or a less complete combination. Cull logs and other logging waste might then find their way economically to the pulp mill or to the wood-distillation plant for charcoal and chemicals. Small-diameter waste would find outlet as pulpwood, chemical wood, or fence posts to be treated for prevention of decay and then marketed, and mill waste, even including bark, may come out finally as wallboard or insulating products. Even logging waste has recently been attacked with considerable vigor in the big timber regions of the West through (1) using portable sawmills set up at the logging site and salvaging much of the smaller diameter material left by power logging of the larger and more valuable cuts; (2) "prelogging" in which the lighter material which would otherwise be abandoned is removed ahead of power logging; (3) "relogging" which is a salvage operation using lighter machinery and following the regular removal of heavy logs.[9]

Among the more interesting products obtainable from wood waste and promising as the results of conservation in the wood industries are roofing felts and building papers from cull wood, cork substitutes from bark and useful in linoleum manufacture, ethyl alcohol and yeast from wood sugars, the latter showing promise as human and animal food, turpentine ex-

[9] Wood Waste in the United States, Report 4, *Reappraisal of the Forest Situation*, 1947, U.S. Forest Service (mimeographed), p. 21.

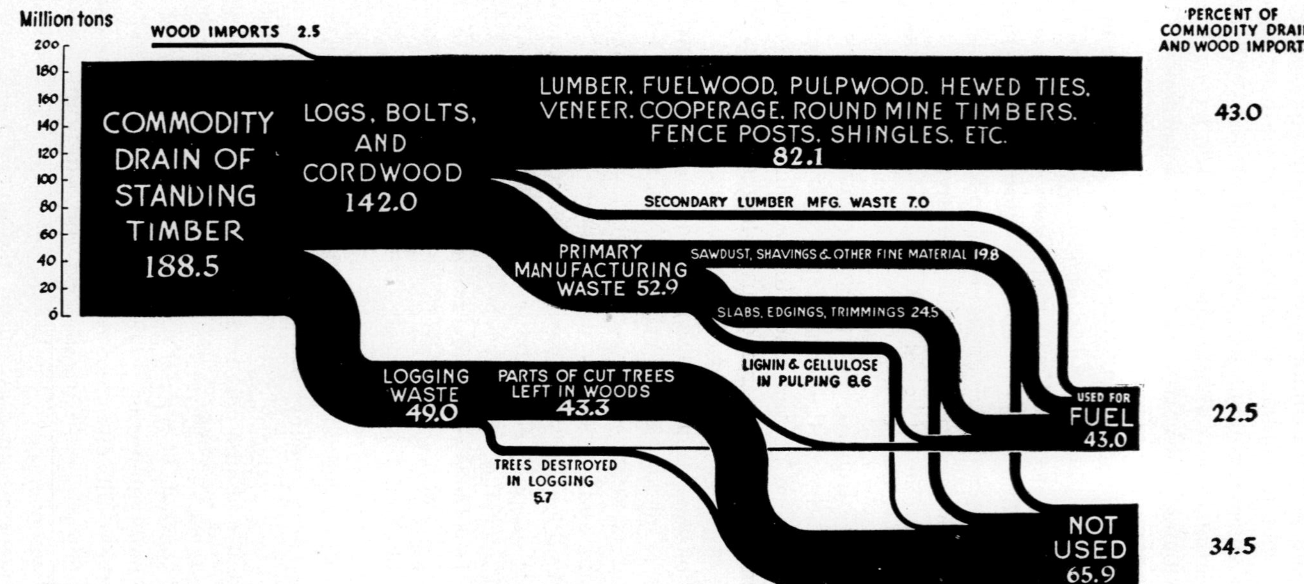

FIG. 88A. Use and waste in logging and manufacturing of all timber products, United States, 1944. (*U.S. Forest Service.*)

tracted by steam and solvent processes, and briquetted waste for more efficient use as household fuel. Besides these, the possibilities of greater demand for charcoal in the fast-growing light-metals industries is encouraging as an outlet for wood waste.

Continuing and intensive research in the field of wood-waste utilization is important. Growing interest in this line throughout the lumber industry is significant. Any prolonging of the life of wood in service through skillful

Fig. 89. Wood-distillation plant of Cliffs-Dow Chemical Co., using low-grade wood. This plant uses daily the equivalent of a pile 4 by 8 feet and a mile long to produce charcoal and chemical products. (*Michigan Department of Conservation.*)

construction and protection from decay and insect attack such as termite damage amounts to waste prevention and to real conservation.

The Future of Forestry

Because demand for the products and services of forests is predicted to increase rather than level off in the next two decades, the program ahead becomes a matter of concern to everyone. Protection and management of existing forests, reforestation of denuded areas with high potential productivity, reconciling the several uses of the total forest resource, progressive control of waste in utilization, and research and straight thinking on ways and means to accomplish such purposes—these are the directions in which effort must be stepped up and maintained.

Protection and Management. Assurance that fire, insects, disease, and storm shall not rob the people of too large a part of the products and services cannot now be given either by public or private forest owners. Losses, however, have been reduced, more and more area is under organized protective effort, and salvage procedures are increasingly effective. While no completely new procedures are indicated in forest-fire control, two items need more attention: (1) definite local, regional, and international coordination of plans, forces, and equipment to meet conflagrations such as the one which hit New England in 1938 (the interstate compact is worthy of study in this situation); (2) increased analysis, study, and effort in preventing fires. Ninety-four per cent of the fires recorded in 1952 were preventable in theory because they were man-caused. It is perhaps safe to say that one-half of them can be prevented in practice as the years go on, even though the *number* of fires has not yielded encouragingly to effort so far. Hazards can be reduced, precautions can be made easier and matters of habit, appeals, while they have the help of the advertising industry, can and must at the same time compete with the most universal and effective commercial advertising that the world has ever known. Use of forest-fire information in public-school teaching holds real promise in preventing forest fires.

Insect and disease control promises to gain effectiveness from the Forest Pest Control Act of 1947 through which prompt action may be obtained in the event of sudden outbreaks. Appropriations under this act, however, must be increased, more entomologists and pathologists must be trained and employed, and modern methods, insecticides, and fungicides must be made fully available as life histories and control programs are worked out. Continuing research is particularly important in these fields in order to determine the need for proclaiming and enforcing quarantines, recommending use of insect- and disease-resistant species for reforestation, and cutting practices which will amount to biological control through timed removal or reduction in number of host species preferred by various insects and diseases. Finding uses for and developing economic methods of salvaging fire- and insect-killed forests and those felled by storms require more study in line with present efforts on the Tillamook burn in Oregon and in the beetle-killed Engelmann spruce in the central Rocky Mountain country.

All this will require heavy investment of public and private funds, but it should be *considered an investment* in the permanent productivity of an indispensable resource.

Management of existing commercial forests is improving, and there need be little worry about the relatively small proportion of such areas that is in the hands of the public agencies. Larger private holdings too are lining up as tree farms, and well-organized corporations are making a good showing in their cutting practices. A disproportionately large acreage in small private holdings presents a less encouraging picture and a tougher problem. Some public regulation of cutting practices is appropriate, for the ax can be a destroyer or a builder and maintainer. Federal laws in this direction have long been opposed by the lumber industry; self-regulation had a trial under the NRA; state laws are rare and weak but perhaps offer the best approach. Until these are perfected and along with their operation, the Federal forest experiment stations offer valuable advice to the industries, many of them employ trained foresters, and self-interest becomes an increasingly enlightened incentive to better private forest management. Farm holdings receive better management

FIG. 90. The porcupine feeds on the bark of forest trees, and injury from this and other animal sources must be taken into account in forest management.

through the work of Federal and state agencies. Such help needs to be intensified.

Reforestation. Contrary to much of the popular belief, tree planting is not our top forestry job in this country. But to bring an estimated 65 million acres of barren or poorly stocked forest land into production, the present effort, at which rate the job will not be completeed for 130 years, must be stepped up. Forest nursery capacity of 450 million trees in 1951—enough to plant about 500,000 acres—may well be doubled, and while farm holdings can be taken care of with stock furnished the soil conservation districts and from state nurseries aided by appropriations under the Clarke-McNary Act of 1924, industrial concerns will have to continue and increase their own nursery and reforestation efforts. Expenditures for reforestation, too, should be considered as investments which will eventually pay off.

Reconciling Various Uses of Forests. There is nothing automatic in the magic phrase "multiple use." It works only when worked at. The same forest can produce timber, game, fur, forage for livestock, water, beauty and restful atmosphere and even maintain itself with mining in operation underneath it. Such a combination of objectives, however, is bound to present conflicts. Priorities must be decided upon and regulations recognizing such priorities enforced. One of the most baffling things currently is the conflict between areas in the forest as dedicated wilderness and the increasing pressure to harvest from such areas any resource that will contribute to local economy. The United States, as the richest democracy in the world, has not yet decided firmly that primitive and inspirational wilderness values have much of a bid to priority except in rare instances. Another conflict arises in umpiring the competition between animals, wild and domestic, on the one hand and trees and water on the other. Rabbits, porcupines, cows, deer, pine trees, farm woodland sprouts, sheep on the range, and city water systems all get into the picture. And the forest usually takes the beating before the unscrambling is effected. Techniques are important in multiple use and so are policies. River-valley and interbureau programs offer a real chance to work out equitable priorities.

Increasing Control of Waste in Utilization. The information on waste in harvesting and manufacturing forest products on pp. 164 to 166 points to the need for continuing research to find uses for parts of trees now discarded in logging and for mill wastes such as sawdust, small-dimension slabs and edgings, and bark. Research alone, however, is not the answer, the adoption of waste-prevention practices requires demonstration and "selling" to operators, many of whom are not in business on a scale to make such practices attractive. Opportunities for the "sales engineer" or the "research missionary" will no doubt increase.

Incentives and Policies to Meet Future Forest Yields. Whether or not the practice of forestry at the hands of private industry contributes its share to future needs of forest products and services is to a considerable extent in the hands of the public. Exploitation of natural resources is not usually too risky a business. Conservation, on the other hand, through intensive management may be risky. This brings questions of ownership, credit, insurance, and regulation into the picture. At present, ownership of commercial forest lands (those which actually produce our timber crop) lines up with Federal agencies, accounting for 89 million acres; states, counties, and municipalities, 27 million acres; private companies and individuals, 345 million acres, of which 261 million are in the hands of owners of less than 5,000 acres each. To assure good management of the latter group is a real problem tied into size of holding, available markets, and the dispensing of needed advice and help. Private owners are in a sense trustees of the forest resources in their hands. So long as they can do the combined jobs of supplying the public with products and keeping their lands productive, their good stewardship entitles them to continue as owners (trustees). Such an arrangement is the only one fair to the people as a whole, and it should govern the action of public agencies in acquiring extensive increased holdings. It should also constitute notice to

FIG. 91. The U.S. Forest Products Laboratory of Madison, Wis. This institution, along with fundamental studies of forest products, works constantly to discover ways of curtailing waste of forest products. (*Photo by U.S. Forest Service.*)

owners that the public expects good management on their part *and* that the public will cooperate as regards grants-in-aid for protection, research, and advice on management problems, and help on credit and insurance. Credit is particularly important to small owners. Insurance not now available is needed by all owners, and that part of the public engaged in banking and insurance has considerable responsibility in these directions. Some public help may be necessary and appropriate.

The future of forestry in this democracy can be assured only as its citizens demand it. The strongest public agencies and the most powerful members of the industry as well need their hands held up through the voice of a public that understands the indispensability of forests.

Forage Resources and Range Lands

The breeding and pasturing of domestic livestock for the purpose of producing meat, leather, and wool are two of the oldest industries known to mankind and ones which have long depended largely upon publicly owned or very extensive privately owned range lands. In the United States more than two-fifths of the entire area of the country was originally land of this character, and the portion now in use lies mostly west of the Mississippi River. It is frequently spoken of as the "Western range," and the long-standing and relatively free-to-the-strongest use of this land by pioneer stockmen has resulted in something more than building up a livestock industry. It has amounted to progressive exploitation of the land and the forage species, which in almost 50 years of management effort by the Forest Service and about 20 by the Department of the Interior has been only partially halted. Moreover, enormous areas both of public and private range lands are still devoid of any real regulation of use by domestic sheep and cattle and are in unsatisfactory condition.

The very fact that more than 42,000 permits to stockmen for the grazing of 13 million head of livestock were approved in 1949 on Federal lands alone emphasizes the need for conserving every available acre of range and of putting a stop to the traditional abuse of the grazing lands.

The figure for all livestock grazed on the Western range would probably reach almost 33 million head, or in terms of animal units (five sheep being considered the equivalent of one steer), the figure would be about 15 million. Slaughtered throughout one year, this number of animal units should keep more than one-fifth of our population supplied with a generous yearly ration of beef and mutton to say nothing of the contribution of wool and leather.

One may well couple these facts to the realization that some of the most heavily used ranges are located on the watersheds of important Western streams and that wild-animal life and people seeking recreation use these ranges. This adds further to their importance as natural resources, particularly because of the dependence of Western agriculture and industry and the actual life of the settlements upon adequate supplies of water for domestic use, irrigation, and power. To a less extent water recreation and hunting come into the picture.

As with other natural resources, the range and its forage form the material foundation for an important segment of our economy. It is not to be taken lightly that some 2 million farm and ranch families obtain a considerable portion of their living from the range livestock business, nor that businesses closely related to the industry add perhaps 5 to 10 million more people whose living is a matter of whether or not the livestock enterprises prosper.

The Nature of the Forage Resources. Natural pasture or range vegetation is more than just grass, although the stockmen would probably be happier if brush species, weeds, sedges, and even small trees did not complete the forage picture. One well-defined range of considerable area may serve to feed the herds or flocks of several owners and may include vast open tracts of grass, patches of sagebrush, mountainsides of chaparral (a term used to designate a type of brush involving many species), areas of open timber and mountain meadows, and finally old burns or forest-fire areas which have come back to grass, weeds, and

FIG. 92. Sheep grazing on Santa Fe National Forest, New Mexico. (*Photo by U.S. Forest Service.*)

brush rather than to forest. The food or, as the stockman says, the "feed" value of species other than grass may vary with the class of stock which graze upon them, and this fact is naturally considered in assigning stock to any given locality. Goats, for example, can do well on leaves and twigs of brush and dwarf timber species. Horses need grass. Sheep sometimes do well on weeds. Cattle will take a certain amount of "browse" or leaf, twig, and seed of brush species, in addition to grass which they prefer. Hogs, of which relatively few are grazed in the West, seek the "mast" or fallen acorns and other nuts from foothill hardwood forests. Larger wild animals, depending upon species and haunts, feed on everything from water plants to twigs and foliage of cone-bearing trees.

Use of the range lands is limited to a considerable extent by the distribution of water as well as by types of vegetation and nearness of grazing grounds to home ranch properties. These among other things have affected the ownership pattern which makes it hard to find large unbroken blocks under single ownership, public or private. Any large units of range may include Federal, state, railroad grant, mining claim and patent, homestead, timber corporation, Indian reservation, and ranch ownerships—all nicely mixed up into a puzzle which adds difficulty to agreement on common policy in grazing use, protection, and rehabilitation. Moreover, it has seemed good business to the stockmen to allow

FIG. 93. Yearling steers in Montana meadow after hay has been cut. Private ranch land with Beaverhead National Forest hills in background. (*Photo by U.S. Forest Service.*)

large stretches of grazing land to remain in public and corporation ownership. In the early days it could be fought for by the large livestock owner against the small ones and by the sheepmen against the cattlemen, and vice versa. So long as it could be used free of charge for the taking and through control of the watering places, there was no need to acquire title nor to assume the obligations of proprietorship. These might include paying taxes, careful use, maintenance of improvements, revegetation of overgrazed areas, closing such areas temporarily to grazing, eradicating poisonous plants, and even cutting down on the numbers of animals grazed on favorite ranges.

Quantitatively, about one-half the area of Western range is privately owned, and of the remainder, one-sixth is state land and five-sixths Federal.

Why the Range Resource Is Depleted. The basic cause of the unsatisfactory condition of the range is overgrazing. Hungry animals feed so heavily that the sod becomes broken and the grasses are eaten down so that no seed is produced. Seed from the less palatable weeds and brush species are then likely to take over and produce a poorer forage if any. Because the grass cover is broken and because of restless trampling of exposed soil, erosion is likely to set in (Figs. 94 and 95). Such rainfall as occurs in the drier range country is likely to be torrential at times, and

FIG. 94. Overgrazed land. Erosion starting to ruin the area. (*Photo by U.S. Forest Service.*)

this aggravates the erosion. Even wind erosion occurs when the native sod has been broken for wheat growing and later abandoned.

Setting the Use of the Range in Order. Until the national forests (then called "forest reserves") were established and put under management, no attempt at regulation of grazing on public lands had been made. Even then, in the first years of this century, the only legal basis for such regulation was contained in the law of 1897 which authorized the Secretary of the Interior to make rules and regulations for the administration of the reserves. This authority was later extended to the Secretary of Agriculture with the transfer of the reserves to that department and their later designation as national forests. Finding itself faced with a grazing occupancy on the national forests, the Forest Service, a bureau of the Department of Agriculture, worked out regulations which the Secretary approved and published, and these still apply on more than 150 million acres of national forest land. They define preferences in the allotment of grazing privileges to former users who are bona fide settlers and who operate dependent ranches, they set grazing fees on a per head and seasonal basis, they define range-management practices required of the permittee and provide a basis for cooperative improvement of the range properties and use of intermingled private land, and finally they define and provide penalties for trespass on the ranges. The courts have upheld the Secretary's authority to make and enforce grazing regulations, and their operation through the years has resulted in beneficial use of the forage on the national forest and in perceptible improvement of the grazing conditions.

Not until 1934 was legislation enacted which would bring about regulation of unreserved grazing lands of the public domain under the jurisdiction of the Department of the Interior. Then the Taylor Grazing Act, which really started working in 1935, brought about the establishment of grazing districts, the adoption of moderate fees, the allotment of range to local users, and actual management of a considerable part of the lands in the Western public land states. The administraton is similar but somewhat less intensive than that of the Forest Service. The control of water figures largely in the allotment of range to various stockmen, and somewhat questionable administrative power is delegated to boards of users. It is fair to say that long neglect of these so-called "Taylor grazing lands" and the far-flung extent of the open range livestock business have made the Department's task of regulation extremely complex and difficult. Furthermore, some of the unorganized public lands without the grazing districts are used on a lease-of-area basis and others without even a lease agreement. Trespass on these lands, which along with the grazing disricts are administered by the Department's Bureau of Land Management, is difficult to control. The bureau manpower is scant, and the areas are vast and scattered. Of course lands used in trespass are likely to be badly abused. As of June 30, 1949, the Bureau of Land Management was responsible for the administration of more than 184 million acres of grazing lands in sixteen of the Western states.[10]

Certain large private holdings in checkerboard pattern where land grants were made to railroads and wagon roads share in the good management of the alternate square miles of Federal range. Livestock of course pay little attention to survey lines, and these are frequently the only boundaries between private and public lands. Permits are issued to stockmen who have obtained leases on the alternate railroad sections and

[10] *Annual Report of the Secretary of the Interior*, 1949, p. 236.

whose stock graze a part of the time over Federal lands. The stock of other owners in turn graze over the railroad lands, and in hewing to the numbers of stock which Federal land will carry, the same formula must be applied to the intermingled private lands. This practice extends in lesser degree to any areas of intermingled public and private ownership. Moreover, it should be understood that the Agricultural Conservation Program, administered by the Production and Marketing Administration of the U.S. Department of Agriculture, provides extensive financial help for conservation practices on private range lands. These include deferred grazing (which amounts to resting the land) and reseeding and in 1947

FIG. 95. The light soils of many Western mountain lands are subject to gully erosion from overgrazing. (*Photo by U.S. Forest Service.*)

affected more than half a million acres of privately owned range lands.[11] Meanwhile, appropriations for similar practices on Federal lands have been meager. In this instance, it appears that the Federal government through its Congress is a better rewarder of the private owner and manager of range land than it is a good proprietor itself.

The impressive part of the picture is the activity, to whatever extent, found in conserving large blocks of both public and private range.

The Demands and Possibilities of Range Conservation. It has been pointed out that range lands have suffered depletion from overgrazing

[11] Landstrom, Karl S., Conservation of the Public Range in Our Public Lands, U.S. Department of the Interior, 1951, p. 14.

and subsequent deterioration of forage and finally from erosion. With this succession of damage, the indicated conservation steps usually included are given in the following order: (1) reducing the numbers of grazing animals using the particular range, (2) preventing further erosion and repairing erosion damage, (3) reseeding the range where necessary, (4) adopting a definite set of good management practices which may include such requirements as development of water, confining stock to appropriate range by drift fences (usually crude fences which supplement natural barriers), systematic salting, eradication of poisonous plants, careful observance of grazing seasons, and using special driveways instead of highways for putting stock on the range and bringing it off.

This sort of program cannot be successfully carried out either by public or private effort alone and certainly not without expert advice and service based on dependable research.

Fortunately some six experiment stations throughout the West combine grazing research with forest research, and findings are shared by all public and private interests. Investigations are constantly being made covering such questions as carrying capacity of certain types of range, best methods of reseeding spent range properties, improved methods of herding and removal of marketable stock to avoid shrinkages in weight, improvement of strains of grazing animals, and eradication of insect and plant pests. Programs of range management and improvement are carried on by the Forest Service on national forest lands and by the Soil Conservation Service through the furnishing of ranch plans where soil conservation districts have been established. Both of these bureaus are in the Department of Agriculture, and the Production and Marketing Administration in the same department is also concerned, as has been pointed out, with subsidizing privately owned range properties. In the Department of the Interior, the Bureaus of Land Management and of Indian Affairs administer the fifty-eight grazing districts under the Taylor Grazing Act, carry on erosion-control work on public range lands and reseeding of the range. The Bureau of Indian Affairs directs and sponsors the grazing use of 40 million acres of Indian forest and range lands which furnish 9 million "cow months" of grazing. The bureau also cooperates with the Bureau of Animal Industry of the Department of Agriculture in the operation of a sheep-breeding laboratory at the Navajo Reservation which has increased the lamb crop and improved the yield of wool. This gears in with a program of reduction of numbers of permitted stock where situations were especialy acute on the national forests. The Forest Service in 1949 reseeded 67,000 acres of grazing lands, bringing the total up to 270,000 acres with special appropriations. This work, of course, represents a considerable capital investment, but it appears to be more than justified with the prospect that carrying capacity will be increased five to ten times. This means strengthening the local economy and increasing the revenues and services from public property other than by grazing.

Contemplated further work on the national forests, as funds become available from special authorizations, include not only the reseeding of 4 million acres of range land but the addition to the vast physical improvements already installed to bring about more efficient use of the range, the construction of 1,500 holding corrals, 30,000 miles of range fence, 23,000 new range-water developments, 9,000 miles of stock driveways, control of poisonous and noxious plants on 439,000 acres and of rodents on 15 million acres.[12] In carrying out this program, advice and actual cooperation of stockmen using the range are sought through their local associations.

With a more difficult task on the Taylor grazing lands and the unreserved public domain, the Bureau of Land Management in the Department of Interior during 1949 made an excellent showing in range improvement and was unusually successful in obtaining financial cooperation from users. Undertakings here were somewhat different in emphasis than on national forests. Grasshopper control, for example, has been attempted on 34,000 acres, rodent control on almost 226,000 acres, control of useless brush species on more than 36,000 acres, seed harvest of more than 5 tons, reseeding of more than 40,000 acres of area which will reach a much larger total as funds are available, 223 water developments, and 46 miles of firebreaks.[13]

While the figures given in the two preceding paragraphs are impressive, they are somewhat lost in the millions of acres where the improvements are needed. And while the financial contributions of the users exceeded the Federal appropriation for improvements on Taylor grazing lands in 1949, there is still room for the users who benefit from these improvements to take a more constructive hand in maintaining these properties which belong to all the people of the United States. The fact that the privately owned range lands are generally poorly maintained presents a problem beyond that of public proprietorship. This will have to be attacked more vigorously than the Soil Conservation Service and the Production and Marketing Administraton have been able to do so far in their cooperative programs.

Grazing and Forage Problems Elsewhere Than in the West. The Forest Service and the various states in their cooperative extension-service work with farm-forest owners have for years pointed out that heavy grazing of farm woods was both poor grazing and poor timber-growing practice. The Soil Conservation Service also recommends frequently in

[12] Report of the Chief of the Forest Service, 1950, p. 41.

[13] *Annual Report of the Secretary of the Interior*, 1949, p. 242.

its farm soil conservation plans that livestock be kept out of the farm woods. More recently the farm foresters, operating out of the offices of state foresters, and financed cooperatively by states and by Federal funds authorized by the Norris-Doxey Act of 1937, have concentrated on helping smaller forest owners to grow more timber. Their work has gone a long way in the control of grazing in farm woods.

Fortunately, however, the work both of foresters and grazing men has not been confined to protecting forests from cattle, sheep, and hogs, but

FIG. 96. Grazed and ungrazed woods, White County, Illinois. There is little reproduction on the grazed side of the fence. (*Photo by U.S. Forest Service.*)

has sought to find and develop forage resources outside the timber-producing lands or to capitalize on some services which grazing can render to timber growing.

Studies in the piney wood of the Southern and Southeastern states made since 1940 by the Forest Service have indicated that grazing, which is an important industry in the South, can be harmonized with timber growing. The benefits of *controlled* grazing are perceptible in eastern North Carolina in more plentiful establishment of pine seedlings, affording a reduction of fire hazard. In Louisiana a study conducted in cooperation with a lumber company indicated that seeding and grazing plowed firebreaks kept the nutritious forage eaten down close to the ground and made a better barrier to the spread of forest fire than the breaks when allowed to grow up to ungrazed vegetation.

Recognizing that scrub oaks and other low-value hardwoods in Louisiana offer no valuable products and prevent growth of grass, experiments in the killing of these species with chemicals have been undertaken. Results show almost double production of grass by weight, and cattle have been able to graze for longer periods at greater carrying capacity.

Range-conservation Policies. In so far as range-conservation policies exist and whether or not they are right, they can be listed about as follows:

1. It is appropriate for the Federal government to administer the forage resources on the land which it holds as proprietor, with the objectives of conserving the forage, seeing that its use is beneficial and fairly distributed, and seeing that such use does not destroy or interfere with the use of other important and intermingled natural resources.
2. It is fair to subsidize the Western livestock industry through the charging of low fees for use of the public range and through financing of improvements to make the range more productive.
3. It is the duty of the public agencies to look into questions of range management to which private enterprise needs answers, but which it is not equipped to solve.
4. It is appropriate for the public agencies to seek ways of reconciling the growing of timber and the grazing of livestock side by side or on occasion on the same area. This is particularly necessary on farm woods and in the South.
5. In spite of the democratic character of our government and the necessity for participation of its citizens in conducting such a government, the need for regulating the acts of citizens in the use of natural resources is frequently apparent and pressing in the national interest. The grazing of livestock on public ranges is one of the activities in which such regulation is indicated.

The Citizen and the Range Resources. Controversies have raged in recent years between certain organized elements of the livestock industry and people who are interested in better management of range resources in behalf of other uses than grazing. Two large livestock trade associations have contended that management of the range is not a matter of public concern outside the public-land states, that stockmen should have a free hand in administering the public range, and even that some of the best of the public grazing lands should be allowed to pass into private ownership at nominal cost.

The stockmen who make their living and serve the rest of us by using natural forage resources are in a tough business, fraught with everything from drought and disease to blizzard and occasional ruinous markets. They are essential to the local and national economies. They are definitely subsidized by moderate fees and range-resource maintenance at public expense. They are indeed trustees of the range whether as users or owners.

The use of the range for raising livestock *is* a beneficial use but not the only one. The ordinary citizen has a real interest in range conservation in terms of the price of meat, wool, leather, and whether or not he can get them at all; in terms of the scenery he wants on his vacation in the West; in terms of wise expenditure of the taxes he pays for irrigation and power reservoirs that shall not be silted full by soil eroded from overgrazed lands; and just possibly in terms of a picturesque segment of American culture which he does not want to see disappearing because of exploited ranges which should be giving it permanence.

Natural Resources Contributing to Recreation

It would be difficult for most people to use leisure time for constructive sport and relaxation, and for obtaining inspiration and adventure that really satisfies, without access to land, water, trees, grass, and wild-animal life. All these make their own contributions to the thing which is called *recreation.* Doubtless the so-called sportsman, who pursues and captures wild game animals and fish, would resent mildly being classified among others who seek recreation. So might the expert mountain climber and the amateur explorer, but these adventurers are certainly no more purposeful than the picnickers, campers, wilderness travelers, sightseers in scenic localities, canoe travelers, or winter-sports and water-sports enthusiasts. Judging from the conversation of the average golfer or baseball fan, *they* may be even less purposeful. At any rate the business of indulging in high-quality outdoor recreation requires space, unusual types of terrain, cover, and environment, and in certain instances recreation must be the dominating use to which these natural resources are dedicated.

For purposes of this discussion city parks and playgrounds, private estates, athletic fields, swimming pools, golf courses, and indoor-sports facilities will be mentioned only, and principal attention will be paid to relatively wild lands and waters some of which are exclusively dedicated to recreation and others of which are used for recreation only as one of a number of simultaneous or alternate uses. The sports angles of wild-animal management including sport fisheries will also be included. This brings the discussion, even under so broad a heading as given to this chapter, nearer to the readily visualized natural resources, as they are usually understood. Certainly such resources can be depleted or they can disappear completely, and to keep them available requires that they be conserved.

Recreation Resources in Private Ownership. Not all land devoted to recreation is in public ownership, and indeed the people of this country would be hard pressed if this were so. Hunters and fishermen, particularly in the heavily populated farming regions, depend largely for their sport upon consent or purchased privilege to enter private property. Even hunting clubs with their own headquarters must frequently lease adjoining lands or waters if they hope to use such resources exclusively. Inland river and lake shores and even the shores of the great lakes and the oceans have passed largely into private ownership, and only by recapturing them or leasing them can the general public share the sort of thing available to the cottage or estate owner or the frequenter of the resort or club.

This situation poses two knotty problems for the landowner to face: (1) To what extent should he allow the general public to use his land for recreation either with or without charge? (2) How can he conserve the natural resources involved without systematic policing of the area and the

Fig. 97. A hunter arranges with the owner of a farm for a day's recreation. He agrees to be careful around buildings and stock. (*Michigan Department of Conservation.*)

users? On the part of the general public the question may be asked, "Are we not entitled to outdoor recreation, and where shall we get it if not on farms and private estates?"

Frequently the latter questions can be answered only by such unsatisfactory rejoinders as: "Buy yourself a piece of land," "Join a rod and gun club with its own land," "Prove to me beforehand that you will clean up your picnic area, abstain from shooting my cow, close gates after you, obey the fish and game laws, be careful with fire, leave some of the flowers and maybe pay me a moderate fee for the day." "There's a resort up the road, why don't you go there,"or "The state park is only 20 miles from here and you can swim in the lake there."

On the other hand, a considerable block of the recreation-seeking public is taken care of on private land either in the form of ownerships of small tracts or of the land becoming available to users with the owner's consent.

Among the more heavily used of these lands are beaches, summer-cottage colonies, resorts, youth summer camps, farm lands supporting upland game species, and those owned by clubs. Many resorts and camps depend upon a *hinterland* in public ownership for the use of their guests whom they house and feed. These enterprisers may themselves own only small, strategically located tracts.

Furnishing Land for Recreation Is a Public Function. Whether the population as a whole thinks of outdoor recreation as a necessity or a luxury, its demands have brought about the establishment at public expense of a great system of parks and playgrounds, varying from the sand lots in crowded districts and the roadside picnic spots, to the national parks and the dedicated recreation areas and wilderness areas in the national forests. This is well-estabished public policy. It has lately been promulgated in a declaration by a National Committee on Recreation Policy, one significant paragraph of which reads:

> Continued conservation of the natural resources of the nation which may be utilized as one of their highest purposes for quality recreation for all the people. These resources include our forests, mountains, waterways, beaches, places of inspiring natural beauty, historic sites, and wildlife.

Certain of these groups of public recreation areas will be taken up and their conservation problems considered.

Parkways. Many people get their outdoor recreation in terms of the scene, and they like change and variety, even though they do not enter or explore wild lands. For these the elongated park characterized by a limited-access road, located to give the best views and following a belt of relatively wild country, is a satisfying facility. The spatial use of land as a natural resource thus comes close to those who may live in crowded communities. The parkway, as such an area is called, may frequently be financed by a county or by one or more neighboring cities. Sometimes such an area will include, along the route, small picnic spots, beaches, wild-animal or wild-flower sanctuaries, canoe ports, winter-sports layouts, and even fishing sites. Space, water, cover, and animal life thereby become involved as recreation resources, and their conservation for exclusive recreation use becomes important. Among the distinctive conservation problems involved are reconciling heavy use in terms of traffic and effect on soil, cover, and animal life with the continuing need to maintain a natural and unlittered scene. Not the least problem is acquiring enough land to keep the parkways attractive and to prevent vandalism.

State Parks. The majority of the states have state park systems. Some of the individual tracts are relatively large and have still a sort of wilderness character although for some reason these particular ones are likely to be called "forest preserves" as in the Adirondacks of New York and in Cook County, Illinois. Areas which are smaller and more intensively used are common and well managed in Iowa, Indiana, California, Oregon, New York, Massachusetts, Minnesota, Virginia, Washington, Texas, and Florida to name only a few. Acquisition and development of these areas were stimulated during the days when Civilian Conservation Corps labor was available during the 1930s. Maintenance of recreation facilities has become a heavy expense in the face of increasing use. Some of the states charge moderate entrance fees to the parks and for special services within.

FIG. 98. A picnic at Gold Head Branch State Park in Florida, Lake Johnson in background. (*Photo by Florida Board of Forestry.*)

The returns from concession contracts are also appreciable and in certain states are earmarked for maintaining the parks.

Conservation problems in the state parks include distribution of human use so that it will neither be too greatly curtailed nor injure the natural resources and facilities; keeping waters clean for sport use and in some instances for fishing; preventing willful destruction of equipment and of plant and animal life; maintaining and improving forest, shrub, and grass cover; and controlling dust, poisonous plants, and to some extent, insect pests.

The National-park System. Perhaps the most symbolic and certainly the most impressive of the natural resources devoted to recreation and inspiration of the people of this country is the national-park *system* which includes many more reservations but none so striking and majestic as the national parks themselves. There are now twenty-eight of these, covering more than 11 million acres in twenty-three states, and attracting annually almost 12 million visitors. The location and area of each are given in Table 5.

Table 5. Information Relating to the National Park System, June 30, 1949

National parks	State	Federal land, acres
Acadia	Maine	28,309.68
Big Bend	Texas	691,978.95
Bryce Canyon	Utah	36,010.38
Carlsbad Caverns	New Mexico	45,526.59
Crater Lake	Oregon	160,290.33
Everglades	Florida	341,969.00
Glacier	Montana	997,695.04
Grand Canyon	Arizona	645,295.91
Grand Teton	Wyoming	94,892.92
Great Smoky Mountains	Tennessee–North Carolina	461,003.79
Hawaii	Territory of Hawaii	173,404.60
Hot Springs	Arkansas	1,019.13
Isle Royale	Michigan	133,838.51
Kings Canyon	California	452,824.82
Lassen Volcanic	California	103,429.28
Mammoth Cave	Kentucky	50,695.73
Mesa Verde	Colorado	51,017.87
Mount McKinley	Alaska	1,939,319.04
Mount Rainier	Washington	241,524.77
Olympic	Washington	846,765.66
Platt	Oklahoma	911.97
Rocky Mountain	Colorado	252,788.28
Sequoia	California	385,100.13
Shenandoah	Virginia	193,472.98
Wind Cave	South Dakota	26,576.15
Yellowstone	Idaho–Montana–Wyoming	2,213,206.55
Yosemite	California	756,440.62
Zion	Utah	94,241.06
Total		11,419,549.74

In addition to the national parks the "system" includes 86 national monuments covering more than 9 million acres and widely distributed; 16 national military parks; 2 national battlefield parks; 1 national memorial park; 6 national battlefield sites; 13 national historic sites; 9 national memorials; 10 national cemeteries; 3 national parkways; and 29,000 acres of national capital parks in and around Washington, D.C. The area of Federal land in the entire system is about 21 million acres and attracts annually more than 26 million visitors. Some of the miscellaneous areas are small and involve, most significantly, land in its spatial sense as a natural resource.

The Real National Parks. The largest of the national parks is Yellowstone, with an area of almost $2\frac{1}{4}$ million acres. Mount McKinley is a close second, with almost 2 million acres. Platt in Oklahoma and Hot Springs in Arkansas are the smallest, each about 1,000 acres in size

FIG. 99. Yosemite National Park, California. Laura Spelman Rockefeller Museum under Yosemite Falls fits the rugged landscape. (*Photo by National Park Service.*)

and questionably classified as national parks considering the specifications of grandeur, wildness, beauty, and setting with regard to natural land and water features. All the national parks but Big Bend, Everglades, Great Smoky Mountains, Isle Royale, Mammoth Cave, and Shenandoah have been created by withdrawing and dedicating land from the public domain. The latter six have been purchased or donated to the Federal government within the last 30 years.

At best the national parks present the scenic masterpieces of this country, with a spatial setting appropriate to such presentation, and indeed a part of it. Considered in this way, such intangibles as beauty, majesty, and grandeur of the scene become natural resources subject, unless conserved, to marring and in some instances, if pressures for commercial use are not constantly resisted, to utter destruction.

FIG. 100. Grand Canyon National Park, south rim. (*Photo by National Park Service.*)

The particular features of the national parks are worth summarizing as follows:

Mountains such as Whitney, Lassen, Rainier, McKinley, and the Great Smokies all located in parks named after them; giant sequoia trees, said to be the oldest living plants and of majestic size and beauty, with their youngsters coming on; monoliths surrounding great glacial valleys such as those of Yosemite; caverns such as those of Carlsbad and Mammoth Cave; geologic erosion on a grand scale as at Grand Canyon; thermal areas such as those in Yellowstone; larger and relatively rare wild animals such as grizzly bear, moose, elk, alligator, eagle, swan, and buffalo; wind-carved and highly colored rock formations; lakes of unusual depth, color, and beauty; waterfalls; great stretches of virgin hardwood and coniferous forests in various of the Western and Southern parks; and archeological sites with structures and evidence of ancient cultures such as the prehistoric copper mines on Isle Royale and the cliff dwellings of the Southwest.

There is hardly one of the greater national parks that is free from continuing pressure for exploitation of its natural resources—water, timber, and forage for domestic animals being the ones most often coveted.

While Hot Springs in Arkansas was withdrawn from settlement and entry and dedicated to the use of all people as early as 1845, that event can hardly be said to be the start of the national-park movement, even though the area was later included in the system. It is generally agreed that the act of 1872 carving Yellowstone out of the public domain as a park and forest preserve put the national-park concept first into law and served somewhat as a model for all subsequent national-park legislation.

The National Park Service finds itself constantly face to face with the tough problem of making the parks widely available to the public "and [the duty] to provide for the enjoyment of same [their resources] in such manner and by such means as will leave them unimpaired for the enjoyment of future generations." This basic purpose involves very careful planning of all roads, structures, and concession quarters; protection of the forests and other resources from fire, insects, and disease, *which frequently in themselves constitute natural phenomena;* resisting constant pressure for the invasion of the parks for exploitation of timber, forage, minerals, and particularly water resources, and storage sites; resisting efforts to legislate inferior areas into the national-park family; protecting the wild-animal life both useful and predatory and seeing that the animal resources do not increase beyond a point where demand for food will destroy valuable cover and even deplete the animal population itself; acquiring of interior private holdings which now offer to the owners opportunity to conduct business, violate development plans, and generally ignore park policies *within* the parks; controlling vandalism which destroys and defaces park property and natural resources.

The purpose of national parks, too, involves equitable distribution of their benefits. Their location and relative inaccessibility makes this difficult from the viewpoints of travel and expense. Ideally every citizen of the country who wants to visit a national park should be able to do so. He is one of the owners. Actually the 12 million who get into the real national parks each year represent only about one-twelfth of the population and this in spite of heroic effort for years upon the part of the National Park

Service to promote and build roads to and within the parks and to bring about the availability of reasonably priced and comfortable subsistence and lodging accommodations.

The conservation problems in the foregoing list are not being neglected nor are they being solved as promptly as deserved expenditure would make possible. The National Park Service which is less than 50 years old as a bureau struggles doggedly with the principal conservation problem, the conflict between heavy use and maintenance of the "unimpaired" condition. Some sacrifices of such condition must be made at the areas of concentrated use and in order to have the parks at all accessible to large

Fig. 101. The Eastern national parks with their spring blossoms offer pleasant recreation on horseback. (*Photo by Tennessee Valley Authority.*)

numbers of people. Development plans are carefully worked out, and constant study is carried on to achieve harmony between man-made facilities and the natural scene.

Methods of extinguishing and the prevention of man-caused fires are highly developed in the national parks, and expert talent is employed. The same is true in protecting the park forests from insect and disease, with full cooperation of the appropriate bureaus of the Department of Agriculture. The National Park Service must depend largely upon the conservation and scientific societies to back it up in everlasting insistence that the commercially important natural resources within the parks are not for material and commercial use. Unless these defenses are continually active artificial emergencies can be pleaded "in the national interest" and away will go majestic forests, towering waterfalls, natural meadows, and even mineral deposits with all the disfigurement which accompany their exploitation. The American people should not be caught awaking some morning to find that they did not believe in national parks after all, because without their exploitation, there might be a tremor of delay in the rate at which their standards of comfort and convenience increase.

Wild-animal life in the national parks is not easy to manage since its increase cannot legally be harvested. It must be protected, but it is deliberately *unmanaged* in the technical sense, the only check on its increase

FIG. 102. A ranger naturalist conducts a hike in Yellowstone National Park, Wyoming. (*Photo by National Park Service.*)

being the presence of predators and death from natural causes. Elk in the Yellowstone and Grand Teton country, however, must be fed in winter and killed by hunters on the borders of the parks or by specially deputized park officials within the parks. This sounds cruel and inconsistent, but it is no more cruel than allowing vast numbers to starve because of overpopulations. Other situations of this sort arise which require heroic means to control.

Small appropriations are available each year for acquiring privately owned tracts within the parks, but progress is slow. Nothing short of complete ownership will assure compliance with national-park policy.

Fair distribution of park benefits appears to people of certain localities to indicate that they should have a national park nearby. Pressure for inclusion of unimpressive areas is still strong and is aggravated by ignorance on the part of the general public concerning national-park specifications. Legislation of this character has to be blocked, and again the scientific societies and the conservation organizations come to the defense.

There is no one answer to the problem of making a national-park visit available to every citizen who wants one. Subsidized tours combined with the "Christmas club" idea have been suggested. Group travel has possibilities which have been little explored. The parks will endure just

FIG. 103. Joshua Tree National Monument, California. Strange rock formations add to the interest in the strange plant specimens. (*Photo by Devereux Butcher.*)

so much travel and use. The problem of inevitably losing out on a national-park visit *is* a conservation problem in equitable distribution but certainly not the only one of that character in our society.

National Monuments. The eighty-six national monuments have been set aside by presidential proclamation under the Act for the Preservation of American Antiquities passed in 1906. The language of the act included the setting aside not only of "historic landmarks, historic and prehistoric structures" but "other objects of historic or scientific interest." This brought into the system not only Cabrillo in California of less than a single acre, Yucca House in Colorado of less than 10 acres, and Mound City, in Ohio of 57 acres, but Glacier Bay and Katmai in Alaska, each covering more than 2¼ million acres. Ordinarily the national monuments are much less impressive than the national parks, but they attract amateur adventurers, budding archaeologists, and many of the sightseer family. Visitors to these areas aggregate around 4½ million a year. Some of the national parks have first been set aside as national monuments. The conservation problems are similar to those of the national parks.

National Forests. Aside from hunting and fishing and a moderate volume of summer camping use by local people, the national forests can almost be said to have had recreation use thrust upon them. They were established primarily for the growing of timber and protection of the watersheds of important streams. Specifically, other uses and resources

FIG. 104. Fishing for recreation on Zigzag Rim, Umpqua National Forest, Oregon. (*Photo by U.S. Forest Service.*)

are not emphasized in the law of 1897 which outlined objectives and purposes of the "forest reserves," but recreation, as in the instance of grazing, has become big business. This was inevitable with the coming of the automobile and the generous program of road building early planned to make the forests accessible for commercial use. The carrying out of those plans has depended not only upon special appropriations but upon return of a part of the revenue from timber sales and grazing to the local counties and to special road- and trail-building funds.

Second only to the national parks in scenic attractiveness and more widely distributed around the county, the national forests have been sought by millions of people for inexpensive camping trips and for day use. Again although fishing is allowed in the national parks, hunting and trapping are forbidden, while all three are allowed in the national forests. Still another pursuit unavailable in the parks and common in the forests is the construction and occupancy of summer homes under special short-term permits for use of the land; these are used heavily by whole families and their guests. Wilderness travel is common in both types of reservation, but the best canoeing water is found in national forests, and much of the extended horseback wilderness travel, aside from that of organized Western mountain clubs, penetrates the dedicated wilderness areas of the national forests.

FIG. 104A. One may get a sense of space and distance from many national forest scenes. View of canyon in Gallatin National Forest, Montana.

Organization camps representing everything from farm youth to young people's church groups operate on national forests, on an area-rental basis, and in rare instances the buildings of an abandoned CCC camp are turned over to an adult organization which in turn makes it available to various youth groups from time to time throughout the season. Resorts of various specifications, usually informal and using the guest-cabin plan, may also operate under area permit. Winter-sports areas and day-use areas for picnicking were built in considerable numbers while CCC labor was available. Both are heavily visited, and some of them are turned over to local communities for operation.

Twenty-six million visits to national forests for recreation were recorded in 1949. Of these 13,200,000 were from users of public camp grounds, picnic areas, and winter-sports areas. The remaining 12,800,000 appeared at resorts, summer homes, organization camps, wilderness areas, and in hunting and fishing areas. The Forest Service maintains no naturalist service for interpreting the country and its resources to visitors and, except on very heavily used public camp grounds and day-use areas and at winter-sports areas, assigns no officer exclusively to the duty of serving recreation users. On the other hand, while merging field duties with the general activities on national forests, specialists in the Washington office staff of the Forest Service and in most of the ten regional office

FIG. 105. Trail riding in the Goat Rocks Wild Area, Washington. Several hundred of these 10- to 12-day horseback trips have been arranged by the American Forestry Association since 1933. (*Photo by James P. Gilligan.*)

staffs are employed both in wild-animal life management and in recreational use other than hunting and fishing.

Conservation problems on the national forests are continually arising. Among them, the reconciling of recreation use with such pressing demands as timber growing and harvesting, grazing of domestic livestock, mining, commercial occupancy of land for stores, sawmills, and mining installations constitute the most serious. The term *multiple use* implies a kind of planning, supervision, and judgment in administration which is not easy and for which manpower is not always available. Furthermore the mere policing of heavily used areas to keep them uninjured, clean, and well serviced with water, shelter, and sanitary facilities is anything but automatic. Distributing the users and on rare occasions charging them a small fee have been the subject of recent experimentation and may prove to be the answer to guaranteeing fairness to all who seek recreation. Along the same line, the equity of renting summer home sites and thus assigning monopolistic use of choice areas may be questioned as increasing demand for mass use appears.

Efforts to conserve the recreation resources on national forests include planning of recreation developments in order best to serve the public and make use of the scenic and sport resources; definite protection of developed areas from invasion by permitted livestock; bringing water supplies to dry but attractive areas; requiring strict adherence to sanitary standards from those who have land under permit; assisting state officers in the enforcement of fish and game regulations; studying and understanding and increasing the fish and other wild-animal resources; resisting constant pressures to invade wilderness country, dedicated and potential, with roads, reservoirs, airplane landing fields, and other developments which would dilute the quality of recreation areas. As in the national-park picture, various organizations with scientific and conservation objectives are active in defending the recreation resources of the national forests.

BIBLIOGRAPHY

Allen, Shirley W.: An Introduction to American Forestry, McGraw-Hill Book Company, Inc., New York, 1950.

American Forests, monthly magazine of The American Forestry Association, Washington, 1930–1953.

Annual Reports of Chief of Forest Service, 1949–1952, Washington.

Annual Reports of the Secretary of the Interior, 1949–1952.

Clawson, Marion: Western Range Livestock Industry, McGraw-Hill Book Company, Inc., New York, 1950.

Forest Outings, U.S. Forest Service, 1940.

Great Lakes Park Institute, Proceedings Fifth Annual Meeting, Indiana University, Department of Recreation, Bloomington, Ind., 1951 (mimeographed).

Landstrom, Karl S.: Conservation of the Public Range in Our Public Lands, U.S. Deparment of the Interior, 1951.

Long Range Agricultural Policy and Programs, *U.S. Dept. Agr., Sup.* 4, 1947.

McKaye, Benton: The New Exploration, Harcourt, Brace and Company, Inc., New York, 1928.

Michigan Conservation, monthly magazine of the Michigan Department of Conservation, Lansing, Mich., 1949–1953.

Planning and Civic Comment, magazine of the American Planning and Civic Association, Washington, 1933–1940.

Resources for Freedom, Vol. I, Report of the President's Materials Policy Commission, 1952.

Shankland, Robert: Steve Mather of the National Parks, Alfred A. Knopf, Inc., New York, 1950.

Smith, Guy Harold, and associates: Conservation of Natural Resources, John Wiley & Sons, Inc., New York, 1950.

Stoddart, L. A., and A. D. Smith: Range Management, McGraw-Hill Book Company, Inc., New York, 1943.

A Study of the Park and Recreation Problem of the United States, National Park Service, Government Printing Office, 1941.

A Survey of the Recreational Resources of the Colorado River Basin, National Park Service, Government Printing Office, 1950.

Thoreau, Henry David: Walden, The Macmillan Company, New York, 1929.

Trees, Yearbook of the U.S. Dept. Agr., 1949.

The Western Range, S. Doc. 199, 74th Cong., 2d sess., 1936.

Wood Waste in the United States, Report 4, *Reappraisal of the Forest Situation,* 1947, U.S. Forest Service (mimeographed).

CHAPTER 5

Wild-animal Resources[1]

Game and Fur Animals

While it is possible to group certain animal forms on the basis of their usefulness for given purposes, many animals sought as the quarries of the hunter or as the producers of coats or hides that may be sold for profit represent other values which are easy to establish though often difficult to measure. Among these are the animals which control harmful insects and rodents. Also included are those which have aesthetic and spectacle value for the attraction of money-spending tourists and for the less easily appraised value of human observation and enjoyment, study, and photographic stalking. On the other hand a grouping such as "game and fur animals" fails to suggest the important fact that many of the fur species are predatory upon game species and constitute real nuisances to the poultry raiser and the livestock grower. By the same token the game species displaced by encroachment of human settlement and activity frequently become destructive of crops if not of other animal species. Here they are said to be guilty of depredations. One must also bear in mind that a lot of so-called game animals are producers of valuable hides and furs and that fur predators furnish hunters with some of their most exciting targets. The examples chosen for discussion under the above heading will attempt to point out these overlapping benefits and nuisance features. Game birds will be included, and further discussion will cover fisheries and miscellaneous animal forms. The role of each grouping in its natural-resource aspects will be emphasized.

As compared with soil, water, air, sunshine, and vegetation, wild animals sought principally for sport, wild meat, and furs are perhaps less essential for survival. Mankind *could* worry along without them. The place of these animal resources in the happiness of men and in the economy of which they are the basis, however, indicates that men have no

[1] At the risk of attempting the impossible in a task of directing thought to an entire field, the term *wild-animal life* will be used in the discussions that follow rather than the looser term of many meanings, *wildlife.*

intention of getting along without wild-animal resources. The 25 million Americans who buy licenses to hunt, fish, and trap and those who hunt without license on their own lands and elsewhere include more hunters right now than can find something to shoot at. And the grumble of the disappointed fur trapper is growing louder. In one group, the waterfowl hunters, there has been a particularly steady increase in number since the close of World War II, some 1,725,000 of them having bought $2 migratory-bird hunting stamps in 1950. In Michigan, which leads the list of states in number of hunting licenses sold, the figure for the latter

FIG. 106. Bringing in the kill. Pisgah National Forest, North Carolina. (*Photo by U.S. Forest Service.*)

reached 1,031,035 in 1951, and even small Rhode Island, at the foot of the list, accounted for 11,488.

Original Abundance of Game and Fur Bearers. Of the forms of wild-animal life now commonly hunted and trapped, one reads relatively little in the stories of early abundance. Rather the passenger pigeon, now extinct, and the American bison, found only in specimen herds at present, are cited as examples. Frequently this is done without comment on the question: "Which shall we accommodate, people or wild animals?" For certainly few people could be happy in southeastern Michigan or like territory if the passenger pigeons maintained a hundred roosts in a single tree and nested at one time over a wooded area of 100,000 acres as they are reported to have done. Neither would the farms and ranches of the

Middle and Far West be in existence if the 15 million bison estimated to have constituted the population in colonial days were still roaming at large.

Even the waterfowl of which there are never enough today to satisfy the hunters are said to have occurred in masses of 50,000 on single limited areas of water and may have perplexed our forefathers in their plans for the next grain crop.

Fur-bearing animals of some dozen or more species constituted significant parts of the fur catch as late as 1821 after almost two centuries of

Fig. 107. Geese feeding and flying over cornfield in Tennessee. The power line in the background was not a part of the original scene when migrating birds blackened the sky. (*Photo by Tennessee Valley Authority.*)

trapping by Indians and of trading by the French and British. One early white hunter and trapper in the Upper Peninsula of Michigan has left us as an estimated list of his catches over a lifetime: 100 bears, 1,000 deer, 50 wolves, 500 foxes, 100 raccoons, 25 wildcats, 100 lynx, 150 otters, 600 beavers, 400 fishers, "mink and marten by the thousands and muskrats by the tens of thousands."[2] (Deer hides are included in the early fur lists although used almost exclusively as leather.) All the animals listed are predators except deer, beaver, and muskrat, and only muskrat, mink, and otter persist sparingly in farming localities with marsh areas at present.

[2] Quoted by James K. Jamison in his book, This Ontonagon Country, 3d ed., The Ontonagon Herald Co., Ontonagon, Mich., 1948, p. 32.

Perhaps it is enough, then, to say that no portion of the globe contained more of the useful wild animals than were to be found in what is now the United States. Certainly the traveler and explorer of those early days must have wondered if mankind could ever challenge the complete possession of the land by animals. Indeed it is said that the French and English had no wish to see the land settled so long as the yield of furs from trading with the Indians and the few pioneers constituted a source of easy profit.

But animals are a product of the land, and in spite of much loose talk about multiple use in land management, the production of *one* crop or the engaging in *one* activity must usually dominate. More human encroachment and more intensive growing of grain, hay, tobacco, cotton,

FIG. 108. This fur animal, the skunk, has a lovely coat but a bad reputation as a predator on domestic poultry, and has an odoriferous means of defense. Nevertheless he is a valuable specimen. (*Photo by Rex Gary Schmidt, Fish and Wildlife Service.*)

fruit, truck vegetables, and other cultivated crops mean less wild land, which all but a few game and fur species must have, if they are to prosper. To a less extent also the ranch livestock business invades the natural habitat of big-game animals and larger fur bearers and aggravates, particularly, the problem of winter range for such forms as elk and deer.

And so, if one considers the numbers of hunters and trappers and the values, whatever they may be, of the game and fur animals, the natural-resource problem might be stated: "How to restore and maintain a supply of these animals sufficient in reasonable measure to meet the demand without too much interference with those human activities which conflict with such a program."

It is surprising to find that quite a satisfactory solution to this problem is possible if the expressions "reasonable" and "too much" can be agreed upon. That happy situation has not yet been reached, but the following examples of game and fur-bearing wild-animal resources and their handling will throw light upon the long struggle.

Factors Which Deplete Wild-animal Resources. It seems appropriate just here to consider the reasons for scarcities and for present distributions of game and fur species. Depletion of original stock may be excusable or inexcusable, depending upon whether one thinks of man as just a factor of environment or as the lord of creation. There is not much doubt as to how the average American feels about these alternatives. He would probably list the following as excusable:

Encroachment on wild-animal habitat by settlement, agriculture, successful drainage projects, industry, and transportation
Breaking game laws without getting caught, particularly if the bag or catch is not wasted
Water pollution if his own acts or business causes it or if it seems too expensive in his opinion to abate
Mosquito control attempted in good faith
Natural disasters, such as droughts, floods, blizzards, and fires
The automobile

Still hoping we had picked the average American, he would no doubt list the following as inexcusable:

Market hunting, particularly to supply early slave forces and construction crews
Water pollution, if it was caused by someone else than himself or his business
Overhunting and overtrapping in the past
Badly planned drainage projects
Predation, by animals he does not like
Difficulties and laxity in law enforcement
Use of poison baits or insecticides without assurance that they are harmless to the animals he wants around
Man-caused disasters of which forest and grass fires are the best examples

Each one of these causes, whether excusable on any grounds or not, deserves some explanation. There is not much chance to argue against encroachment features if the expanding economy idea is valid, and most Americans believe that it is and that our standard of living must be steadily improved. Luxury furs and hunting trips are a part of that standard, but they, in turn, can be acquired only by making a living with something extra to spend. New factories, roads, air fields, farms, golf courses, and real-estate subdivisions challenge the right of wild animals to occupy the land, and the owners in turn challenge the hunter in his pursuit of whatever game remains. Encroachment upon habitat is a most serious depleter of game and fur-bearing species.

Sportsmen of the better class are law-abiding and sometimes even militant against the game-law violator, but too common an attitude toward law is that the crime consists of getting caught. Game and trapping laws are hard to enforce, and sometimes the laws themselves are not based on complete knowledge of the need for protection and management of the species concerned. Law violation is a cause of depletion and a serious one.

It was pointed out in the chapter on water that waste transportation is one of the inescapable and important uses of water. Moreover, it is so well established that this use has occurred without general protest or

FIG. 109. This slow-moving "critter" often gets in the way of an automobile. His coat is only moderately valuable as opossum fur. (*Photo by John D. Guthrie, courtesy U.S. Forest Service.*)

regulation until recent years. Pollution may result by way of untreated sewage or of industrial, shipping, and mining wastes, many of which are actual poisons, or (less frequently designated as pollution) of soil washing. Stream and other types of pollution are particularly destructive to fisheries but also affect the fur animals, many of which occupy marsh and stream-bank areas. Waterfowl also suffer through the destruction of food and cover and from actual poisoning.

Anyone who has suffered the tortures of a mosquito-infested area will be likely to believe in heroic methods to abate this nuisance, and yet the oil films, sprays, and other devices used may well make water intolerable to fur animals and to waterfowl, and might on occasion pollute the only source of water available to larger game animals.

The destructiveness of droughts, blizzards, and fires on game and fur-bearing animals is evident not only in their effects on food and cover but in the actual toll of the animals themselves. All forms suffer.

Our average American is likely to consider an automobile a necessity and whatever interferes with its operation a nuisance. Safety in driving usually precludes care to avoid hitting slow-moving or suddenly appearing animals. Rabbits, muskrat, opossum, and skunk are often killed on the highways, and even larger animals get into the list now and then and may wreck the car and the driver as well as themselves. In the neighborhood of and within the national parks of the West, officials make the interesting statement that automobiles have the combined forces of bobcats, coyotes, and foxes beaten in the toll taken of small mammals. Anyone

FIG. 110. The coyote is an outcast and is generally considered a predator. He does however contribute something to the control of rodents on the Western range. (*Photo by National Park Service.*)

who travels will remember pavements strewn with mangled woodchucks or marmots, squirrels, chipmunks, jack rabbits, and cottontail rabbits.

Market hunting is universally outlawed in this country but was probably a principal cause of depletion of birds and the larger game animals. To a greater extent than our American can imagine, the meat fed to early slave labor was usually wild, and the buffalo should be credited with a considerable part in the building of the transcontinental railroads. The size and weight of the buffalo made mass killing of these food animals for workers a regular occupation around the construction camps.

Mountain lions, foxes, wolves, mink, and bears take their toll of their game and fur animal brothers and are particularly severe on the young. These predators, however, do not constitute an important factor of depletion and are themselves a part of the fur and game resources.

Drainage projects are not always undertaken with full knowledge of the soils to be reclaimed or the full effects of lowering water levels over large areas. Waterfowl and fur animals such as the muskrat are frequently, thus, robbed of necessary conditions for life and reproduction. Drainage for mosquito control may produce similar results.

Use of the poison baits and insecticides may bring about the death of large numbers of birds and rabbits instead of the pest species for which they were intended. This is not, however, a very important factor of depletion.

Man-caused disasters are rare except in the case of forest fires, which are obvious destroyers of food, cover, and animals. Controlled use of fire and cover types resulting from fires may, on the other hand, benefit certain game animals eventually.

Finally overhunting and overtrapping in the past should be set down as one of the greatest of depleting factors. Of course it overlaps market hunting and has been most common in areas where people live off the land rather than raise enough for their needs.

Big-game Animals. Deer, elk, antelope, moose, bear, and mountain lion (also called panther and cougar) are the big animals pursued by the hunter at present in this country. By far the most plentiful of these are deer, and so naturally they are the most commonly hunted. Those herds persisting or restored in the northeastern part of the country and extending through the Lake states of Michigan, Wisconsin, and Minnesota range over forested and cutover lands and spread to some extent over farms and orchards. They "yard up" in winter, concentrating in cedar swamps if available, and they have their troubles as their populations increase and browse species become overgrazed. Restrictive hunting laws have usually spared too many does and resulted in a deer population beyond the carrying capacity of the land in winter. In milder climate such as that found in the Piedmont and mountain country of the South, the problem of food is not serious (1) because the population of deer is small as the result of years of overhunting and (2) because the winter-feeding problem does not bring about destructive concentrations. In the Western timbered plateau and mountains, deer find refuge and food during the warmer months in the high areas but must seek the foothills when heavy snow comes. This is painfully true of elk also. Crowded out of their winter range of open grasslands by fenced ranches, they have reached numbers which are not yet held down appreciably by hunting or systematic slaughter. Antelope seek more open and usually lower country and must win their battle with the fences or die.

In all these situations the history of the herds and their management is similar. First there is a period of heavy depletion from overhunting. Then there occurs a long stretch of scarcity of animals for the hunter whose demands eventually bring about expensive and usually fruitless attempts to restock the areas artificially or to use restrictive measures only. Finally, in desperation, more range is made available at public expense and food and cover conditions are improved to care for a limited game population. The latter can be achieved only by population control with kill quotas and flexible regulation on season, sex, and number allowed to each hunter. What needs to be done can be determined by research. How to get it done is another matter running squarely into pressure for questionable practices in order to keep plenty of animals immediately available to

FIG. 111. Elk on San Juan National Forest, Colorado. This large-game animal has lost much of its winter range to ranching operations and presents a problem of overpopulation. (*Photo by U.S. Forest Service.*)

hunters and into political and law-enforcement difficulties of administration.

Hunters probably bag bear more often when hunting deer or elk than when on organized bear hunts. Bear have had so little legal protection (outside the national parks) that no complaint of scarcity as game animals is heard. Rather, the predatory and marauding habits of these interesting animals often lead mankind close to practices of persecution.

Hunters do go on trips particularly to get mountain lion, and it is likely that these stealthy predators will not always be available to sportsmen. The livestock industry will see to that.

Small Nonmigratory Game Animals. Quail, grouse, pheasants, wild turkeys, rabbits, and squirrels are sought principally by the small-game hunter and constitute the bulk of the take in farming country. Both open fields and wooded areas are essential for these forms, and brushy vine-grown fence rows are especially needed as cover and protected travel ways. Except for the nut- and edible seed-bearing species, trees are less essential to these animals than shrubs and young forest reproduction which comes into open spaces and edges. Logs and hollow trees are used for dens and nests, and brush piles after logging get plenty of use by rabbits. Enforced seasonal and bag limits have put these game resources in less danger than big-game species, although there is much speculation over population cycles. These have not yet had sufficient study.

Fig. 112. Rabbits need places to hide and nest. This one is on the Santa Rita Range Reserve, New Mexico. (*Photo by U.S. Forest Service.*)

Migratory Birds. By far the most talked-of game species are ducks, geese, and other migratory waterfowl. Many of our song and insectivorous birds are also migratory, but few figure in the hunter's plans. Migratory waterfowl have no unusual food, cover, and breeding-ground requirements except that these essentials must be spread out over long fly ways, and lack of them has put the birds at the mercy of habitat changes and of hunters who were abroad before essential restrictions were in force. Even today one seldom hears of a hunter coming home with one duck. Figures obtained by the Fish and Wildlife Service however in 1949 indicated an average daily bag of 1.9 birds to the hunter who was out on the average of 5 days a season and who, with his kind, accounted for a total kill of 17 million waterfowl. This total, involving principally mallard, pintail, and black ducks, amounted to about 27 per cent of the birds in the Pacific fly way, 22 per cent in the Central, and 10 per cent in the Atlantic.[3]

Improved transportation, ingenuity in the manufacture and sale of arms and ammunition, increasing numbers of hunters, baiting, drainage, and other types of habitat destruction, diseases such as botulism and fowl cholera, water pollution, and just plain overhunting within and without the law—all these have had their part in reducing the numbers of migratory birds and on the problem of keeping the present-day hunters happy.

FIG. 113. Muskrat in spillway is a part of the objective of an Illinois soil conservation farm plan. His kind are the principal producers of fur in the Middle West. (*Photo by Soil Conservation Service.*)

That this practice has not ended is attested by the fact of the arrest and conviction of three persons in California in 1949 who possessed and were endeavoring to sell 800 wild ducks. This number is the equivalent of the combined daily bag of 200 sportsmen.[4]

And while the hunters worry about ducks and geese, those who love the antics and calls of such nongame waterfowl as herons and loons know

[3] Wildlife Conservation Activities of the Federal Government 1949, Hearings before the Sub-Committee to Investigate Wildlife Conservation, Committee on Expenditures in the Executive Departments, U.S. Senate, 81st Cong., 2d sess., 1950, p. 3.

[4] *Ibid.*

that these forms also have their feeding, hiding, and breeding troubles. Smaller forms, either of waterfowl or of songbirds, appear to have fewer difficulties although certain of them, such as snipe, curlew, meadowlark, woodcock, and doves, have suffered in the past from overshooting.

Fur Animals. Some thirty animals are taken for furs in the United States proper, not counting as more than one animal the various species of any particular form. Among these the most frequently captured include muskrat, raccoon, mink, beaver, fox, skunk, otter, marten, fisher, weasel, rabbit, hare, coyote, wolf, opossum, badger, wildcat, lynx, and bear. In

FIG. 114. Beaver at his "house" in Rocky Mountain National Park. This interesting and valuable fur animal needs waterway and the sort of forest cover that will serve as food. (*Photo by National Park Service.*)

addition to these, Alaska yields furs from seal and blue fox principally.

The fur bearers as a class have a fine, soft undercoat for warmth as well as a crop of longer guard hairs useful for shedding water. These hairs are plucked or sheared when the hides are processed as furs. Some furs, such as those of rabbits and hares, mat easily and are more useful for the manufacture of felt of the sort used in hats. Other furs are not subject to matting and find their way into fur garments and trimmings. Once used extensively for male garments, furs are now more often luxury items in coats, capes, and separate pieces for women. Prices vary with style, but some idea of persisting values may be obtained from the fact that Alaska, purchased in 1867 from Russia for $7,200,000, had produced up to 1947 fur crops worth

$100,000,000. Two public auctions of Alaska furs, held in the fiscal year 1952 (July 1, 1951, to June 30, 1952), yielded $4,044,324.[5]

The muskrat, a small water-loving vegetarian, is the most commonly captured fur animal in the United States proper. It inhabits most of North America except the Southeast coast and is of one species only save for the Louisiana and Texas forms. The muskrat inhabits stream banks, and builds "houses" or "cabins" consisting of cone-shaped piles of cattail stalks and other vegetation, the tops extending a foot or two above water level in swamps and shallow waters. Three to five and sometimes as many as eight young are produced in a litter. Good muskrat localities will yield five peltries (skins) to the acre each year. The muskrat's enemies are the mink and the otter, both valuable fur bearers themselves. Throughout the northern part of the Middle West, particularly, muskrats are trapped in the swampland on and surrounding marginal farms, and the crop is counted on to furnish a part of the yearly farm income.

Raccoon and mink rank next in number taken annually in the United States and along with otter and beaver require much the same waterway habitat as supports their more plentiful neighbor the muskrat. The raccoons, however, use hollow trees rather than waterfront accommodations for housing. The other fur bearers listed are likely to range over wider territory. Seals, a distinctive and important source of fur, are migratory animals herding a part of the year in the Pribiloff Islands, off Alaska, and are not subject to trapping under license. Their management is discussed on p. 260.

Managing Wild-animal Resources

Conserving the wild-animal resources of the country is a matter of understanding and management. Excellent progress has been made in both directions in late years. Every wild animal experiences stages in its development where it needs help in terms of food, shelter, protection, or some other service amounting to manipulation of environment or assuring temporary freedom from capture. Providing this service to wild animals, based on knowledge of life history and habits, is the business of management. Discussions of it will appear in the literature under such headings as Game Management, Wildlife Management, and Fisheries Management. Certainly considerations of cover, food, and water figure heavily in the picture, while restriction of the kill and controlled increase in the take of surplus animals are matters of cost and management which are difficult to enforce and which call for flexibility in policy. Ownership of wild animals, residing as it does in the states, complicates the business of management, because the animals furnishing some 75 per cent of the game and fur harvest in the United States spend most of their lives on farms. If the

[5] *Annual Report of the Secretary of the Interior*, 1952, p. 315.

public assumes the task, public agencies must work on private land. If the private owner takes over, he is dealing with animals which he does not own.

Specific Practices in Wild-animal Management. *Protection.* Historically, the attempts to conserve wild-animal resources have usually started with regulation of the kill, and this has usually meant restrictions in the form of laws or administrative regulations affecting bag limits on number which any hunter or trapper may take in a day or season; sex, particularly as regards big-game animals and certain game birds; age and size; season; time of day; arms, traps, and other gear; length of time the captured animal may be in possession; sale, shipment, and importation of game; and permitted hunting, trapping, and fishing areas. All these restrictions are designed to protect animals from constant pursuit and capture by men. Properly worded and enforced, many of the regulations have worked well, but at best their principal positive effect is to give the animals a chance to catch their breath, breed, and grow without being under continual bombardment. The restrictive approach to conservation here is largely negative. Improvement of environmental conditions in such an approach is ignored.

Improvement of Cover. Wild animals require many types and arrangements of vegetation for purposes of shelter and hiding while nesting, breeding, feeding, and even migrating. Edges of forests, marshes, and waterways are most commonly needed on wild land. Added to these, on cultivated land, are brush- and vine-grown fence rows, unharvested patches of grain and hay, shocked corn, brush piles, irregularly planted patches of shrubs and evergreens, and reflooded areas which have once been drained and abandoned. These happy (for the animals) combinations of cover are not always sightly. Frequently their maintenance is contrary to clean farming, roadside maintenance, and the development of golf courses, landing fields, and other large space requirements. Here as in all conservation efforts, the questions of priorities arise. Only by the most careful planning can the needs of animals, space users, intensive agriculture, and sometimes even forestry be reconciled. Actual planting of trees, shrubs, and vines for cover as well as food purposes has been promoted successfully for the past few years on farms throughout the eastern half of the country. This practice was undertaken first through cooperation of states, farm owners, and sportsmen's groups, with the universities and state colleges doing much of the necessary research work. The plans worked out by the soil conservation districts also include frequently a section on improvement of food and cover resources.

Improvement of Food Conditions. While food and cover problems overlap and are tied in to control of game populations, the question of food for wild animals is perhaps of greatest popular interest. Starvation among big-game animals serves to dramatize the problems, and heavy winter storms are bound to interest large numbers of people in artificial methods of supplying food such as scattering hay for big game and grain for game birds and songbirds. Not so well understood is the constant necessity of tailoring animal population to the food supply and of acquiring and improving wild lands to support the number of animals demanded by

FIG. 115. Teeth marks of elk on quaking aspen. Rocky Mountain National Park. An indication of shortage of food. (*Photo by National Park Service.*)

hunters. Efforts at improving food conditions vary all the way from raising hay for Wyoming elk and synchronizing cedar logging with season of greatest need for deer browse in the Lake states to planting of food patches of soybeans, berry bushes, and small grains or influencing farmers to leave unharvested crops. The judicious use of fire is said to have helped the quail in the South and is finding favor elsewhere as a stimulator of the growth of food-bearing vegetation. Putting the brakes on indiscriminate drainage so that marsh food plants as well as water levels can be maintained is a good stroke of management applying to fur bearers. It may be generally said, and the statement defended, that artificial supplying of food to wild animals is less successful in the long run than controlling population and extending natural food areas. In either case a vast amount of information on food habits, populations, and carrying capacity of the land must be constantly sought through research.

Assuring a Water Supply. Aside from the indispensability of water for waterfowl and marsh-inhabiting mammals in the humid portion of the

Fig. 116. Water is essential to game management. This marsh on a Western national forest serves beaver, waterfowl, and big game. (*Photo by U.S. Forest Service.*)

country, upland game birds and big-game animals must have water provided in arid regions. Thus the Chukar partridge introduced from Hungary and first released in central Nevada appears to be well adapted to hot desert areas but must have water developments to assure survival. Nevada sportsmen and the state game officials are cooperating with the Bureau of Land Management in water development for these birds. Similarly, the states of California, Arizona, and New Mexico have constructed numerous quail-watering projects under permit from the Bureau of Land Management. These facilities consist of small fenced areas with paved catchment basins for impounding small quantities of water for game birds, principally quail and doves. Some effort is made to locate stock-watering developments so as to serve the needs of range game animals.

Obtaining Censuses of Wild Animals. It is obvious that any allowable kill of wild animals should be based on the numbers constituting the resource at any time and place. But animals do not care to be interviewed, and ingenious methods of counting have to be worked out. Actual counts of both big game and smaller forms are made by sending trained observers over the land afoot in systematically covered routes, by supplementing such efforts through using well-trained dogs, by airplane surveys, and by analysis of figures on the season's licensed kill. Censusing is, of course, a kind of research and an important one.

FIG. 117. It is 4 A.M. on the Pisgah National Forest, in North Carolina. These hunters are being issued numbers and safety red shawls in a controlled deer hunt. (*Photo by U.S. Forest Service.*)

Controlled Hunts to Reduce Overpopulations. A depenable census will sometimes indicate need for reduction of populations of big-game animals, and the controlled hunt will frequently accomplish the necessary kill. It works like this: The number to be removed is decided upon. A hunt for which drawings will be held is publicly advertised, or dependable licensed sportsmen are notified. An appropriate number of names are drawn, the fortunate hunters report to a specified entrance point at a given date, are checked in, transported to various points in the area, and picked up with their kill later in the day. Successful hunts of this sort have been held in recent years for deer on the Pisgah National Forest in North Carolina, on the San Andreas Mountain Game Range in New Mexico, and in Plumas County, California.

Providing Special Refuges and Preserves. In addition to the closed-season regulations, wild animals need areas in which they may be unmolested even during open season, and this is particularly true for migratory forms requiring rest "stations" during travel. The larger refuges provide safe breeding grounds and serve as areas of supply from which the excess numbers "spill over" to territory where they may be hunted. Refuges may be Federal, state, or private as far as ownership and management is concerned and may vary in size from a million acres to less than one acre. National and state parks serve as animal refuges indirectly, and even a cemetery or a small posted estate may make a real contribution to continuing supplies of wild animals.

Refuges and "sanctuaries," as certain of them are called, should not be confused with game preserves, which are increasing in number and are operated as paid hunting enterprises. Preserves may consist either of rented land managed by some gun club for its own members or of large areas privately owned by clubs or individuals and closed to all but club members or paid guests, Any efforts to increase the wild-animal population other than waterfowl, on preserves, must be undertaken at private expense and is consequently likely to be neglected. On the other hand the gun pressure inside the preserves is well distributed even though little contribution to the general hunting situation of the nearby territory results. To get around the unfairness of a preserve system to the less fortunate hunter, some of the states provide extensive public hunting grounds, largely through the use of Federal grant-in-aid funds.

Artificial Propagation and Restocking. To the layman, one of the most obvious ways to keep up the supply of wild animals seems to be rearing them artificially on game farms and using them to restock areas where they are scarce or absent. Frequently it will be contended that some form, plentiful in another country, should be introduced. So strong is the sentiment for introduction and restocking that many of the states operate game farms at great expense. The most common effort is to increase the numbers of upland game birds, the quail, prairie chicken, and wild turkey being representative of the native species used and the Hungarian partridge and the ring-necked pheasant of the exotic forms. Perhaps the greatest success has been achieved with pheasant, particularly in farming areas of the Middle West. Many local gun clubs are interested in their own hatching and release operations. But we have much to learn if propagation and restocking from game farms are to reach a justifiable stage in this country. Meanwhile, we may be thankful that the introduction of exotic species is sharply regulated by Federal law; such important nuisances as the starling, English sparrow, and European carp have taught us a lesson.

Closely related to and somewhat more successful than the game-farm restocking devices are the projects of transferring surplus animals from one locality to another where environmental conditions are promising. The reestablished deer herds of Vermont and Pennsylvania are successful examples, and the moving of beaver and wild turkeys in various localities has given good results. Strangely enough, the National Park Service has made a number of "plantings" of wild animals and appears to consider the procedure entirely within its policy of presenting the plant and animal life in a manner opposed to artificially managed relationships. Thus a small planting of three or four elk about 1925 in the Blue Ridge Parkway of Virginia and North Carolina was reported to have increased to about thirty-five adults and five calves by 1950. Seventy-five of the Yellowstone

FIG. 118. Fox on Datil National Forest, New Mexico. Trapped for fur and as a predator, this fellow is still a valuable individual in game management, keeping down the diseased and crippled of other species. (*Photo by U.S. Forest Service.*)

antelope herd also were removed about 1950 to the Theodore Roosevelt Memorial Park in North Dakota and twelve bucks released in Wind Cave National Park, South Dakota. Furthermore, plantings of antelope were made in Big Bend National Park, Texas, in 1947–1948, and plantings of bighorn sheep are contemplated. Of forty-four deer removed from Grand Canyon National Park in 1952, thirty-nine were released in good condition at the Santa Rita Mountain "transplant site."

Control of Predators. It is quite natural for disappointed sportsmen or for habitual lawbreakers to rationalize a dwindling game-animal supply by blaming the situation on some predator. Enthusiasm for bounty laws, crow shoots, coyote drives, and other attacks on suspected predators is well known in almost any locality where hunting is an established sport. The marauding of certain wild animals on poultry and young livestock affords further reason to pursue and annihilate all predators whether or not they are proved guilty. Wolves, mountain lion, coyotes, and bears are definitely a problem to the livestock ranchers and to hunters of big game, and some evidence piles up against hawks, owls, foxes, skunks, and turtles for destroying domestic poultry and the eggs and young of upland game and waterfowl. Where these sorts of predation get out of hand, there is justification for the employment of paid trappers working for public agencies and for including predators as a part of the sportsman's quarry. But the predators have their uses, and they are frequently persecuted. While they do kill numbers of desirable animals, it is scientifically established that they perform useful services in capturing diseased and crippled specimens and in devouring insects and undesirable rodents and reptiles. What predators actually devour can be determined by examination of stomach contents after they are killed. It is well established that of the crow's diet of animal matter, which is about one-fourth of the total, about two-thirds consists of crop-destroying beetles, grasshoppers, locusts, crickets, and other insects. Four Michigan crows when killed were found to have been digesting collectively 85 June bugs (May beetles), 72 wireworms, 123 grasshoppers, and 438 small caterpillars.[6] This chalks up a pretty good service record. Analysis of 2,222 coyote stomachs in California recently indicated the following food breakdown: rodents, 26.5 per cent; birds, 4.6 per cent; plant material, 4.0 per cent; and miscellaneous items, 10.5 per cent.[7] This is not too damning a disclosure, and even if it were worse it is well to bear in mind that fraud, failure, and even harm to the desirable species frequently characterize bounty-payment systems and that paid professional trappers are more successful and more economical. In using the latter, such results of research as are available can be employed to see that the control methods really effect control.

Research in Wild-animal Management. Knowledge of the life histories of all wild animals, beneficial and predatory, is indispensable to good management of wild-animal resources. In addition to such knowledge, managers must understand feeding and breeding habits, cover and water requirements, predator, disease, and disaster relationships, actual populations and their fluctuations, and the long-run effects of laws and regulations covering various species. Such knowledge cannot be picked out of the air. It must be won by patient and skillful research and, what is even more difficult, passed out and "sold" to the hunter, trapper, fisherman, farmer, general public, and even to natural-resource administrators

[6] Black, C. T., Ebony Robin Hood, *Michigan Conservation*, **22**:13, March–April, 1953.

[7] *Pittman-Robertson Quarterly*, vol. 13, January, 1953, for July–October quarter 1952, p. 16.

themselves. Fortunately, interest in such research is high in this country, and funds from Federal, state, and private agencies support nearly a score of research units at as many state agricultural colleges. These in particular are maintained in cooperation with the Fish and Wildlife Service of the Department of the Interior and the Wildlife Management Institute, a private nonprofit enterprise. In addition, graduate studies at a number of universities, usually where wildlife management is taught as a part of a natural-resource curriculum, attack important problems each year. Numerous important studies have been made over the past 50

FIG. 119. Fox farm at Lake City, Minn. Fox farming is a risky but in some localities a well-established business. (*Photo by Fish and Wildlife Service.*)

years by the Federal bureaus concerned with wild-animal resources, and fortunately again, these have covered more than just the game and fur-bearing species.

Fur Farming. The actual husbandry and systematic breeding and pelting of fur animals such as silver foxes, mink, chinchilla rabbits, and to a lesser extent and by less intensive methods, muskrat, constitute a considerable industry. The annual yield now amounts to hundreds of thousands of valuable pelts. Such fur-farming procedure is a far cry from usual wild-animal management practices. It can be considered as conserving natural resources only in the sense that it helps to supply fur to a market which must otherwise be served by hard-pressed wild stock.

Federal Agencies and Wild Animals. In addition to the Fish and Wildlife Service in the Department of the Interior (a bureau made up by combining the earlier Bureau of Biological Survey in the Department of Agriculture and the Bureau of Fisheries in the Department of Commerce), some four other bureaus are concerned with wild-animal resources. In the Department of the Interior, the National Park Service is charged, among other duties, with the protection of wild-animal forms in the parks for their educational and spectacle values, and the Bureau of Land Management must deal with the conflicts between livestock grazing and wild-animal occupancy on the Taylor Grazing Districts. The

FIG. 120. Bull elk on winter feed ground, Yellowstone National Park. (*Photo by Joe Joffe, courtesy National Park Service.*)

Forest Service in the Department of Agriculture in managing the more than 150 national forests finds wild animals on its domain, both desirable and undesirable, including about one-third of the big-game population of the United States, and this bureau must reconcile other land uses with those serving the game and fur species. Also this agency must to some extent service a vast army of hunters every year, estimated at 2,030,000 in 1950, and help to enforce the game laws. In the Department of Agriculture, too, are the Soil Conservation Service, interested in assisting farmers to make the most of wild-animal resources in their soil conservation districts and farm plans, and the Bureau of Animal Industry, concerned with wild-animal diseases and parasites. Besides all these the Department of State is called upon to negotiate treaties covering international aspects of wild-animal–resource administration.

Private Agencies Concerned with Wild-animal Resources. There are probably more than a thousand local rod and gun clubs under various designations which concern themselves with the promotion of better hunting and fishing. A considerable number of them are seriously engaged in conserving the resources which serve them, through connection with national organizations. These in turn influence legislation both directly and through their cooperation with state fish and game agencies. But before there were any national organizations, state groups of private citizens

FIG. 121. Rocky Mountain goat at lick in Glacier National Park. (*Photo by John C. Phillips, courtesy National Park Service.*)

constituted the "game commissions" in Delaware, North Carolina, and South Carolina, and these groups were active not only in obtaining legislation but in enforcing it. Among the early groups were the Massachusetts Fish and Game Protective Association, organized in 1874; the Delaware Game Protective Association, incorporated in 1879; the first Audubon Society in New York, 1886; the League of American Sportsmen, 1898; and The American Game Protective Association, 1900. The two latter groups were powerful in the legislative field for many years previous to 1925, and the National Association of Audubon Societies which in 1902 grew out of the earlier New York group is still active in the protection of nongame species and in the promotion of popular education.

Among the private national groups active in wild-animal conservation at present besides the National Association of Audubon Societies are the following: The Izaak Walton League of America, organized in 1922 and particularly militant on pollution control, in opposition to high dams which it feels are unjustified economically, and in promoting acquisition of wildlife refuges and inviolable wilderness areas; the North American National Wildlife Conference called first by President Frankin D. Roosevelt in 1935 and combining in an annual meeting all wild-animal interests; the Wild Life Management Institute which operates somewhat as a foundation, promoting education and research; the National Wildlife Federation, a publishing and educational group; and the International Association of Game, Fish, and Conservation Commissioners. The American Forestry Association should also be mentioned for its publicizing and support of legislation affecting wild-animal conservation.

How Wild-animal Administration Is Financed. One of the great accomplishments of game-conservation agencies is the firm establishment of the license fee as a source of funds for administering game resources. Laws covering this feature have long been in effect in all the states, and additional revenue on a Federal level has come from the Migratory Bird Hunting Stamp Act of 1934. Under this law hunters of migratory waterfowl buy a stamp which is attached to their state license. Recently the fee has been raised from $1 to $2. The revenue is used for acquiring and administering refuges and for research. Still another Federal source of funds comes from the Pittman-Robertson Act of 1937. Under this act, amounts each fiscal year "equal to the revenue accruing . . . from the tax imposed by the . . . Revenue Act of 1932 on firearms, shells and cartridges," are set aside to constitute "the Federal aid to wildlife-restoration fund." This fund is allotted to the states on the basis of area and on number of paid hunting licenses issued and may be used for acquisition of land, construction of facilities, and research related to wild-animal restoration. A similar act in the fisheries field, known as the Dingell-Johnson law, was passed by the Congress in 1950. This law makes available to the states on a matching basis, the monies raised from the excise tax on the sale of fishing tackle. It may be used for such purposes as the purchase of public fishing sites, fisheries research, and the improvement of environmental conditions. Occasionally private funds from individuals or groups are sought to cover such things as emergency winter feeding or the buying of some special area for which public funds are not immediately available. The conservation of wild-animal resources, however, is not entirely self-supporting, and both state and Federal appropriations are required. Examples of special Federal authorizations in this direction include the Upper Mississippi River Wild Life and Fish Refuge Act of 1924, the Bear River (Utah) Migratory Bird Refuge Act of 1928, the General Migratory Bird Refuge Act of 1929 as amended in 1935, and the Cheyenne Bottoms (Kansas) Migratory Bird Refuge Act of 1930.

Important Legislation Affecting Wild Animals. In addition to a great number of regulatory acts passed by the various states in the past 50 years, attention should be called to the following Federal laws:

The Lacey Act of 1900, which extended certain powers of the Secretary of Agriculture and contained regulations on interstate and foreign commerce in wild birds and other animals. The enforcement features of this act were strengthened by amendment in 1935.

The Migratory Bird Treaty with Great Britain (on behalf of Canada), signed in Washington and after ratification proclaimed Dec. 8, 1916. This treaty or "convention" lists game, insectivorous, and other nongame birds, provides for close seasons which put an end to spring shooting, and agrees that legislation for carrying out all terms will be sought by the contracting powers in their own countries.

The Migratory Bird Treaty Act of 1918, giving full effect to the treaty. A similar one was enacted by the Canadian Parliament in 1917. The validity of the latter and the constitutionality of the former have been established by court decisions.[8]

The Migratory Bird Treaty with Mexico, signed in Mexico City and after ratification proclaimed Mar. 15, 1937. Provisions of this treaty are similar to the one with Canada, plus the interesting prohibition of hunting from aircraft. Appropriate amendment of the Migratory Bird Treaty Act of 1918 was approved in 1936, pending ratification of the treaty with Mexico.

The Wildlife Refuge Exchange Act of 1935, providing for the acquisition of refuge lands privately owned in exchange for other Federal lands or products from Federal lands, when the public interest will thus be served.

The National Forest Fish and Game Sanctuary Act of 1934, granting authority to the President to establish refuges by proclamation within the national forests with the approval of state legislatures in the states involved. This act is important because of the vast area of the national forests and their wild-animal populations.

The Wildlife Coordination Act of 1934 as amended in 1946, designed to reconcile objectives of various bureaus in the construction of flood control and power and irrigation works in any river valley and recognizing that there is plenty of chance to interfere with the best interests of wild-animal resources. This situation received the attention of the Congress as early as 1934, when the so-called Wildlife Coordination Act was first

[8] *State of Missouri v. Ray P. Holland,* 252 U.S. 416; *United States v. Lumpkin,* 276 Fed. 580; *King v. Russell C. Clark,* Supreme Court of Prince Edward Island, Michaelmas term, 1920.

approved. It provided that consideration should be given to the effects on wild-animal life of the construction of public works and that, before construction, the bureaus concerned with wild-animal resources should be consulted. Unfortunately the law does not require the construction agencies to hold up or to abandon projects. Some progress was achieved in attempting to reconcile the operation (rather than the construction) of the Bonneville and Grand Coulee Dams with the conservation of the salmon resources of the Columbia River, but in general the results of the law have been disappointing. Since the amendment of the act in 1946,

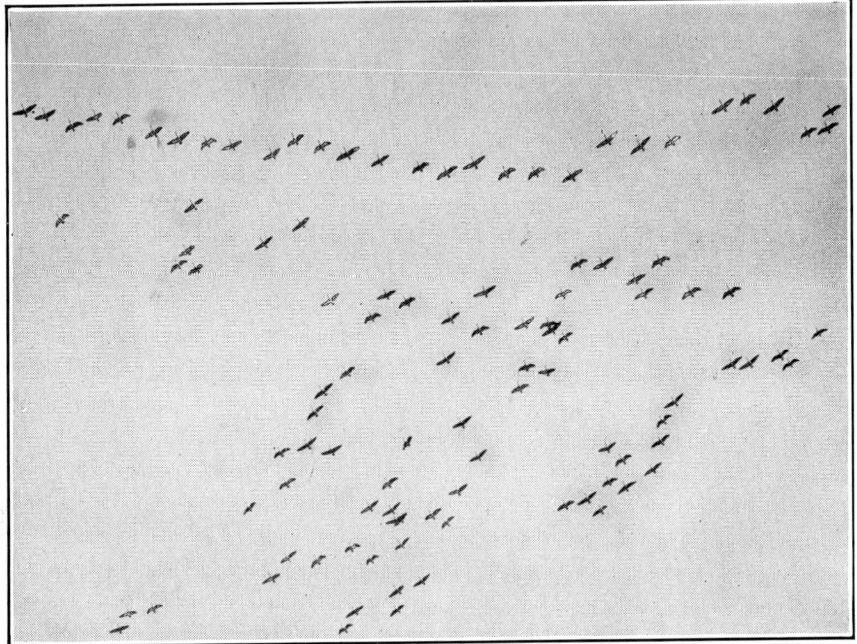

Fig. 122. The Migratory Bird Treaty Act of 1918 protects birds such as these Canada geese. (*Photo by Paul A. Moore, courtesy Tennessee Conservation Department.*)

interdepartmental committees have been set up in the Columbia, Missouri, and other river valleys, but they have power only to advise. The Bureau of Reclamation in the Department of the Interior and the Office of Engineers in the Department of Defense, which are the construction agencies, usually dominate the committees, and the rush of their interests allows little time for study and adjustment of wild-animal resources to the vast changes which occur with the construction of power, irrigation, and flood-control works.

However, among the 1,000 water-use projects examined since 1946, by the Fish and Wildlife Service, a number have received the attention of the Congress. Among them are the following: Grays Lake and the Bureau of Reclamation's Palisades Reservoir in Idaho. The latter, once a superb wildlife area, has experienced since 1925 a drastic shrink in wild-animal habitat through the lowering of lake levels by diversions for irrigation. Recommendations for restoration and management of this area as a Federal-state project have been made, and legislation to that effect has been introduced. Purchase of flood-water rights of the grasslands on a similar area located in the Central Valley Project of California threatens a considerable area of adjacent waterfowl habitat unless water supplies are reserved from project use. Here a joint report by the Fish and Wildlife

FIG. 123. Chipmunk—the bane of the camper's life but an interesting and amusing form that deserves protection.

Service, the Bureau of Reclamation, and the California Department of Fish and Game recommends water development for waterfowl management in the lower San Joaquin Valley. Should the Congress approve the recommendations for these two areas, they will represent the first clear-cut cases when allocations of water for wild-animal life are being planned in connection with reclamation projects.[9]

Certain Important Miscellaneous Federal Acts Affecting the Conservation of Wild-animal Resources. Penalties are set in special laws as follows:

[9] Dieffenbach, Rudolph, River Basin Activities of the U.S. Fish and Wildlife Service, address before Western Association of State Game and Fish Commissioners, Glacier National Park, June 15, 1952 (mimeographed), U.S. Department of the Interior.

capturing or disturbing wild animals, nests, eggs, or Federal property on refuges, act of March, 1909, as amended 1924; assaulting Federal Officers and resisting arrest, act of 1934 as amended 1936; importation, unlawfully, of plumage, skins, and game, Tariff Act of 1930; setting fires on the public domain, act of 1909. Certain treaties affecting whales and seals, both sea-going mammals, are discussed under Fisheries on pages 257 to 260.

Neglected Wild Animals. The conservation, or even the control, of certain of our wild-animal forms receives relatively little official attention

Fig. 124. Young great gray owl, a controller of rodents. (*Photo by O. J. Murie, courtesy Fish and Wildlife Service.*)

in this country, and yet a majority of our citizens are not hunters, trappers, or fishermen and may be much more interested in this miscellaneous neglected group. The list will include songbirds, reptiles, scavenger species such as gulls and buzzards, and certain of the harmless insects, some of which are of great beauty, unusual forms such as armadillos, alligators, porcupines, prairie dogs, field mice, jack rabbits, and lizards, ferrets, pack rats, bats, eagles, condors, and even horses and burros that have gone wild over the years. What a motley parade they make! They are here listed unsystematically with the purpose of calling attention to their number, variety, and difficulty of classification. (The reader is spared a separate discussion of fleas, bedbugs, cockroaches, lice, ants, flies, rats, mice, and other of the accursed "wild animals" but not because they are not wild.)

Aside from the more common songbirds, snakes, turtles, and very small mammals, about the only place the general public sees many of the forms mentioned here is in a museum, a zoo, or a bird store. And yet they are all a part of the natural scene, and many of them are parts that we should not lose. Their services cannot be appraised in definite material terms, their nuisance characteristics are hardly greater than those of their game and fur-bearing brothers, and they have to depend on their Audubon Society and other nature-loving friends. But they repay with antics, color, movement, song, dance, roar, and scream, reminding us that this is a living world. One of their strongholds is the national parks, another the small public and private nature sanctuaries maintained under dozens of designations. Still another is found in the thousands of back-yard feeding stations for birds. Laws, too, are of some help, but in most states protective legislation concerns itself with the more commonly known game species.

The Future of Wild-animal Resources

As far as natural resources are concerned in any culture, their conservation is a matter of conscious or unconscious decision on priorities. In terms of modern technological development, the extension of a city or an industrial area may appear to be more urgent than maintaining forest, vacant land, or even farming areas which would support wild animals. When the chance arises to raise cash crops by draining a swamp rich in wild-animal resources, the animal life may seem unimportant. And certainly the impoundment of water for the various defensible purposes of power, irrigation, flood control, or even municipal water supply may mean the doom of many animal forms whose favorite habitat will be buried under water. Similar alternative situations could be multiplied almost without limit. A blunt query, "What do you want, payrolls or fish?" was reported during a recent state campaign against industrial stream pollution. That is oversimplification at its worst, but the rejoinder might well be, "What will it cost to have both?" A lot of people in this richest country in the whole world are asking just that, which seems to prophesy a few good breaks for the animals.

The Need for Understanding. Many of our mistakes in managing natural resources can be blamed on ignorance both of facts and of their significance. Some of the well-known exaggerations of fishermen, bear hunters, and even of amateur research men suggest that, after all, the term "true facts" in the vernacular of the advertising people may have its uses. Surely wider public understanding of the things discussed briefly so far in this chapter is to be hoped for and cannot but be helpful in achieving successful management of wild-animal resources. But how can such knowledge be made common property?

First of all there is no substitute for public-school education even if it goes no deeper into wild-animal conservation than elementary courses in nature study or, at most, courses in high-school biology. Where the public-school systems recognize the value of translating such courses into the language and principles of wild-animal conservation, there is a tremendous start on educating the public. Such effort is increasingly widespread as public-school teachers in science, vocational training, and the social studies become equipped and interested themselves. Of all natural

FIG. 125. Egrets in flight over the rooking east of Okeechobee, Fla. (*Photo by Hugo H. Schroder, courtesy American Forests.*)

resources, too, animals have perhaps the strongest appeal to children. A National Committee on Policies in Conservation Education has operated for several years past in promoting teacher training and introducing conservation slants into the fields of secondary education mentioned. More and more courses in conservation of natural resources are becoming available to undergraduate college students. Few of these in other than preprofessional programs are required, but they are popular and widely elected. The matter presented on wild animals is usually an important feature. Graduate work in forty or more institutions offers opportunity for developing professional technicians, teachers, and administrators in the wild-animal resource field. The total college crop, undergraduate and graduate, is, however, relatively small and serves only to leaven the vast public whose support must be won.

The task of educating the public outside the schools and colleges is by far the most difficult. It requires the use of every device of communication. Here is a list of the facilities now used to do the job and, in some instances, to grind a business ax at the same time: the sportsmen's and a few of the trade associations with their magazines, news releases, efforts to influence legislation, public meetings, various cooperative projects with public agencies, and in rare instances, their codes of outdoor behavior for their members; the considerable group of outdoor writers who have their special pages or columns in all the leading newspapers and who

Fig. 126. Spring peeper—one of the dwarf tree frogs. (*Photo by American Museum of Natural History, courtesy American Forests.*)

have their own organization; the variously sponsored radio and television programs which vary all the way from bedtime stories to popularized reports on the latest researches; the financial contributions to contests, researches, and general education, and the advertising material of the arms, ammunition, and gear manufacturers; the youth organizations and vacation camps; and not the least effective, the visual and publication materials, programs, and tours available from the public agencies and from such organizations as the Wildlife Federation and the National Audubon Society.

All this sounds like a vast concerted effort at public education, but it is at best scattering, difficult to unify, and only slowly effective against the competition it meets in all channels and against established attitudes such as "my license entitles me to bag and creel limits,"or "the violation

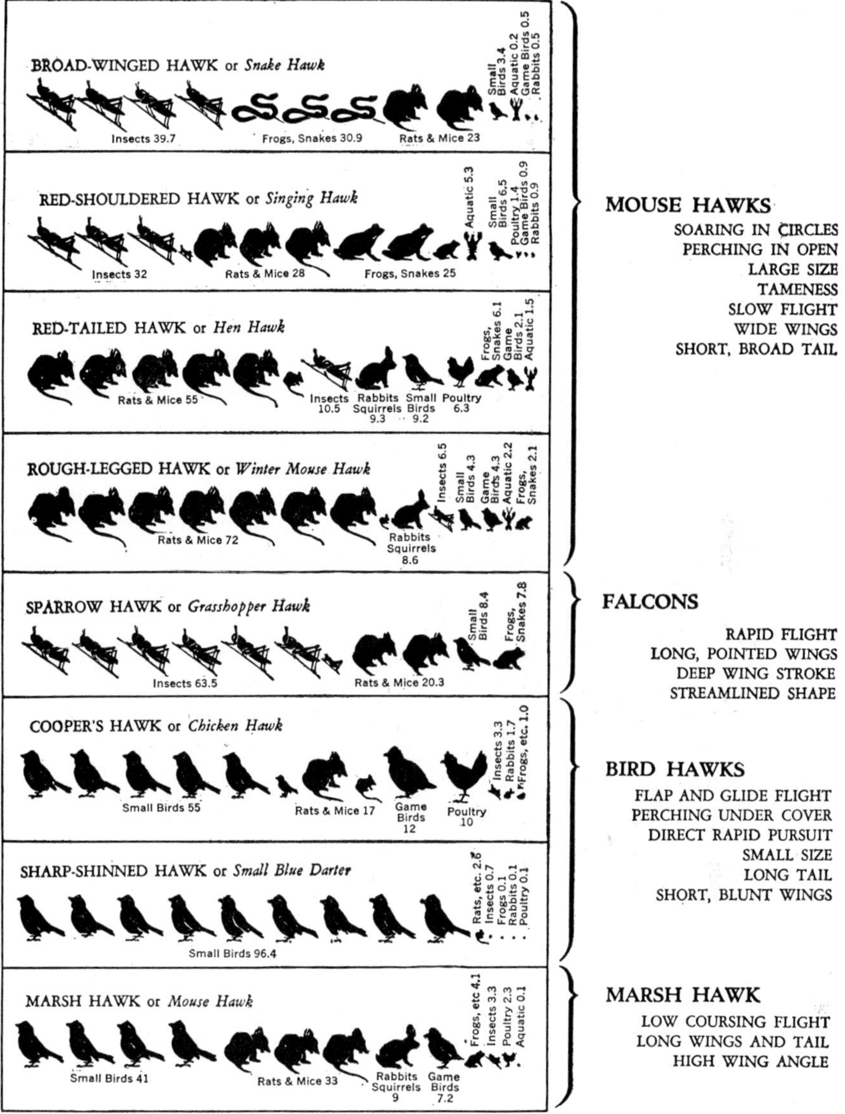

FIG. 127. What hawks eat. Based on Circular 370 U.S. Department of Agriculture, "Food Habits of Common Hawks," covering content of stomachs of 5,185 hawks. (*National Association of Audubon Societies.*)

consists of getting caught," or "I don't hunt or fish, why should I worry?" or "it's wrong to kill animals under any circumstances," or "it's better to throw away the kill than to be called a meat hunter," or "wild animal life is the most important of all the natural resources." But while desirable action may even lag behind public information and understanding, there will be little wild-animal or any other kind of conservation without it. It is our biggest single task because it makes possible the support of needed research and action programs.

The Need for Flexible Policy. The various states with their duties of administering the wild-animal resources have included in actual laws many regulations and decisions which might well be left to the "commissions" trusted with the task of conserving these resources. Sportsmen frequently find themselves appointed to these commissions, and "politics" seems to figure less and less in their selection and that of other interested but untrained citizens. But many commissioners are too busy to give the necessary time and thought to a resource which is continually fluctuating in quantity and behavior and as regards gun pressure. On the other hand, wherever policy making is taken seriously and worked at conscientiously, certain discretionary power may well be delegated to commissions so that seasonal and other emergencies and changes can be dealt with promptly. The fixing of open and closed seasons and of bag limits, the allotment of earmarked funds as between enforcement and perhaps research, and the choice of technical personnel are all examples of situations where flexibility of policy and discretionary administrative power can be useful.

The Need for Continuing Research. While interest in and financing of research are encouraging in the important hunting states, there is much to be learned of fundamentals such as life histories and habits and new problems arising daily in the conflicts of land use, the influences of weather, disaster, and last but not least in that thing that might well be called "the life history and hunting habits of the sportsman." Research programs, therefore, must be maintained and strengthened.

The Need for Law Enforcement. Hardly a year goes by in which there is not a report of the killing of some state or Federal game warden or field agent, and it is safe to say that the record of the more common violations of game and fish laws each year fails to cover the actual number which occur. In spite of advances in conservation education, according to the Fish and Wildlife Service, and a growing awareness of need for protection, game-law violations have risen as hunting pressure has increased. From a record of 4,929 cases of violations involving Federal forces in 1952, more than 4,000 were cooperative prosecutions under state laws, and 673 were violations of the Migratory Bird Treaty Act. Even the Migratory Bird Hunting Stamp Act chalked up sixty-five violations. The most efficient use of an inadequate number of agents is made by temporary assignment to emergency areas. This has considerable effect in preventing violations.[10] Many of the states with efficient staffs of enforcement officers have trouble in bringing violators to justice.

[10] *Annual Report of Secretary of the Interior,* 1952, pp. 333–334.

Other Needs for the Future of Wild-animal Resources. Overlapping to some extent the needs for understanding and for more flexible policy, research, and law enforcement, the future welfare of wild-animal resources requires increased area of public refuges and hunting grounds, reconciling of conflicting departmental objectives (here a case in point is the use of wildlife areas by the Department of Defense), and perhaps an increasing appreciation of the value of wild animals aside from their usefulness as targets. Only as wild-animal resources gain recognition of some definite and enduring place in the natural-resource priority list can we be assured of their ultimate survival along with our technological advances.

Fisheries

With more than 17 million licensed anglers for sport abroad in the land, representing better than 100 per cent increase in a single decade, and

FIG. 128. Fish pier, Boston, Mass. Unloading a catch of mackerel. (*Photo by Fish and Wildlife Service.*)

with a commercial fishing industry taking a 4.6-million-pound catch in 1948, worth 325 million dollars to the fishermen and retailing for almost a billion dollars, the fisheries of this country represent an important natural resource with plenty of conservation problems. And regardless of the difficulty of giving away any part of the catch which the enthusiastic fisherman for sport brings home, or which he contributes to an overloaded camp larder, *his* total contribution to the food of the country is probably almost as impressive as it is costly. It is estimated that fishery products are exceeded only by beef and pork as leading protein foods in the world, and in many countries of the world they rank first. The 1948 consumption in the United States was 11 pounds per capita, whereas in Finland it was about 50 pounds. Nor should it be forgotten that valuable oils, fertilizers, raw materials for plastics, glues, and feeds for poultry make up an imposing list of by-products from commercial fisheries.

FIG. 129. Experimental logging across salmon stream in Alaska to prevent accumulation of barrier. (*Photo by Dow V. Baxter, School of Natural Resources, University of Michigan.*)

The term *fishery* may therefore include not only the business of capturing fishes in the form most commonly understood, but the taking of shellfish, whales, kelp, and other resources of the sea and of inland waters.

The Nature of the Fishery Resources. Fishes are more mysterious than most of the other of the natural resources because of their habitat and the migratory routes of key species which hide them from easy observation and study. They ignore man-made boundaries between political units. They are particularly vulnerable to modern technology both with regard to instruments for capturing them and to interferences with their environment and migrations by dams, pollution, and drainage.

Fishes respond remarkably to husbandry and its many artificial devices, but only as the life histories and needs of the species are understood. Demand for both commercial and sport fishes has increased steadily since the early days of settling the country.

Factors Which Deplete the Fisheries. As in the instance of other natural resources, exploitation by man has depleted the supply of many of the important fishes. It has occurred on the assumption, if any, that the resource is somehow automatically renewable on a sustained-yield basis without any help from mankind. Notable examples of reduced annual

FIG. 130. Discharge of pulp cooking liquor from a paper mill into stream. This is particularly harmful to fish in sluggish streams. (*Photo by Michigan Water Resources Commission.*)

catch are common. These include cod from North Atlantic waters which in about 70 years has decreased from almost a 300-million-pound annual catch to less than 100 million pounds; a 50 per cent decrease in the lobster catch from New England waters; a negligible present catch of whitefish from Lake Huron, which had a thriving fishing business in the 1920s; the small catches of Pacific coast pilchard (sardine species) in recent years compared with the former catches which led others in the United States in number; and a situation where the Atlantic salmon, once important commercially, is now only a sport species in United States waters.

Barriers in streams have long interfered with the free movement and the spawning habits of certain fish species, several of them, such as salmon and shad, being of real commercial importance. Usually these barriers are dams of various types, from the early small grist-mill power dam to the enormous structures for impounding waters for irrigation and power in the West, which challenge the imagination as engineering accomplishments. Indeed it is a question whether the increased demand for power in the Northwest will not force a choice between use of water in a truly multiple sense, including fish production as an important function, and permanent destruction of this resource, on the theory that hydropower is the more important and that the public cannot have both.

Marooning is a matter of fish finding themselves trapped in pools and other high-water impoundments which dry up eventually and in irrigating ditches and even out on fields which are being watered from ditches where the intake is not properly screened. Rescue of fish stranded in such instances is sometimes practiced, but it is difficult and costly.

FIG. 131. Lake trout with lamprey and scar—just to rear of center. (*Photo by Michigan Department of Conservation.*)

Pollution of water occurs from many sources and in almost every instance tends to deplete the fisheries of the waters concerned. Perhaps the most common source is domestic and municipal sewage, insufficiently treated or not treated at all and entering the public waters to leach from them the life-giving oxygen. Industrial wastes including so-called pickling liquors from steel plants, sulfite and other refuse from paper mills, poisons from plating works, oil refinery, coal-mine, and atomic-pile wastes, and a host of others which may be relatively free of bacteria, but are full of taints and poisons—all these present relatively new problems. Industrial wastes from packing and other food-processing plants, of course, may also carry harmful bacteria but are most often of concern because of their oxygen demand. Finally the silt carried into streams, lakes, and reservoirs from farm and other lands makes the water intolerable to preferred kinds of sport and commercial fish species and may be considered a kind of pollution. The reader is referred to page 71 for a general discussion of the problems of the inevitable use of water for the transportation of waste.

Drainage of land for agricultural or occupancy purposes obviously removes water and interferes with the fish populations of ponds, lakes, and sluggish streams, which characterize the marshes.

Natural enemies, including predators, are probably not so important in the depletion picture as the other factors listed, but occasionally the invasion of waters by a new form, such as the parasitic sea lamprey in the Great Lakes, will reach serious proportions and threaten an entire industry.

Closely related to the predator problem is the invasion of fresh waters

FIG. 132. Feeding young trout in a hatchery. A liver mixture is used. (*Photo by Michigan Department of Conservation.*)

by so-called "trash fish." A recent example of this is the appearance of the alewife, or river herring, in Lake Michigan. This is a fish native to the North Atlantic waters and important there in the fish canning and by-products industries. It is relatively worthless, however, in the lakes and may be a serious competitor of the lake herring which has established value. Previous to the opening of the Welland Canal, this species was unknown above Niagara Falls. Another aspect of the trash-fish problem is seen in the manner in which carp, suckers, and similar species come to predominate in many inland waters from which predacious game species are depleted.

General Devices Used to Conserve Fisheries. As in all efforts to conserve wild-animal resources, legal restrictions of various kinds have been much more common than any other positive devices to increase the productivity of the resource. With only limited knowledge of certain fishes, laws and regulations have been established as the easiest and the only immediate means available. Enforcement is, however, anything but easy, and ways of "getting around" such regulations are frequently discovered. General restrictions on capture involve catch quotas (sometimes spoken of as "creel limits" in sport fishing); limits on types of gear, on season

FIG. 133. Farm pond in Barbour County, West Virginia. Impounding water in this manner and planting to warm-water fish is a positive measure of fishery management. (*Photo by Hermann Postlethwaite, courtesy Soil Conservation Service.*)

and intermittent closures, on size of specimens taken, on time of day, on territory over which fishing may be done, and on fishing without purchase of a license. Most of these measures apply both to sport and commercial fishing. Where they are based upon knowledge of life histories and habits, and are really enforced, they have been effective. Their greatest promise lies in their employment to match current and localized situations. Recently older laws restricting size, season, and creel limits are being relaxed, particularly on warm-water fish, to retard overpopulation and stunting which is so common in these forms.

Positive measures of fishery management also include operation of hatcheries from which young fishes are planted in waters where they may develop; manipulation of native environment in terms of increased food, shelter, freedom of water from siltation and from predators; and the digging of new ponds or impounding waters in which fishes may be produced as a crop.

Just how these methods work may be more clearly discussed under descriptions of individual fishes which follow.

Examples of Important Commercial Fishes. *Salmon.* Few Americans are unfamiliar with canned salmon for the salmon, based on five species —red, king, coho, pink, and chum or dog—makes up the largest catch by

Fig. 134. Salmon going upstream to spawn, in Alaska. (*Photo by W. H. Case, courtesy U.S. Forest Service.*)

weight of any of our commercial species. Some 85 per cent of the catch is packed. The balance is sold fresh, frozen, smoked, or cured. Almost 90 per cent of the domestic production of salmon comes from Alaska, and this comprises close to 50 per cent of the world's production. Only one other commercial species, the masu, is known in the Pacific, and it inhabits Asiatic waters. The Atlantic salmon is important now only as a sport fish except in a few localities in the Maritime Provinces of Canada.

The salmons are so-called *anadromous* fishes. This means that they must have stream spawning grounds, that they migrate, spend their growing years at sea, and return to their native streams finally to spawn. Here the grounds must be of gravel with a consistent and moderate flow of clear, cool water, the conditions and distance of the grounds upstream varying with species. The adult Pacific salmon die after spawning. The eggs incubate in the gravel, and the young, 2 months after hatching, reach the stage called fry and begin the search for food. Within the next 4 years, depending upon species, the young have migrated to the sea, and within periods of 2 to 7 years, survivors of the various kinds have swarmed in season back up their native streams—that is, unless some barrier constructed meanwhile has stopped them. But life is a struggle from the start. Some birds, fish, and other animals feed on salmon eggs. Ducks, other water birds, and fresh-water fishes devour young salmon if the

FIG. 135. Salmon cannery, Tongass National Forest, Alaska. (*Photo by Dow V. Baxter, School of Natural Resources, University of Michigan.*)

latter have escaped death by earlier enemies or disease. Sea lions, seals, whales, and certain kinds of large fish prey upon growing salmon in the ocean. At the mouth of streams, on the return migration, the most efficient capturing gear man can devise awaits them. Finally, on their way upstream, bears, wolves, gulls, eagles, and other natural enemies feed upon them. Only the "escapement" is left to spawn. It cannot take unlimited abuse from the construction of man-made barriers and from unscreened irrigation and power diversions.

In spite of all this, the statement is made by the Fish and Wildlife Service, concerning one single fishing area, that "intelligent management of the resources, based on scientific knowledge, would increase the over-all production in Alaska by at least 50 million pounds, worth some 10 million dollars annually."[11] Since some 70 per cent of Alaska's tax revenue comes from the salmon industries, such an opportunity should prove a good public investment. In the Pacific Coast states the opportunity to increase the catch is less promising because of rapid industrial development, with its dams and other encroachments.

An appraisal of conservation opportunities and devices would indicate that restrictive laws and regulations, varying with the different states, provinces, and territories, are useful, if not always the best, and moderately well enforced. This is perhaps more evident in Alaskan waters than in the three Pacific Coast states, where varying laws and regulations permit less unified management.

FIG. 136. Looking down fish ladder at Bradford Island on the Columbia River. (*Photo by Lawrence E. Griffin, courtesy American Forests.*)

Salmon hatcheries established in 1870 have been somewhat disappointing as an improvement on nature. They have been abandoned in Alaska and confined in the states and provinces to producing stock for two kinds of streams. The first are those streams so far depleted as to need help if they are to recover at all. The second are those streams which may be modified to make new spawning grounds available, and thus justify restocking.

[11] Fishery Resources of the United States, S. Doc. 51, 79th Cong., 1st Sess., 1945. p. 3.

Barriers present a difficult set of problems in getting the spawning migrants around or over the dams and getting the young salmon fingerlings safely downstream past the gauntlet of spillways, turbines, and deeply submerged outlets of storage reservoirs. Fishways are used for these purposes and may consist of fish ladders made up of a staircase-like

FIG. 137. Commercial catch of salmon in barge headed for cannery in Tongass National Forest, Alaska. (*Photo by Dow V. Baxter, School of Natural Resources, University of Michigan.*)

cascade of rectangular pools arranged at rising intervals of 1 to 2 feet so that the fish can make their way upstream. This device sounds simple, but it is expensive and requires that the fish be attracted to the entrance and that quantity and speed of water flow be carefully regulated. Imagine a self-respecting salmon, however, finding himself in a lock similar to those used for navigation, a bucket hoist, or a tank truck! These devices are used occasionally. High dams such as the Shasta on the Sacramento

River, the Grand Coulee on the Columbia, and a new one proposed on the Cowlitz river in Washington are practically impassable. They pose the question, "Power or salmon?" So far, in spite of man's ingenuity, artificial propagation below the dams, fooling or trying to educate the salmon, and attempts to develop safe conduct through the dams themselves, with all the mangling and pressure problems involved, the answer seems to be, "Power is more necessary than fish, so let's forget the salmon." This does not mean that heroic attempts to solve these problems have been given up entirely, but rather that power has first consideration.

FIG. 138. Even the power of a salmon to jump a low cataract or rapids is not enough to get it over a dam without the use of a fish ladder. (*Photo by Dow V. Baxter, School of Natural Resources, University of Michigan.*)

Prediction of the salmon crop on a yearly basis is possible and important if the catch is to represent the advisable population control on spawning grounds. Overcrowding of spawning grounds means lower production and survival. Such prediction therefore contributes to conservation in a positive sense. Upon its accuracy hinges the real management of the resource. This is how it is done: First the number of spawning adults must be estimated or counted as they make their way upstream to spawning grounds (a tough kind of census to take); next the resulting number of young must be determined on their way downstream (and this is not easy); finally these counts must be studied in the light of carefully obtained knowledge of stream and ocean conditions which are actually proved to affect survival. All this must be done for *each* stream population *each* year. The conservation of this resource still awaits a twelvefold expansion of laboratory and research facilities and personnel, and yet there is every reason to believe that the investment would pay handsomely. One of the newest of the international commissions, the North Pacific Fishery Commission, was established in 1952, involving Canada, the United States, and Japan and concerned with equitable distribution of fishing rights in waters used by these three nations.

Haddock. Haddock is another fish well known to American consumers whether it appears on their tables as fillets, finnanhaddie (smoked), or as fish flakes. It is the most valuable of all the North Atlantic coast fisheries, and its peak production, which came in 1929, reached 260 million pounds. Authorities agree that overfishing is responsible for a drop to 140 million pounds in recent years. Haddock do not spawn until 3 or 4 years old. At that time they have come to weigh 2 to 3 pounds, and gathering on the Nova Scotia, Newfoundland, or New England banks, the schools spawn their eggs into relatively deep surrounding waters where they are fertilized and drift until incubation. Early life periods are spent in drifting until the bottom existence is started. Hazards to young include possible exposure to severe conditions of depth through adverse currents, but the most important problem arises from the increased catch of smaller fish which have not reached the spawning stage. In 1928 only 9 per cent of the catch was made up of fish weighing less than 2 pounds. By 1941 this had risen to 47 per cent. Studies by the Fish and Wildlife Service indicate that the spawning stock should be nearly doubled if adequate sustained production of young is to be achieved. Strangely enough the simple expedient of taking no fish under 2 pounds would allow many to grow to spawning age, and it is estimated that the catch might so be increased eventually by 15 per cent. (Too radical methods could presumably increase population too greatly and bring about eventual depletion from lack of food supply.) But so far there are only voluntary agreements by a few fishermen to cooperate on size limits, modification of gear, and sustained effort, in general, to increase spawning stock. No state laws or other regulations require compliance with suggested changes. Whether the increase of convincing evidence that this program is to the interests of the fishing industry will be heeded depends somewhat upon testing out the conclusions of scientists and upon further investigations of young-fish-saving gear and methods of measuring populations. But, as in other natural-resource–shortage situations, a tough problem here is to get the support of the public and the industry for a promising program of action. One hopeful development is the 1952 agreement by the Northwest Atlantic Fishery Commission, which had been established in 1951, on the increase of mesh sizes to allow the escape of young. This agreement went into effect in 1953.

Pacific Sardine, or Pilchard. This group of herring-like fishes (called sardines when canned) is the basic resource for the largest fishing industry in the Western Hemisphere. Pilchard are widely distributed in temperate coastal waters throughout the world and are known as pelagic fish, that is, those inhabiting surface offshore layers of water. Habitually traveling in large schools or shoals, the range of the group covers the entire Pacific coast of the United States and extends beyond to Mexican and Canadian waters. The catch yielded some 420 million pounds annually of processed food meal, oil, bait, and other materials in prewar

FIG. 139. Biologist measuring haddock to obtain information from commercial catch on age and fluctuations in catch from year to year. Many measurements are of course taken and recorded. (*Photo by A. H. Fisher, courtesy Fish and Wildlife Service.*)

years. The years 1946 to 1948, however, showed disastrous reductions in catch, thought to be due to poor production and survival of mature fish from 1940 through 1945 and to possible unexplained changes in migration and availability of the pilchard population.

The life history and habits of sardines are becoming better understood through cooperative studies of various public agencies, and yet more observations on oceanic conditions affecting spawning, of fluctuations in food supply, and of the effect of weather upon fishing luck are needed.

Sardine spawning occurs mostly in March and April in the open sea 50 to 300 miles offshore. A single female may produce as many as 35,000 eggs three times a season. This is a population safeguard, necessary because of the high mortality of the young. Fertilization takes place in open water, the hatch follows in about 3 days, and the young eventually become free swimming and feed upon minute plant and animal life known collectively as *plankton*. Fluctuations in food supply and deep-water temperatures take a heavy toll, and the habit of swimming in schools allows heavy catches for bait while the young are feeding close to shore. (The bait is used for catching tuna and mackerel—both important fishes.)

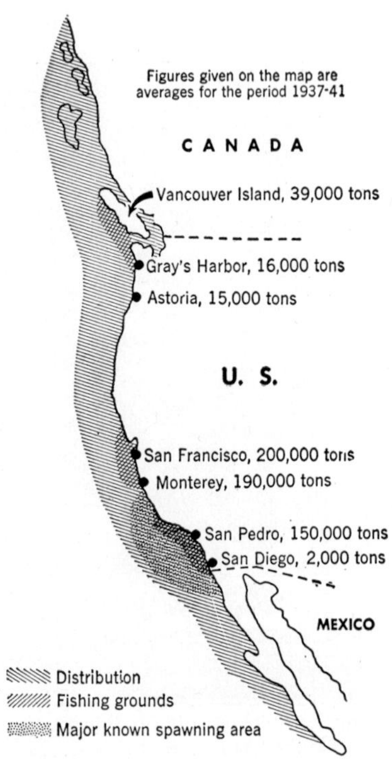

FIG. 140. Map indicating distribution, fishing grounds, and major known spawning area of West coast sardines. (*Courtesy Fish and Wildlife Service.*)

Specimens of more than 7 inches in length are wanted by the commercial fishermen who do their fishing far offshore.

Three effects of intensive fishing must be considered in maintaining a conservation program for the pilchard: (1) reduction of the total number of fish, with a resulting smaller catch for a given amount of fishing effort and investment; (2) reduction in average size of fish caught so that effort must be intensified and more fish caught if tonnage is to be maintained (this might also require changes in processing equipment); (3) reduction in the numbers of spawning stock with disastrous results in sustaining the annual yield. To meet these situations, vastly more must be learned of the habits of the fish making up this resource and of oceanic conditions which affect fluctuations in the catch. A program with this in mind is getting under way with Federal, state, and private participation. Legislative control is confined to waters under the jurisdiction of California and is so far confined principally to utilization of the catch. There are closed seasons not on fishing but on the use of sardines for canning and for reduction into industrial products. This affects the management of fishing boats and processing plants but has little effect upon sustaining the resource itself. Only through greater knowledge, sought as mentioned above, may intelligent and effective restrictions be drawn and enforced if needed.

Recent researches supported by California state and private agencies and by the Federal Fish and Wildlife Service indicate that decline of the sardine catch in recent years may be a fluctuation due mainly to a succession of poor spawning season and to an unexplained natural mortality of adults. Good catches in the 1951 season appear to indicate a substantial recovery.[12]

Mackerels. Both the true Pacific form and the horse mackerel, which belongs to a family known as jackfish, are caught from California ports by certain of the pilchard fishermen and others, and together they account for more than 85 million pounds annually of products sold fresh, salted, canned, and smoked, and worth more than 1¼ million dollars to the fishermen. Sport fishing for mackerel from pleasure barges is also important and unhampered by legislative restrictions. As with pilchard the only regulations in force concerning mackerel have to do with utilization of the catch, no part being allowed for reduction to industrial products except the trimmings and offal remaining from canning. There are no restrictions on catch, gear, or season. Investigations so far have revealed location of spawning grounds, migration habits (through the capture-tagging-release-capture device), and spawning ages and habits. Use of the resource is, however, increasing, but practically nothing is known of the proportion exploited annually. The same is true of the Atlantic mackerel, the Spanish mackerel, and the king mackerel, all caught off the Atlantic coast. These appear as important fresh-fish products, and the latter because of speed and fighting power is a favorite game fish. Atlantic mackerel during World War II appeared increasingly also as a canned product, but violent fluctuations in the runs hamper the industry in sustained catch and use of this valuable food fish. The greatest need for conserving the resource in the sense of use while maintaining productivity is further knowledge upon which to predict each year's potential catch. This much is known, that in spite of amazing egg produc-

[12] McHugh, J. L., and Elbert H. Ahlstrom, Is the Pacific Sardine Disappearing? *Sci. Monthly*, **72**:377–384, June, 1951.

tion, as high as 500,000 by a single female, mortality of young fish is high. This is thought to be due to mysterious recurring scarcities of food or to drifting, caused by unfavorable winds, away from grounds where survival conditions are favorable.

The mackerel fishery in general appears to illustrate an attitude of exploiters toward an apparently inexhaustible resource which might be expressed as "what we don't know won't hurt us." Apparent abundance also represents an opportunity to learn of the resource and how to conserve it, before it exhibits dangerous decline.

Cod. This fishery should be mentioned, not only because of its historical importance during the past centuries when its catch was our principal salt fish, but because of its present importance in the fresh fish marketed and in its value for liver oils (also taken from pollock, hake, and haddock) as a source of vitamin D. The Atlantic cod fishery contributes a catch of some 85 million pounds a year. The fish inhabits the same kinds of bottoms as haddock, runs to greater size, and moves about to a greater extent. The skins are a source of high-quality glue. Understanding of daily variations in catch and maximum utilization of this apparently plentiful resource await basic studies not yet undertaken. The true Pacific cod, lingcod, and sablefish are all taken in Pacific waters and marketed fresh, frozen, and (except lingcod) salted. All are underutilized. In the case of the true Pacific cod this is partly due to the distance of Alaskan waters, where it is taken, from processing centers. The resource offers opportunity for development of marketing techniques which would make it comparable to the Atlantic cod fishery. The quick-freezing method is one of the most promising for better utilization of this resource. Pollock which has a distribution similar to that of cod is marketed in Atlantic waters but awaits utilization from the Pacific.

Ground Fishes. Among the "ground fishes," of which cod is one, rosefish or redfish is now sold regularly on the market as packaged fillets. It is found in New England waters and has become second only to haddock in volume of catch. Intensive fishing appears to indicate decline as stocks of older fish are caught. Rosefish is one of few commercial species which give birth to live young. They reach maturity at the eleventh year, and it is important that so-called seed stock be undisturbed and allowed to grow rather than to be taken as a part of the catch. Popularity on the market has stimulated fishing, however, so that more and more of the younger specimens are taken. Studies by the Fish and Wildlife Service are under way to determine best management methods and adoption of a practicable program to maintain maximum sustained yields. Modifications of gear and better understanding of the seasonal movements of mature rosefish are among the measures being considered.

Halibut. This large form of flounder should be considered here because it is well known in the fish markets and because its exploitation has been turned to conservation through international cooperative means. First taken from the North Atlantic banks, a catch of more than 14 million pounds has declined to about 1 million pounds in contrast to a catch in the Northern Pacific waters of more than 50 million pounds annually. On the other hand, heavy and unregulated fishery in the Pacific banks brought about a decline in landings from 69 million pounds in 1915 to 43 million pounds in 1931. This is the more significant because halibut livers and viscera furnish important amounts of vitamin-rich oils.

As early as 1916, signs of depletion indicated that international action would be necessary to regulate halibut fishing, and in 1924 a treaty between Great Britain and the United States set up an International Fishery Commission which undertook a study of halibut resources. This treaty was changed and strengthened in 1930 to prescribe regulatory powers and modified further in 1937. Again in 1953 this agreement was amended to broaden further the commission's powers. One of the provisions had to do with catch quotas for each of four Pacific coast areas where the seasons were closed when the quotas had been filled. Another prohibited all fishing for halibut in a particular area where the fishes were of small size. Good management under these arrangements has increased the catch more than 100 per cent in two decades.

Menhaden. Another herring-like fish similar in habit and life history to the Pacific sardines, but used little for human food, the menhaden constitutes a fishing industry which centers in the Middle Atlantic states but has been important along New England and southward. The three species are pelagic and travel in dense schools. At two years they have reached a length of 7 to 10 inches and are increasingly rich in oil up to maturity, which is believed to be the third or fourth year. They are taken in great quantities for fertilizer, oil, and livestock and poultry feeds. Menhaden roe, the unspawned eggs, saved out and frozen, salted, or canned is used for human food. The oil is important in the manufacture of linoleum and rainproofing garments. One-fourth of all the marine-animal oils produced in the United States and one-third of all the fish meal used in poultry and livestock feeds are products of the menhaden industry. As with many other fishes, the importance of the catch to national economy indicates need for greater knowledge than is available if conservation of the resource is to be assured. No legal restrictions are imposed upon menhaden fishermen at present. Information is badly needed on migration, location of spawning grounds and of grounds where the young develop, food habits and resulting oil content, parasites said to sterilize the male, and the relation of oceanic climate to fecundity, survival, and welfare of seed stock.

Tunas. These fishes rank next to salmon in the canning industry, where the waste is worked into industrial products consisting principally of meal and oil. The livers are a source of high-potency vitamin oils. Aside from their commercial values, the tunas are a favorite quarry for sport fishermen. The four Pacific tunas—bluefin, skipjack, yellowfin, and albacore—are the most valuable. The Atlantic tunas, while serving a high value as game fish and reaching large size, have darker coarser flesh than the Pacific forms and are not important commercially. Fishing for Pacific tuna is done principally from clipper vessels, stocked with sardine and other small fish as bait which has been obtained close to shore. Barbless hooks

Fig. 141. Seining for menhaden near Beaufort, N.C. (*Photo by Frank Dufresne, courtesy Fish and Wildlife Service.*)

and short poles are used when schools are attracted to the boats by release of quantities of bait. When the fish run large, two or more men may work together with separate rods attached to the same line. While it is known that tunas are widely distributed throughout the world and that they range over great distances, relatively little is known of their life histories and habits, and the extent of the resource. In view of the rapid expansion of the fishery in recent years, this is unfortunate. It is probably the reason that the only conservation measures in force so far are rather weak international agreements on so-called "conservation zones" and on exchange of information, although there is hope in the commission recently activated by North American countries. Limits are imposed in California waters on maximum and minimum sizes of fish to be caught, and certain areas for sport fishing are reserved. Even the limitations on size are dictated more by sizes which can be handled economically by the industry than by sound conservation considerations. Recently enacted tariff provisions on tuna, imported into the United States, has caused ill feeling among Latin-American countries whose fishermen have found this country their best market. This sort of situation does not help to bring about the international conservation effort necessary if this valuable and wide-ranging resource is to be understood and conserved.

Fishes of the Great Lakes. Not all commercial fishing is confined to ocean species. The Great Lakes, which with their connecting waters form the largest single fresh-water area in the world, have long been famous for their commercial fisheries of lake trout, whitefish, and herring, and they present even more difficult problems of conservation. The most valuable fish is the lake trout which at peak reached a catch of 10 million pounds annually, worth more than 3 million dollars at prewar prices. Overfishing, lack of uniform restrictive regulations in waters off the various states and provinces, and lately the predation of the sea lamprey, have reduced the catch sharply. Size limits are considered generally inadequate for the protection of immature fish, and the effectiveness of artificial propagation has not been fully explored. Some progress has been made in control of the sea lamprey.

Whitefish because of demand as one of the finest fresh-water fishes has been badly overfished in the Great Lakes, and regulations governing catch have almost uniformly failed to recognize the weight at which spawning age is reached. This weight is well known for some localities, varying from 2.4 to 3.8 pounds. Large numbers of immature fish have appeared in the catch. The use of the deep-trap net has been especially disastrous and has been more or less outlawed.

Lake herring, which are related to the whitefish, are taken in greatest volume in the Great Lakes and marketed salted and smoked. No size limit is in effect for herring, but the average age of specimens in the catch is younger than formerly. Limitation on size of net mesh has been in force generally. The size of the herring population is not known, and tremendous variations in catch are common from year to year, as evidenced in a drop from 717,000 pounds in 1939 to 25,200 pounds in 1942.

More needs to be known of the life histories and habits of commercial Great Lakes fishes, and concerted action in their administration and protection is needed. Out of a United States–Canada Convention signed Apr. 2, 1946,[13] has come a draft of a treaty not yet ratified by the United States up to January, 1953, but which it is hoped will result in some restoration of Great Lakes fisheries. It should be noted that, altogether, some half a

[12] Senate Executive C,, 79th Cong., 2d sess., 92 Cong. Rec. 4092.

dozen other fishes than those discussed figure importantly in the Great Lakes catch.

Conservation of fresh-water commercial fishery resources including those of the Great Lakes, the Mississippi Valley, and the larger coastal streams is now largely a matter of restricting gear and season and the continuous application of the results of research by state and Federal agencies. Efforts to control the sea lamprey in the Great Lakes is an example of the latter.

FIG. 142. Trout fishing, South Platte River, Pike National Forest, Colorado. (*Photo by U.S. Forest Service.*)

Fresh-water Sport Fishing. Some twenty or more groups of fresh-water fishes furnish the bulk of the sport fishing in the United States. Relatively few fishermen have the time or money for ocean or bay fishing for the larger sport varieties. The inland cold-water fishes most commonly sought are the trout, among which are represented both introduced and native forms. It is well to get them sorted out as to name and requirements. The brook trout native to eastern North America has been widely introduced into Western streams and into lakes where bottom waters are cold and rich in oxygen and free of predatory fishes. They vary greatly in appearance with differences in waters. The rainbow trout, native to turbulent Western streams, is hardy and can stand relatively warm water and heavy fishing. A variant sea-run form known as steelhead is taken commercially as well as for sport. The brown trout is a hardy form introduced from Germany some 70 years ago. It is widely planted, can stand relatively high temperatures, and is now interbred with an English form known as Loch Leven, also introduced into the United States. The group known as cutthroat or black spotted trout includes a native Rocky Mountain form, a sea-run form taken in Pacific coast waters, and several locally named trout with distinctive appearances such as the cutthroat. Among these are the famous California golden trout. The lake trout or "Mackinaw," as mentioned earlier, is sought for sport as well as for market.

Most of the trout require waters of low temperature. Except for lake trout, they are spring spawners and utilize tributary streams for this purpose. They are taken for sport principally with fly and light tackle.

Other cold-water fishes taken for sport include grayling and smelt. The grayling, now extinct in Michigan waters where it was once plentiful, occurs in the headwaters of the Missouri and in Arctic waters including Alaska. It is closely related to the salmons, but it is usually under 12 inches in length at maturity. The smelt, native to New England rivers and introduced into the Great Lakes, is prized for food and taken both commercially and for sport. Early spring spawning runs afford exciting opportunity for dipping this small silvery fish if one can find footing among the crowds of fishermen at the sport centers.

Important warm-water fishes include sunfishes, several varieties of bass, yellow perch, crappie, northern pike, pikeperch or walleye pike, catfish, bullheads, and carp. All are native in United States waters except the carp which was introduced from Europe where it had long ago been brought from its native waters in China. It is caught commercially, is usually considered a nuisance in sport waters (except by bow-and-arrow fishermen), and is extremely hardy.

Most expert warm-water fishermen are after black bass, either the largemouth variety found in ponds, warm lakes, and the quieter streams, or the smallmouth form which runs smaller and requires clearer, cooler, gravel-bottom waters. The black bass are good fighters and are usually taken by fly or plug with light tackle. They are nest builders, and the male guards the eggs and fry. Of the two, the largemouth bass is the more diligent "baby-sitter," and also reaches greater size than his smallmouth kinsman.

The sunfishes include the bluegill and pumpkinseed, known collectively as "bream" in many localities, and the rock bass. They are perhaps the most widely distributed sport fishes, bream particularly being well adapted to stocking and serving as a forage fish for bass without undue depletion. The combination of bluegills and bass make up perhaps the most common stocking for the thousands of farm ponds constructed as a part of soil conservation district activities throughout the nation. The "still fishermen" count sunfish as an important resource.

Yellow perch, important as a commercial species in the Great Lakes, has a high percentage of survival of the young and sometimes overpopulates small bodies of water and becomes stunted. It is easily taken by still fishing but furnishes a fair amount of sport.

The conservation problems which characterize the warm-water sport fishes are not so much a matter of maintaining the quantities, except in polluted waters, but of understanding life histories and adjusting interrelationships of the various species and of human fishing pressure.

FIG. 143. Bass fishing below Norris Dam. (*Photo by Tennessee Valley Authority.*)

Sport fishing must withstand increasing rod pressure every year and can be assured only through legal restrictions, stocking, environmental improvement, the creation of new fishing waters, and public education. Perhaps no wild land sport has a greater number of devotees.

Shellfish Resources. *Oyster.* Perhaps the best known shellfish is the oyster. This valuable natural resource contributes almost 90 million pounds of meat annually to the nation's supply and is characterized by conservation probems which have persisted for more than a century. More than half the present yield comes from oyster farming, which is comparable in efficiency and trouble to land farming, but usually far exceeds the income per acre from the latter. The oyster farmer leases barren and unutilized areas of sea floor, usually in protected bays, obtains seed oysters from public reefs, and plants them on the leased bottoms. Depending upon such factors as acreage, quality of bottoms, distance from shore, prevalence and control of pests, costs of transplanting, protection from trespassers, and labor, returns of 100 bushels or more per acre may be expected. Oyster farming is common in Delaware and Chesapeake Bays, Louisiana waters, and to a lesser extent along the Northwest Pacific coast. Public oyster grounds are vast in extent but even under persisting state regulation have declined steadily in output.

FIG. 144. Young oysters attacked by starfish. Shell is opened by steady pull of sucker-equipped feet, and the starfish then inserts its own stomach into the shell and digests the meat of the oyster. (*Photo by J. V. Engle, courtesy Fish and Wildlife Service.*)

The life history of the oyster is interesting. An inhabitant of shallow waters, it may be found on muddy grounds but prefers a hard, stable bottom. Oysters vary greatly in size and in the appearance of the shell. On overcrowded grounds they assume a vertical position, and the shells, which are long and thin, form large clusters. On hard bottom the shells are smooth and round. They adapt themselves to wide range of saltiness in the water. Usually there is about a 50-50 ratio of sexes. They breed in summer, and the adult female may spawn as many as 500 million eggs in one season. Mortality is so high, however, that few of the hatching larvae reach a size where they can attach themselves to clean rocks or other hard objects to grow and accumulate a shell. Feeding occurs by straining large quantitites of sea water through the gills, to obtain the minute organisms which it contains, and continues only during the warm months. Oysters feed at a slower rate when even slight pollution of the water occurs, and thus fail to reach marketable size. They contain, when mature at 2 to 5 years, about 20 per cent of solids by weight and 5 per cent glycogen; the meat is nourishing and digestible.

Among the predators which attack the oyster, the starfish accounts for several million dollars' loss a year. It is able to open even a large oyster shell by the strength of its sucker-equipped feet. It then inserts its own stomach into the shell and digests the oyster.

Methods of harvesting oysters vary from hand picking with grabs in parts of the South to the tongs and multiple dredges common in the Middle Atlantic coast or the suction dredges of Puget Sound. All these devices must be operated with skill, usually acquired only from long experience. Even though self-interest dictates care in method and in design and construction of gear, rapid destruction and decline have characterized the exploitation of the million acres of public reefs and rocks open to fishing by those who hold state licenses. Decline is probably due in a large degree to the rate at which harvesting occurs. Loss from breakage of shells and from forcing the oysters into the mud because of inefficient gear are also in the picture.

Shrimp. In point of value, quantity taken, and number of men employed, the shrimp fishery of the South Atlantic coast and the Gulf of Mexico is the most important in those regions. Its continued prosperity will require more attention to the life histories and age classes captured than it has commanded so far. There are three varieties, common, grooved, and sea-bob. The latter is used only locally; most of the catch is of the common variety and is taken at less than 1 year of age. In real life the shrimp looks more like a monster than it does in a cocktail. Shrimp spawn from early spring until early fall, depositing the eggs in open water. When they hatch, the young find their way to the shallow bottoms and grow rapidly. Many of them are fed upon by various fishes, but enough escape to move eventually into deeper waters, and the larger ones migrate from colder to warmer waters. Here they mature and by spring are ready to spawn in open water. Large catches of smaller shrimp in nursery ground waters close to shore during summer months mean a heavy depletion of immature specimens. The same is true of certain winter months in shore waters where the only shrimp present are still those too small to migrate. Conservation of the resource suggests year-round fishing in the outside gounds where the larger specimens are found and a closed season in certain winter and certain summer months for inside waters where too many immature but fast-growing shrimp make up the population.

Lobsters, Crabs, and Clams. Other important shellfish industries include the following: American lobster which provides full and part-time employment to more fishermen than any other New England fishery and

FIG. 145. Icing down the catch of shrimp, near New Orleans, La. (*Photo by Fish and Wildlife Service.*)

which poses the interesting conservation problem of protecting large spawning females. The Atlantic coast blue crab fishery, from which both soft-shelled (captured at one of the many moltings with shell discarded) and hard-shelled (not a separate species) crabs are sold fresh in Eastern markets and to a less extent as canned crab meat. More needs to be learned about sharp natural fluctuations in the total stock and about safe methods of marketing fresh crab meat. Clams, both soft and hard or littleneck, the latter ranging somewhat farther into deep water than the former which is only taken on tidal flats and beaches, come almost entirely from public beds. Management of clam grounds suffers from polluted waters and lack of positive cultivation measures which offer real opportunity to maintain and increase productivity. Sea and bay scallops, the rock crabs, mussels, and spiny lobsters also figure in shellfish production, and all require better knowledge of their life histories and habits if they are to be conserved as resources.

Fig. 146. This barnacle-encrusted lobster is larger than those usually caught along the Atlantic seaboard. (*Photo by Fish and Wildlife Service.*)

Other Products of the Sea. While most of the animal products from ocean water are fishes, two interesting mammals figure prominently in the yield—whales and seals. Sponges also, conveniently designated as "marine animals of simple form," contribute their skeletons.

Whales. Capturing some 8 million dollars' worth of whales annually about 100 years ago, the United States whaling industry employed around 40,000 people, operated more than 700 vessels, and represented an investment of 40 million dollars. Ten years ago the industry operated 3 ships, employed 59 people, represented an investment of less than 1 million dollars and a yearly catch worth $44,000. Bad management of the natural resource itself was partly responsible for this decline, but it was of course hastened by a surprising lack of enterprise in whaling and processing methods and by the capturing of the illuminating-oil market by the petroleum industry. Other countries have developed more efficient whaling methods, almost complete utilization of the catch, and have even developed valuable human food products from whales. The use for whale oil in the United States is principally for the manufacture of soap. The cruder forms of this product in turn are used in insect sprays. In Europe edible fats, ointments, leather and fiber dressings also employ whale oil, and it also finds limited use as a lubricant for machinery. An average-sized whale will yield, in addition to oil, a considerable quantity of

FIG. 147. Whales off the southeast coast of Alaska. Tongass National Forest in background. (*Photo by Dow V. Baxter, School of Natural Resources, University of Michigan.*)

whalebone, used in Europe for brushes, artificial hair, feathers, and mattress stuffing, some three tons of "meal" for cattle or poultry food, and a ton of guano for fertilizer.

The whale population has been definitely overexploited for many years with little attempt toward any kind of management of the resource until a committee of experts at the call of the Economic Committee of the League of Nations met early in the 1930s and drafted an agreement which, after being ratified by seventeen countries and acceded to by eight, came into force in 1935. Its provisions covered the protection of whales in general, prohibited the taking of calves or females accompanied by calves, and required full use of captured carcasses so far as practicable. These regulations were expanded and strengthened by an

International Conference for the Regulation of Whaling, held in London in 1937. Approved in 1938 by the governments of South Africa, Argentina, Australia, Great Britain, Eire, New Zealand, and the United States, this agreement forbade operation of factory ships on calving grounds, strengthened protection of the hard-pressed humpback whale stocks in the antarctic and established a whale sanctuary west and northwest of Cape Horn. Also under this agreement and the later Whaling Convention of Washington, 1946, whaling vessels must be licensed by their governments and each factory ship must carry an enforcement officer to assure compliance with the international agreement and the particular national license.

The future of whales as a natural resource is not yet assured, and repeated restrictive agreements hardly keep pace with the improvements in gear and capture. The last stand of whales is the antarctic, and even stronger international measures will have to limit size and numbers taken and seasons and places where operations are permitted.

Seals. Highly valuable for their fur and for by-products of oil meal and even food used locally, seals are seagoing mammals which make up an important and well-managed natural resource. The largest herd occupies the Pribilof Islands off the coast of Alaska in the Bering Sea and unlike the one on the Kuriles claimed by the Japanese and those of the Commander Island claimed by Russia, the Pribilof Island herd has been managed under international agreement and has steadily increased in numbers and value since 1911.

The life history and habits of seals have made their conservation difficult in the past but have also served as the key to maintaining and increasing the productivity of the resource. Mating and breeding occurs in late summer following return from migrations which have taken the females as far south as the California coast and the bulls to the Gulf of Alaska. The bulls arrive in early summer, the most powerful acquiring the best grounds near the shore and establishing harems of forty to sixty females. The mature surplus bulls establish themselves in the immediate rear and await the arrival of the younger females which are left to them by the tired old harem masters who have fought off their rivals, worn themselves out, and also surrendered some of their females. A third colony back on less favorable grounds is occupied by the younger bachelor bulls, of which there are a large number and from which the annual kill is made. Meanwhile the mothers have given birth to their pups—usually single births—and busied themselves after breeding by swimming far out to sea in search of food. The pups may go along or stay at the rookery with the assurance that the mother will return to find and nurse her own pup if he has not been trampled by the harem master in his battle with rivals. Things get a bit crowded after the young females arrive in August, and within 4 months the arctic weather has driven the whole herd including the pups, which are on their own at 2 months, into the sea for migration. There is a considerable loss of pups at best.

Following out this story it will be seen that seals of both sexes and all ages are at sea for a major part of their lives, and this fact, coupled with

FIG. 148. Bull seal and the start of his harem. Note other groups in the top of the picture. (*Photo by Jas. C. Ward, University of Michigan Forest Pathology Expedition.*)

the habit of feeding and then resting afloat, makes them easily vulnerable to capture while resting at sea. This kind of hunting is known as "pelagic" sealing and has resulted in past years not only in a heavy kill but also a heavy loss of carcasses with their valuable hides. It was this very type of exploitation which reduced the Kurile and Commander Island herds almost to extermination and cut down the Pribilof herd, once estimated to number more than 3 million, to less than 150,000.

Taking their cue from practices of the Washington and British Columbia Indians who learned to creep up on the sleeping seals by canoe, some 100 ships of Canadian, Japanese, and American sealing fleets were operating in the 1890s and are estimated to have taken almost 1 million skins between 1868 and 1911. Counting the losses, including pregnant females and their nursing pups, this figure should perhaps be doubled at least. The Russians had placed some restrictions in earlier years on numbers which could be taken, but the successful restriction of pelagic sealing under the four-nation treaty of 1911 was the stroke which reestablished the Pribilof herd and kept it at about its former size. The provisions of this agreement were bold and have been well enforced. The old Bureau of Fisheries and later the Fish and Wildlife Service have carried out the systematic harvesting of skins after a prescribed 5-year period during which no seals were to be taken. The first systematic kill was made in 1918 at the rookery from the young bulls, and in accordance with the treaty the revenue from the sale of skins was divided among the four nations, Great Britain (Canada), Japan, Russia, and the United States. A certain number of the 3-year-old bulls are left for breeding, and care is exercised not to kill breeding bulls or cows. The United States provides housing, schools, employment, food, and clothing for the native population, and the whole picture represents a well-ordered natural-resource management enterprise. In 1941 the Japanese abrogated her claim on the argument that seals were injuring her commercial fisheries and Russia gave her entire attention to the Commander Island herd. The division of revenue in accordance with a provisional agreement of 1942 now stands at 80 per cent for the United States and 20 per cent for Canada. The present population is estimated to have increased to 1,500,000 animals. Sales of skins during the fall and winter of 1951–1952 brought in a gross sum of almost 4 million dollars. Blue fox skins, also taken on the Pribilof Islands, yielded a gross of $4,802. In addition to the skins, by-products produced in 1951 included 40,000 gallons of oil and 351 tons of meal. The sale of a portion of the latter brought in a gross of about $76,000. A considerable amount of seal meat is used by the native population.

There is not a better example of the rehabilitation, maintenance, and sound management of a natural resource to be found than that of the Pribilof seal herd.

Sponges. The sponge fishery of the United States is confined to the upper west coast of Florida and the lower coast south of Fort Myers and extending to the keys at the southern tip of the state. It is thought that certain areas between these two limits contain sponges, but so far no fisheries have been prosecuted between Fort Myers and Tampa.

The sponge of commerce is the skeleton of a marine animal and consists of a mesh of fine resilient fibers. The rest of the animal consists of soft tissue through which extends a system of canals and chambers. Minute microorganisms are captured in this system as the water in which they travel flows through it. Reproduction occurs during the warmer months. Eggs produced and fertilized within the body are released as larvae which attach themselves to rocks after they have reached the sea floor. The entire life history of sponges, however, is little understood. They are thought to grow slowly, to be subject to periodic disease, and to be declining in numbers if figures on yields per unit of fishing effort are

FIG. 149. Boats from sponge-fishing fleet and unloaded catch. Tarpon Springs, Fla. (*Photo by Fish and Wildlife Service.*)

any indication. They also are known to be successfully cultivated from cuttings in the Bahamas and British Honduras.

The best known and most valuable of the sponges are the sheep's-wool type which must have certain qualities as to texture, fineness, durability, absorptive capacity, shape, and size. They are used in many of the arts including surgery, brick and tile laying, painting, leather dressing, and as household and vehicle-washing conveniences.

As far as the sponge fisheries are now understood, the measures relied upon to conserve them are restrictions on size, gear used, and diving procedures. The hooking and trampling of sponges by divers is regulated to prevent waste from tearing and crushing.

Sponge fishermen must consecrate their olfactories to the business, since the separation of the dead canal system from the skeleton can come about only as the former decays, with resulting disagreeable odors.

The key to a prosperous future for the sponge fisheries, which represent a take worth more than 2 million dollars a season, lies in better knowledge of life histories, diseases, rate of reproduction and growth, and in the promise of unexplored grounds.

BIBLIOGRAPHY

Annual Reports of the Secretary of the Interior, 1945–1952.

Bachrach, Max.: Fur: A Practical Treatise, rev. ed., Prentice-Hall, Inc., New York, 1947.

Carson, Rachel L.: Fish and Shellfish of the South Atlantic and Gulf Coasts, *U.S. Fish and Wildlife Service Conservation Bul.* 37, 1942.

———: Food from the Sea, *U.S. Fish and Wildlife Service Conservation Bul.* 33, 1943.

Dambach, Charles A.: Conservation of Wildlife, Chap. 18 in Conservation of Natural Resources, Guy Harold Smith, ed., John Wiley & Sons, Inc., New York, 1950.

Federal Wildlife Conservation Activities, 1950, Report of the Committee on Expenditures in the Executive Departments, S. Rept. 317, 82d Cong., 1st sess., 1951.

Fishery Resources of the United States, S. Doc. 51, 79th Cong., 1st sess., 1945.

Gabrielson, Ira N.: Wildlife Conservation, The Macmillan Company, New York, 1941.

———: Wildlife Refuges, The Macmillan Company, New York, 1947.

Graham, Edward H.: The Land and Wildlife, Oxford University Press, New York, 1947.

Hamilton, W. J., Jr.: Chaps. 11, 12, and 13 in Conservation in the United States, A. F. Gustafson and associates, Comstock Publishing Associates, Inc., Ithaca, N.Y., 1949.

Jamison, James K.: This Ontonagon Country, 3d ed., Ontonagon Herald Co., Ontonagon, Mich., 1948.

Lagler, Karl F.: Freshwater Fishery Biology, William C. Brown Company, Dubuque, Iowa, 1952.

Leopold, Aldo: The American Game Policy, in *Transactions, Seventeenth American Game Conference,* Wildlife Management Institute, Washington, D.C., 1930.

McHugh, J. L., and Elbert H. Ahlstrom: Is the Pacific Sardine Disappearing? *Sci. Monthly,* **72**:377–384, June, 1951.

Martin, Howard H.: Fisheries for the Future, Chap. 19 in Conservation of Natural Resources, Guy Harold Smith, ed., John Wiley & Sons, Inc., New York, 1950.

A National Plan for American Forestry, S. Doc. 12, 73d Cong. 2d sess., 1933.

Palmer, E. Laurence: Fieldbook of Natural History, McGraw-Hill Book Company, Inc., New York, 1949.

Report of the U.S. Bureau of Fisheries, in Report of Special Committee on the Conservation of Wildlife Resources, S. Rept. 1203, 76th Cong., 3d sess., 1940.

Shoemaker, Carl D.: Report on Federal Conservation Legislation, in Proceedings of the Forty-first Convention, International Association of Game, Fish and Conservation Commissioners, Rochester, N.Y., Sept. 10 and 11, 1951.

The Status of Wildlife in the United States, Report of the Special Committee on the Conservation of Wildlife Resources, S. Rept. 1203, 76th Cong., 3d sess., 1940.

Tressler, Donald K.: and James McW. Lemon, Marine Products of Commerce, 2d ed., Reinhold Publishing Corporation, New York, 1951.

Trippensee, Reuben E.: Wildlife Management, 1st ed., McGraw-Hill Book Company, Inc., New York, 1948.

Van Hise, Charles R., and Loomis Havemeyer, eds., and associates: Conservation of Our Natural Resources, The Macmillan Company, New York, 1930.

Westerman, Fred A., and Albert S. Hazzard: For Better Fishing, Department of Conservation, Lansing, Mich., 1945.

CHAPTER 6

The Mineral Resources[1]

The minerals served mankind first in the form of crude tools and as means of storing up wealth. In relatively recent times they have become sources of warmth and energy. Today they are used increasingly as the materials of technology in its thousands of directions from drugs and caustics to airplanes and metal-frame buildings. More than most people have come to realize, too, minerals are the bases of much of our labor saving and luxury equipment. One could go on almost indefinitely listing uses in which minerals are today indispensable, including surgery and winding up with national defense.

In the economy of the country the mineral resources play a big part. Almost a million men are employed in mining alone, and this figure extends to well over 3½ million with the addition of the number required by the mineral manufacturing industries. The 1949 figure for value of mineral production the United States runs to nearly 14 billion dollars.

In the face of such facts, it is amazing that mineral resources are taken as a matter of course so far as demand is concerned and dropped like a hot potato when it comes to thinking and acting on questions of their conservation. The brilliant inventor and the unselfish public-spirited conservationist alike frequently ignore the fact of irreplaceability in their mad rush for new uses of mineral resources. New discovery, use of substitutes, and general human ingenuity have so far taken care of threatened shortages, but one may well question whether they can continue to do so.

The least that can be asked of a thoughtful citizen of a democracy is that he keep himself informed, that he challenge indefensible waste of mineral resources, and that he support conservation measures in their management. This is true even though he should fail within his lifetime to achieve the ultimate in comfort and convenience.

[1] Most of the factual material for this section was obtained from three sources: The 1949 *Minerals Yearbook*, *Annual Reports of the Secretary of the Interior*, and *Resources for Freedom*, Vols. I and III, the Report of the President's Materials Policy Commission. These works are more fully listed in the bibliography at the end of the chapter.

In order to understand mineral resources it is well to consider some of the accepted classifications. Perhaps the simplest of these is mineral fuels, metals, and nonfuel metallics. These general classes are subject to various breakdowns, and this is also true of the whole resource group. For example, coal, iron, and copper are sometimes spoken of as *basic* and all others are *contributory* in terms of industrial economy; or certain minerals are called *strategic* because they are necessary for national defense and are likely to be in lean supply, while others are *nonstrategic;* again the minerals known to world trade may be *primary* as products of first capture from nature or *secondary* as products of recovered scrap or by-products.

Some idea of the variety of mineral resources may be obtained from study of a generalized classification according to physical, chemical, and use characteristics as shown in Table 6.

National Mineral Policy. Whatever the United States may have in the name of mineral policy is made up of unrelated laws dealing with (1) mineral-land disposal; (2) tariffs on imports to protect domestic producers from foreign competition in the sale of those minerals which are ample in supply or those whose production needs to be stimulated; (3) authorization of surveys to locate, test, and rarely to develop new deposits of those minerals which are scarce and needed; (4) purchasing output at artificially high prices to relieve mining distress; (5) maintaining government monopoly on certain materials or on federally owned property but providing procedures for their development by private enterprise and thereby obtaining public revenue; (6) allocating strategic minerals in wartime; (7) encouraging mild self-regulation by mineral industries, usually aimed at production control to maintain prices; (8) stockpiling strategic minerals in time of war or preparation for war; and (9) negotiating agreements for importation of strategic minerals from foreign sources. Of these items the only ones which put any particular emphasis on conservation of mineral resources are 3, 5, and 6. Theoretically, item (1) which has to do with mineral-land disposal should operate to conserve these resources, but weak enforcement of patent requirements and superficial appraisal of mineral values under these laws have led to widespread fraud and sometimes to wasteful exploitation and inequitable distribution of public resources.

Recommendations of policies for the various mineral resources were made in 1933 by a special "mineral inquiry" under the leadership of C. K. Lieth, but little legislation has resulted and a new set of recommendations is contained in the President's Materials Policy Commission Report of 1952. The latter are comprehensive, and among other things they urge (1) the speeding up of fact gathering and analysis by the Bureau of Mines and the Geological Survey. This would include provision of funds

Table 6. Generalized Classification of Minerals According to Physical, Chemical, and Use Characteristics

					Examples
Minerals	Metals	Ferrous	Iron		Iron ore
			Ferro-alloying		Manganese ore Metallurgical chromite Molybdenum
		Non-ferrous	Base		Copper Tin Mercury
			Light		Aluminum Magnesium Titanium
			Precious		Gold Silver Platinum
			Rare		Uranium Radium Beryllium
	Non-metals	Mineral fuels	Fluid	Liquid	Petroleum
				Gaseous	Natural gas
			Solid	Hard coal	Anthracite Semi-anthracite
				Soft coal	Bituminous Lignite
		Other non-metals	Building materials		Sand and gravel Stone Cement materials
			Chemical materials		Sulfur Salt Chemical chromite
			Fertilizer materials		Phosphate rock Potash Nitrates
			Ceramic materials		Clay Silica Feldspar
			Refractories		Silica Fire clay Refractory chromite
			Abrasives		Sandstone Corundum Industrial diamonds
			Insulating materials		Magnesia Asbestos Mica
			Pigments and fillers		Ocher Clay Diatomite Barite
			Precious and semi-precious stones		Gem diamond Amethyst Amber

SOURCE: William Van Royen, Oliver Bowles, Elmer W. Pehrson, The Mineral Resources of the World (Copyright 1952 by Prentice-Hall, Inc., New York) reproduced by permission of Department of Geography, University of Maryland, and the publisher.

for a complete census of the mineral industries in 1954 and every 5 years thereafter (already authorized but not financed). (2) Acceleration of topographic and geologic mapping of the United States and Alaska by the Geological Survey (authorized but weakly supported by appropriation) and intensive study of procedure and instruments of mineral exploration. (3) Revamping of the entire mining claim and lease systems to eliminate opportunities for fraud without discouraging legitimate prospecting and mining.

A considerable program of piecemeal legislation is continually before the Congress without too much attention being paid so far to the commission's statesmanlike recommendations.

State Mineral Policies. All the important mineral-producing states have their own laws which comprise their particular mining policies. Some of them attempt to regulate mining, and many have to do with tax provisions and other incentives to production. Safety laws vary widely, and those which are pointed toward conservation of minerals are principally in the fields of petroleum and natural-gas production.

The treatment of minerals which follows will be necessarily confined to three groups—the mineral fuels, the metals, and the miscellaneous nonmetallics.

THE MINERAL FUELS

Sometimes spoken of as the "fossil fuels," coal, petroleum, and natural gas appear to have been furnished to the human race with all of Nature's talent for variety and storage. They come solid, liquid, or gaseous in form and along with sunlight, falling water, and animal strength have been our sources of energy. In spite of all the potentialities of atomic energy, we shall probably be demanding the mineral fuels in increasing amounts as long as they last. Their conservation is most difficult, not only because of their irreplaceability and of human habits of wasteful use, but because their discovery and capture is expensive and even dangerous to human life. Their capture and use is also accompanied frequently by necessarily brutal wrecking of landscapes and by pollution of air and water. But their conservation is necessary not only for energy purposes but because human health and convenience are tied in to the use of hundreds of their products and services all the way from aspirin to the treatment of wooden railroad ties for durability.

Coal

It is fortunate that coal, which in many ways may be thought of as the most important mineral, is relatively plentiful, for it has been mined in this country in recent years at the rate of almost 1,000 tons a minute and used or exported at about the same rate. It has been said, however, that our coal reserve represents a solid cube 15 miles on each edge, and that only one corner of it has been used up. But it happens that this is the most valuable corner.

Coal has been known in what is now the United States since 1679 when the French missionary Father Hennepin recorded its presence along the Illinois River. News traveled slowly in those days, however, and the coal-mining industry has been in operation only since 1814. The first large-scale mining was reported in Virginia in 1822, although small shipments

FIG. 150. A coal-cutting machine starting to undercut coal at the face of an Ohio mine. The blade, with its teeth which move at high speed, can be operated either horoizontally or vertically. (*Photo by Bureau of Mines.*)

from the Virginia mines had been sent to New York as early as 1758 and coal had been used in Pennsylvania in 1769.

Second only in dollar value to petroleum on the basis of annual mineral production, coal constitutes the greatest tonnage of any mined product. It is burned to generate most of the electrical power used in the United States and to produce most of the artificial gas. It contributes to the manufacture of steel in the form of coke, a solid residue after it has been heated and certain by-products have been removed. The sulfa drugs, nylon, and plastics used for the manufacture of thousands of useful articles are all products of coal. The list may be continued to include fertilizers, insecticides, and food preservatives. In modern life, coal is indispensable.

Origin and Occurrence. Coal is of organic origin and differs in this sense from the metals. It is the result of centuries of accumulation of plant material which grew luxuriantly in past ages in the periods of generally mild, moist climate. Layer after layer of dying vegetation accumulated in the form of leaves, branches, and trunks which gradually changed to peat such as is cut, dried, and burned in European countries and used in the United States for soil conditioning, packing material, and other purposes. Ordinarily the accumulations of such material would decay rapidly but only in contact with oxygen. This was cut off as the peat became deeply buried and subjected to pressure from the weight of upper layers and of water and silt as it sank below swamp and ocean levels. Gradually the vegetation and its residues were buried deeper until seas overflowed the ancient swamps from whose waters and floods still greater layers of silt and mud increased the heat and pressure. All this compressing with its accompanying heat turned the accumulations slowly into coal, which is now mined after millions of years. Limited deposits were subject to movements of the earth's crust in mountain-range upheavals. This brought about increased pressures and greater heat and produced the "high-rank" coals such as anthracite.

Rank is a term applied to coal which signifies the relative proportions of fixed carbon, moisture, and volatile (easily vaporized) material. In general, rank increases as moisture and volatile material decrease, with an accompanying increase in fixed carbon.

For purposes of general understanding it is sufficient to list the ranks from high to low as follows:

1. Anthracitic (three groups of anthracite)
2. Bituminous (five groups)
3. Subbituminous (three groups)
4. Lignitic (lignite and brown coal, the latter unconsolidated)

If lignite were to become anthracite, the following approximate changes would have to occur over a million years or so[2]:

	Lignite	Anthracite	Change
Fixed carbon, per cent.........	**33**	92	59 (increase)
Volatile matter, per cent.......	26	5	21 (decrease)
Moisture, per cent.............	41	3	38 (decrease)
Total (ash-free basis)........	100	100	

Lignite, of which there are vast deposits in eastern Montana, the Dakotas, and Texas, is a relatively soft coal which may vary from light

[2] Sherman, Allan, and Allen B. Macmurphy, Facts About Coal, Bureau of Mines, U.S. Department of the Interior, 1950, p. 2.

brown to almost a black but which always leaves a brown mark when rubbed over a white surface. It runs as high as 40 per cent moisture when first mined, slacks easily, and is difficult to store. It is not yet important in American mineral economy but has potential value for improvement through drying, briquetting, and for the production of gas, synthetic liquid fuel, or as an improved coal under steam boilers, and locally for household heating.

Subbituminous coal is black and resembles the well-known bituminous or "soft" coal commonly used for heating throughout the Middle West. Its

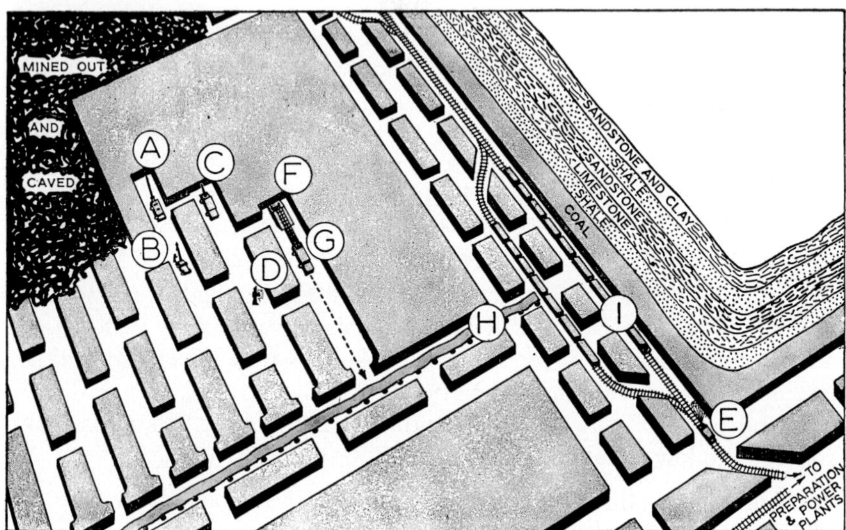

FIG. 151. Diagram of modern coal mine. (*A*) Cutting machine, (*B*) roof bolting machine, (*C*) drilling machine (for blasting), (*D*) safety inspector, (*E*) rock duster (dilutes coal dust to prevent explosion), (*F*) mechanical loader, (*G*) mine shuttle car, (*H*) conveyer belt, (*I*) underground railroad. Surface works including a giant ventilating fan are not shown. (*Adapted from* 1952 *Bituminous Coal Annual, courtesy Bituminous Coal Institute.*)

moisture content of 15 to 30 per cent is lower than the best-quality lignite, but it slacks easily in contact with air and is subject to the same difficulties of storage. For this reason it has limited use except locally. Deposits of subbituminous coal are widely distributed in the Rocky Mountain region and in western Washington.

Bituminous coals, with which most people are familiar and which are most widely used industrially and for transportation power, vary sharply in their make-up and in the way they burn. In appearance they may be either dull or lustrous black. Industrially and from the standpoint of efficient use for the many heating purposes, it is important to know which bituminous coals will "coke," that is, leave a porous gray residue when heated in ovens with little air and relieved of certain volatile and liquid components. Coke is a clean efficient household fuel and is used in the smelting of iron ore and the manufacture of steel. The recovered by-products from its production are the source of many useful materials, and their use represents good conservation. Some of the otherwise efficient bituminous coals burn to an ash or powder instead of coking and are therefore more difficult to utilize fully. The various bituminous coals are widely distributed.

Anthracite or "hard" coal is the least abundant and most adaptable coal for domestic use. It is slow burning, compares favorably in heating power with the best rank bituminous, and produces less soot. It is black and lustrous in appearance and leaves a considerable volume of very light-weight ash. The smaller sizes of anthracite are used to some extent industrially.

It is well to bear in mind that both composition and heating power are used in classifying coal into "ranks." The term *British thermal unit* (B.t.u.) is frequently encountered, and it means the amount of heat required to raise the temperature of 1 pound of water 1° Fahrenheit. *Ash* consists of the mineral impurities incapable of becoming gaseous and devoid of fixed carbon.

Knowledge of the ranks of coal is important to the coal industry because of the variation in usefulness and the consequent differences in profit when the product is marketed. Such knowledge is also important in conserving coal since the higher ranks are likely to be used up first, and because actual waste, rationalized as economically unavoidable, varies with the exploitation of the different ranks.

Distribution of Coal Resources. There are six coal "provinces" in the United States, all but one of which, the Gulf province, extend into Canada. Fifty-one per cent of the reserves are of bituminous rank, and the greatest volume is in the Rocky Mountain province, wholly within the United States. Then comes the Northern Great Plains province, the Interior province, and the Eastern province, with the Pacific and Gulf provinces constituting poor fifth and sixth places, respectively. Sub-bituminous makes up 31.4 per cent of the reserves, lignite (in better coal equivalent) 16.8 per cent, and anthracite only 0.8 per cent. The Eastern province in terms of *volume, concentration of area, and quality combined* is the most important and supports the greatest single volume of production. The Eastern and Interior provinces contain about one-third of the nation's reserves.

The wide and general distribution of coal resources in the United States is fortunate for the people and the industries using coal in terms of the prices they pay, since rail transportation is an important item of expense. Also the occurrence of both coking coal deposits and gas coals alongside of iron deposits has been an important factor in the location of steel-production centers. Birmingham, Ala., is a good example. In like manner the location of Detroit and Cleveland, both important steel and industrial centers, are almost midway between the Lake Superior iron-ore deposits and the Appalachian region of the Eastern coal province.

Distribution of coal resources in the United States is no indication of rates of production. Thus Pennsylvania, the leader in production, ranks eleventh in estimated tonnage of deposits. West Virginia is second in tons produced but seventh in estimated deposits.

Loss and Waste in Managing Coal Resources. In mining, preparation for market, and utilization, loss and waste of coal may be said to be more common and more significant than in the management of many of the other natural resources. The forms or arrangements and the depths at which deposits occur present a handicap to full recovery. Highly competitive exploitation and marketing, along with lag in development and adoption of efficient utilization equipment, result in waste at almost every turn. Nor is the ordinary householder any too anxious to utilize heating coal fully in firing practice.

Coal is mined by sinking vertical shafts to underground deposits, reaching them by openings in side hills which makes removal possible horizontally, using "slope" openings when deposits are tilted, and by stripping of the overburden of rock, soil, and vegetation from shallow deposits. The latter method makes possible almost full recovery of the coal and thus amounts to good coal conservation, but what it does to the landscape is anything but conservation of soil and space resources.

Poorer recovery may result from shaft mining since thinner deposits are usually bypassed in reaching the thicker ones which may lie deeper. Eventually, caving in makes it impossible to recover the thinner beds later. It is generally considered prohibitive in cost to take out a bed of coal less than 15 inches in thickness for the higher ranks or less than 36 inches for lignite. Depth of deposits and occurrence of impurities are also limiting factors, 3,000 feet being considered the maximum depth at which coal may be mined economically. Loss also occurs in pillars of coal left to support the mine roof in the "room-and-pillar" method of removing the coal (see Fig. 151). These pillars may be 50 to 80 feet thick or thicker and as long as the rooms between them, which are usually 14 to 30 feet wide. These rooms are made by removing the coal loosened by cutting and blasting. In the more efficient mines the pillars are largely removed from the rear of the deposit forward to the foot of the shaft after the rooms are exhausted. This may allow the roof to cave as the work retreats. In some instances the pillars are left as mining ceases. In general the first method is the better conservation practice but somewhat more dangerous to human life. Timber supports are used along with coal pillars in both methods, and both apply to shaft and to those with horizontal entryways.

In strip mining there is no need of timber or coal pillar support because there is no "roof" to the mine. The overburden, as noted above, is removed, piled first to the rear or side of the operation (and thereafter in areas from which coal has been removed). The coal is then loosened and removed with little loss. The problem here is to leave the mined area in shape for some sort of use rather than a shambles of upside-down material. Leveling for pasture development, reforestation without leveling,

FIG. 152. Land reclamation after strip coal mining in Indiana. Lakes are formed by damming up the final cuts made by drag lines or power shovels used in uncovering coal seams. Four-tenths of all mined land in Indiana has been revegetated and one-tenth devoted to recreational development. (*Photo by Indiana Coal Producers Assoc., courtesy Bituminous Coal Institute.*)

and development of fishing, boating, and other recreations where water has accumulated furnish opportunities for conserving the areas.

Waste and loss in the preparation of coal for market occurs in the separation of coal from attached slate or other noncombustible impurities after it has been mined, in washing, and in the slacking of unmarketable finely divided coal.

In final utilization, for whatever industrial or household purpose, incomplete combustion is a problem which must be met by modern heating equipment and by thoughtful and careful operation of such equipment. Two ways in which the householder may save money and save coal resources are the use of coke when available, which when properly fired is more efficient than coal, and the use of the power-operated stoker which feeds coal fires efficiently and, by aid of forced draft, accomplishes almost complete combustion. Stokers are also used by the industries.

From a business-management standpoint it should be noted that the coal-producing industry is highly competitive, costly in terms of human life, and subject to labor troubles in which both management and labor have failed to achieve measures of cooperation which society has a right to demand of them.

It is well to remember also that the very nature of the industry brings it into conflict with the conservation of certain replaceable natural resources in terms of air and water pollution, blighting of surface space resources, and the disarranging of otherwise productive soil.

Ownership of Coal Resources. Before 1873, when the first coal land law was enacted by the Congress, public lands underlain with coal were sold as agricultural lands and any coal involved became the property of the purchaser. Enormous areas of coal-bearing land thereby passed into private ownership in Ohio, Kentucky, Illinois, Missouri, and Kansas. Coal lands farther east had been disposed of similarly by the states which owned them. The coal statute of 1873 provided for the sale of known coal lands at prices "not less than ten dollars per acre" for lands farther than 15 miles from a railroad and "not less than twenty dollars per acre" for lands within 15 miles from a completed railroad. Only 160 acres were to be sold to any individual, but associations could purchase 160 acres for each member. No attempt was made to classify or evaluate the lands, and the Department of the Interior read "not more than" for "not less than" so that $10 and $20 became the standard prices up to 1906. During this period in spite of the provisions of the law, vast areas of coal lands were still sold as agricultural land. The total of all lands so disposed of approaches 100 million acres.

A new interpretation of the plain language of the law was put into force by the Department of the Interior in 1906 so that rates of $75 to $100 per acre were charged, and in 1909, $100 to $300 were the prevailing rates. Even at these prices the actual coal cost the producer only a few cents a ton, which was but a fraction of its value in terms of royalties per ton paid in the West by operators to private proprietors of coal lands.

Thus the disposal of much of the coal-bearing area in the United States is the old story of fraud and neglect so common with respect to timber and agricultural lands. And while it may be argued that private enterprise has not done so badly in making coal available to the people of the country, it is fortunate that President Theodore Roosevelt, prompted by the report of the short-lived National Conservation Commission appointed upon the recommendation of the 1908 White House conference of governors, withdrew from settlement and entry 80 million acres of public lands thought to be coal bearing. This was in 1909, and out of these and additional withdrawals since that time some 35 million acres have been classified definitely by the Geological Survey as coal lands, with about 24 million acres still to be classified. Previous to these withdrawals President Roosevelt had withdrawn in 1906 almost 9 million acres of coal-bearing lands.

FIG. 153. Drilling for blasting with charged Chemechol tube, a modern nonexplosive device for breaking down coal by the force of compressed gas produced by chemicals in a reusable tube. (*Photo copyrighted by DuPont Magazine, courtesy Bituminous Coal Institute.*)

The buying rush on Western lands was halted by the enactment of the Mineral Leasing Law of 1920 covering nonmetallics on the public lands. Under this law the Federal government assumed obligations of proprietorship and specified a lease procedure whereby operators could recover coal, petroleum, potash, phosphate, and other nonmetallics and would be required to use certain conservation measures and to pay the Federal government on a royalty basis, either in money or in kind. Some of the Indian lands bearing coal are managed under a similar procedure by the Federal government in behalf of the tribes.

The Mineral Leasing Law of 1920 is the only important step taken by the Federal government which challenges wasteful exploitation of the country's coal resources.

Conserving Coal Resources. Since coal is the first one of the truly irreplaceable natural resources so far considered in this text, it is well to remember that coal like other fuels is destroyed when used. Only in a limited sense is it "capitalized" or put into form for continuing use. It differs here from the metals, clays, and building stones which may go on serving mankind in one or another form for centuries after being mined. Coal does get into the form of plastics, textiles, and in small quantities becomes a part of steel, but it is used mainly as fuel. How then can coal be conserved? Certainly mankind cannot "grow" any more coal. People can, however, avoid some of the inexcusable waste and be fair enough to future generations to leave them some of the deposits, particularly of the higher ranks which are in relatively short supply. Much along this line can be done if the public wants it done. Here are some of the ways to conserve coal:

1. Promote the avoidance of waste in mining. The long room and pillar method has been mentioned. Removal of pillars will be done by operators only if it pays. Limited subsidy might be considered here as an incentive and is probably the only one that would bring about the mining of the thinner beds above thick ones.

2. Promote avoidance of waste in preparation. Here the dredging of streams to recover washing wastes for briquetting offers some opportunity for profit, and indeed when the market is good, as many as 1 million tons a year have been recovered. Mechanical cleaning, washing, and sizing covered only 5 per cent of the bituminous coal produced in 1925 as against almost 40 per cent in 1950. This will have to keep pace with the increasing proportions of impurities and of finer sizes resulting from mechanized mining. Research by the Bureau of Mines in this general direction deserves full and continuing support.

3. Improving quality of lignite by drying treatment and using it as fuel for power production in remote localities. Experiments by the Bureau of Mines are progressing in this direction in Texas. (It has been suggested by those who are disturbed over the increasing number of high dams for power, with their many problems of conflict with conserving wild-animal life, that the vast lignite resources can compete with water in the production of power if water for steam plants is available. The lignite would not be marketable for other purposes.)

4. Allocating coking coals as far as possible to coke production in modern by-product ovens. It will be claimed that this is done wherever it is economically possible and convenient. Action of this kind with regard to many natural resources has not been uncommon in time of war and might well be invoked in the event of sharply shrinking supply.

5. Exploring courageously and fairly various regulatory practices on coal exploitation and production as an alternative to nationalizing the

industry. One experiment along this line has been made. The industry was given its chance in the Guffey Coal Act (Bituminous Coal Act of 1937) which said in effect: "Try self-regulation through a commission, as a means of getting some order into a wastefully competitive business which seems always to be in trouble. Take a look too at your management-labor situation in behalf of the public interest." The act was to be in effect for 4 years, and in 1941 it was extended for 2 years and then for 90 days more. It was allowed to lapse in 1943, and was disappointing in its results. This was the Federal-industry approach. Perhaps regulation on a state basis may be worked for as a more promising approach, but while nationalization of natural-resource industries is repugnant to American political thought, it is not beyond the range of possibility with regard to coal even in a democracy.

6. Continuing the Mineral Leasing Law of 1920 in force as a fair and successfully tested procedure by which the Federal government can discharge its obligtion as a proprietor of vast coal and other deposits. There is considerable talk of weakening it by amendment or of repeal in favor of passing Federal mineral lands into private possession. The stipulations contained in these leases covering conservation practices by holders is the one really effective means now in force to conserve as well as to develop the coal resources which belong to all the people. Coal leases continue to be a small but steady and important proportion of all mineral leases issued under the law.

7. Requiring by Federal or local law certain equipment and/or practices designed to curtail waste in building heating. Such regulations might apply to all above certain minimum space-heating requirements and might even, through local building codes, require adequate insulation. Centralized heating could be used to a greater extent also with real fuel saving.

8. Pushing research into various improvements in coal exploitation and use, including such undertakings as burning coal deposits underground to produce fuel gas. Significant progress in the latter is reported from field-scale experiments by the Bureau of Mines in cooperation with a local power company in Alabama.

9. Requiring or promoting cooperation in accomplishing rehabilitation of the surface in strip mining. Certain states now require the posting of a bond by operators on an area basis in order to assure such action. Others promote voluntary action through advice and other forms of mild subsidy. In general, however, the problem is not solved. State regulation appears to be most promising.

10. Working for and accomplishing the enactment of uniform coal-mine safety laws to conserve human lives and powers as well as coal. Over and over, responsibility for shocking disasters is dodged because regulations

are neither adequate nor uniform. What is defined as a gassy mine situation in one state, for example, should be so agreed upon in another, but it is not. Until 1952, the fine work of the Bureau of Mines could lead only to recommendations, not to adoption and enforcement of practices. State regulation has fallen down on this problem although the use of "permissible" (tested) blasting devices and explosives recommended by the bureau are quite generally adopted by the industry. Some real progress is looked for from the passage of the new Federal Coal Mine Safety Act of 1952. This strengthens the earlier law of 1941 by authorizing Federal enforcement of safety recommendations. It is only fair to say that considerable improvement did occur after 1941.

Present Status and Future Outlook for Coal Resources. While competition from petroleum and gas has reduced the general demand for coal throughout the past 25 years, demand for the production of electrical power and for coke is increasing, and in the latter instance coke for metallurgical uses can be produced in sufficient quantity only from coal. This and other special uses in which coal is free from competition accounts for 20 per cent of the total coal consumption. Thoughtful investigators believe generally that coal will figure more and more importantly in the increasing energy demands of the country. More economical production of coal and increasing cost of producing competing fuels bid fair to overcome, eventually, any shrinkage in the traditional demands for this useful fuel.

With estimaed total reserves of 2,500 billion short tons (2,000 pounds), one-half of which is subject by present standards to economic recovery, the 1950 production of 556 million tons would appear to indicate that more than 2,000 years would be required to exhaust the resource. It should be borne in mind, however, that coking coals account for 15 to 20 per cent of the *production* while constituting only 2 per cent of the *reserves;* that steel, electrical power, and chemical industries will have increasing coal demands; and that eventually diminishing reserves of oil and natural gas will put new burdens on the coal resources.

Mechanization in mining marked by such devices as coal-cutting machines, mechanical loaders and belt conveyers to move more rapidly the products of continuous mining, and strip mining—all these have increased productivity per man day and have made considerable contributions to the reduction of waste.

In war or peace, coal is indispensable, and its conservation merits the attention not only of industry and government but of every citizen.

Petroleum

If for no other reason than the development and well-nigh universal ownership of the automobile and its variations in this country, petroleum is an indispensable natural resource. Our present economy would be paralyzed without it. Transportation, space heating, agriculture, mining, power production, and the chemical industries all draw heavily on the petroleum reserves. Representing less than one-tenth of the nation's energy supply in 1900, petroleum and natural gas have become the source of more than one-half the present energy supply. In 1950 the people of this country used 2⅓ billion barrels of petroleum. This amounts to 6½ million barrels a day, and this is three times the amount used in 1925. Comparative consumption for 1929 and 1950 is indicated by uses in Table 7.

Over the next 25 years the demand of this country is estimated by the above commission at double the present requirements. More than 8 per cent of the present domestic consumption comes from imports, and this is net (after subtracting exports).

The petroleum industry, starting in 1859 with the bringing in of the first paying well by a certain Colonel Drake in Pennsylvania, chalked up a production of half a million barrels in 1860. Ninety years later, in 1950, production had increased 4,000-fold and demand for particular products had changed radically. Originally kerosene for lighting had been principally in demand, and not until after the First World War did gasoline take the lead. By 1951, demand for distillate, a heavier product, and residual fuel oil combined exceeded slightly the demand for gasoline, as it had done for a short time about 1929. A slowly rising price for crude oil has been overcome by improvements in the refining of motor fuels and lubricants. Much is made today in the news of discovery exceeding production, and this is a fact. It is far from a fact, however, that discovery trends indicate adequate reserves indefinitely, in the face of rapidly increasing demand.

Origin and Occurrence of Petroleum and Natural Gas. The notion that oil is likely to be found "anywhere" might well have been held by early settlers in the United States. Petroleum skimmed from the surface of springs is known to have been a part of the Indians' medical stores, and petroleum seeps and water pollutions are reported to have plagued the colonists. Guesses as to how oil occurred underground were as common as they were inaccurate, and only in relatively recent years have the petroleum geologists and other scientists put discovery on a basis of scientific knowledge.

Petroleum is a product of buried marine sediments and as such is distributed more widely than present production centers would indicate. This is because accumulations are found only where a combination of source beds, formations adapted to storing accumulations, and underground traps that can hold them are found. This combination is somewhat rare, but here and there vast quantities of organic materials, prob-

Table 7. Consumption of Petroleum Products in the United States, 1929 and 1950

Item	1929	1950
	Millions of barrels	
Total domestic consumption:	940	2,375
Annual	940	2,375
Daily	2.6	6.5

Use	Percentage of total 1929	Percentage of total 1950
Transportation:		
Highway	36	36
Railroad	9	5
Water	10	6
Air	*	2
Total transportation	55	49
Residential and commercial	6	19
Industry and agriculture:		
Manufacturing and mining	15	14
Generation of electricity	1	3
Manufacture of gas	2	2
Agriculture	3	4
Total industry and agriculture	21	23
Miscellaneous†	12	3
Nonfuel uses	6	6
Grand total	100	100

SOURCES: 1929—Adapted from Bureau of Mines *Report of Investigations,* 4805, W. H. Lyon and D. S. Colby. 1950—Bureau of Mines, *Annual Petroleum Statement,* No. P 347; and *Mineral Market Report,* MMS 2003. Table appearing in *Resources for Freedom,* Vol. III, Report of the President's Materials Policy Commission, 1950.

* 0.05 per cent.

† Not allocable. The decline in this category from 1929 to 1950 undoubtedly reflects more complete statistical information for 1950.

ably of both plant and animal character, have been subject to millions of years of change from heat and pressure. The resulting compounds of hydrogen and carbon together with varying impurities, colorless to black in appearance, flow from the ancient muds to domes or traps formed by tilting, faulting, or folding of the earth's crust (Fig. 154). It is at such points that petroleum can be obtained by drilling. Along with the oil, natural gas occurs and serves, when pools are reached by drilling, to force the oil to the surface. The gas itself is valuable as a fuel of high efficiency

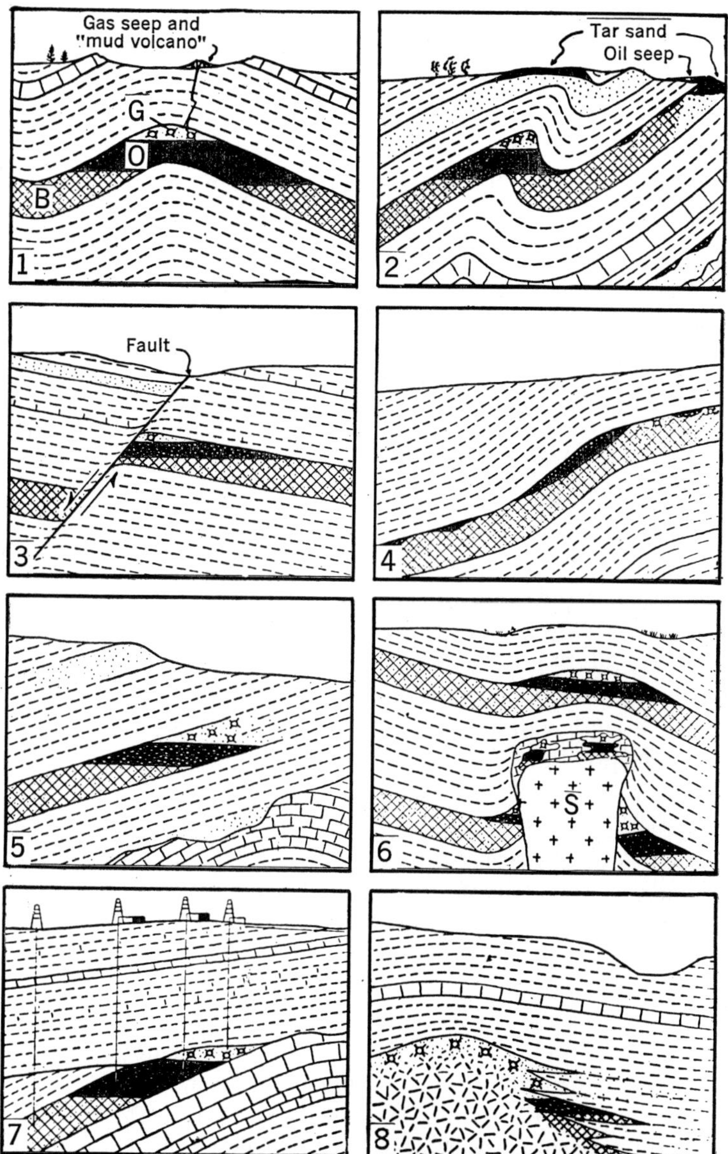

FIG. 154. Common types of oil traps: (1) symmetrical anticline; *G*, sand saturated with gas; *O*, sand saturated with oil; *B*, sand saturated with brine; (2) assymmetrical anticline (3) sand sealed by fault; (4) monoclinal fold or structural terrace; (5) lensing sand, *e.g.*, sandstone grading into shale; (6) salt dome, oil accumulations in upturned sands at side, in cap rock and gently flexing overlying sand; (7) oil accumulating at an angular unconformity; (8) buried granite hill. [*T. S. Lovering, Minerals in World Affairs (copyright 1943 by Prentice-Hall, Inc., New York), p. 150. Reproduced by permission of the publisher.*]

and for the manufacture of certain derivatives, one of which is carbon black used in printer's ink, in the manufacture of rubber articles, and elsewhere in the arts.

Petroleum occurs commercially in twenty-five of the forty-eight states, and natural gas is produced in most of the fields. The major provinces and districts designated on the map on page 284 rank from top production downward as follows:

Mid-Continent
Gulf coast
California
Illinois–Southwest Indiana
Rocky Mountain
Appalachian
Michigan
Lima–Indiana

While the gas provinces and districts are not identical with those of oil, natural-gas production as well as reserves occur principally in decreasing abundance in the same order as the geographical distribution, namely, Mid-Continent, Gulf coast, California.

Ownership of Oil Resources. In the United States the commercial development of oil resources is relatively young, and this has meant that much of the land under which oil lies has passed, by one procedure or another, into private ownership. Furthermore, under our system of government, the owner of the land is usually the owner of its subsurface resources. This situation preceded the discovery and development of many state and federally owned oil lands and, combined with certain misconceptions about the occurrence and behavior of oil deposits, led to wasteful exploitation. Both oil operators and owners of oil land were inclined to believe that petroleum was "galloping around underground like a wild animal" and that it should be pounced upon while it was under certain ownerships and leases. It thus became customary to drill wells on each one and so seek a quick "flush" yield, with resulting rapid decline in the amount of oil obtained. Of course this system or lack of system exhausted the gas which had served to force out the oil. Pumping could be resorted to in some of the wells, but the general effect was to abandon wells from which production had shown a sharp drop. During the 1920s geologists and engineers became increasingly well informed on the "reservoir-energy" function of natural gas, and such knowledge as existed earlier was made use of in drafting the Mineral Leasing Act of 1920. Stipulations written into oil leases under this law were aimed at better drilling practices on Federal lands, and in recent years many of the states have taken account of the need for requiring that state-owned oil properties be operated under similar leases. Ownership, then, has been an important consideration both in the depletion and conservation of petroleum resources.

Factors Which Deplete Oil Resources. As with coal, it must be remembered that petroleum is an irreplaceable natural resource and that it does not get its share of attention as to need for conservation.

Ownership and expense of drilling set the stage for wasteful exploitation, and certainly too many wells, badly spaced, have reduced the production life of the older fields. Certain of the fields showed a decrease

FIG. 155. Carefully spaced oil wells in the Trapp Pool near Susank, Kans. Wheat fields occupying same land. [*Photo by Standard Oil Co. (N.J.), courtesy American Petroleum Institute.*]

from peak production of as much as 90 per cent in 3 years, due mainly to the dissipation of gas drive as it is frequently called.

Competition and resulting overproduction, particularly in the early days of new discovery, have been common, with inevitable waste in marketing and consumption.

Two world wars have stepped up demand in turn, and strangely enough both have stimulated the domestic demand. Oil operators and merchants will point out that one cannot produce without a market and emphasize the benefits which production volume and resulting lower prices have brought to society. But they can hardly contend that waste has not characterized the industry and its marketing procedure.

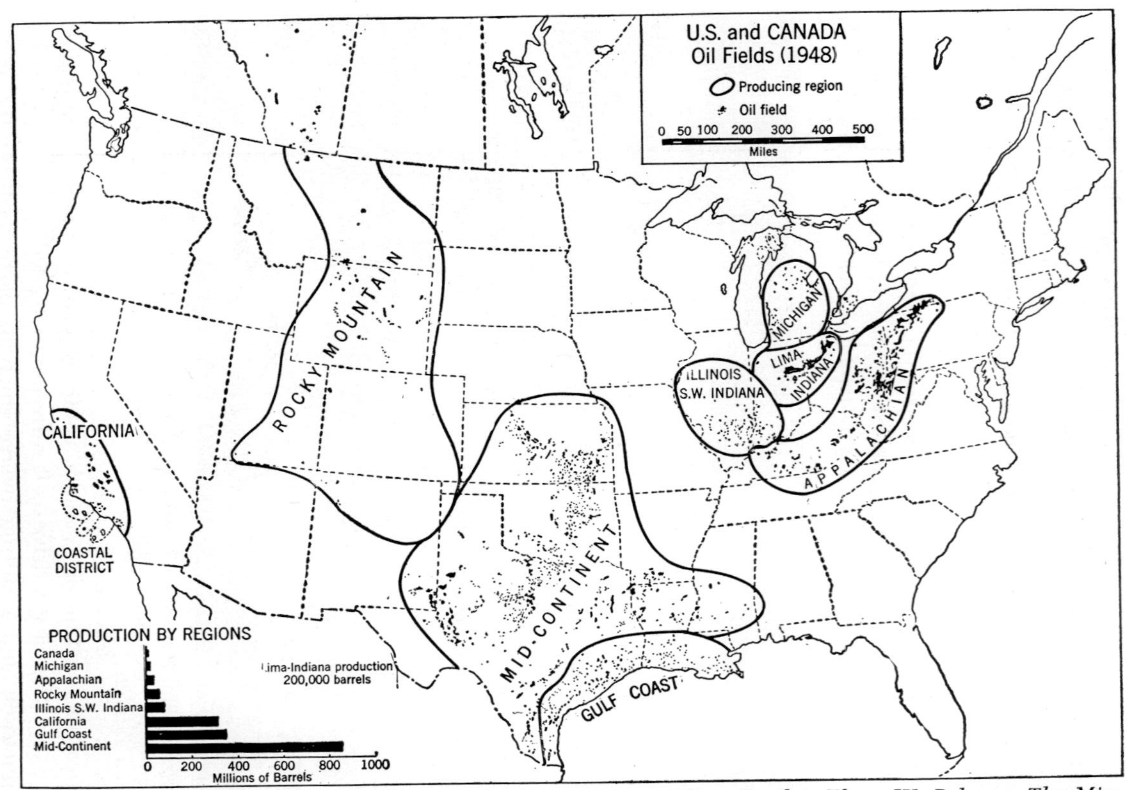

FIG. 156. Map of United States oil fields. [*William Van Royen, Oliver Bowles, Elmer W. Pehrson, The Mineral Resources of the World* (*copyright* 1952 *by Prentice-Hall, Inc. of New York*), *reproduced in simplified form by permission of Department of Geography, University of Maryland, and the publisher.*]

The design of the internal-combustion engine in its myriad uses has of course improved tremendously since the turn of the century, and more powerful engines are appearing continually. Failure to achieve lower consumption of gasoline, however, in the development of the automobile engine, so that lesser amounts of petroleum would be required, is characteristic of the automobile industry in this country, and change would probably greatly depress the petroleum industry. The recent popularity of the smaller European automobiles in the United States indicates a mild rebellion against the cost of operating the conventional type of automobile and may affect slightly the demand for gasoline. At any rate the opinion may be risked that automobile transportation today consumes much more gasoline than could be made to do the job if some attention were given to more economical engines, and particularly to lighter weight cars.

The growing use of fuel oil for household heating and for power production brings convenience but, along with it, wasteful consumption of petroleum. The product required is not just a refinery residue but contains valuable constituents subject to recovery. It is known that the rapid development of oil-burning heating equipment was stimulated by the need to find a market for fuel oil when inventories of the latter began to pile up. Industrially, the use of petroleum has competed strongly with coal, which is much more plentiful.

The very nature of the petroleum industry with its high costs of discovery, drilling, and refining and its competitive character have made waste difficult to avoid. High rate of consumption has been a corollary of constant productive capacity. All this means that any effort to curtail consumption as a conservation measure is doomed to failure. That is why conservation stops at the field or at the latest in the refinery.

Possibilities of Conserving Petroleum Resources. With the "known economic reserves inadequate" according to the President's Materials Policy Commission and the two phrases "discoveries geologically likely—though not necessarily adequate" and "synthesis progress expected" as the only optimistic comments, the people of the United States may well be concerned with the possibilities for reducing waste and making one barrel of oil do the work of two. The following are some of the directions in which effort can be speeded up:

1. Improve recovery from present producing oil fields through operation of pools cooperatively or by legal requirement, as units. Agreements of this sort provide for efficient well spacing and best use of "reservoir energy" or "gas drive." Other provisions include "repressuring" or returning gas or water to the underground oil formations, "acidizing" or using acid to open up the less porous "sands" and increase oil flow, and "fracturing"—all these to bring otherwise irrecoverable oil to the drilled well.

State regulatory laws have been successful in bringing about these practices.

2. Process natural gas at the well for the production of gasoline and other liquids, generally used by the industry. This measure has real possibilities.

3. Attack transportation losses by better inspection and maintenance of pipeline equipment and by land shipment instead of water shipment wherever possible during war periods.

4. Prorate production on a voluntary basis by the industry so long as it works to prevent flooding the market and so encouraging waste. This may be accomplished by law if necessary.

5. Perfect and keep available the methods of obtaining oil from coal and from oil shale, both of which are vastly more abundant than petroleum. Research and development work by the U.S. Bureau of Mines in the hydrogenation of coal for the production of oil (Bergius process used extensively in Germany) and in gas synthesis (Fischer-Tropsch process) have led to an estimate that gasoline and other products can be made from Wyoming coals at prices competitive with petroleum products. And while these findings are challenged by the National Petroleum Council,[3] they indicate progress and promise of a generous chance for supplying petroleum substitutes. Likewise the Bureau of Mines has experiments under way in the production of oil from oil shale on a demonstration basis at Rifle, Colo. The bureau has estimated that oil-shale deposits located principally in Colorado, Utah, and Wyoming represent a possible oil content of some 500 billion barrels which might be recovered at several times the cost of producing natural petroleum and that 80 billion barrels of this could be produced at cost only slightly higher than the present costs of finding and producing petroleum. In this estimate the study of the National Petroleum Council agrees that a daily production of 200,000 barrels could be marketed at about 2 cents a gallon higher than comparable grades of natural petroleum products on the Los Angeles market. The council does not appear too enthusiastic, but several of the oil companies have oil-shale holdings and are said to be planning future operations.

Right here, though, an oil-shale industry runs into another natural-resource problem. The deposits are located in dry country. Even water enough to supply the necessary labor-force community is none too plentiful. Oil from shale therefore may be a question of water supply. Location of plants in sparsely populated territory also introduces difficulty in marketing until natural petroleum production shrinks and lessens present competition.

6. Develop and manage publicly owned reserves. Under the Mineral

[3] Official industry advisory group to the Secretary of the Interior.

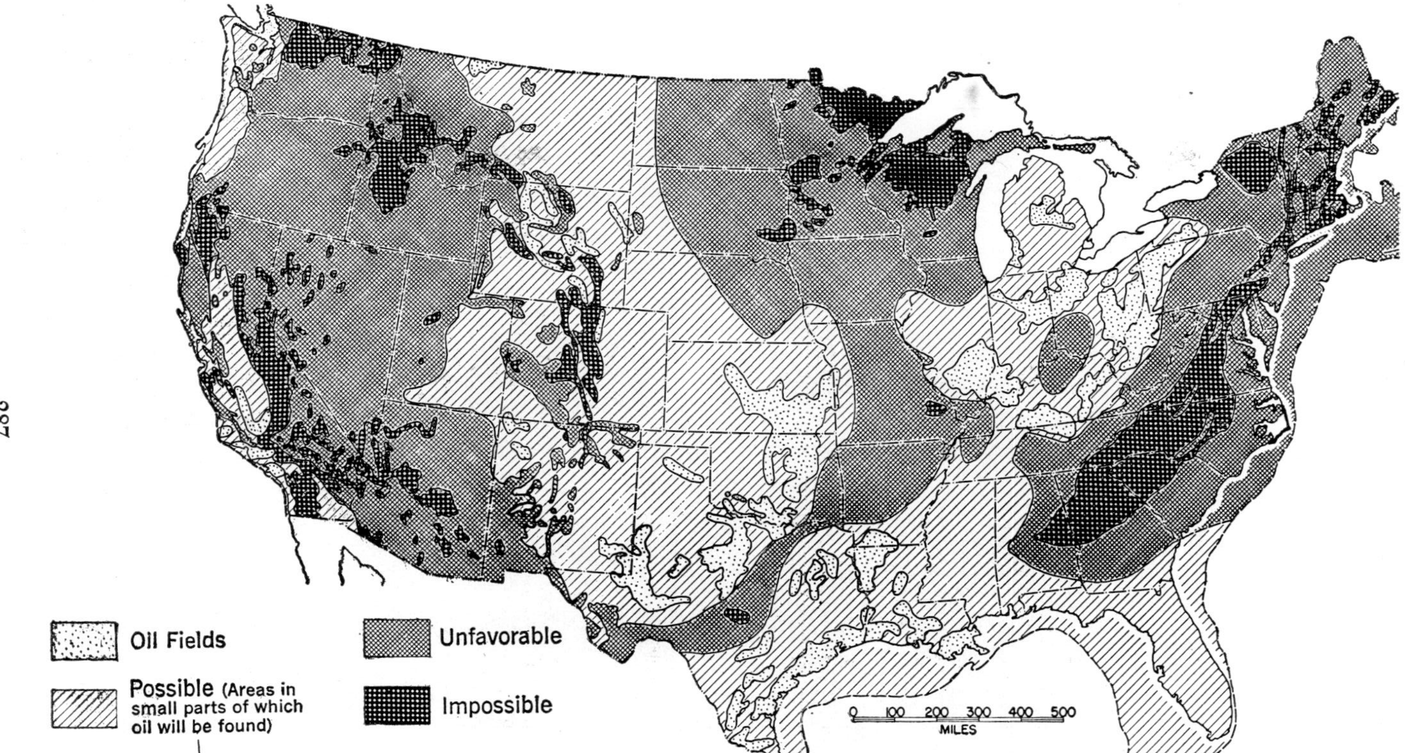

FIG. 157. Map of United States oil possibilities. [*William Van Royen, Oliver Bowles, Elmer W. Pehrson, The Mineral Resources of the World* (*copyright* 1952 *by Prentice-Hall, Inc., New York*), *reproduced by permission of Department of Geography, University of Maryland, and the publisher.*]

Leasing Law of 1920, oil-prospecting permits and oil leases must be used in accordance with good conservation practice. As mentioned on page 275 this is one of the few regulatory devices in the hands of the public. This system should be continued and, in modified form perhaps, applied to the *outlying* submerged lands of the continental shelf over which the

FIG. 157A. Diesel-operated rig 7 miles off Louisiana shore. Quarters, storerooms, storage tanks, and all other facilities for maintaining this rig are included. Oil is taken off in barges and brought to mainland. [*Photo by Standard Oil Co. (N.J.), courtesy American Petroleum Institute.*]

Federal government still has control. Those submerged lands which passed to the states by the law of 1953, within their historic boundaries, will need appropriate legislation for their exploitation. Some of these states already have experience along this line within their land boundaries, notably California, Texas, and Louisiana. These various submerged lands, state and Federal, are estimated to be underlain with oil resources running into the billions; their development is beset with unusual expense and difficulty, and drilling works would be vulnerable in time of war. Low royalty rates and other incentives will probably be necessary to encourage private enterprise to develop them.[4]

7. Encourage new discovery. It is highly questionable as to whether new discovery can be called conservation. Certainly, however, it serves to replenish the steady draft on reserves and should be considered. Discovery efforts have increased tremendously in the past few years. In 1939 fewer than 3,000 exploratory "holes" were drilled, and for every one that became a producer 8.5 proved dry. Thirteen years later, in 1952, some 12,425 exploratory holes were drilled with one producer for every 4.8 dry ones. The average depth of drilling was 4,476 feet, although extreme depths of more than 3½ miles have been reported. One well has been drilled to a depth of 20,600 feet.

In the past much was heard of the so-called "doodle bug" which meant any sort of gadget alleged to be useful in indicating the presence of oil and belonging to the same family as the sticks used in "dowsing" for good water-well location. In recent years, scientific methods known as *geophysical* have been developed and used widely in exploration for oil. The information obtained by these methods has to do with promising rock formations beneath the surface, rather than with the actual presence of oil itself. Their usefulness, however, is proved and they include among others the "artificial earthquake" or seismographic method. Successive charges are exploded a short distance below the surface, and the time of the rebounding shocks is recorded by delicate instruments so that the occurrence of a dome in a hard underground stratum, for example, may be plotted (see Fig. 158). An instrument known as a *magnetometer* and another known as a *gravity meter* are useful in obtaining information as to the character of underground rock formations. The former is towed behind an airplane or carried otherwise in a definite pattern of paths over the surface, and the recordings are plotted for underground mapping. But most of the exploration for petroleum as well as other minerals is the slow, careful, and systematic work of the geologist with his hammer, and there is much left to be done. Oil is not obtained without drilling, but this can be done now with less guesswork than formerly, though hardly with less expense. Reserves that lie deeper than the present producing zones and possible horizontal reserves between producing fields offer chances for further production of both oil and gas.

8. Import oil from other countries. This, too, is hardly conservation if,

[4] The question of Federal as against state jurisdiction of the nearby submerged lands has been settled by law but not in the minds of many citizens who believe that the resources belong to all the people rather than to the particular states. The controversy is a good example of the difficulty of determining what amounts to equitable distribution in managing natural resources in a democracy.

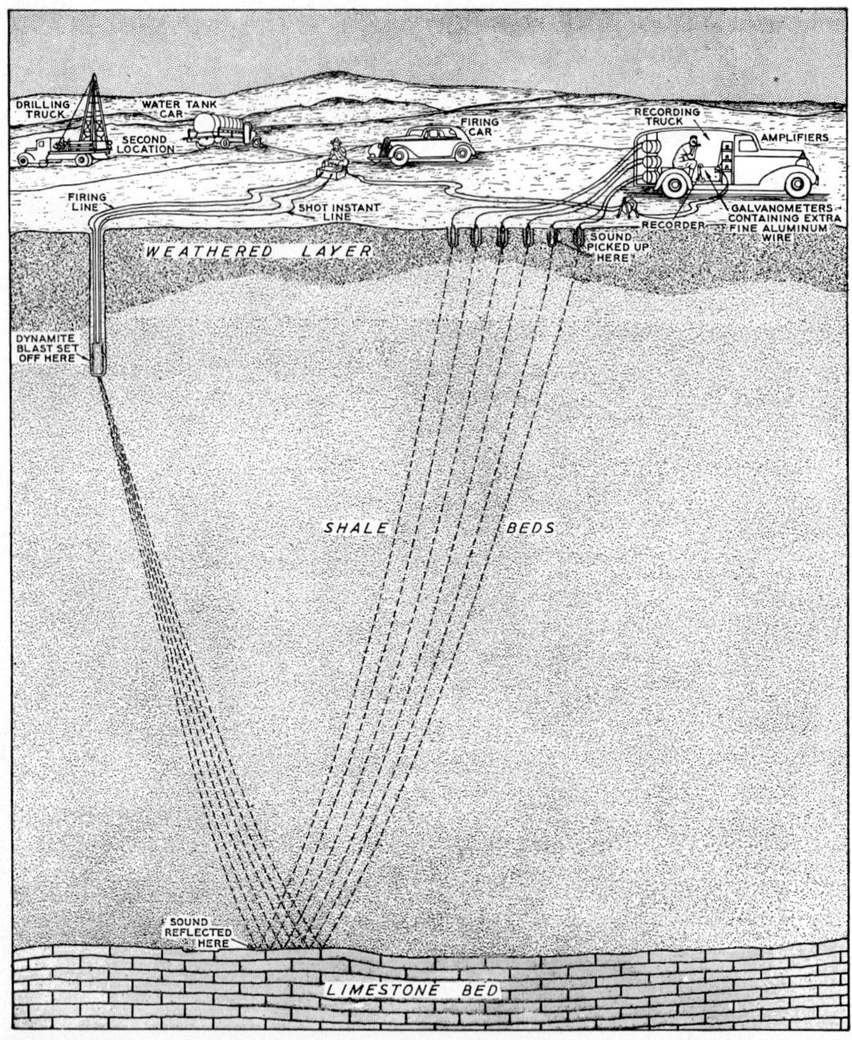

FIG. 158. Diagram of seismographic method of exploration for promising oil structure. An artificial earthquake is set off by a blast, and the reverberations are recorded for interpretation. (*Askania Corporation of America.*)

as we must, we think only of those natural resources available within the United States. Ships are lost, international agreements are broken, and eventually dependence on importation of so essential a product carries the seeds of war.

Trends and Prospects for a Continuing Oil Supply. Landes points out that the petroleum industry operates upon a small inventory and gambles, as does its consuming public, on ability to continue discovery. But he calls attention further to the three directions in which we must look, present reserves, undiscovered deposits, and finally "technological reserves" which include developing dormant supplies at great depth and the manufacture of synthetics.[5]

Items 7 and 8 above indicate our main chances to avoid a trend toward failure to meet the 1975 demand *if we depend on crude oil only.* The diagram in Fig. 159 indicates the most recent speculations on crude-oil production, and even the most optimistic curve falls far below the demand.

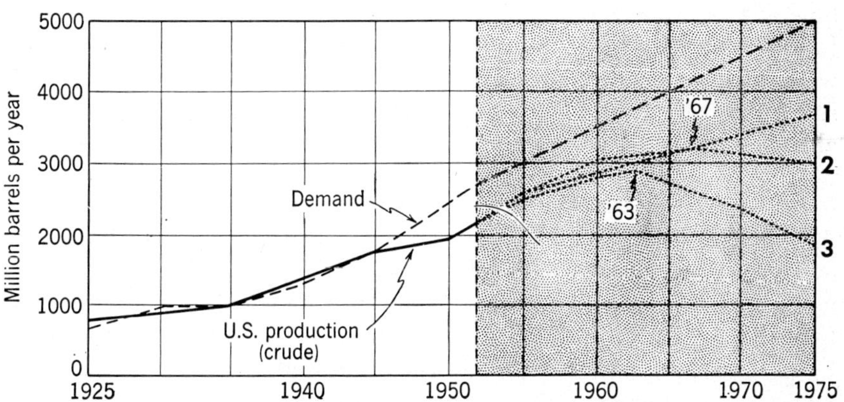

Fig. 159. Three possible trends in U.S. crude-oil production. (*Courtesy the President's Materials Policy Commission.*)

Recoverable reserves in 1951 (exclusive of 4.7 billion barrels of natural-gas liquids) were estimated at 27.5 billion barrels. As against the sum of these two ($27.5 + 4.7 = 32.02$) the 1950 consumption by the United States was 2.375 billion barrels. Something will need to happen fast on this basis, if new discovery is to win the 15-year race. History of discovery and drilling so far would indicate that it may be won.

Meanwhile the American people have the opportunity to understand their petroleum resources more fully, to discard the idea that waste of gasoline and fuel oil is unimportant, and to insist that an efficient liquid-fuel industry can be reconciled with increasingly intensive conservation practices.

Natural Gas

Because it is largely free of inert nitrogen, is clean, produces no residual waste products, and requires no storage space on the premises of the consumer, natural gas is the most efficient of the natural fuels. It is

[5] Landes, Kenneth K., Petroleum Geology, John Wiley & Sons, Inc., New York, 1951, pp. 601–602.

also used to blend with gas manufactured from coal and petroleum, and where available direct from the fields it is relatively inexpensive.

Moreover, it is an important raw material for the chemical industry. But it has not always been easy to capture or to handle and distribute. For these reasons and because of the early attitudes toward waste of natural resources, natural-gas waste represents to date one of the most dramatic pictures in the entire natural-resource field. Dr. Charles R. Van Hise, whose book *The Conservation of Natural Resources in the United States*[6] was the first one published exclusively on the subject, pointed out in 1910 the five ways in which natural gas was being wasted at that time.[7] (1) Losses from high-pressure gas wells before drillers knew how to cap them. If lighted and allowed to burn, as many of the gas wells were, there would be a caving of rock around the casing, a sinking of the surface, and the development of a veritable flaming lake. For a considerable time, 70 million cubic feet of gas a day was estimated to be thus wasted in one Louisiana field. (2) Losses in connection with oil wells which are frequently also gas wells. Here the lack of easy markets and difficulty of capture have resulted in the practice of allowing the gas to escape or to be "flared" (lighted and burned as it escaped through pipes a safe distance from the derrick). Van Hise comments that all attempts to halt this practice by law had been defeated by 1910, save in Indiana. (3) Loss in pipeline transmission to market. In the early days of the industry, construction and inspection of pipelines were indefensibly careless when one considers that as far back as 1907 the country was utilizing 400 billion cubic feet of natural gas a year. (Transmission losses in 1950 still amounted to 171 billion cubic feet.) (4) Loss related to allocating gas to uses for which more plentiful fuels such as coal were readily available. Here the use of gas for generating steam power is challenged. This particular loss is significant today and is receiving some attention where there is sharp competition for gas by industry, as against the demands of the householder. (5) Loss in the disproportionate amount of natural gas used inefficiently to produce carbon black. Crude methods of recovering the sootlike deposit from deliberate burning of gas and the slightly improved "channel" process will produce considerably less than the modern furnace plant process, but the former are still widely used. This loss of natural gas is both dramatic and important, since the 1949 consumption of natural gas for carbon-black manufacture was about 428 billion cubic feet from a total residential and commercial consumption

[6] Van Hise, Charles R., The Conservation of Natural Resources in the United States, The Macmillan Company, New York, 1910, pp. 56–60.

[7] Those who feel that we need not worry about conservation of minerals will lick their chops over Van Hise's prediction that the natural-gas supply would be short by 1930, but at the rates it was being wasted in his day he might have been uncomfortably correct. Curtailing waste has proved to be good conservation.

of about 1,340 billion cubic feet. Use of carbon black in the United States ranks highest in rubber manufacture followed in order by that of ink, miscellaneous products, and paint.[8]

From the years of heavy surplus of natural gas at the fields and corresponding unsatisfied demand at distant localities, this excellent fuel had come in 1951 to supply 18 per cent of our total energy needs as against 4 per cent of lesser need in 1920. Greater supply from increased discovery of both oil and gas, improved gathering and transporting facilities, reduction in price, and performance have all figured in this remarkable increase in the use of natural gas and may have unconsciously brought about increasing conservation. One remarkable development is the fact that the disposal of natural gas is subject to regulation, not only by state public-utility commissions but also by the Federal Power Commission. The latter has been roundly challenged in recent efforts at legislation, but most of the objections have been against interference with prices and volume of business. In general, regulation has helped to conserve the resource.

It is probable that there is a market ahead for all the natural gas that the country can produce, whether it continues to be less expensive than other energy sources or not. Its very efficiency and convenience can cause it to compete successfully. While the Mid-Continent, Gulf coast, and California were mentioned on page 282 in order of the abundance of natural-gas occurrence, it is produced in more than twenty-five of the states. Production for 1950 saw Texas heading with 52 per cent, Louisiana next with 13 per cent, California at 9 per cent, and Oklahoma at 8 per cent. The Appalachian field including Pennsylvania, West Virginia, Ohio, Kentucky, and New York accounts for less than 6 per cent. The actual future of the natural-gas business appears to rest upon four courses of action which may require increased public regulation. The President's Materials Policy Commission lists these as follows *without emphasizing need for increased regulation*[9]:

1. Stimulate maximum discovery of natural-gas resources.
2. Avoid waste in the production of natural gas and ensure that full advantage is taken of the driving force of natural gas in lifting oil in order to get maximum economic recovery of the oil and gas.
3. Improve the pattern of use so that relatively more gas goes to those uses in which it has a special advantage and relatively less to those which could be served just as well by other fuels.
4. Lay the basis for an orderly transition to other fuels at that distant but inevitable date when natural-gas production falls off.

[8] *Minerals Yearbook*, 1949, Bureau of Mines, U.S. Department of the Interior, 1951, pp. 192–202.

[9] *Resources for Freedom*, Vol. III, The Outlook for Energy Sources, Report of the President's Materials Policy Commission, 1952, p. 16.

Because these "challenges to our natural-gas economy" are so clearly stated by the commission, the means by which they may be achieved should be discussed here.

Present incentives for discovery are powerful and are reflected in exploring activity for gas as well as for oil. Prices, demand, and tax provisions are all favorable.

Except under the Federal Mineral Leasing Law of 1920, governing exploitation of oil and gas as well as other nonmetallic minerals on the public domain, regulation of the natural-gas industry is in the hands of the state so far as waste reduction is concerned. While such regulation is anything but uniform and needs to be improved, it augurs well for higher standards and better operating practices.

Allocating natural gas to its highest use is subject to more than market forces and improved distribution and processing facilities. Unusual profit incentives will be necessary to obtain action in this direction by the industry, and Federal and state policy will have to give a hand.

The following uses represent the breakdown which will need readjusting, with the consumption by each for 1950[10]:

Use	*Billion Cubic Feet*
Residential	1,198
Oil and gas field	1,187
Carbon-black plants	411
Petroleum refineries	455
Portland cement plants	97
Electric public-utility power plants	629
Other industrial (food, paper, chemical, clay, etc.)	1,661

Adjustment to an eventual shrinkage in supply will result in grasping at imports from Canada and Mexico, at a much cheaper substitute gas from coal (if it can be developed) than is now available, and eventually, at the harnessing of solar energy. Of course the promise of atomic energy is ahead, but this is also a natural-resource problem with a far vaster research and development frontier to be conquered.

Proved economically recoverable reserves of natural gas at the end of 1950 were 186 trillion cubic feet, or about twenty-six times the 1950 production of 7.1 trillion cubic feet. One estimate of future discoverable and recoverable reserves arrives at 510 trillion cubic feet,[11] but nobody has estimated future annual consumption.

Consideration of natural gas and its equitable distribution brings up the interesting question as to why its distribution and marketing fall in the public-utility field along with hydroelectric energy, whereas other indispensable mineral resources and even some of the replaceable resources are not so considered. Certainly the experience of this democ-

[10] *Ibid.*, pp. 17 and 18.

[11] Terry, L. F., The Future Supply of Natural Gas Will Exceed 500 Trillion Cubic Feet, *Gas Age*, Oct. 26, 1950, p. 58.

racy in regulating, trade, transportation of the two natural resources—one a service, water power, and the other a fuel, natural gas—will be useful in developing future policy.

THE METALS

Tools, transportation, laborsaving devices, and any one of a thousand taken-for-granted luxuries would be unavailable in the modern sense and in the present world without the metals. Men were sharply limited in helping themselves when the tools they used were of stone, wood, or bone. Likewise communication and transportation were slow and uncertain before steam and mineral fuels were harnessed in metal trappings. Thousands of slaves did the relatively small volume of physical work, and very few enjoyed any measure of luxury before metals came into the laborsaving picture.

Metals are usually combinations of elements, lustrous in native form, opaque, often heavy, ductile or malleable so that they can be melted by heat, drawn, or hammered into various shapes, and capable of conducting heat and electrical current.

Human imagination can hardly picture the origins of metals, and indeed a human being would hardly have lasted in a ringside seat while the processes were going on. Great outpourings of molten volcanic rock were pushing and bubbling out over the surface of this planet. Other masses trying to get out of the interior were forcing the rock crust apart and filling up the cracks. Volcanic waters and vapors came from this commotion. Saturated with metallic elements in solution, these waters in contact with other waters, air, and material masses set up violent chemical reactions from which the metals were assembled and deposited to cool over the ages. Through countless millions of years the metals which now serve humanity, in fountain pens and all the way to diesel locomotives, were formed without the help or cooperation of men, and men cannot add to the total supply.

Metals as a natural resource are irreplaceable. They cannot be managed for sustained yield in the manner applicable to forests or wild animals. Sometimes they cannot even be captured for human use at reasonable expense and effort. In use they are frequently destroyed and consumed in prodigal quantities. It is important to remember, however, that the greatest opportunity for conserving metals is at the stage of use, for in the uses of greatest volume some of the metals are recoverable for "secondary" use. Indeed scrap recovery is depended upon to a considerable extent to keep the steel mills of the country operating. Table 8 will indicate examples of uses in which metals may or may not be recovered.

Usually a metal, whether it is an alloy or not, is named for the principal element in its make-up, and the same is true of the natural-resource form or ore in which it occurs. One of the old and commonly used classifica-

Table 8. Selected Uses of Metals—Recoverable and Irrecoverable

	Recoverable	*Irrecoverable—relatively or wholly*
Iron:		
	Construction	Paints
	Transportation	War
	Tools	Chemicals
Copper:		
	Electrical equipment	Paints and sprays
	Automobiles	War
	Miscellaneous alloys and utensils	Chemicals
Lead:		
	Construction	Paints and sprays
	Miscellaneous alloys and utensils	War
	Electrical equipment	Chemicals
		Gasoline mixtures
Zinc:		
	Miscellaneous alloys and utensils	Paints
		Galvanizing
		Chemicals
Gold:		
	Coinage	Paints and leaf
	Jewelry	Drugs
	Objects of art	Stained glass
		Dentistry
Silver:		
	Photography	Plating and leaf
	Coinage	Dentistry
	Objects of art	Surgery

tions is "major" and "minor" based on volume of use, indispensability, and value, or some combination of these characteristics. The major metals thus are listed as iron, copper, lead, zinc, gold, and silver. The minor metals are all the others, of which aluminum, manganese, and platinum are examples. Still another way of classifying emphasizes the "light" metals, although "heavy" is not so frequently applied to those such as iron, gold, and lead. The light metals include aluminum and magnesium as examples. The metals also appear in the total mineral classification such as "basic" which includes only coal, iron, and copper and "contributory" covering all other minerals.

In Table 8, only the major metals are included, and these will be discussed one by one. Occurrence and use will be taken up under each.

Iron

Because of its strength, hardness, malleability, availability, and numerous other distinctive qualities, iron is considered the most useful of all metals. Certainly it represents the greatest volume of use in cruder forms and in its highly processed form as steel. Ore production totals more than 100 times that of copper, the next metal in terms of tonnage produced. Total domestic reserves of "commercial" iron ore, which means material cosidered usable under present economic and technologic conditions, as of 1951, are estimated by the U.S. Geological Survey at 6,435,558,000 short tons. Consumption in 1949 amounted to around 85 million tons, and it is likely that by 1975, at which time the President's Materials Policy Commission believes consumption will be more than doubled, this reserve will be reduced at least a third. On the basis of this kind of arithmetic, the reserves within the United States would keep industry supplied for about 40 years. Imports, however, from Venezuela, Cuba, Liberia, and the Quebec-Labrador area will no doubt increase significantly. Also, to the extent that lower grade domestic ores can be "beneficiated" or raised in quality by concentration and other procedures, imported ores will have to compete with them as an addition to the domestic reserve. Finally, there is the chance that increased scrap recovery and reuse will affect the rate at which reserves are exhausted.

Occurrence and Ownership of Iron Resources. Iron ore occurs in five great districts in the United States: (1) Lake Superior with 47+ per cent of ore of better than 50 per cent iron content[12]; (2) Northeastern with 17+ per cent of ore of 60 per cent iron content; (3) Southeastern with 25 per cent of 35 per cent ore; (4) Southern with 1+ per cent of 45 per cent ore; (5) and Western with 9+ per cent of 50 per cent ore.

Iron is mined in all these districts at present, some thirty-six mines each producing more than 1 million tons of crude ore annually. More than three-quarters of the production comes from open-pit mines, where the overburden is removed and the ore taken out by shovel. The 1949 production came from the following states in order of highest production to lowest:

1. Minnesota
2. Michigan
3. Alabama
4. New York
5. Utah
6. Texas
7. Wisconsin
8. Pennsylvania
9. Georgia
10. New Jersey
11. Wyoming
12. California
13. Missouri
14. Nevada
15. Virginia

    Washington (ranked fourteenth in 1948—no data for 1949)

In general, iron deposits are privately owned in the United States, and the important deposits are practically all controlled by large corporations.

[12] Does not include low-grade taconite ore which at present is considered of commercial quality when concentrated.

This fact is significant so far as any public regulation of iron mining is concerned. Various state and Federal tax laws are generally favorable to the industry and constitute the only means at present by which conservation practices may be required by the public. (The Mineral Leasing Law of 1920 does not cover the removal of metal deposits from the public domain.)

Conserving Iron Resources. Relatively few people are in the iron business, but practically everyone uses iron. The large-scale conservation efforts will have to be made by the industry and the industrial manufac-

FIG. 160. Railroad approach to an open-pit iron mine near Hibbing, Minn., on the Mesabi Iron Range. (*Photo by Bureau of Mines.*)

turers of iron products. This will occur only, however, with the demand and the cooperation of the public. The following list of ways in which iron may be conserved as a resource may seem to involve only the industries, but the attitude of the ultimate user is important in every one.

Improved Mining. While there is need in underground mining to leave pillars of ore for safety as in coal mining, the losses in recovery from this angle are less important than might be supposed. Recovery in general is good, and open-pit mining represents real conservation at the mining stage. It is also the method by which most of the mining is done. Mechanization as a means of reducing the cost of mining will make possible better total ore recovery as well, including lower grades.

Beneficiation. Improving the grade of ore by crushing, washing, and sizing, mechanical removal of rocks of varying sizes, magnetic separation of ore from impurities, mixing low- and high-grade ores, and sintering or pelletizing to suitable physical character for blast furnaces are known as beneficiation practices. In the sintering process, fine material is pressed into larger sizes. The effect of these procedures is to increase the iron content of the ore and adapt it otherwise to form and concentrations which will permit economic shipment and use. More than 15 million tons of "sinter," the term used to designate the product of sintering and

Fig. 161. Three blast furnaces at a steel plant in Chicago, Ill. Piles in the foreground are heat-resisting brick to line the furnace. (*Photo by Bureau of Mines.*)

pelletizing, was produced in 1949 in this country. In the same year, 39 per cent of the total ore production was shipped to beneficiation plants en route to the consumer. Investigations of the flotation process have recently been reported in the experimental treatment of low-grade taconite ore. In this process, finely ground ore is treated with water and chemicals to produce a froth in which the metal is captured and by which the inert material may be discarded. If successful in the treatment of iron ore as it has been in treating zinc and copper ores, another beneficiation procedure is available.

Scrap Recovery and Use. Unlike the mineral fuels, iron can be used as secondary material or scrap. So important has this practice become in steel manufacture that in 1949 and the 2 previous years, more scrap than pig iron (the crude product of smelting iron ore) was used. Price has much to do with collection since the small dealer who collects farm and household scrap can operate only when demand is high and the price good. The so-called "home scrap" is that which accumulates at the plants using scrap against that which is purchased and is of course an important part of the total used. Industrial scrap from chemical and other industries is also important. Wartime interest in scrap collection not only helped the industry and the defense effort but cleaned up a lot of local dumps and eyesores.

The individual can make some contribution here to the conservation of iron by seeing to it that worn-out iron articles are routed to junk dealers. Even the community scrap drive is a conservation stroke.

Maintaining the Life of Manufactured Articles. Again, unlike the mineral fuels, iron can be "capitalized" in the sense of being manufactured into useful form and, with good care, made to serve longer and more efficiently. Of course in an expanding economy, styling and improvement (real and claimed) keep people continually buying replacements and scrapping good equipment. This makes "business" and is one of the wasteful practices which Americans, above all people, justify in the name of progress. But good care of steel articles from the kitchen knife to the farm tractor is still good iron conservation. Various coatings to prevent rust include paints, tarlike coatings, gun-metal finish applied by superheated steam processes, greasing of tools in storage, and finally galvanizing. (The latter process by which iron is coated with zinc is questionable as a conservation practice, since zinc is relatively scarce).

Improving Usefulness by Alloys. Hardening, toughening, and otherwise improving the serviceability of iron manufactured into steel has long been practiced and results frequently in making one ton of steel do the work of two. Manganese, tungsten, molybdenum, nickel, and vanadium are examples of metals added to iron for these purposes, manganese being required in greatest volume. Conservation of iron by these practices also makes imperative the conserving of the alloy materials themselves.

Substitution of Replaceable and More Abundant Materials for Iron in Use. Wood, stone, concrete, clay products, and plastics all serve well in many uses to which iron and steel are now put. Poles, bridge and derrick timbers treated for durability, roof trusses, industrial office and home furniture, laminated and plywood structural members are often available and serviceable as substitutes for iron and steel, and the materials used in their manufacture can be grown in continuous supply on the soil. Stone and concrete with iron reinforcement are practically industructible and relatively plentiful as original or fabricated natural-resource materials. Their use in bridge and building construction in place of steel is good engineering and good conservation. Brick, tile, and pipe as clay products are frequently as useful if not so convenient as steel. Glass during the Second World War was used in place of tin-plated steel for food containers. Plastics, many of which are made from fiber or very plentiful natural materials, are common in utensils, automobile accessories, and even construction. All these substitutions can extend our reserves of iron but probably will not if the salesman of iron and steel products can help it. Conservation by substitution therefore runs squarely into our competitive

FIG. 162. White hot steel pours from a 35-ton electric furnace at a western Pennsylvania steel plant. While the most expensive, the electric furnace is increasingly used because much greater control of temperature is permitted and the finest quality steels and alloys can be produced. The furnace is tilted for the pouring. (*Photo by Bureau of Mines.*)

system. In emergency periods, substitution can be brought about by rationing.

Further Discovery and Importation. These two lines of action are mentioned together because they amount to alternatives to conserving our present known national iron resources and are not properly conservation procedures in themselves. While little is heard of exploration for new iron deposits in the United States, such explorations are under way. Rich deposits have attracted American capital both for exploration and development in Liberia, Venezuela, and the Quebec-Labrador area particularly. Iron ore from these localities will be water-borne to this country, and the Quebec-Labrador development emphasizes the inevitable construction of the St. Lawrence River Waterway, whether or not the United States participates. Principal imports of iron ore, up to the present, have come from Canada to which neighbor exports have also been generous.[13] Thus the United States in terms of its iron industry finds global self-sufficiency the answer to impending national scarcity of iron resources, and such a statement is not a bad way to sum up the situation. It should be remembered that the President's Materials Policy Commission sees a 73 per cent increase in demand for iron ore over 1950 consumption by the time 1970–1980 is reached.

Copper

As one of the earliest metals captured for the use of mankind, copper has become an indispensable industrial material if, indeed, only the electrical and automobile industries were to be considered. But copper finds outlet in thousands of articles and conveniences from tea kettle to poison sprays. It is used both in the "capitalized" and wasting senses as indicated by examples in Table 8. Scrap recovery is high, use as an alloy metal is important, and its place in the chemical industry is well established. Copper also is a national-defense necessity. While it occurs as almost pure metal in occasional deposits, its recovery from ores is expensive, and such economic perplexities as depression in the mining industry occasioned by the recovery of too much competing scrap are not unknown. In the late 1930s the United States became a net copper-importing nation, and since that time consumption has not been met by production of domestic ores. Consumption for the year 1950 was estimated in this country as 3.6 per cent of its known reserves.

Occurrence and Ownership of Copper Resources. Copper deposits occur in twenty-eight states and in Alaska. Mine production in 1949 found Arizona in the lead, with 48 per cent of the total for the country. Utah ranked second with 26 per cent; Montana, New Mexico, Nevada, and Michigan came next in the order given and acounted collectively for 23 per cent. Thus these six states produced 96 per cent of the 1949 total. Alaska, California, Colorado, Washington, and Idaho are also steady, if relatively small, producers. The fact that 78 per cent of the copper ore produced in 1949 came from open-pit mines gives some indication of its occurrence with respect to depth. The ores frequently yield other metals such as silver, zinc, and lead. The treatment of the ores for concentration is common near the mines, and the richer ores are often smelted directly. Copper occurs widely throughout the world, and imports come from a

[13] It would seem that the 1939 export of more than 3½ million tons of scrap iron, at least half of which went to Japan, was good *business* but not good conservation or good national-defense policy.

dozen or more countries of which Canada, Cuba, Chile, Cyprus, Northern Rhodesia, and the Union of South Africa are among the most important.

Conserving Copper Resources. The growing deficit in consumption over production of copper in the United States presents a need for conservation which is at present somewhat clouded by a generous world production, and yet there are plenty of opportunities to extend our domestic reserves through conservation practices. The industry is alive to most of these. They may be listed as follows:

Fig. 163. Copper mining on "the richest hill on earth," Butte, Mont. (*Photo by Bureau of Mines.*)

Improved Recovery in Mining. The efficiency and thoroughness of copper mining is a credit to the industry so far as recovery is concerned. The very fact, previously noted, that most of the ore comes from open-pit mines would indicate that loss is thus avoided. Underground recovery also has generally been high, and increased mechanization offers the principal chance for improvement in cost of recovery.

Treatment and Use of Progressively Leaner Ores. Because the percentage of copper in many ores is very low (from 0.64 in some Southwestern ones to 4.11 in certain of those in Montana), the treatment of ores to produce concentrates is common at the mines. Flotation (described on page 299) is one of the important concentration methods. In 1948–1949 the amazing figure of 93 per cent of the material smelted was made up of concentrates. Only 3 to 4 per cent was considered rich enough ore for direct smelting. Some 3 to 4 per cent was recovered by leaching, a process whereby water is run through the ore and the copper obtained from the drip. Smelting also frequently takes place at the mining centers and by various methods has become very efficient. It should be mentioned here that copper mining and treatment of the ores constitute anything but conservation of space and landscape. Smelter fumes which kill vegetation, and which may be treated to some extent for by-products, are still

FIG. 164. Flotation cells in a copper concentrator in Western United States. (*Photo by Bureau of Mines.*)

an air-pollution problem. Slag and other waste products are ugly, disorderly, and space-requiring. Open mining pits are useless when abandoned, ugly, and unavoidable.

Recovery from Mining Wastes. One form of mining waste offers an opportunity for reworking and thus recovering additional copper. The terms "tailings" and "stamp sands" are encountered in local and statistical jargon. The former are rock dumps in which some copper-bearing waste occurs, and the latter consist of finer wastes from the mills where ore is crushed for concentration. When price incentives are sufficient, these materials can be made to yield significant amounts of copper.

Scrap Recovery. In many uses the manufactured copper either in relatively pure or alloy form is easy to recover, and the scrap business is of real importance as a conservation measure. Sometimes the recovered material is used in the alloyed form, but in terms of copper content almost one-seventh of the total copper produced in 1949 was "secondary" from scrap. Here is an opportunity, as with all metals, for the individual to see that discarded copper articles reach the scrap dealers. Strangely enough, however, our copper economy is so delicately rigged that the appearance of too much scrap in any one year has had the effect of depressing the mining industry.

Fig. 165. Pouring molten copper into molds to form bars for shipment. A refinery in the United States. (*Photo by Bureau of Mines.*)

Allocating Copper to Its Highest Uses. In time of war the citizens and the industries accept a measure of rationing applied to scarce and strategic materials. In peacetime such rationing or allocation would be considered something of a persecution, and yet copper in an insect spray is conceivably a more important use than copper in an object of art. The first destroys the copper in use, the second "capitalizes" it. On the other hand a copper paint or coating is a less essential use than copper in bombs and shells stockpiled for future national defense. Both are wasting uses. Finally, copper for wiring and for equipping diesel locomotives and ships could easily be proved more important than copper for roofing. Both of these are "capitalizing" uses. Theoretically, and perhaps practically in the future, public action to ration or allocate copper equitably to various uses is good conservation, and this could lead to the development of substitutes. Steel shell cases for military use are examples of such substitutes.

New Discoveries and Imports. As observed in the instance of other mineral needs, filling them by new discovery and more particularly by imports will extend total domestic reserves but can hardly be termed conservation, save in the sense of equitable distribution both as among the present nations of the globe and in the sense of the present as against future generations. Both discovery and imports, however, are important, and while discovery in this country has been mainly contiguous to present workings, American capital has figured significantly in foreign discoveries. Imports have been necessary from the time of the Second World War and will probably be unavoidable in the future. These imports are, of course, *net,* exports being considered in reporting them.

The Outlook for Copper Supply. With the prediction of an increased demand of 43 per cent by 1970–1980 over the 1950 consumption of copper exclusive of scrap in this country and with importation, new discovery, or the more drastic moves of rationing and special allocation as the assumed remedies for shortage, copper-supply policy amounts to no definite policy at present. These and other findings of the President's Materials Policy Commission need to be made known to the people of this country and by them to the policy makers.

Lead

From the lead-plate cushion under a great skyscraper to give it certain qualities of stability in spite of motion, to the hundreds of tons of lead blown wastefully into the air from the tetraethyl motor fuel, lead appears to be indispensable in the modern world. It has served mankind as metal in ammunition, bearings, alloys in brass and bronze, storage batteries, pipe, cable covering, and type. In pigments it is well known in white and red lead and as a base in blended colors. In chemicals it appears in drugs, sprays, and tetraethyl fluid for gasoline. Miscellaneous uses include galvanizing, lead plating, and ballast. Because of its versatility, reduction of use in one direction—plumbing, for example—is replaced by increase in a new field such as sprays, batteries, and gasoline.

The bottom of the barrel seems to be in sight with regard to domestic reserves of lead. The 1950 domestic production amounted to 6 per cent of the known reserves. Net imports have always been large and in 1949 amounted to more than one-third of the total consumption.

Occurrence and Ownership of Lead Resources. Lead is mined in twenty-two states, the highest production occurring in thirteen of the Western states and Alaska. The West Central states come next with Missouri leading, and those east of the Mississippi constitute a poor third.

By individual states Missouri, Idaho, and Utah are in the lead and account for 65 per cent of recent years' mine production. Lead is often found in ores containing zinc, copper, gold, or silver in various combinations. On a world basis the United States, Canada, Mexico, and Australia have accounted for nearly three-fourths of the world output in recent years. Lead

FIG. 166. Lead-zinc mine in Missouri. A mechanical shovel loads ore on one level, a locomotive works at a higher level, and drillers sink blast holes from a catwalk high up near the roof. (*Photo by Bureau of Mines.*)

is mined however in thirty-one countries. Deposits in this country are practically all in private ownership, and should an important deposit be discovered on public lands, no policy except passing it into private hands exists.

Conserving Lead Resources. Perhaps the greatest difficulty in conserving lead resources lies in the irrecoverable uses to which it is put. Mining and separation from other metals and rock wastes are highly developed. In our economy, price affects mining and smelting procedures considerably, and only as imports may become more difficult and prices higher will the more radical conservation practices be adopted. Hopeful signs, however, are the reworking of chert rock dumps for lead-bearing materials, the general use of flotation for better recovery of lead in ores more valuable for copper, zinc, and silver, and the recovery of secondary lead from storage batteries, metal articles, and from gun-club areas. Substitution of titanium and barium for lead in pigments is increasing.

The Future of Lead Resources. Lead is classified under the heading of Known Economic Reserves Inadequate by the President's Materials Policy Commission, and it is noted that while geological discoveries are likely they are not necessarily predicted to be adequate. As in the case of copper, our alternative appears to lie in heavy importation which may or may not be good global conservation. Certainly any economic procedure that will extend our domestic reserves should be a definite part of a so-far-lacking national mineral policy.

Zinc

Galvanizing, which is a process for coating iron electrolytically or by dipping it into molton zinc, to protect it from rust, has long been the principal use of zinc and has made it almost indispensable. Brass which is an alloy of copper and zinc and the so-called zinc-base alloys used in dies and die castings constitute the second use in volume. Other uses include rolled zinc for fabrication of many articles, zinc oxide, used in paints and as a drug, wet batteries, removing silver from lead, light-metal alloys, and many miscellaneous small uses such as fertilizer and zinc chloride treatment for the preservative treatment of timber. In most of these uses it is irrecoverable, and domestic reserves are being reduced at the rate of about 3.8 per cent a year. Discovery of new deposits is likely but not sure, and reserves are inadequate for present technological needs. Deposits of economic importance occur in some twenty states of the union, the heaviest production coming from the tri-state area, Oklahoma, Kansas, and southwest Missouri. Idaho, New Jersey, New York, Arizona, and Tennessee also figure prominently in the zinc-production picture. Among the other countries of the world Canada, Bolivia, Mexico, and Peru are leading zinc producers.

New zinc deposits are being developed in Nevada and New Mexico which may add appreciably to reserves. About the only other means of extending domestic reserves would be the more general use of substitutes for zinc now employed in galvanizing. More plentiful paints, tarlike compounds, and "gun-metal" finishes offer possibilities, but because they would hurt an established business, and are less serviceable, their increasing use is unlikely.

Table 9. Domestic Supply Position of Selected Mineral Materials

Known economic reserves adequate for well over 25 years

Magnesium	Lime	Gypsum
Molybdenum	Salt	Borax
Coal	Sand	Barite
Phosphate	Clay	Feldspar
Potash		

Known economic reserves inadequate

Discoveries geologically likely—though not necessarily adequate:

Copper	Vanadium	Petroleum
Lead	Tungsten	Natural gas
Zinc	Antimony	Sulfur
Uranium		

Beneficiation progress expected:

Iron	Beryllium	Fluorine
Aluminum	Thorium	Graphite
Titanium	Oil from shale	

Synthesis progress expected:

Oil from coal	Gas from coal

Little or no known economic reserves, significant discoveries not expected

Beneficiation progress expected:

Manganese

Synthesis progress expected:

Industrial diamonds	Quartz crystals
Sheet mica	Asbestos

Significant beneficiation or synthesis not expected:

Chromium	Tin	Platinum
Nickel	Cobalt	Mercury

SOURCE: *Resources for Freedom*, Vol. I, Report of the President's Materials Policy Commission, 1952.

Some zinc scrap is recovered, and reuse of this material is of course good conservation. About half as much secondary zinc was produced from scrap and chemical compounds in 1949 as the amount produced from mines in the United States.

Importation seems to be the only course ahead to assure adequate supplies of zinc.

Gold

Because of its scarcity, beauty, resistance to corrosion, and other distinctive characteristics, gold has served throughout the ages as a standard of value and until recent years was not only minted into coin but widely used for that purpose. Compared with other major metals in terms of total resources, usefulness, and indispensability, the world would perhaps miss it less than any. On the other hand, industrial consumption has recently assumed considerable importance, and use in the arts increased rapidly during the Second World War. Also while much of the supply has been allocated to monetary use, this portion of the supply is in the form of government stockpiles from which it may be released to industry and the arts without smelter or refinery preparation. In 1949 the net consumption by industry and the arts totaled more than one and one-half times the new gold produced from domestic mines. The actual net industrial consumption amounted to about 109 million in gold dollars. The

FIG. 167. Steel gold dredge in California. Agricultural land is overturned for the gold that lies under it. (*Photo by Bureau of Mines.*)

use of gold in the arts goes far back in history. In modern times, high marriage rate and generally high wages have created a heavy demand for gold articles along with other luxuries. Gold has long been used in dentistry, and recently its compounds have come to be used in medicine, notably in the treatment of arthritis. Gold leaf on the domes of public buildings and in the window signs of prosperous business and professional firms seems to do a lot for morale, but these uses are neither essential nor large in volume. This interesting metal, however, is not only a symbol but an economic good and should be conserved.

It occurs in eighteen of the states and in Alaska. In order of production the rank is South Dakota, California, Utah, Alaska, and Nevada. Among the Eastern states, Pennsylvania, Tennessee, North Carolina, and Georgia produce small amounts.

Gold occurs in gravel deposits and in underground ore deposits usually with quartz both alone or with copper, silver, lead, or zinc. It is mined as "placer" when free gold is washed from the gravel using hydraulic methods, or by dredge which also treats the gravels, and as ore which must be crushed for various separation procedures. The Utah production comes largely as a by-product from the mining of copper ore in the West Mountain (Bingham) district. Recovery is generally high.

Gold resources may be conserved principally in the utilization stage. Mining requires little improvement, and if there is more gold to be found, the age-old incentive to quick wealth will keep the prospectors hunting. Scrap recovery is well organized, and gold in "capitalized" form, particularly in the arts and in coinage, is subject to little wear. "Seniorage" which is loss from wear of coinage in use has been taken care of by the Federal withdrawal of gold coin from circulation. Losses from ship sinkings, hoarding, and the death and burial of people will have generally to be written off.

The release of stockpiled gold by Federal authorities for use in industry and the arts gives a measure of control and represents good conservation.

Silver

While used and valued to some extent in the same manner as gold, silver has a much wider industrial use and is actually generally in circulation as coinage. Its bid for a place among the major metals calls to attention its indispensability in the photographic industry. In the arts it is also indispensable as surgical material and finds considerable use in dentistry. Like gold its use in objects of art reaches back beyond written history.

Silver is produced in twenty-three of the states and in Alaska. The principal producers rank as follows in order of volume: Idaho, Montana, Utah, Arizona, Colorado, and Nevada. Among the Eastern states Vermont, Pennsylvania, Tennessee, Illinois, and Michigan are interesting but of little importance. Silver occurs in various ores and is a by-product at many mines from the recovery of copper, zinc, and lead. Neither silver nor gold were included in the studies of the President's Materials Policy Commission of 1952.

The most promising conservation measure for silver is recovery from industrial and other uses. Significant amounts are now salvaged from motion-picture and other photographic film, and silver scrap is important in the scrap-metal market. Mining and treating methods are generally efficient. Seniorage, or wear, is high on silver coins, and in the event of severe shortage some saving could be made here by larger issue of paper currency. This, however, would hardly be necessary unless some rationing to the luxury industries had been first explored. Silver is an important material and should not be wasted.

The Minor Metals

Aluminum. Following discussion of the six major metals, aluminum assumes next importance in terms of volume used and growing importance. Much of this importance arises from its use in building and by the airplane industry because of its high strength-weight ratio and convenience in handling. Airplane manufacture in 1949 accounted for more than one-half of the entire amount used for transportation equipment. Trucks, automobiles, railroad tank cars and passenger units figured strongly in the balance. Power cable, foil for insulation and packaging, and even experimental gas pipeline represent other rapidly developing uses. Also in November, 1949, aluminum was added to the list of strategic materials for stockpiling. In many of these uses, excluding foil and paints, the material is recoverable, and strangely enough aluminum scrap is an important item of export. In total consumption the United States is a net importing nation.

While aluminum is widely distributed in the clays of the United States, it occurs commercially as bauxite in the form of ore principally in Arkansas, Alabama, Georgia, and Virginia; 1949 production in terms of dried ore was 1,196,337 long tons. (A long ton is 2,200 pounds.) Reserves of economically recoverable ore on the same basis were estimated in 1947 by the Bureau of Mines and the Geological Survey at 36,341,000 long tons. Other abundant world sources are Hungary, the Gold Coast, and British Guiana. Certain deposits in Haiti and in Jamaica are promising, with three companies producing. Little is heard about further domestic discovery or of the use of lower grade ores.

Conservation of domestic aluminum resources includes reduction of waste in beneficiation plants and general improvement of beneficiation methods to make possible the use of leaner ores. Cheaper and more abundant power will also make possible the reduction of leaner ores. Scrap recovery is a possibility for increased conservation although war losses are high, and will again be high if there are great wars in the future.

Eventually the United States will probably depend even more fully on imports.

Tin. With a domestic production including that of Alaska of less than 1 per cent of the 1949 domestic consumption, and with solder, automobiles, tin-plated food packages, and various alloys depending upon an adequate supply, it is no wonder that people were asked to save tin cans (which are tin-plated only) during the Second World War. In the years 1940–1944, almost one-eighteenth of the amount of tin consumed in this country came from secondary material recovered from saved scrap which was handled by detinning plants. For this scarce and versatile metal, it is not easy to find satisfactory substitutes, and while Alaska offers promise of future discovery and profitable development, the tiny production in the states appears principally as a by-product of the mining of molybdenum in Colorado, copper in Nevada, and as one of the products of a rock known as pegmatite in South Dakota. Probably because cassiterite, the most common mineral of tin, is heavy and frequently occurs in pebble form, much of the tin mining is of the placer type, in which the pebbles are washed out of gravel deposits and shipped to smelters. The distinctive weight of this mineral may also account for the fact that it was easily separated and used by ancient peoples.

Specifically the uses of tin are confined almost entirely to six items: (1) tin plate, which is the material most people know as tin, and terneplate, a similar product plated with a tin-lead alloy; (2) solder for sealing tin-plate joints and used in other metalwork; (3) bronze, an alloy of copper and tin; (4) babbitt, a soft metal alloy used in plumbing and bearings; (5) tinning and type metal. These five accounted for 95 per cent of the consumption, and the remainder (6) goes mostly into tin chemicals. Manufactured tin imports come to the United States from fifteen countries, Malaya, Belgium-Luxembourg, Portugal, Belgian Congo, China, and the United Kingdom ranking in order of volume received in 1949. Three other countries supply tin concentrates for smelting in this country. These in order of volume are Bolivia, Indonesia, and Thailand. The low-content concentrates from Bolivia increased from the time of the opening of a federally owned smelter at Texas City in 1942, but the United States, always the heaviest consumer, smelts only 23 per cent of the world production of ore as against more than 50 per cent smelted by the British Empire and lesser amounts by the Netherlands, Belgium, and China.

Since tin is so essential and next to gold and silver the most costly of the commonly used metals, its conservation is of first importance. So far little progress has been made in this direction. Three of the chances which need further research and study are the following: (1) Finding substitutes in which aluminum for foil and collapsible tubes and glass for food packaging have already figured importantly offers possibilities. Ironically enough the use of tin plate for beer cans has increased sharply over the traditional bottle long used and made of less essential materials. Just how the merchandising of lubricating oil in small tin-can units can be rationalized may well also be considered. Solders with lesser tin content than usual have been developed. (2) Improvement in concentration of low-grade ores has not kept pace with the treatment of such ores as copper and lead, and recovery from lode mines particularly can be greatly improved. (3) Wider adoption of the electrolytic plating process which uses less tin for the product of equal serviceability than the hot-dip method has good possibilities.

As far as new discovery is concerned, only Alaska appears to offer promise for the United States. Elsewhere explorations in Malaya, Belgian Congo, and Bolivia are rumored to be encouraging.

Mercury. As the source of a detonating agent for explosives and as a material used in control instruments, mercury (quicksilver) was one of the seven minerals mentioned as "strategic" and listed for study by the Bureau of Mines, in the Strategic Minerals Act of 1939.[14] Encouraging results have been obtained by these studies in terms of domestic occurrence and recovery possibilities. A slump in prices following the Second World War, however, has put the United States back into the position of a heavy net importer. Besides the two mentioned, mercury finds a number of other uses of which electrical apparatus, pharmaceuticals, agriculture (insecticides and disinfectants), paints, chemicals, and dental preparations are the leading ones.

Mercury occurs in a large number of minerals but is obtained only from cinnabar, a sulfide ore, worked early in some Western mines for the sulfur rather than the mercury. Domestic production comes from California, Oregon, Arizona, Arkansas, Idaho, and Alaska. Italy and Spain lead the world in production and with Mexico furnish the United States with the bulk of its imports. Possibilities of conservation lie in making profitable the mining and treatment of low-grade domestic ores and promoting the use of substitutes for dental and antiseptic uses and for paints. Porcelain, sulfa drugs, and base paints using other metals are respective examples of such substitutes now finding considerable favor.

Manganese. Because of its service in steel manufacture, of counteracting sulfur and producing changes which improve quality, manganese is a most important strategic material. More than 96 per cent of the domestic consumption goes into the metal-manufacturing industries. On the other hand only 10 per cent of the total amount consumed in 1949 was produced by domestic mines. Other important uses of manganese include manufacture of dry battery cells and use in chemicals. Domestic ores vary widely in manganese content and of the meagre production hardly any contain the 48 per cent of metallic manganese desirable as a major proportion of furnace charges of ore. Blending of the domestic low grades with high-grade imported ores to manufacture ferromanganese alloys or progress in beneficiation of domestic ores before shipment appear to be the only ways that their quality can be made sufficient for use in steel manufacture. As long as foreign ores are readily available, the United States will depend upon them. Brazil, Gold Coast of Africa,

[14] The others were antimony, chromium, manganese, nickel, tin, and tungsten. The list now includes more than fifty.

Cuba, and India are the main sources of imports. The U.S.S.R. also has generous deposits. Montana, Minnesota, and Arkansas are the largest domestic producers.

Conservation of manganese resources cannot gain from use of substitutes because so far none have been developed. Mining recovery and by-product recovery from slags and from treatment of zinc ores is good. This leaves beneficiation of low-grade domestic ores as the most promising future conservation measure. Severe emergency might be expected to force such practice.

Nickel. Resistance to corrosion and usefulness in hardening, toughening, and strengthening steel make nickel indispensable even though almost the entire amount used in the United States must be imported. The steels containing nickel are especially adapted to use under high-temperature conditions such as obtain in jet engines. Such domestic production as there is comes as a by-product of smelting copper ores. Formerly, also, small amounts of nickel ore were obtained as a by-product of talc production. A considerable amount of nickel is also recovered from scrap, but the total domestic production is hardly a tenth of requirements. That from primary sources is considerably less than 1 per cent. Fortunately a friendly neighbor to the north, Canada, is the world's heaviest producer, and the United States is her top customer, taking about 85 per cent of the total production. At the rate of consumption in 1947, these Canadian deposits are estimated to last for about 50 years. Other countries from which imports come are Cuba and New Caledonia.

Conserving nickel is largely confined to the ways in which it is used and reused. Technology is well advanced, but satisfactory substitutes are so far not available except in some plating procedures and in the limited use of molybdenum.

Molybdenum. Abundant in the United States, indispensable in the manufacture of molybdenum steel and gray iron, and serving as a substitute for certain scarce alloy metals, molybdenum has been used increasingly since World War I. It is particularly valuable in producing high-speed and stainless steels. In the latter it is used with chromium and nickel and may replace the scarcer tungsten. It is also used in steels subject to high temperatures in performance and so becomes important in jet aircraft engines. Steel manufacture employs about three-fourths of the total consumption, the remainder finding outlet in the manufacture of gray iron, malleable castings, ceramics, in chemical and electrical industries, and in a small but effective role as fertilizer.

Molybdenum occurs with other metals, notably tungsten, copper, gold, and silver, principally as molybdenite of which there are large deposits in Colorado and New Mexico. Copper mines in Utah, Arizona, New Mexico, and Nevada yield molybdenum as a by-product, and the same is true of tungsten operations in California. Even at wartime rates of consumption, the reserves in the United States which are the largest in the world are estimated to last for several hundred years. Possible further discoveries are likely, and improvements in concentration methods of handling the ores offer good conservation opportunities. It is interesting to observe that this metal, which is abundant, helps to replace tungsten and nickel which are less plentiful and becomes a conserving agent in making iron more serviceable and durable in the form of high-speed alloy steels.

Tungsten. Because of its important but small-volume use in electric-lamp and radio-tube filaments and in fluorescent lamps, tungsten is somewhat better known popularly than other alloy materials. By far its greatest use, however, is in steel for cutting tools, automotive valve steels and special heat-resisting alloys employed in jet-propulsion devices, gun-barrel liners, and armor-piercing projectiles. Tungsten salts are used in tanning leather and to some extent in pigments. Tungsten occurs as *wolfram*, its crude mineral form, in various ores containing 0.5 to 2.5 per cent wolfram and is usually beneficiated to a 60 per cent shipping concentrate. California is the leading domestic producer followed by North Carolina, Nevada, and Colorado. Six other states produce smaller amounts. Reserves are considered inadequate. At the height of the Second World War in 1945 consumption reached more than 14 million pounds but had shrunk to about 5 million in 1949. Imports that year totaled 6¼ million pounds, and domestic production was less than 3 million. China, Burma, Portugal, Bolivia, and Korea are the principal foreign sources. As noted earlier, molybdenum which is more plentiful than tungsten serves to some extent as a substitute for it in steel manufacture. And while further discovery of deposits is predicted, importation and substitution will probably have to be resorted to in the future.

Vanadium. Versatile and recoverable from numerous ores, flue dusts, and asphalt-using industries and also occurring as an ore, vanadium is so important strategically that information concerning it has been withheld in recent years for security reasons. It is a hard metal with a high melting point, and about 90 per cent of the domestic consumption goes into high-speed and other tool steels, other alloy steels, and into metal purification. The remainder is used principally in other metal alloys. Production is developed chiefly in Peru, the United States, southwest Africa, and Northern Rhodesia. Domestic ores are mined in Utah, Colorado, Nevada, and New Mexico. Small quantities of vanadium are recovered in the mining and treatment of phosphate rock, iron, and chrome ores and from processing bauxite for recovery of aluminum. Economic reserves are inadequate, and conservation will probably take the direction of more thorough by-product recovery from known and potentially promising metal processing.

Other Alloy Metals. Cobalt, beryllium, and titanium are other representative metals used in alloys and which are insufficient in domestic supply. Each serves other uses, titanium for example serving mainly as a pigment. Because these and similar metals may serve to increase serviceability or serve as substitutes for other metals widely used, continued research in the beneficiation of their ores and the development of their uses is needed.

Platinum-group Metals. In spite of the fact that the jewelry trade has long been the principal outlet for platinum, a group of metals made up of palladium, osmium, osmiridium, rhodium, ruthenium, and iridium are also in demand for dental, medical, electrical, and chemical use. Most of them are recovered from other metallic ores, notably those of gold and copper. Alaska and California are the leading producers. (Gold, which has been heretofore discussed as a major metal, is sometimes included in this group.)

Uranium, Radium, and Thorium. Because it can be used for the manufacture of atomic bombs and has possibilities of extensive use for industrial power production, uranium is an important key to ruin or to the good life. At present its use for other than military purposes is largely confined to medicine. The ore from which it is obtained is pitchblende in which it is associated with other metals such as copper, bismuth, lead, cobalt, and silver. Carnotite, the domestic ore from which uranium is produced in the Colorado plateau, is associated with sandstone and low-grade material which has been identified in oil shales. Carnotite yields around 1 per cent uranium compounds, a similar percentage of vanadium, and much smaller amounts of radium. Data on reserves and rates of military use are of course for security reasons unavailable. It is probable, however, that progressively leaner domestic ores will be tapped at an early date. Production and marketing throughout the world are generally in public control. In the United States the official body in control is the Atomic Energy Commission.

Radium is used in the treatment of tumors and cancer, in the manufacture of luminous paint, and for exploring metal articles for defects. It is obtained from pitchblende and other uranium ores, and its production and conservation are linked with uranium.

Thorium, unlike uranium and radium, is obtained from a mineral known as monazite, occurring in certain sand and gravel deposits. Domestic deposits occur in gold-bearing gravels in Idaho and in sands of northeastern Florida. Thorium was formerly used principally in the manufacture of gas mantles and in ceramics. Its present value is its radioactive characteristic which makes possible its use with uranium to extend the supply of the latter. Throughout the world it is of course subject to the same public control as uranium. Whatever is done to exploit or to conserve these fissionable (multipliable in terms of energy) metals is a matter for which the public, in the form of its governments, cannot escape responsibility.

NONFUEL NONMETALLIC MINERALS

While most of the serious conservation problems in the mineral-resource field have to do with fuels and metals, other products, many of which are accepted as inexhaustible, pose problems of their own conservation and of the interferences which their exploitation present in conserving other resources. Water pollution, scarred and disorderly landscape, and space requirements for waste materials are examples of these interferences. Use as substitutes for less plentiful materials, indispensability in the building trades and in the recovery and treating of natural fuels and metals, replacements for nutrient materials removed by crops, and medical and food-seasoning use are examples of values demanding that the resources themselves be conserved.

In the following discussion only a few examples will be covered, and these will be chosen on the basis of the conservation problems which they raise. Uses will of course overlap, in such broad groups as building materials, salts, abrasives, and refractories (heat- and corrosion-resisting materials).

Building Materials

Mineral building materials include sand and gravel; clays; special cement materials such as limestone, shales, and marl; materials from which lime is prepared including oystershell; gypsum; and the various special building stones, such as slate, granite, marble, sandstone, and limestone. Even in this breakdown there are several overlaps.

Sand and Gravel. Of all the earth's natural resources, sand and gravel would seem to be the least exhaustible and perhaps, with the exception of air, the most widely distributed. But there are actual instances where sand is "manufactured" from massive sandstone to meet a scarcity of nearby supplies of natural sand, and crushed rock is a well-known product.[15] Certain special sands for glass manufacture and foundry use must meet exacting specifications, and more than 90 per cent of all sand and gravel produced for commercial use requires special preparation. Moreover, because of the universal demand and the transportation expense, most of the sand and gravel is used locally. Widely distributed deposits are thus essential.

Aside from building, which is the largest use, paving is the only other

[15] *Rock Products*, **52**:56–59, July, 1949.

one that is at all comparable in volume. Glass manufacture, molding (foundry), engine use, and grinding and polishing are typical requirements. Gravel is employed in paving, building, and as railroad ballast, in the order given.

Supply problems are less important in the sand and gravel picture than conservation conflicts which their exploitation brings about. Gravel pits are landscape scars, and seldom are they put to constructive space utilization after being worked out. Necessary washing operations and consequent siltation and gravel waste pollution of streams have become the subject of legislation in certain states. Ponds for the collection of "tailings" and finer wastes from aggregate works are in use to meet this conservation problem *of water.* Occasional efforts made to level, screen, or otherwise make gravel and sand pits eventually available for spatial use are on record. One Michigan city has a public stadium in a former gravel pit, and here and there one is used as a sanitary fill when city waste is buried and packed beyond the reach of rats and without danger to water supplies.

Other Minerals Used in Concrete Construction. As mentioned above, the natural materials used in manufacturing portland cement—the product which with sand and gravel supplies a vast construction industry with concrete—are limestone, cement rock,[16] clay or shale, and marl. Blast-furnace slag is also used. These are all relatively plentiful although not always distributed advantageously for local use. In order of volume consumed in cement manufacture, the materials rank as follows: limestone, clay, and shale combined, 72 per cent; cement rock and pure limestone, 22 per cent; blast-furnace slag and limestone, 5 per cent; and marl and clay, 2 per cent. The average weight of materials required to produce a barrel (376 pounds) of portland cement is 654 pounds, and the total 1949 consumption amounted to nearly 68 million short tons. This included small amounts of a dozen or more miscellaneous materials such as flue dust, calcium chloride, and grinding aids.

Except for reasonably full recovery and as an outlet for certain by-products of other industries, no program of conservation covers these important materials.

Resources from Which Lime Is Produced. Because lime is cheap and widely useful but finds its greatest utility in building, a word should be said here concerning the importance of limestone, marl, and oystershell from which it is principally produced. As in the case of portland cement, adequate local deposits or supplies of these materials specifically available for making lime are desirable. Fourteen of the states produce the

[16] "Cement rock" is a term applied to rock containing adequate proportions of lime and other compounds for use in cement making. It is not so uniform or as "pure" as limestone.

bulk of the lime sold and possess within their boundaries the largest deposits of the raw resources. Ohio, Pennsylvania, and Missouri lead in order of volume and account for more than one-half of the production of manufactured lime annually. The total is more than 1½ million short tons. Some of the uses for lime which are not generally known include manufacture of glue, varnish, and rubber and the refining of petroleum, salt, and sugar. Two contributions which it makes to conservation of water are purification and prevention of pollution through treatment of sewage and trade wastes.

FIG. 168. Cement rock workings in Kern County, California. (*Photo by Kern County Board of Trade, Bakersfield.*)

Clays. In addition to the common clays used in cement manufacture, which amount to 19 per cent of all clays produced, building requires a considerable proportion of the refractories (heat-resistant brick and tile), which consume 15 per cent of the clays produced, and practically all, except drain and sewer tile, of the heavy clay products such as common brick and tiles for walls, floors, and facing. (Aside from building, clays are important in pottery, rotary drilling muds, coating paper, and filtering and decolorizing oil.) From a conservation viewpoint, clays are useful in treating scarcer natural-resource materials and in the manufacture of heavy products which may to some extent substitute for steel construction. Exploitation occasions little waste, but no particular conservation efforts are in force.

Building Stone. In their native form, unmanufactured save for shaping, sandstone, granite, marble, limestone, and slate are valuable building materials, used at one step from the natural-resource stage. Cut stones, slabs, and mill blocks (which include a small proportion of refractory stone) constitute the largest use and their consumption amounts to more than 10 million cubic feet annually. In addition to structural efficiency, much of this stone is used for decoration and dignified effect, which no one would question as a cultural contribution, in public, religious, and business buildings and monuments.

Use of the various building stones in terms of tonnage and value and including other small-volume uses rank about as follows:

Tonnage	*Value*
1. Slate	1. Granite
2. Limestone	2. Limestone
3. Granite	3. Slate
4. Sandstone	4. Marble
5. Marble	5. Sandstone
6. Miscellaneous	6. Miscellaneous

Slate is produced in greatest volume in Vermont, Maine, New York, and Pennsylvania. Limestone for building comes from Indiana and Missouri chiefly. Granite in considerable amounts is quarried in some twenty-five of the states, the leading ones of which are Georgia, Massachusetts, Vermont, Pennsylvania, Maine, and North Carolina. Architectural sandstone is produced principally in Ohio, Pennsylvania, Tennessee, and New York in the order given. Tennessee accounts for more than one-half of the production of marble, followed by Arkansas, Maryland, and Colorado. Miscellaneous building stone includes light-colored volcanic rock, mica schist, greenstone, and others, among which a large variety of local field stone is represented.

Conservation of building stone involves little that the ordinary citizen can do. On the other hand, those who quarry and merchandise this material have steadily improved exploitation practices in the general directions of *channeling*, which cuts and removes stone in shapes and sizes appropriate for use without wasteful dressing, instead of employing the older and more wasteful blasting practices, and of finding use for broken and small-sized material. The latter finds outlet as crushed stone for highway construction and in the production of concrete for many other construction purposes. Quarrying is perhaps less likely to leave ugly landscape scars than the exploitation of sand, gravel, and other of the minerals, and quarries with their clifflike walls and accumulations of water have recreation and scenic potentialities which merit more attention from land-use planners.

Abrasives

An industrial nation such as the United States operates with sharp tools and minute measurements, and it could not do this without grinding, sharpening, drilling, and polishing materials. From the hand-operated grindstone of the colonial farm to the emery wheels and sanding belts and drums of today, emery, sand, other silicon-containing materials, corundum, garnet, pumice, and industrial diamonds have had to be found and prepared for abrasive duty.

Of the dozen natural abrasives produced domestically, ground sand and sandstone, pumice and pumicite (volcanic materials), and quartz lead in volume. All are abundant. Natural alumina abrasives include corundum and emery; the former is largely imported from South Africa. The latter is produced in relatively small amounts domestically, but is almost indispensable in such uses as saw sharpening. The most important natural carbon abrasive is the industrial diamond, of which the United States has no deposits or reserves. Artificial abrasives made of silicon and aluminum compounds offer substitute possibilities. No organized program of conservation of the rarer abrasive materials is in force.

Salts

Displaced ocean floors and ancient inland lake beds have left numerous deposits now considered indispensable to human welfare. Common salt, known to most people only as food seasoning, potash and phosphorus, thought of usually as fertilizing materials only, borax, "mineral-water" ingredients, and various drugs, used widely but taken for granted, form the natural-resource base for vast industries and a considerable world trade. Most of these resources are classified as "known reserves adequate" and require only brief consideration.

Common Salt. While the world and the domestic reserves of the materials from which salt is produced seem inexhaustible, the industry has its conservation problems; one of these has to do with the severe corrosion produced by salt on the metal equipment used in processing and in which the material is used industrially. Here it is not salt itself but metals as natural resources which must be conserved. Some progress is being made on the latter problem through development of corrosion-resistant linings and platings which not only conserve equipment but keep the salt solutions purer. More than 15 million short tons of salt were sold or used in the United States in the average year from 1945 to 1949. Michigan, Ohio, New York, Louisiana, and Texas lead in the order given. In terms of table and household use, consumption amounts to about 5 pounds annually per capita. Industrial uses such as bleaching and the manufacture of glass and various chemicals require around 70 per cent of the total domestic production.

Salt is mined as block and granular material and pumped out as brine either natural or artificially dissolved. The brine is then evaporated and the residue refined. Some salt is recovered by pumping in and evaporating sea water. It seldom occurs without being associated with other materials such as bromine, iron, or magnesium compounds. In some countries it is used for household and table purposes with only superficial refinement.

Miscellaneous Salines. Calcium chloride, well known for its hygroscopic and antifreeze characteristics, has many uses and is produced in many domestic localities from natural brines. Demand for bromine, which also comes from natural brines including sea water, is increasing because of its use in antiknock gasoline. Iodine, used in photographic emulsions, animal feed, iodized salts, drugs, and dyes, is recovered from waste oil-field and other brines and may be recovered from seaweed.

Sodium carbonate and sodium sulfate, extensively used in the glass, soap, and paper industries and variously as refining materials, are widely distributed and in adequate supply. Borax and other boron minerals in addition to extensive household use have become an item in the fertilizer industry and are finding increasing use in the hardening of certain metals. Reserves are adequate.

Phosphates. The United States has long been the largest producer and exporter of phosphates in various forms and has adequate supplies to meet the heavy domestic demand for phosphate fertilizer. The older southeastern fields in Tennessee, Kentucky, South Carolina, Florida, and farther west in Arkansas have in recent years been supplemented by discoveries in Utah, Montana, Idaho, and Wyoming. Lately, export trade finds vigorous competition from North African producers. Western deposits are largely located on public lands and are operated under the Mineral Leasing Act of 1920. Domestic consumption occurs mostly in states east of the Mississippi. These factors of export competition and long freight haul are not too good for the phosphate-mining business but do put the brakes on wasteful exploitation. Aside from the 80-odd per cent of use for fertilizer, phosphate materials find their way into such varied uses as stock and poultry food, rodent poisons, tracer bullets, matches, and poison gases.

Much of the mining of phosphate rock in the Southeast is by open-pit methods which results in high recovery but ruined landscapes.

Stipulations in Western Federal phosphate leases include conservation features.

Potash. Unlike phosphate, potash had to be imported into this country previous to the First World War, when supplies from the rich Stassfurt fields were cut off from import. This stimulated discovery through congressional appropriation, and deep but rich deposits were found in New Mexico. It is interesting that the discoveries were made in drilling for oil. There is now a thriving American potash industry, handicapped somewhat by location distant from greatest demand but backed by resources adequate for many years ahead. Potash is essential as a plant nutrient, and more than 90 per cent of total consumption is used for agricultural purposes. The remainder is used principally by the chemical industries.

Imports in 1949 amounted to less than 4 per cent of total consumption. Most of the domestic deposits are on Federal lands, operated under the

FIG. 169. Aerial view of potash workings near Carlsbad, N. Mex. Mine head and refinery are seen below and at left of center, tailing or waste dumps are seen in large white area and in dark area below, huge storage sheds are seen at right of center. (*Photo by American Potash Institute, Inc.*)

Mineral Leasing Law of 1920, and operators are required to use conservation procedures in mining. Some production comes from natural brines from wells in private ownership.

Other Nonmetallic Minerals

Certain important nonmetallics such as feldspar, graphite, sulfur, fluorspar, mica, and asbestos defy classification and should be taken up separately.

Sulfur. Consumption of domestic native and by-product sulfur, having increased from almost zero in 1900 to 4¾ million long tons in 1949, has recently emphasized the consideration of reserve problems. Sulfur occurs in almost pure form as crystals, masses, and powders and in combination with certain metals as pyrites (sulfides). Its uses vary from chemicals, fertilizers, and insecticides and pulp and paper manufacture which account for more than three-fourths of total consumption, to such products as rubber, explosives, and paints. Much of the industrial consumption is in the form of sulfuric acid. Thus the figure for sulfur consumption for 1949 is 3½ million long tons and for sulfuric acid more than 10 million tons. Texas with three-fourths and Louisiana with one-fourth of the supply produce practically all the domestic native sulfur. Ores and by-product sulfur come from many localities. In spite of shrinking reserves the United States exports a net of almost 1½ million long tons of sulfur a year. Pyrites, a metallic-appearing sulfide mineral, has approached production of a million long tons a year and is an additional source of sulfur and sulfuric acid. As a substitute source of native sulfur, its use constitutes good conservation. By-product sulfur is recovered in the flotation treatment of copper, lead, and zinc ores and from smelter fumes and from natural gas and oil. The smelter fumes are a nuisance in smelter centers, and their treatment to produce sulfuric acid yielded about 167,000 tons in 1949. This process is not particularly profitable, but some of the cost can be charged off against prevention of damage to vegetation. Likewise, current interest in smog control will no doubt bring about by-product treatment of industrial sulfur gases from urban industries. Sulfur is also recovered in the treatment of "sour" natural gas in oil fields, from coke manufacture, and from oil-refining gases. All this by-product business amounts to conservation with some of the expenses paid and adds to the domestic sulfur reserves when industry decides the practices can be used "economically."

Fluorspar. Important in steel and glass manufacture and in the production of hydrofluoric acid which has many industrial uses, fluorspar is mined principally in Illinois and Kentucky. Reserves are inadequate, and more than one-third of the amount consumed in this country must be imported. Some progress may be looked for in beneficiation of lean material.

Graphite. With high consumption and inadequate reserves of natural graphite, hope for improvement in beneficiation of ores and for the manufacture of artificial graphite from coal appear to be the directions which conservation must take. Uses range from foundry batteries, lubricants, and crucibles to the "lead" in the everyday pencil. Production of natural graphite in the United States in 1949 amounted to somewhat more than one-third of consumption. Imports included both natural and artificial graphite and were almost double the figure for natural graphite consumed.

Asbestos. Length of fiber, which adapts it for weaving into textiles, fire resistance, and filtering value are qualities which give asbestos a wide variety of uses. Aside from insulation, the use for brake lining is perhaps best known by the average citizen. In 1949 domestic production, mainly from Vermont and Arizona, supplied only 8 per cent of the amount consumed. Canada is the principal source of imports. Lower grade asbestos is produced in several states, and some progress is reported in developing synthetic substitutes, one project having been inaugurated in 1949 at Norris, Tenn., by the Bureau of Mines.

Mica. Used all the way from roofing and paint to electric insulation and Christmas-tree snow, mica has become one of the indispensable minerals. It occurs naturally in sheets which split into very thin transparent layers. Its property of nonconductivity of electricity and heat make sheet mica of special value. Unfortunately it is scarcest in this form, and domestic reserves are insignificant. Scrap mica can be used for many industrial purposes such as manufacture of wallpaper, dusting powder, automobile tires, and the production of paints and plastics. Domestic sheet mica comes mainly from North Carolina and New Hampshire. Scrap mica, suitable for the ground product, not only comes from shop and factory wastes but is recovered from the washing of kaolin, a ceramic clay. Imports of all grades of mica are heavy and expensive. They come principally from India and Madagascar. Some progress is being made in producing a synthetic mica under the sponsorship of the Office of Naval Research.

Kyanite. This porcelain-like mineral and sillimanite are representative of a group of minerals used for insulating spark plugs, of which the United States imports about one-half of what it consumes. There is some promise of new discoveries.

BIBLIOGRAPHY

Annual Reports of the Secretary of the Interior, 1950–1952.

Bituminous Coal Annual, Bituminous Coal Institute, Washington, D.C., 1949.

Investigation of National Resources, Hearings before sub-committee of Committee on Public Lands, U.S. Senate, May 15, 16, and 20, 1947.

Landes, Kenneth K.: Petroleum Geology, John Wiley & Sons, Inc., New York, 1951.

Lovering, T. S.: Minerals in World Affairs, Prentice-Hall, Inc., New York, 1943.

Minerals Yearbook, Bureau of Mines, U.S. Department of the Interior, 1949.

Resources for Freedom, Report of the President's Materials Policy Commission, Vols. I and III, 1952.

Sherman, Allan, and Allen B. Macmurphy: Facts about Coal, Bureau of Mines, U.S. Department of the Interior, 1950.

Stutzer, Otto, and Adolph C. Noé: Geology of Coal, University of Chicago Press, Chicago, 1940.

Van Hise, Charles R.: The Conservation of Natural Resources in the United States, The Macmillan Company, New York, 1910.

Van Royen, William, Oliver Bowles, and Elmer W. Pehrson: Mineral Resources of the World, Prentice-Hall, Inc., New York, 1952.

CHAPTER 7

Human Powers as Natural Resources

Because the use of human beings for the benefit of themselves and other human beings is a use of services which flow from human powers, and because there is nothing unnatural about human beings, the term *human powers* will be used in this discussion rather than the more common term *human resources.*

Man of course assumes that he is the lord of creation and that all other elements or resources of nature are for his benefit. He may object to the very natural urge of the coyote to prey upon his sheep, but actually he uses his own powers and those of others to prey upon the coyote and perhaps even to use its hide for a garment. Other of his powers and those of his fellows are used for higher purposes such as maintaining the health of his family, moving natural-resource materials about in commerce, educating his children, generally understanding his environment, and on rare occasions even attempting to keep some of his wild-animal brothers from extinction.

What then *are* these human powers? Some of them are physical, others are mental. Ely[1] has classified them as

Those of the body.
Those of the spirit.

He subdivides the latter into moral and intellectual, and there is no reason why the former, also, should not be subdivided. So that the following classification, incomplete and overlapping, might result:

- Human powers
  - Those of the body
    - Power to reproduce
    - Strength
    - Dexterity
  - Those of the spirit
    - Power to think and to reason
    - Imagination
    - Power to distinguish between right and wrong
    - Power to inspire and to lead

[1] Ely, Richard T., and associates, Foundations of National Prosperity, The Macmillan Company, New York, 1923, p. 48.

A moment's thought will suggest that some of these powers can easily get out of hand as far as the good of mankind is concerned, and certainly the way in which the material resources of the earth have been handled is an example of this. Moreover the powers themselves are somewhat analogous to material natural resources in the sense that they may be wasted, depleted, and reduced in productivity, and may frequently be inequitably distributed in terms of talent needed at varying times, places, and by different groups. Examples will suggest themselves: a skilled and promising scientist drafted as a private in fighting forces, an overstaffed enterprise during a time of scarcity of manpower, or a surplus of labor for one industry and scarcity in another requiring different skills, side by side; disease and unsafe working conditions cutting down the producing power of a training or manufacturing force; lack of medical and teaching services in a fast-growing pioneer community with poorly paid and irregularly employed medical and teaching talent in older, larger communities.

On the positive side human powers may be analogous to material natural resources because subject to efficient use through proper training and allocation, with minimum waste; to improvement in skill and output through training, supplying with proper tools, and guiding in the expenditure of effort; to redistribution through planning, forecasting need, and possibly decentralizing certain industries; to better distribution in a social sense, by such procedures as extension courses in centers away from main educational plants, group hospitalization, traveling and decentralized service forces for widely used mechanical devices, and to forecasting the need for training workers in new fields.

Factors Which Waste and Deplete Human Powers

Dr. Thomas Carver, in *Foundations of National Prosperity*,[2] lists disease, vice, idleness, and dishonesty as depleting factors affecting "human resources." He wrote at a period when the automobile and other mechanical devices were neither so common nor so bloodthirsty as at present (although industrial and household hazards *were* common); so he has little to say about accidents. Nor does he talk about wars, disasters, or overpopulation. These latter make up quite an addition to the list, and each is worthy of at least brief discussion.

Disease. The age-old ravages of disease are of course obvious destroyers of men and at times take the lives of valuable individuals at their most productive periods. Human powers are thus depleted, and the talents of many are deflected from producing economic goods and services to care of the afflicted. Still another angle of depletion exists in the reduced energy or human power of those in ill health who still must

[2] *Ibid.*, pp. 275–323.

work. It is a far cry from the plagues of the Middle Ages when the average city inhabitant could count on only five pints of water a day for all purposes to the present stage of medical and sanitary service. But it still is not far enough. The losses of time, in general employment, from the common cold alone runs into astronomical figures. Tuberculosis, cancer, heart ailments, arthritis, and poliomyelitis, among others, strike down thousands of valuable members of society each year and occasion vast expenditure of human energy and treasure which might otherwise be turned eventually to more productive use.[3] Such use could probably consist most constructively of preventive medicine and improved sanitation.

Accidents. Few reforms get more publicity or put out more effort than accident prevention, and yet figures compiled by the National Safety Council for 1951 indicate a total of 94,000 deaths by accident of which 37,300 were caused by motor vehicles, 28,000 occurred in homes, 15,000 were caused by nonmotor public vehicles, and 16,000 were occupational. (Figures are rounded approximations, and duplication between motor vehicle, occupational, and home accidents is eliminated in the total.) Wage losses from motor-vehicle accident injuries alone in 1951 reached $1,150,000 and medical expense amounted to $90,000,000. It is hardly likely that this depleter of human powers can be reduced in the face of the mania for greater speed and more power and the economic limitations observed in employment of engineering talent and physical improvements, to say nothing of the effectiveness of legislation and law enforcement. Much of this record appears to be an inevitable accompaniment of the standards of production and of living which Americans demand. As the demand mounts, the average American might well take time off to think that the automobile and its imperfect operation alone account for one death every 14 minutes and one injury every 24 seconds.

Vice and Crime. While there is probably a great degree of natural rebelliousness and of battle against frustration in mankind as a whole, and while vice is superficially defined as meanness by those who suffer from it, it is somewhat a corollary of substandard health and living conditions and of boredom. Vice, therefore, as a depleter of human powers, overlaps disease and idleness. Aside from the waste and destruction of economic goods occasioned by theft, arson, and general racketeering, for example, it is well to remember that the talents of otherwise valuable members of society are frequently turned to use as master minds for the planning and executing of crime. Again the vast army of persons required to police and care for criminals, captured and at large, require the use of human powers in disproportionate volume. This may not appear to be

[3] Exclusive of deaths among the armed forces overseas, tuberculosis for example was fatal to 22.2 per 100,000 of population for 1950 and the figure for diseases of the heart was 354.4 per 100,000, according to the Federal Security Agency.

waste when the necessity for maintaining order and protecting society is considered. The number of people, however, required to achieve such results is appalling.

Idleness. There has been a good deal of talk throughout the ages of the pleasure of having nothing to do. The sluggard of Biblical times represents one extreme. The talented individual of the modern world who has the means to live without working, and chooses to do so, represents the other. Between the two there are vast resources of human powers unused either voluntarily by those who possess such powers, or because there is no opportunity for employing them. By far the greater depletion occurs of course among those individuals who choose to be idle. Their talents, or powers, are frequently more valuable than those of the "unemployables," be the latter diseased, unskilled, disadvantageously located, imprisoned, or incurably lazy.

Referring again to Professor Carver's excellent essay, this situation can be reduced to a matter of ideals and interests, both of which may be influenced by training and education. Carver draws attention to an Indiana farmer who apparently gets his satisfaction out of life by producing economic goods. The goods he produces are hogs. As one observes his operation, it seems to go something like this: The sale of his hogs brings in more money than he needs to live on and so he spends the surplus for more land, upon which he raises corn to feed more hogs, which bring in more profit, which he spends to buy more land to grow more corn to feed more hogs—and so on far into the twilight along the Wabash. By this time, the observer—an intellectual no doubt who likes his bacon for breakfast—begins to smile and to feel that something is wrong. But the fact remains that the farmer is producing economic goods.

The intellectual retires to his study and starts thinking about Michelangelo, who worked feverishly and persistently throughout his life, not only in art but in other fields. His total accomplishment for the satisfaction of his fellowmen, both culturally and economically, is almost beyond human comprehension. He also was a producer whose satisfaction came through creative effort.

Slowly the following diagram[4] begins to take form:

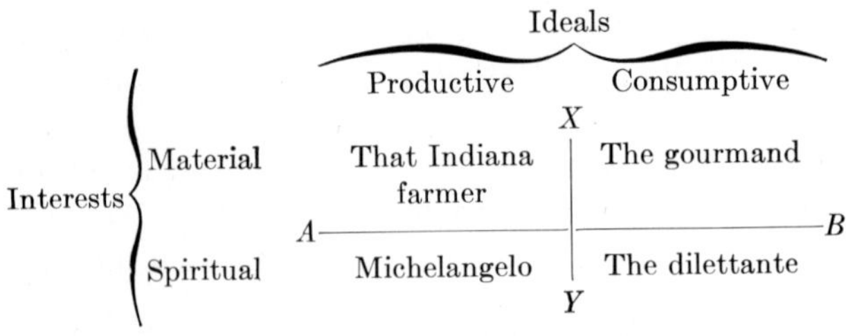

[4] Ely and associates, *op. cit.*, p. 295.

Under those whose ideals are consumptive in this picture appears the gourmand or glutton who apparently lives to eat and drink. He would be in a tough spot if it were not for the producer to his left. Below him is the dilettante who dabbles with art and science but only for amusement. Probably he rationalizes his program by assuming that he inspires the producer of art by serving as a consuming audience.

This diagram is not reproduced to belittle artistic and scientific achievement or, in other words, to compare material and spiritual production. It *is* useful to demonstrate that the line *XY*, which separates the voluntarily idle and unproductive possessor of powers from the voluntarily occupied producer, regardless of the quality of his powers, is important. The line *AB* on the other hand is not so important. The world has not yet suffered too much for lack of consumers of really essential economic goods. But the strike of the producer, either on the part of labor or management, has frequently caused suffering.

This is a long argument to indicate that idleness is a depleter of human powers, but it should be pointed out that mankind has not courageously faced the problem of making it simple for all who want to work to be employed constructively.

Dishonesty. Credit, safety of property and person, peace among men, organizations, and nations are all founded upon adherence to standards of honesty as well as on signed legal agreements with penalties prescribed for violation. There is no complete substitute for the will to keep one's word, even to his hurt. Dishonesty, therefore, with its chance to disrupt order and safety is a depleter not only of the powers of the liar but of those of his fellowmen to whom he is untrue. In this connection the conservation of natural resources and of human powers requires courageous facing of the dangers surrounding the modern code of dishonesty from which may be extracted such passages as: "The end (always) justifies the means." "The crime consists of getting caught." "If I don't take it somebody else will." "What he doesn't know won't hurt him." And perhaps (with a warped meaning), "God helps the man who helps himself." Perhaps mankind was endowed with the power to rationalize, so that he could maintain a sense of validity in a turbulent world, but he still has an obligation to strive for intellectual honesty.

War. Regardless of the mental and moral gymnastics by which war is rationalized, and of the total positive results of war in the development of a civilization, war does destroy in vast measure the resource consisting of human powers. Moreover the quality of human powers destroyed is high in terms of vigor, courage, and potential contribution to the good of society. It is not the old, worn-out, or unemployable surpluses of population or human powers that go to battle. It is a select group, often the best, particularly in terms of health, intelligence, and strength. What this expenditure purchases must also be charged with the destructive use of vast quantities of treasure and natural resources with minimum recovery. One of the developments that is to be hoped for and worked for is a program of waging peace with somewhere near the energy that nations wage war.

Disasters. Flood, earthquake, hurricanes, and other natural phenomena which constitute disasters are dramatic and persistent. And while they are relatively unimportant in the total picture of the depletion of human powers, it is defeatist to say that these as well as the disasters caused by mankind—wrecks, fires, mine disasters—cannot be attacked and their depletion of human powers reduced. The reader is referred back to the discussions of flood control on page 117 and mine safety on page 277.

Overpopulation. One human power that has concerned a number of recent writers and thinkers in connection with conserving natural resources is mankind's power to reproduce. Theoretically this brings about a continuing flow into the world's reservoir of human powers. Actually it may add to populations which are ill fed and proportionately unproductive. Even in a great democracy such as the United States with relatively small percentage increase of population annually, there are sections where disproportionate population increase is accompanied by irregular and inadequate food supply and living conditions generally. Increase in numbers of people, therefore, does not necessarily mean increase in the total resource of human powers.

Almost all the voices raised in behalf of population control are speaking of world population, and while the United States faces a lesser immediate population problem than other countries, her food-producing resources will be increasingly called upon to help the vast portion of the globe which is now inhabited by undernourished people. By similar token the rapidly expanding and space-requiring advances in her technology will lessen rather than increase her own self-sufficiency. In a sense, therefore, talk of world-population problems is talk of this country's conservation and production problems and of the demand for an increasing supply of human powers. For any who wish to confine their thinking to the United States alone, it is well to bear in mind that each 24 hours we have about 6,200 more mouths to feed. This figure is net and is derived from the subtraction of 1,486,000 deaths in 1951 from 3,758,000 births.

On a global scale[5] a population of 2.2 billion includes one-third at least of such a number who are undernourished, and those inhabiting almost two-thirds of the area of the globe account for an annual increase in population ranging from 1.25 to 3 per cent a year. At a rate of 1 per cent

[5] Huxley, Julian, Population and Human Destiny, *Harper's Magazine,* Vol. 201, pp. 38–46, September, 1950.

a year, the population will double in two generations, and that is the present approximate rate. Some examples will make this figure even more startling: Haiti with a population of 3.5 million on 10,000 square miles of badly abused land has doubled its population in 30 years. Japan with a 1.5 per cent increase annually has double the population it had 60 years ago. Italy has increased its numbers 50 per cent in 50 years. And the U.S. Department of Agriculture declares that, for the decade 1939–1949, world population has increased at a greater rate than world food production.

On the whole then it appears that simply increasing population may well amount eventually to decrease rather than increase of human powers.

Conserving Human Powers

Because a harvest of human powers or even an inventory cannot be expressed in tons, board feet, or kilowatts, the means of conserving such powers must also differ from those used to conserve material natural resources. On the other hand, the items of (1) use with minimum waste, (2) increase in productivity, and (3) equitable distribution are still subject in some degree to remedy. The over-all cure is made up largely of research, education, and sounding out a positive, if qualified, answer to the old inquiry, "Am I my brother's keeper?" Specifically, society has a number of tough jobs on its hands. *Disease* yields remarkably to the application of the results of long-drawn-out and patient research. More than a score of associations and foundations are active in promoting and supporting research, prevention, and treatment involved in as many important diseases. The following are examples of research, educational, and action programs which deserve mention: The death rate from tuberculosis in the United States was cut in 6 years by one-half, but 30,000 persons still die annually, 250,000 active cases are recorded, and an estimated 150,000 go unrecorded. Promotion of the wholesale chest X-ray examination by health agencies resulted in more than 15 million examinations with one to two active cases found in every 1,000. Cities of more than 100,000 may obtain free X-ray service from the U.S. Public Health Service, and much of this work is financed by the National Tuberculosis Association from proceeds of the sale of Christmas seals. Funds allocated to almost 3,000 state, county, and city units are also used partially for education. Steady and promising research on the origin and treatment of cancer has long been under way and has recently been accelerated in the field of atomic energy. The American Cancer Society declares that the number of lives saved from cancer can be doubled if people see their doctors earlier and if doctors become more familiar with known means of detection and treatment. Among the educational efforts of this society was the showing in 1951 to more than 1 million women of a film on breast cancer, produced by the Society and the National Cancer Institute and endorsed by the American Medical Association.

Large-scale inoculations with gamma globulin as a prophylactic against the paralytic form of poliomyelitis were begun in 1951 and continued in 1952 and 1953 by the National Foundation for Infantile Paralysis. Results are encouraging.

Other groups working for the prevention and treatment of disease include associations and foundations concerned with heart ailments, diabetes, leprosy, arthritis, and rheumatism, and eye banks for sight restoration.

While the above are somewhat spectacular, the quiet and persistent work of thousands of physicians, nurses, research workers, visiting nurses, mental hospital workers, and good neighbors forms an effective attack on suffering and disease.

And with all the bitterness which has developed in the argument over socialized medicine, a democracy is the very place where people may look for more nearly universally available medical care with proper compensation and incentive for professional improvement to the physician and a minimum of abuse by the recipient.

Idleness, particularly involuntary idleness, poses a problem for society in general which can be met. In the great depression following the crash in 1929, employment was furnished to millions on a vast public-works program. Sarcastic and bitter criticism was leveled at many of these public enterprises, and yet with all the jibes hurled at some of the best citizens in the country, who found themselves employed by WPA and other agencies, they showed little evidence of "making a career of being publicly supported." For as recovery developed, these same involuntarily unemployed left the public rolls as fast as they could obtain private employment. Normally, the unemployed in the United States do not represent any great proportion of the workers, and frequently the "unemployables" comprise a considerable part of the number. Here, as well as in a general situation, education to equip and allocate workers in all fields has no substitute. While it is hardly true that "the world owes me a living," it may very well be true that "democracy owes me *the opportunity, as a good citizen,* to earn a living." Excellent work is done by certain organizations in finding work for which handicapped and aged persons are adapted.

One direction in which too little progress has been made is that of according respect to a conscientious and productive worker in *any* useful occupation. Let the poet respect the charwoman and the statesman the garbage man, or let the "self-made" businessman tolerate the professor, and vice versa (see diagram, page 330).

Vice and Crime, it is pointed out, are often results of substandard conditions of health and living, and certainly are stimulated by boredom resulting from having nothing interesting to do in leisure hours. A part, if only a small one, therefore, of the remedy is in the hands of society. And when slums are replaced by decent housing, or racial discrimination is dispensed with in employment, or playgrounds are furnished at public expense, they need not be considered failures if at first they seem to be unappreciated and if the first decent wages of the tenants are spent for a showy automobile. The reconditioning of embittered youth may take several generations, but it is worth working at. Education can do much also to lessen tendencies to crime. There is a long way to go in prison reform.

Dishonesty. Just how *honest* one can be and still make a living is a question that bothers many a possessor of considerable human powers. Unfortunately he often concludes that "virtue is its own (read 'only') reward" and that this is not enough. Or he may conclude, as did the lad trying to remember the Sunday School text, that "a lie is an abomination unto the Lord, but a very present help in time of trouble." But because the keeping of one's word is so important in human and even international relations, a radical change in the present-day habits of adults who set an example for their children is one of the few hopes for the emergence of an honest generation.

Accidents. These command the attention of the newspapers, police, hospitals, and the National Safety Council, and there is a healthy preoccupation with accident prevention. The two approaches, safer gadgets and relentless education, both pay off. The potentialities of wise legislation have not yet been fully realized.

War, unless it is defined as a biological phenomenon, has little chance of going out of style unless the causes of war can be recognized and eliminated. The United Nations bids fair to make steady, if slow and irritating, progress in this direction.

Disasters. These overlap accidents but are also due to natural phenomena. Research, legislation, and planned or restricted occupancy of flood plains and lake shores offer some hope of forecasting and escaping.

Overpopulation. Increase in numbers of people was given only one alternative by Malthus whose thesis was that population tends to outrun the means of subsistence. That alternative was moral restraint. Since then, alternatives of new land discovery, improvement in crop production, food from the sea, development of synthetics, and general natural-resource conservation have been offered on the positive side. They are not yet exhausted, but their use is not too encouraging on a global basis. On the restrictive or negative side, birth control is generally advocated by the "neomalthusians," as the recent writers have been called. So great is interest in this alternative that the well-known planned-parenthood movement is prospering in the United States and there is an International Planned Parenthood Committee with offices in New York and London. The committee is interested in promoting the furnishing of birth-control information and the establishment of clinics. It also publishes information on sterilization, mass migrations, and on the progress in meeting religious opposition to birth control. The matter of eugenics has still far to go.

In the foregoing discussion, education has been frequently mentioned. It is a broad term and should be so understood. Education occurs both in and out of school. There is no substitute for that obtained in either way. The tools of communication, measurement, reasoning, and analysis are perhaps best acquired in school. Attitudes, habits, viewpoints and, unfortunately, prejudices build up outside school, in family, gang, club, and business. An educated man should be informed, know where to acquire needed facts, and have ability to reason out a healthy sense of values. On the vocational side it is no discredit to education to say that he should have mastered certain skills even if some of them are only manual. These are the releasers and maintainers of human powers.

BIBLIOGRAPHY

Cain, Stanley A.: Food and People: A Second Look at Malthus' Principle of Population, in Resources and Policy, Current Issues in Conservation, Lee S. Greene and René de Visme Williamson, eds., reprinted from *Jour. Politics,* **13**:315–324, August, 1951.

Ely, Richard T., and Ralph K. Hess, Charles K. Lieth, and Thomas Nixon Carver: Foundations of National Prosperity, The Macmillan Company, New York, 1923.

Huxley, Julian: Population and Human Destiny, *Harper's Magazine,* **201**:38–46, September, 1950.

Kellogg, Charles E.: Opportunities for World Abundance, in Resources and Policy: Current Issues in Conservation, Lee S. Greene and René de Visme Williamson, eds., reprint from *Jour. Politics,* **13**:325–344, August, 1951.

Mather, Kirtley F.: Enough and to Spare, Harper & Brothers, New York, 1944.

News of Population and Birth Control, No. 14, May, 1953, International Planned Parenthood Committee, New York.

Vogt, William: Road to Survival, William Sloane Associates, New York, 1948.

World Almanac, 1953.

Index